Praise for *Manifesta*

"Amy Richards and Jennifer Baumga[rdner] [show us] the fruits of this wave of feminism—intended and unintended, media mess and truth—for a new generation. With wit and honesty, *Manifesta* shows us the building blocks of the future of this longest revolution."

—Gloria Steinem

"Great news from the front—feminism lives! Bold, independent, generous, and cautionary, *Manifesta* leaves no doubt that for a new generation of women the F-word is not only speakable but shoutable and singable."

—Alix Kates Shulman

"*Manifesta* is an exciting and important contribution to the growing body of Third Wave literature. Richards and Baumgardner speak the language of a new generation of feminists, proving once again that young women are committed to continuing to work passionately for social justice."

—Rebecca Walker, editor of *To Be Real: Telling the Truth and Changing the Face of Feminism*

"Richards and Baumgardner have spent years as participants in and observers of the feminist movement, and now they have their say, asking new questions and coming up with provocative answers. They do it with wit, confidence, and superior insight. *Manifesta* will reinvigorate armchair feminists and recharge activists of all ages."

—Barbara Findlen, editor of *Listen Up: Voices from the Next Feminist Generation*

Jennifer Baumgardner and Amy Richards

ManifestA

Jennifer Baumgardner (right) is a former editor at *Ms.* and writes regularly for *The Nation*, *Jane*, *Nerve*, and *Out*. Amy Richards (left) is a contributing editor at *Ms.* and a co-founder of the Third Wave Foundation, an activist group for young feminists.

MANIFESTA

MANIFESTA

young women,

feminism,

and the future

JENNIFER BAUMGARDNER

AND

AMY RICHARDS

FARRAR, STRAUS AND GIROUX
NEW YORK

Farrar, Straus and Giroux
19 Union Square West, New York 10003

Copyright © 2000 by Jennifer Baumgardner and Amy Richards
All rights reserved
Distributed in Canada by Douglas & McIntyre Ltd.
Printed in the United States of America
Designed by Jessica Shatan
First edition, 2000

Library of Congress Cataloging-in-Publication Data
Baumgardner, Jennifer, 1970–
    Manifesta : young women, feminism, and the future / Jennifer Baumgardner
and Amy Richards.
        p.   cm.
    Includes bibliographical references and index.
    ISBN 0-374-52622-2 (alk. paper)
    1. Feminism—United States.   2. Young women—United States—Attitudes.
I. Richards, Amy. II. Title.

HQ1421.R53 2000
305.42′01—dc21   00-026492

Grateful acknowledgment is given for permission to reprint from the following:
From "Parents Are People" by Carol Hall. Copyright © 1972 by Free to Be Foundation. Assignment 1999 Otay Music, Corp., and Daniel Music (ASCAP). All
rights reserved. Reprinted by permission of Otay Music, Corp. From "Hour Follows Hour" by Ani DiFranco. Copyright © 1995 by Righteous Babe Music. All
rights reserved. Reprinted by permission of Righteous Babe Music.

To feminists everywhere—including those of our generation who say, "I'm not a feminist, but ..." and others who say, "I am *a feminist, but* ... "—with the faith that young women will transform the world in ways we haven't yet imagined.

Contents

Acknowledgments

A special thank-you to everyone who made this book possible:

To Tara Brindisi, who spent her summer afternoons and fall weekends calling the Bureau of Labor Statistics and burrowing in the stacks of the New York Public Library to help us check facts. To Meghan Weber, who sought us out because she believed in the book and wanted to help in any way she could—even if it meant transcribing.

To Elizabeth Birdsall, whose frequent trips to New York from Virginia became filled with helping us edit; to Barbara Findlen, whose own anthology, *Listen Up*, was a first indication that young feminists had something to say, and who helped us to articulate concisely what we had to say; to Nina Chaudry, who gave us the benefit of her graduate degree in journalism, and her unwavering editorial eye; to Becky Michaels, who managed to cheer us on while simultaneously saving us from our bad sentences; and to Suzanne Braun Levine, who brought her experience as editor of *Ms.* and the *Columbia Journalism Review* to bear on our manuscript.

To our mentors at *Ms.* magazine, Marcia Gillespie, Barbara Findlen, and Gloria Jacobs, women of talent and integrity who gave us our first breaks as writers and editors.

A special thank-you to Gloria Steinem, who acted as if it was normal—even fun—to have intergenerational sleepovers/writers' workshops at her house for a year, and who offered her services as a combination historian and feminist librarian, while still remaining a firm believer that we know more about our generation of feminism than she does.

To Jim Smith, Rebecca Spence, and Julie Pershan for last minute help, and to Ali Price and Jenny Warburg for photos.

To others who have fed us, housed us, and lent us a car: Wilkie McCoy and Tim Cook, Julie Parker, and Amy Ray.

To Barbara Seaman, a feminist fairy godmother who pushed us to do this book, and is an original cheerleader (and font of history) for Third Wave feminism.

To Becky Kurson, who didn't need us to emulate her personal feminism in order to acquire our book for Farrar, Straus and Giroux; to Denise Oswald, who inherited this project with grace, insight, and patience; and to FSG, a publisher that doesn't believe the only good feminist book is an anti-feminist book.

To our smart agent, Jill Grinberg, who always smiles, wooing even anti-feminists and book publishers, and then wows them with her professional mettle.

And to all the gorgeous and righteous women who gave their time so we could include them or their work in this book: Kathleen Hanna, Jane Pratt, Carol Gilligan, Sabrina Margarita Alcantara-Tan, Tali Edut, Ophira Edut, Marcelle Karp, Debbie Stoller, Laurie Henzel, Christina Kelly, Mary Clarke, Janelle Brown, Dawn Lundy Martin, Winter Miller, Nomy Lamm, Phyllis Chesler, Elizabeth Wurtzel, Katie Roiphe, Farai Chideya, Amaryllis Léon, Susan Ray, Julie Semones, Melissa Huffsmith, Tanya Selvaratnam, Sandy Fernandez, Shannon O'Kelley White, Vivien Labaton, Lisi Grinberg, Sarah Lucia Hoagland, Hagar Scher, Letty Cottin Pogrebin, Becky Michaels, Mavis Gruver, Phyllis Rosser, Nia Kelly, Nancy Gruver, Molly McKinnon, Alyza Bohbot, Rachel Ostovich, Isabel Carter Stewart, Lisa Silver, Anastasia Higginbotham, Elisabeth Subrin, Tammy Rae Carland, Betsy Reed, Julie Felner, Ginia Bellafante, and many others who talked with us or wrote books and articles that informed this one.

AMY THANKS:

My mother, Karen Richards, whom I respect and love, and whose confidence and strength, sometimes in the face of adversity, made me who I am—and thus made everything in this book possible. To my auntie, Janet McNeill, whose sense of humor inspires my own. To my friend and colleague Gloria Steinem, whose conviction that everything you do matters made me believe in my own experiences enough to write this book. To everyone at the Third Wave Foundation, but mostly my everyday co-strategist Vivien Labaton, who had to work double time while I worked on this. She made me laugh, cry, think, and angry just when I needed it most. To Marianne Schnall of feminist.com, and to the thousands of people who have E-mailed me at Ask Amy and entrusted me with their stories. To friends—especially Elizabeth, Michelle, Becky, The Julies, Pilar—as well as those listed above, who were patient with me for the entire year that I said "I can't, I have to write." They not only understood this but enjoyed the gradual appearance of the book as if it were a new friend brought into the fold. Among those friends is also Brent Garcia, who was understanding and supportive of the time I needed to take to write this book—and loved me every step of the way.

JENNIFER THANKS:

My parents, Cynthia and David, who manage to be cool, loving, honest, and supportive parents without being my "friends" and trying to smoke pot with me. My sisters, Jessica (who has the brain of Woody Allen trapped in the body of Cameron Diaz) and Andrea (who has the brain of Annie Hall trapped in the body of Annie Hall), who make me laugh until I am hysterical. My two grannies, Gladys and Effie. Steven Daly, who gave me early encouragement to write a book. My circle of friends, who are really family: Marianne Jensch, Gillian Aldrich, Erin Wade, Jeff Hull, Anastasia Higginbotham, Alexandra Shiva, and the Bars, Bares, and Needhams. And, last but not least, Amy Ray, the most liberated woman I know.

Introduction to Jennifer

I was walking in the East Village on my way to meet my best friend, Marianne, and I passed one of my favorite neighborhood restaurants. The sun was high and bright, a breeze was blowing, I liked what I was wearing—the world was good. That is, until I was confronted with the Trustafarian hipster (read: white guy with dreads, likely to be living off a trust fund) who works the register at this restaurant. A "front of the house" member of the service industry, he was standing outside the door, yapping loudly into his cell phone, while the Mexican kid who actually does the work, did the work. For some reason, the fact that the privileged gals and guys, with their overdyed hair and thrift-store glad rags, were up front at this trendy chow wagon, while the short brown men in their black-checkered food-prep pants and white shirts hustled behind them, set me off. By the time I hooked up with Marianne, I was frothing at the mouth. This is the kind of anger I associate with men, with privilege, with the reasons that the he-girl of anger, Valerie Solanas, was driven to write the *SCUM Manifesto*, not to mention shoot Andy Warhol. I couldn't get it out of me. It was like a virus. I had road rage—and no car.

Some kind of rage percolates in my veins even though I generally want to be liked. My fury, like road rage, is that generalized sense of your blood pressure elevating frighteningly because what you presumed was going to go smoothly (no traffic out to the airport) is in fact riddled with barriers. But there is a difference between the random road rage of personal frustration (which I occasionally indulge in) and the healthy anger that is a response to injustice. For example, the fact that I got paid $1.50 per word (on the high end) writing for a Condé Nast magazine, while an ex-boyfriend was paid more than $2 provokes a dignified pique—as does the fact that I can barely bring myself to ask for more money. Jann Wenner and his boys' club at *Rolling Stone* sucking off a band like Limp Bizkit offends me (as does the fact that there isn't a competing magazine called *Roxanne* run by women). The gang of white male late-night talk-show hosts perturbs me. (Is there a *reason* women have shows only during daylight hours?) The fact that women aren't equal in the U.S. Constitution or that the Hyde Amendment means that millions of dollars a year have to be fundraised (women's unpaid labor) so that poor women can get abortions does, too. It makes me angry that abortion is treated like a privilege rather than a right (as if having your uterus scraped so that you don't have to take on the responsibility of someone else's life were akin to getting to drive your parents' BMW at age fifteen). *AAARGH!*

Righteous is the word for my anger, and I distinguish it from road-style rage in another way. Road rage is impotent. There is nothing you can do if you're sitting in traffic, bumper to bumper, with other enraged weekend warriors. You chose to be there, no prejudice was enacted in trapping you there, and no amount of screaming will change anything. But my righteous rage in the face of bare-assed wrongs is only as impotent as I am. I have an inner Valerie Solanas *and*, because of the fluke of timing, family, and my own efforts, I have the tools of feminism at my disposal.

Yes, I was raised in a home where my sister called me a lesbian at age five not because she was clairvoyant but because she read the word in an article in *Ms.* I had a stay-at-home mom, who somehow made it clear that it wasn't her *job* to make dinner or pick us up from basketball or dance class the minute we called. I had a breadwinning dad, a doctor, who never acted as if he wished his three daughters were sons. I was raised in Fargo, North Dakota, went to public school, and was suspended for being truant during my senior year. Like most women who relate to feminism, I hated the sexism of high school (though I didn't have a word for the date rape, focus on boys' sports, and petty cruelty back then). My sisters and I are all feminists, which we learned from our mom, who learned it from *Ms.*, her women's group, reading Marilyn French's novel *The Women's Room,* and, most of all, from her own life. My first radical act was, at fifteen, biking to the Fargo Women's Health Clinic with $200 I fund-raised from a senior's college account so that my sixteen-year-old sister could get an abortion. Although I was proud to have been able to get a girl I loved out of a jam, I never anticipated how devastated my parents would be when they found out that we didn't turn to them in this moment of teenage crisis. Their sadness led to my first radical insight: My sister didn't fail to tell them because she thought *they* would judge her—they didn't have to. Any girl who gets pregnant feels like a chump, like a native New Yorker taken in a shell game on Broadway. It's too embarrassing to make it into a family affair. Making public, even to my parents, my sister's choice to determine the course of her life would have been misconstrued as having "screwed up." In other words, the women's movement ensured that my sister had the right to an abortion, but the feminist interpretation of *choice* didn't make it onto the coattails of *Roe v. Wade.*

When I was twenty-six, I walked out on my job as an editor at *Ms.* magazine, my first real job. I had loved it there more than anywhere since the womb, but by the time I left the sight of the harried editors, the stained and airless offices, and the constant crises had made me ill. After years of declining working conditions under hostile male owners—long hours, low pay, bungled editorial processes that alienated writers, a harrowing year of stiffing writers, and being asked to sit in for the beleaguered company receptionist so that the poor woman could go to the bathroom—I got out. I packed my files and left without saying goodbye. For a while, I was really bitter toward *Ms.* for not standing up to the owners or striking until the writers got paid, ideas I trumpeted like a lonely, clueless cheerleader. The writers did eventually get paid, over the course of two years, through a covert system of padding future assignments and the editorial budget, as well as through Gloria Steinem, who used her own fees to pay them. If the magazine's editors had quit in protest, the writers would never have recouped their fees. So all's fairly well that ends fairly well. *But* I wanted us to be cool and brave and righteous. Like Ani DiFranco—or at least freaky and noticeable like Courtney or Roseanne. Instead, I felt that we were passive-aggressive, insecure, and, to paraphrase Flo Kennedy, a bit too eager to eat shit and call it chocolate. We were martyrs. We were *unliberated.*

My first instinct after this insight—*The women who tell you to rebel and strike are hypocrites!*—was to write a tell-all book. But soon, as I started making it on my own outside the *Ms.*-utero, my analysis began to complexify. True, *Ms.* was the dysfunctional family I had never had, but there was a story behind that story, too. *Ms.* had battered women's movement syndrome. That poor girl was pushing thirty and she couldn't get a break; she was treated like shit by a sexist industry and then ignored by the many feminists who were her natural constituency. Feminists, let down by *Ms.,* had then rushed out to rip it to shreds for not filling the gaping holes (in self-esteem or ambition) left by sexism, something a single magazine simply could not do. Feminists my age, Girlies with tight clothes and streaky hair, who made zines and music and Web sites, exhibited the confidence and self-worth that I craved from *Ms.* But part of what was free about them seemed to be that they weren't taking on anything they might have to lose. Soon I looked at the world outside the shabby, radical-chic offices of *Ms.* and realized that the whole movement was in a kind of crisis: the people who are creating the most inspiring feminist culture and the people who have a working knowledge of feminist political change haven't met yet.

One night in the late fall of 1997, Amy and I got extremely drunk on huge glasses of wine at a downtown bar and decided to collaborate on a book about our generation of feminism. *Ms.* wasn't effectively getting the news out there to our peers (people often asked both Amy and me if *Ms.* was still around); nor did we necessarily feel represented by the fresher, younger, Jell-O–shots versions of feminism, like *Bust* and *Bitch* and the many Girlie webzines. Ultimately, while we believed that confidence and culture are key, we knew it was political consciousness (and an understanding of power and a commitment to action) that was going to wake up the women's movement.

So we began writing. I was doing this for a living anyway, but writing a book is hard work. All the time I spent procrastinating felt harsher and more guilt-inducing than it did when I was writing a magazine piece. However, for all the tedium and transcribing, the late nights and the coffee-induced acne, writing about one's feminist peers and predecessors is a gift. At times, I felt that I shouldn't be paid for it because I would want to get to know the women in this book anyway. Fortunately, I wasn't paid much.

Four years ago, when I was still at *Ms.* but had just learned about *Bust,* the editors of that zine asked me to interview Björk, the Smurfy Icelandic pop star, for their issue on motherhood. I was perhaps a little naïve in assuming that she and I would connect on some ethnic level simply because my matrilineal family also hails from lava-laden Iceland, but her dismissiveness of contemporary feminism weirded me out. Trapped in my own earnestness about Third Wave feminism, I found myself asking a lot of goody-two-shoes questions about being a single mother. I wanted to know what had led Björk to divorce the father of her son after only a year of marriage. "Why suffer?" she said, and picked her nose.

Although I was actually raised on the Protestant philosophy

of "No pain, no gain," "Why suffer?" was to become a part of my personal manifesto. Because I said "Why suffer?," I didn't psych myself out by thinking that to write a book means one has to lock oneself in a tiny apartment for a year, sleep all day, chain-smoke American Spirits, and write in a paranoid blaze during the vampire hours. Because Amy and I said "Why suffer?," we went to Cuba, organized intergenerational readings, attended sample sales, and wrote a fucking book—all in the service of keeping joyful while figuring out what's wrong with the patriarchy and the movement.

I consciously brought "Why suffer?" into my personal manifesto because the cult of martyrdom is sold to girls like cigarettes, and sometimes from the most unlikely sources—the women who should be our natural allies. Although I wish the Girlie feminists in this book would organize as well as they onanize, they have created a joyful culture that makes being an adult woman who calls herself a feminist seem thrilling, sexy, and creative (rather than scary, backbiting, or a one-way ticket to bitterness and the poorhouse). I think Girlie-style feminists are unfairly maligned for this act. I also think that being an adult woman in the world requires not just saying "I believe in equal pay for equal work" but knowing how to fight for it, dragging womankind closer to that and many other goals.

I feel that I should end this introduction to our joint work with my own freshly minted words of wisdom. When Amy and I got the book contract, I was ecstatic but nervous. We were friends and comrades in arms—what were we doing risking it all by co-writing a book? Would I hate how she writes—and vice versa? Worse, would she and I end up hating each other? Suing each other? It turns out that there was no spark of anxiety in my own soul that someone else didn't want to fan into a bright, leaping flame of paranoia. A mentor of mine, who has yet to write any book, congratulated me when she heard about the deal, and toasted it this way: "Here's to your *next* book, which you'll be *ready* to write alone." Another Second Waver, whose books I had read, looked at me with a knowing and concerned smile when she learned about our book and said, "Important books aren't co-written, you know." I was too polite to mention the eight unread books she wrote after her one groundbreaker. There were more undermining comments, and I don't know if two men who chose to collaborate would have provoked this kind of questioning, but the point is that Amy and I had to learn to write together, to compromise, and I couldn't put in a bunch of personal moments from my own life (which are the most gratifying to write). We couldn't be precious about language or slang or word choice—not if we wanted to get the book done and refrain from destroying our friendship. Thinking back over the past year and a half, what I am proudest of is that we negotiated that tricky space of compromise and mutual creation. I think it's even cooler that we had fun, taxed our brains, and treated each other well throughout the whole process. If we had rage, it was righteous.

This book, then, and writing it with a friend whose brain and politics I admire, is in defiance of people who think there's only one way to write a book. I hope that after you read it you'll go and create a zine or a broadsheet or a film or music or an article for the paper or write a *book*. And if you want to do it as an act of sisterhood with a girl (or a boy) who's fierce like you, but in different ways, more power to you. We women, especially we feminists, are still trying to become what we believe in. So get equal pay for comparable work, down with the virgin/whore complex, know your body the way you know your Judy Blume books, fight for the right to love whom you choose, and, in all things, fight for equality. You could take less, but why suffer?

—*Jennifer Baumgardner*
New York City, 2000

Introduction to Amy

I think of myself as an activist first and a writer second. I write to bring to light otherwise subliminal messages that are concealed within a culture that pretends to be ignorant of them. I write to give voice to those who need to be heard, and don't yet have a forum for exposing injustices. I write to honor the individuals who are beacons of light in our midst. This book is a bigger version of all these motives.

I am not quite sure how I came to be a feminist activist and writer. I was born into a good working-class family in central Pennsylvania. In my childhood community, the examples of what I could do with my life were pretty much limited to getting a high-school diploma, and maybe later a teaching certificate, or embarking on another "female" profession. My mother's commitment to giving me lots of opportunities meant that in the seventh grade we moved to Massachusetts so that I could get a better education—and, hopefully, stop skipping school and spending every weekend (and all of my baby-sitting money) at the roller-skating rink in the misguided belief that making an impression on the hulky boys was what mattered most to my future standing in life. With this move, I did get a better education—along with exposure to new opportunities. But, to fit into my small New England neighborhood, I left behind the girl with feathered hair and tight Jordache jeans with a comb stuck in the back pocket. I became a preppy teenager with plaid shorts, Izod shirts, straight hair, and an attitude of middle-class privilege. I realize that this aspect of my upbringing is what most informs my activism. I have access and humility, *and* an understanding that the world isn't so neatly divided between the haves and the have-nots.

My first dose of actual activism came in April 1992, a few days after the Rodney King verdict was handed down. South Central Los Angeles was on fire, and I was a twenty-two-year-old sitting in a small New York City apartment with eight other people, trying to figure out what we could do to make the world a better place. I was about to graduate from college and was still insecure enough to believe that everyone in that room but me had their life all wrapped up, like the pretty packages showcased in Martha Stewart's catalog. I was convinced that the twenty-something women and men in the room were going to become lawyers, educators, movie directors, and authors. On the other hand, I was going to be back at Christie's auction house (where I had been an intern) peddling art that I should have been creating and feeling sorry for myself because I wasn't rich enough to actually buy it.

Later, I discovered that I really was like all those other ambitious people in the room. We had been pulled together by a common thread: we wanted to play a role in making our generation more accountable politically and socially. A voter-registration drive, we concluded, was the best way to do that—and thus our planning began. We started this work wide-eyed and with an honest-to-goodness belief that anything was possible. After a few weeks, the small group fine-tuned our vision into Freedom Summer '92. On August 1, 1992, we departed New York City on three buses carrying 120 primarily young people on a cross-country voter-registration drive.

Since that Rodney King day, I have gotten out of bed every day with a commitment to equality and justice, and a passion for putting people in touch with information and for putting good ideas into the hands of those who can execute them. Most of this I learned directly from Gloria Steinem, who has been a boss, a friend, and a mentor while I honed my own activist and organizing skills. If you had asked me what I was doing back then, I would have explained only the detail of my days, because I did not yet know that being either a feminist or an activist could be my full-time calling and career. Co-founding the Third Wave Foundation, a national organization for young feminists, initiated my interactions with other idealistic and political people across the country, all of whom wanted to be connected to other feminists. In New York City, a cadre of activists wanted to meet regularly, so we instituted member meetings covering a range of topics. Before long, I was putting all of these individuals in touch with one another and with information that could get them started with organizing in their own communities. Upset by the lack of voter participation among young people, we launched a voter-education program called Why Vote?—in hopes that we would be able to get these should-be voters hooked by showing them how they could influence the issues they cared about. Each step of the way, we were identifying problems and finding creative solutions, while bringing more and more like-minded people to Third Wave and vice versa—introducing Third Wave to people who didn't yet know that they needed such a network in their lives.

My other activist undertaking is Ask Amy, an on-line feminist advice column, which has been featured at feminist.com since 1996. "*You've Got Mail*" greets me most mornings and has also become a sort of good-night blessing—or curse, depending on how much mail I have and what wee hour of the morning it is. After three years, I have relationships with thousands of people who have written to me. Our conversations are often born of desperation—a twelve-year-old in Pakistan who believes she's ugly or a fifteen-year-old in California who was raped by her stepfather. Others are just looking for help with a report, or for historical information about the women's movement. Then there are still others who are looking to yell at someone about how much they want all feminists to crawl under a rock and die. But those are usually counterbalanced by a note from someone thanking me (and feminism) for being there.

There are also the off-line individuals in my community, like the people I sit next to on the subway who ask about the two bracelets I wear every day: one in protest of parental-consent laws and the other opposing the Hyde Amendment. My explanation is typically greeted with a glare of disapproval or a smile of support. I thrive on these everyday occurrences, because they prove that nothing in life is random. I walk away from most of these chance interactions with a new friend, a new enemy, or a new way of explaining something.

These are examples of my inadvertent mission in life, which is to collect and share information. Call it good fortune, great instinct, or overattention verging on obsession, but I love disseminating information to anyone I believe needs it, wants it, and will make something of it. There is no rhyme or reason to my information gathering. The only requirement is that it intrigue me enough to hold on to it, believing that someday, somewhere, I will find a way to put it to good use. There have been a few moments when I thought I'd kept something unnecessarily—an E-mail query from a woman who wanted to become a pipe fitter, for instance—but, sure enough, I usually find a reason for it; in this case it was an article on a Journey Level pipe fitter named Darlene Owens. It's like the card game Concentration, where satisfaction comes from finding the perfect match. Other examples are the scraps of paper I rip out of magazines or newsletters and deliver to friends and colleagues daily; a coffee-stained computer printout with interesting prison statistics; and the business card of a woman I met in Cairo in 1994 whose video camera recorded people speaking about birth control, fertility, and sexually transmitted diseases. Eventually, she showed her tape to illiterate women in rural Africa, and I know that one day I'll get a request for just such a tape.

The primary residence of all these examples is my office, but there is also the cute striped plastic Peruvian bag I carry with me at all times, just in case I need something or get stuck in an elevator or in traffic with a little extra time to work. I used to describe these habits as chance occurrences, but with the help of other people's insights into my life I've come to realize that collecting and making connections are my activism. I am a conduit through which information and ideas pass, or the recycler—taking in the bad and trying to make it good. For want of a better word, I have come to describe myself as a producer, though a film or TV show has yet to be the result. Perhaps I am an organizer, a change agent, or some other description yet to be coined.

Like Third Wave and Ask Amy, *Manifesta* is an example of cause and effect. It was created to fill a gap in the lives of young women, like me, who yearn for a connection to feminism. Unfortunately, most of the books that have been published about feminism in this generation have tried to convince readers that young women are somehow lacking in activism and are even antagonistic to the feminists who came before them. This was counter to what I saw every day. Accurate examples do exist, but most of them either cover a specific issue—the media or growing up biracial, for example—or are anthologies that address many issues without offering a sustained argument. The thread in this book is my observation that feminism is out there—manifesting itself in individual people's lives, and often in the lives of people who don't even know they're living it. I've also become a repository for other people's stories about their feminism and their activism—and it's only fair that I share them.

This book was born also of conversations that helped me push barriers in my own life, specifically talks I've been privileged to have over the past seven years with my co-author, Jenny, a close personal friend and colleague. Our conversations began simply enough—as two recent college graduates living and working in New York City—and were often prefaced by "Hey, want to go check out this new band?" As our professions grew, so did our conversations. When Jenny was a junior staff person at *Ms.* and I was Gloria Steinem's assistant, we would look to each other to confirm ideas that we knew deep down were good but that we were still too impressionable to have total confidence in. As we moved along in our careers, we began to own our own ideas. Jenny had moved on to writing, and I was spending more time on political research for the pro-choice political-action organization Voters for Choice, setting up a database clearinghouse on indigenous issues for First Nations Development Institute, trying to take the Third Wave Foundation in new and more bold directions, and immersing myself in Ask Amy.

Jenny and I were no longer a part of each other's daily lives, but we'd sneak time together every few weeks, sometimes over coffee but mostly over glasses of wine that would grow into bottles of wine. We continued to look to each other for confirmation and a reality check. Before long, I found myself saving up ideas I wanted to explore, things I wanted to know more about, until I could see her. It was as if we were having an intellectual affair—meeting at odd hours in smoke-filled bars to steal time together in the middle of our busy lives. On one such night, the idea to do this book together was conceived. We were each working on separate book proposals—mine more Feminist Activism 101 and Jenny's more cultural and critical. After confirming that a book with both these components was exactly what had been missing from our reading, we began Manifesta.

The idea of writing a book wasn't so daunting, since I had quite literally lived through Gloria Steinem's writing of Moving Beyond Words. I knew the process—the sleep deprivation, the blurry vision, the familiar delivery person who brings a can of Coke or a pint of ice cream at odd hours, and the endless yellow stickies. What I also knew was that every detail had to be accurate and confirmed in order for people to take you and your argument seriously. Gloria is a consummate reporter, journalist, and fact checker, and this is what makes her work accessible, timeless, and valuable. So, beyond learning the quirky sides of writing, I'm hopeful that the latter wore off on me as well.

Since March 1998, when Jenny and I started this project, we have often been asked how we managed to write a book together: "How could you two possibly agree enough to write the same book?" This was a logistical and an emotional question—and perhaps a political one, too. The most basic ingredient has been the tried-and-true respect we have for each other, and for each other's ideas. It's not so much about agreeing to agree as agreeing to disagree, and also to use the different strengths we've brought to this book. And, throughout all my experiences, whether I was organizing a cross-country voter-registration drive, launching a national organization, responding to questions at Ask Amy, or being a catalyst for feminist activity, there has been one constant lesson: no good project was ever executed alone. *Manifesta* was no different. Collaborating came easily to us, largely because of our collaborative pasts—Jenny's as an editor at *Ms.*, and mine as an organizer of meetings for Third Wave. We started out thinking that we would each write different chapters, then edit the other's work. After our first chapter exchange, however, we decided to write together.

Over the course of about eight months, we spent part of almost every day sitting across from each other—Jenny decked out in some hand-me-down-from-her-mother-Pucci-style dress, hunched over the computer, while we thought out loud. I read from our edits on paper, attempting to look semiprofessional in autumn-colored skirts, tights, and T-shirts. Sitting between us was our pathetic but addictive sustenance: cheese and coffee (iced in the summer months and hot in the spring and fall). And flowing between us were more important nutrients: ideas born and confirmed. Just when we were approaching a tense moment, we would break out in laughter about a glaring typo, how self-righteous one of us was choosing to be at a particular moment, or how disgusting we felt after eating an entire pan of

Rice Krispie Treats. Those moments of laughter, honesty, and support were ingredients necessary to our project, and, I believe, to any feminist setting.

Though Jenny and I are the authors of this book, it was made possible only by the people who inform its pages and remind us that feminism is a necessary part of every person's life. We have taken the good ideas and the horrendous stories confided to us, put them together with our ideas, and transmitted them to you, the reader. My friend the Native American activist Rebecca Adamson once said to me, "The mark of a good idea is when you can't remember whose it is." Perhaps this is what the poet Victor Hugo was trying to convey when he said, "There is nothing as powerful as an idea whose time has come." Those quotes still make me accountable for my ideas, but they remind me that an idea is good only when there is a constituency that's ready to hear it. Many of the concepts in this book might feel like yours. I hope you spend some time saying, "Hey, I've had that idea." It's this unspoken connectedness that I believe is out there. This book is meant to expose our conversations for what they are—part of a big, visible, passionate movement.

I hope the existence of this book will lead to similar conversations in your own life—and to making feminism your own.

—*Amy Richards*
New York City, 2000

MANIFESTA

A Day without Feminism

We were both born in 1970, the baptismal moment of a decade that would change dramatically the lives of American women. The two of us grew up thousands of miles apart, in entirely different kinds of families, yet we both came of age with the awareness that certain rights had been won by the women's movement. We've never doubted how important feminism is to people's lives—men's and women's. Both of our mothers went to consciousness-raising-type groups. Amy's mother raised Amy on her own, and Jennifer's mother, questioning the politics of housework, staged laundry strikes.

With the dawn of not just a new century but a new millennium, people are looking back and taking stock of feminism. Do we need new strategies? Is feminism dead? Has society changed so much that the idea of a feminist movement is obsolete? For us, the only way to answer these questions is to imagine what our lives would have been if the women's movement had never happened and the conditions for women had remained as they were in the year of our births.

Imagine that for a day it's still 1970, and women have only the rights they had then. Sly and the Family Stone and Dionne Warwick are on the radio, the kitchen appliances are Harvest Gold, and the name of your Whirlpool gas stove is Mrs. America. What is it like to be female?

Babies born on this day are automatically given their father's name. If no father is listed, "illegitimate" is likely to be typed on the birth certificate. There are virtually no child-care centers, so all preschool children are in the hands of their mothers, a baby-sitter, or an expensive nursery school. In elementary school, girls can't play in Little League and almost all of the teachers are female. (The latter is still true.) In a few states, it may be against the law for a male to teach grades lower than the sixth, on the basis that it's unnatural, or that men can't be trusted with young children.

In junior high, girls probably take home ec; boys take shop or small-engine repair. Boys who want to learn how to cook or sew on a button are out of luck, as are girls who want to learn how to fix a car. *Seventeen* magazine doesn't run feminist-influenced current columns like "Sex + Body" and "Trauma-rama." Instead the magazine encourages girls not to have sex; pleasure isn't part of its vocabulary. Judy Blume's books are just beginning to be published, and *Free to Be . . . You and Me* does not exist. No one reads much about masturbation as a natural activity; nor do they learn that sex is for anything other than procreation. Girls do read mystery stories about Nancy Drew, for whom there is no sex, only her blue roadster and having "luncheon." (The real mystery is how Nancy gets along without a purse and manages to meet only white people.) Boys read about the Hardy Boys, for whom there are no girls.

In high school, the principal is a man. Girls have physical-education class and play half-court basketball, but not soccer, track, or cross country; nor do they have any varsity sports teams. The only prestigious physical activity for girls is cheerleading, or being a drum majorette. Most girls don't take calculus or physics; they plan the dances and decorate the gym. Even when girls get better grades than their male counterparts, they are half as likely to qualify for a National Merit Scholarship because many of the test questions favor boys. Standardized tests refer to males and male experiences much more than to females and their experiences.[1] If a girl "gets herself pregnant," she loses her membership in the National Honor Society (which is still true today) and is expelled.[2]

Girls and young women might have sex while they're unmarried, but they may be ruining their chances of landing a guy full-time, and they're probably getting a bad reputation. If a pregnancy happens, an enterprising gal can get a legal abortion only if she lives in New York or is rich enough to fly there, or to Cuba, London, or Scandinavia. There's also the Chicago-based Jane Collective, an underground abortion-referral service, which can hook you up with an illegal or legal termination. (Any of these options are going to cost you. Illegal abortions average $300 to $500, sometimes as much as $2,000.) To prevent pregnancy, a sexually active woman might go to a doctor to be fitted for a diaphragm, or take the high-dose birth-control pill, but her doctor isn't likely to inform her of the possibility of deadly blood clots. Those who do take the Pill also may have to endure this contraceptive's crappy side effects: migraine headaches, severe weight gain, irregular bleeding, and hair loss (or gain), plus the possibility of an increased risk of breast cancer in the long run. It is unlikely that women or their male partners know much about the clitoris and its role in orgasm unless someone happens to fumble upon it. Instead, the myth that vaginal orgasms from penile penetration are the only "mature" (according to Freud) climaxes prevails.

Lesbians are rarely "out," except in certain bars owned by organized crime (the only businessmen who recognize this untapped market), and if lesbians don't know about the bars, they're less likely to know whether there are any other women like them. Radclyffe Hall's depressing early-twentieth-century novel *The Well of Loneliness* pretty much indicates their fate.

The Miss America Pageant is the biggest source of scholarship money for women.[3] Women can't be students at Dartmouth, Columbia, Harvard, West Point, Boston College, or the Citadel, among other all-male institutions. Women's colleges are referred to as "girls' schools." There are no Take Back the Night marches to protest women's lack of safety after dark, but that's okay because college girls aren't allowed out much after dark anyway. Curfew is likely to be midnight on Saturday and 9 or 10 p.m. the rest of the week. Guys get to stay out as late as they want. Women tend to major in teaching, home economics, English, or maybe a language—a good skill for translating someone else's words.[4] The women's studies major does not exist, although you can take a women's studies course at six universities, including Cornell and San Diego State College.[5] The absence of women's history, black history, Chicano studies, Asian-American history, queer studies, and Native American history from college curricula implies that they are not worth studying. A student is lucky if he or she learns that women were "given" the vote in 1920, just as Columbus "discovered" America in 1492. They might also learn that Sojourner Truth, Mary Church Terrell, and Fannie Lou Hamer were black abolitionists or civil-rights leaders, but not that they were feminists. There are practically no tenured female professors at any school, and campuses are not racially diverse. Women of color are either not there or they're lonely as hell. There is no nationally recognized Women's History Month or Black History Month. Only 14 percent of doctorates are awarded to women. Only 3.5 percent of MBAs are female.

Only 2 percent of everybody in the military is female, and these women are mostly nurses. There are no female generals in the U.S. Air Force, no female naval pilots, and no Marine brigadier generals. On the religious front, there are no female cantors or rabbis, Episcopal canons, or Catholic priests. (This is still true of Catholic priests.)

Only 44 percent of women are employed outside the home. And those women make, on average, fifty-two cents to the dollar earned by males. Want ads are segregated into "Help

Wanted Male" and "Help Wanted Female." The female side is preponderantly for secretaries, domestic workers, and other low-wage service jobs, so if you're a female lawyer you must look under "Help Wanted Male." There are female doctors, but twenty states have only five female gynecologists or fewer. Women workers can be fired or demoted for being pregnant, especially if they are teachers, since the kids they teach aren't supposed to think that women have sex. If a boss demands sex, refers to his female employee exclusively as "Baby," or says he won't pay her unless she gives him a blow job, she either has to quit or succumb—no pun intended. Women can't be airline pilots. Flight attendants are "stewardesses"—waitresses in the sky—and necessarily female. Sex appeal is a job requirement, wearing makeup is a rule, and women are fired if they exceed the age or weight deemed sexy. Stewardesses can get married without getting canned, but this is a new development. (In 1968 the Equal Employment Opportunity Commission—EEOC—made it illegal to forcibly retire stewardesses for getting hitched.) Less than 2 percent of dentists are women; 100 percent of dental assistants are women. The "glass ceiling" that keeps women from moving naturally up the ranks, as well as the sticky floor that keeps them unnaturally down in low-wage work, has not been named, much less challenged.

When a woman gets married, she vows to love, honor, and obey her husband, though he gets off doing just the first two to uphold his end of the bargain. A married woman can't obtain credit without her husband's signature. She doesn't have her own credit rating, legal domicile, or even her own name unless she goes to court to get it back. If she gets a loan with her husband—and she has a job—she may have to sign a "baby letter" swearing that she won't have one and have to leave her job.

Women have been voting for up to fifty years, but their turnout rate is lower than that for men, and they tend to vote right along with their husbands, not with their own interests in mind.[6] The divorce rate is about the same as it is in 2000, contrary to popular fiction's blaming the women's movement for divorce. However, divorce required that one person be at fault, therefore if you just want out of your marriage, you have to lie or blame your spouse. Property division and settlements, too, are based on fault. (And at a time when domestic violence isn't a term, much less a crime, women are legally encouraged to remain in abusive marriages.) If fathers ask for custody of the children, they get it in 60 to 80 percent of the cases. (This is still true.) If a husband or a lover hits his partner, she has no shelter to go to unless she happens to live near the one in northern California or the other in upper Michigan. If a woman is downsized from her role as a housewife (a.k.a. left by her husband), there is no word for being a displaced homemaker. As a divorcée, she may be regarded as a family disgrace or as easy sexual prey. After all, she had sex with one guy, so why not *all* guys?

If a woman is not a Mrs., she's a Miss. A woman without makeup and a hairdo is as suspect as a man with them. Without a male escort she may be refused service in a restaurant or a bar, and a woman alone is hard-pressed to find a landlord who will rent her an apartment. After all, she'll probably be leaving to get married soon, and, if she isn't, the landlord doesn't want to deal with a potential brothel.

Except among the very poor or in very rural areas, babies are born in hospitals. There are no certified midwives, and women are knocked out during birth. Most likely, they are also strapped down and lying down, made to have the baby against gravity for the doctor's convenience. If he has a schedule to keep, the likelihood of a cesarean is also very high. *Our Bodies, Ourselves* doesn't exist, nor does the women's health movement. Women aren't taught how to look at their cervixes, and their bodies are nothing to worry their pretty little heads about; however, they are supposed to worry about keeping their little heads pretty. If a woman goes under the knife to see if she has breast cancer, the surgeon won't wake her up to consult about her options before performing a Halsted mastectomy (a disfiguring radical procedure, in which the breast, the muscle wall, and the nodes under the arm, right down to the bone, are removed). She'll just wake up and find that the choice has been made for her.

Husbands are likely to die eight years earlier than their same-age wives due to the stress of having to support a family and repress an emotional life, and a lot earlier than that if women have followed the custom of marrying older, authoritative, paternal men. The stress of raising kids, managing a household, and being undervalued by society doesn't seem to kill off women at the same rate. Upon a man's death, his beloved gets a portion of his Social Security. Even if she has worked outside the home for her entire adult life, she is probably better off with that portion than with hers in its entirety, because she has earned less and is likely to have taken time out for such unproductive acts as having kids.[7]

Has feminism changed our lives? Was it necessary? After thirty years of feminism, the world we inhabit barely resembles the world we were born into. And there's still a lot left to do.

CHAPTER ONE

The Dinner Party

THE FIRST SUPPER

In the beginning was the Word, and the Word was Consciousness. Feminist consciousness—understanding that women can and should be whole human beings, not measured in relationship to male supremacy—is, was, and will always be the soul of feminism. In the seventies, Jane O'Reilly called this experience the "click," as in women "clicking-things-into-place-angry." In the nineties, on celluloid, Thelma's moment of consciousness came when she said to Louise, "Ah feel a-wake," and for the next hour these two women had the power of clarity and righteousness—the kind of righteousness that makes you blow up a leering truck driver's eighteen-wheeler or lock a macho policeman in the trunk of his squad car. Epiphanies about sexist injustices don't happen in a vacuum (though they may be caused by a vacuum). Women often see that an experience was a result of sexism only if another woman, or group of women, says, "Yeah, I get told to smile by random men as I walk down the street, too. Why are they doing it, and why do I apologize for not smiling?" Reading women's real experiences in books and magazines can provide the same click of recognition.

11

All of us begin our life with a child's sense of fairness, but it's soon socialized out of us. Raising our consciousness is something we have to work on—and what comes out of that work is the very foundation on which social-justice movements are built. In the sixties and seventies, women across the country woke up their consciousness, often realizing that the civil-rights movement and the peace movement were led by men and didn't give a thought to women's human rights. They knew suddenly that there needed to be a cultural revolution to purge women's heads and men's hearts of the notion of male supremacy. Then our generation came along, and took its first breath of air in a new atmosphere, one where women's expectations and freedoms were soaringly, thrillingly different.

It's poignant to look back, seeing how much harder the lives of the women who came before us were, and to imagine the clicks that erupted during other generations. Making a big leap through history, what if this clicking of consciousness had begun at the beginning of Western history? With feminism added, would the women in the Bible have put up with being unliberated scapegoats who got blamed for most of the evil in the world yet don't even merit a listing in the Good Book's index? Imagine how the Bible would read if these women had had a chance to get together for dinner, just the girls, and talk.

After the ladies loosen up around the table, Mary Magdalene would begin by talking about sex workers' rights, and returning belly dancing to its origin as an exercise for giving birth. Leah and Rachel would resolve their longtime sisterly competition by ditching Jacob, the man their father married them both to, and agitate for women to be able to inherit their own property. Rather than being synonymous with evil, Jezebel would be lauded for her business acumen. Hagar would receive palimony and child support from her lover, Abraham. Sarah, Abraham's wife, might even befriend Hagar, Abraham's concubine and Sarah's slave; at the very least, she would empathize. Bathsheba, tired of looking for love from a poetic boy who couldn't commit, would have the presence of mind to leave King David. Delilah would teach them about orgasms and exhort her friends to make sure they got what they needed in bed. Lilith would be full of first wives' club advice for Eve, and Eve would be pontificating about the politics of housework. Eve would also recognize that she had been framed, and refuse to take the Fall for her man or her God. Ruth wouldn't be saying "Whither thou goest, I will go" to her mother-in-law or anyone anymore; she'd be blazing her own trails. Meanwhile, they'd all begin to question why the hell Lot's wife was turned into a pillar of salt when her husband was busy offering up their virgin daughters to the marauders. (And why the hell she didn't have a name.) Perhaps they'd start a Mothers Against Raping Children chapter in Judea. After they realized that they could change their lives locally, they'd hunker down and organize with other women. Their daughters would be born into a whole new world. Who knows what greater good would come from future dinner parties?[8]

The universe is made of stories, not of atoms.
—MURIEL RUKEYSER

Thirteen men got together for the most lauded dinner party in patriarchal history: the Last Supper. However, thirteen women around a table tend to be regarded as something a bit less positive—a coven comes to mind. (Of course, anyone who knows anything about Wicca knows that covens are benevolent, that thirteen is a lucky and powerful number, and that spells work like karma: whatever you send out will come back at you.) Women breaking bread together has probably always been a sort of consciousness-raising group with food—a time to vent, learn from one another, and organize.

In the 1970s, groups of women began coming together intentionally to focus on consciousness-raising, or CR, which was a staple of Second Wave feminism, pioneered by Redstockings, an early New York radical women's liberation group. At these informal meetings, usually in their homes, women shared their secrets, stories of injustice, and mundane frustrations—most of which could be chalked up to sexism. They sought to become aware of male supremacy, and to politicize their lives. For example, a woman might tell her CR group that she never had orgasms, something that she had blamed on her own "frigidity." The other women in the group would offer their own tales of not getting satisfaction, and they'd think, We can't *all* be neurotic and frigid. At a subsequent meeting, they might read Anne Koedt's article "The Myth of the Vaginal Orgasm" and realize there was no such thing as frigidity, only inattention to the clitoris.[9] CR was designed to be a radicalizing process, a way of spurring women to change the world and of transforming the personal into the political.

The feminist implications of this sort of gathering were clear to the artist Judy Chicago in the late seventies, which is why she called her most famous installation "The Dinner Party." In Chicago's work, a triangular table the size of a neighborhood swimming pool was set with customized, labia-inspired place settings for thirty-nine of the most iconic women in Western history, thirteen on each side of the triangle. Dinner guests such as Sacagawea, Sappho, and Susan B. Anthony weren't even contemporaries, yet Chicago brought them together the way disparate men of note always come together in the history books, forming a narrative of accomplishment.[10]

In addition to being an ideal concept for one of the most famous pieces of feminist art, the women's dinner party is an appropriate setting for brainstorming about the state of feminism. Whether it's volunteering at a women's shelter, attending an all-women's college or a speak-out for Take Back the Night, or dancing at a strip club (an arena in which the only authentic relating goes on among the ladies—just ask anyone who has worked at one), whenever women are gathered together there is great potential for the individual women, and even the location itself, to become radicalized. This was probably the most important, but least appreciated by the media, benefit that came out of Lilith Fair, the all-women's music tour that played summer shows across the United States from 1997 to 1999. Audience members could meet new allies, for instance, and were often introduced to the feminist organizations in their community. Also, performing on that tour was the first time that women like Bonnie Raitt, Me'shell Ndege'ocello, and Sinéad O'Connor met each other. Before Lilith, these musicians had felt, perhaps, isolated from other women in the industry. After Lilith, many of them began playing on each other's records and sitting in on each other's tours. A whole new women's music community was created out of the ladies' space that was Lilith.

Today, the feminist movement has such a firm and organic toehold in women's lives that walking down the street (talking back to street harassers), sitting in our offices (refusing to make the coffee), nursing the baby (defying people who quail at the sight), or watching TV shows (*Xena*! *Buffy*!) can all contain feminism in action. For women of the Third Wave—that is, women who were reared in the wake of the women's liberation movement of the seventies—a good dinner party (or any gathering of women) is just as likely to be a place to see politics at work as is a rally. It's a place to map a strategy for our continuing liberation, because, as with every wave of feminism, our politics emerge from our everyday lives.

The concept for this chapter came out of a fierce faith that this honest communicating among women is a revolutionary act, and the best preface to activism. Of course, not all dinner parties are intentionally subversive. Women also use these gatherings as an excuse to sit down and talk with some interesting stranger they admire, or to develop ideas by having intellectual trysts with other women. (As *we* did for years before deciding to write this book.) This need to get together for girl talk begins over soggy Tater Tots in the grade-school cafeteria, continues through endless confabs on the phone or on sports teams during high school, and is grabbed throughout adulthood in book clubs or beauty parlors, while lifting weights at the gym or running through Target or at work.

The two of us have had a dinner-party circle together since around the time we first met as peons at *Ms.* magazine in 1993. For two years, we had a makeshift coven to which we invited a revolving group of eleven other women. We'd drink wine out of big purple goblets and consume huge potluck meals while we cast freestyle spells. (The spells consisted primarily of lighting candles and sending a kiss around the circle; we were novices.) Most of us had left our own religion or allowed it to lapse, and we were searching for spiritual rituals that had meaning for us. We were also searching for the kind of community, held together by shared morals and values, that many people get from religion. After casting the circle, we'd dive into some serious CR—discussing our deepest fears, for example; anxieties we had never shared with anyone. Because everyone was equally vulnerable, no one was really vulnerable, and the honesty poured forth. The wine poured forth, too, so much so that on one humid night we ended up singing to the moon from a New York City garden apartment, ecstatic in our drunken sisterhood, until the neighbors yelled down at us to shut up. After a while, we realized that the covens were mostly an excuse to get together and talk about intellectual and personal ideas in a concentrated way. So we ditched the Wiccan stuff but continued to have dinners with interesting new batches of women. Intense friendships were born at these parties, business deals conceived, ideas sparked, and contacts exchanged. Generally, we got energy and support to initiate all of the projects and ambitions we secretly, or proudly, held. Together, we bore witness to all manner of coming-of-age moments: getting an abortion, landing record and book deals, breaking up, tying the knot, becoming or owning up to being queer, leaving a first job, losing a parent, preparing to have kids, becoming or owning up to being straight, miscarrying, coming out about being rich or poor, and falling in love—all were mourned or celebrated or hashed out at our dinner parties.

The ideas for this book began to unfold around that table, and the questions that came up at these gatherings confirmed its premise: that feminism is out there, tucked into our daily acts of righteousness and self-respect. Feminism arrived in a different way in the lives of the women of this generation; we never knew a time before "girls can do anything boys can!" The fruits of this kind of confidence are enjoyed by almost every American girl or woman alive, a radical change from the suffragettes and bluestockings of the late nineteenth century, and from our serious sisters of the sixties and seventies. We also have the benefit of knowing from recent history that consciousness-raising must precede action, just as research precedes a breakthrough. In exchanges with one another, women learn that we are the real experts—often more so than the paid experts, who have studied but not experienced the subject at hand. If a woman has gone through a divorce, for instance, researched the best way to get an abortion, asked for a raise, or is having sex at the age of sixteen, she knows something that could help another woman. For these women, and for anyone born after the early 1960s, the presence of feminism in our lives is taken for granted. For our generation, feminism is like fluoride. We scarcely notice that we have it—it's simply in the water.

As our peers charge toward equality and liberation, we watch them contribute their defiance to a historic narrative. Third Wave feminism's contribution to women's history builds on the foundation of the Second Wave. It is the thousands of little girls with temporary tattoos on their arms, and Mia Hamm soccer jerseys on their backs, who own the bleachers at the Women's World Cup, just as much as the few writers and leaders who have attained prominence. Our activism is in the single mother who organizes the baby-sitting chain on Election Day so that all the housebound mothers can vote. Our revolutionary act is in the twenty-nine-year-old woman's challenge to her doctor's blithe directive that she get a hysterectomy to deal with fibroids in her uterus.

The only problem is that, while on a personal level feminism is everywhere, like fluoride, on a political level the movement is more like nitrogen: ubiquitous and inert. There is still no Equal Rights Amendment, so women are not equal to men within the Constitution. The wage gap is still wide (a twenty-six-cent-per-dollar discrepancy on average). Women and girls E-mail Ask Amy, Amy's on-line advice column, every day, brimming with stories of injustice at work, at the doctor's office, in their homes: a binational lesbian couple who can't legally marry and thus they can't both be citizens of the same country or live together permanently; an eighth-grade girl who can't join her school's wrestling team; or a longtime sales associate who deserves to be promoted to assistant manager at Petsmart but is told that a woman's place is at the cash register. These women know that these incidents are unfair. What they don't have is a sense that there is a movement that has changed and will continue to change marital law, wrestling, or the Petsmart status quo.

What young feminist-minded people often lack is a coherent declaration that can connect the lives of individual women to the larger history of our movement. We need to transform our confidence into a plan for actually attaining women's equality. We were born into a feminist history. What we need is a Third Wave feminist manifesta.

THE PERSONAL IS STILL POLITICAL

"Feminism has overpersonalised the political and overpoliticised the personal, and in the process has lost sight of its two great, longstanding goals: political equality and personal freedom," wrote the British journalist Natasha Walter in her 1998 book, *The New Feminism*. To be sure, "the personal is political" is the most used—and most abused—motto to come out of the Second Wave. But as a concept it's too important to be allowed to languish in misunderstandings. A buzz phrase of the early radical groups, "the personal is political" was invented by members of New York Radical Women and documented in an article of the same name by Carol Hanisch, a member of the group. Later, in Robin Morgan's introduction to her 1970 best-selling anthology, *Sisterhood Is Powerful*, she popularized the idea: "Women's liberation is the first radical movement to base its politics—in fact, create its politics—out of concrete personal experiences." One such shared "personal issue" was the fact that many women underwent illegal abortions and were made to feel ashamed rather than outraged that this common, and much needed, procedure was illegal and unsafe. Consciousness-raising groups and speak-outs transformed this shame into an acknowledgment that unwanted pregnancy was a systemic, sexist problem, as was the criminalizing of abortion.

More recently, the witty *Nation* essayist Katha Pollitt reflected on the term for an April 1999 piece in *The New York Times Book Review*. In "The Solipsisters," Pollitt complained about the recent spate of self-absorbed books on women's condition. "The personal is political was a way of saying that what looked like individual experiences with little social resonance and certainly no political importance—rape, street harassment, you doing the vacuuming while your husband reads the paper—were part of a general pattern of male dominance and female subordination." Political action was needed to remedy these inequities. Almost immediately, this phrase was misinterpreted to mean that what an individual woman *does* in her personal life (like watching porn, wearing garter belts, dyeing her hair, having an affair, earning money, shaving her legs) undermines her feminist credibility and can be levied against her, like a fine. Thus it has sometimes been used to restrict women, rather than to free us. (Of course, for the same reasons that these once-taboo lifestyle activities shouldn't be held against feminists, these rebellious acts or personal choices shouldn't be construed as the same as political activism. Moreover, when you find yourself choosing what the patriarchy promotes, it's worth asking yourself if it really is a choice.) Gratitude is due to Pollitt for this part of her clarification, but she continues in her critique of this generation's feminist writers: " 'The personal is political' did not mean that personal testimony, impressions and feelings are all you need to make a political argument."

This is where we add a qualifier to Pollitt's analysis: It may not be all you need, but testimony is where feminism starts. Historically, women's personal stories have been the evidence of where the movement needs to go politically and, furthermore, that there is a need to move forward. Anita Hill's tale of being subjected to crass sexual overtures from her boss galvanized thousands of women in 1991, many of whom began to come forward with their own stories of egregious behavior from their employers. The media and even some feminists fail to apprehend this first step when they criticize, such as Pollitt appeared to be doing, the Third Wave propensity to explore women's personal stories in essays and memoirs. Recent Third Wave anthologies—*To Be Real: Telling the Truth and Changing the Face of Feminism, Am I the Last Virgin? Ten African American Reflections on Sex and Love*, and *Listen Up: Voices from the Next Feminist Generation*, as well as *The* Bust *Guide to the New Girl Order* and *Adiós, Barbie: Young Women Write About Body Image and Identity*—are the foundation of the personal ethics upon which a political women's movement will be built. The maligned memoir—which when written by a woman is often referred to as "confessional"—is more than a diary entry that has been typeset. Memoirs like *Mama's Girl* by Veronica Chambers, *Prozac Nation* by Elizabeth Wurtzel, and the memoiresque study of teen sexuality *Slut! Growing Up Female with a Bad Reputation* by Leora Tanenbaum, are all introducing Third Wave women's experiences into the cultural atmosphere.

The First Wave battles for the vote and later the Equal Rights Amendment (ERA), and the Second Wave effort to establish reproductive freedom, job equality, plus the leftover goal of the ERA, overflowed into women's personal lives. Unlike the women who took part in the First and Second waves of feminism, young women today feel as if they live their feminist lives without clear political struggles, which begs the question What are the goals of the Third Wave? The core belief in legal, political, and social equality hasn't changed much since English writer Mary Wollstonecraft's *Vindication of the Rights of Woman* in 1792. Third Wave's goals are derived from analyzing how every issue affects this generation of young women. We have inherited strategies to fight sexual harassment, domestic abuse, the wage gap, and the pink-collar ghetto of low-wage women's work from the Second Wave, which identified these issues. Together, we are still working on them. And we have modern problems of our own. Prominent Third Wave issues include equal access to the Internet and technology, HIV/AIDS awareness, child sexual abuse, self-mutilation, globalization, eating disorders, and body image (witness the preponderance of Third Wave feminist writing that centers on the last issue, from *The Beauty Myth* in 1991 to *Adiós, Barbie* in 1998 and a handful of recently published anorexia memoirs). Sexual health is of special concern to young women, because we now tend to have more partners and to be more sexually active at a younger age (and are more likely than not to have a sexually transmitted disease). The choice of whether to have a baby is under siege for our generation. Teenagers and young women may have their children taken away from them based on any excuse; gay couples are often denied access to adoption and "couples-only" sperm banks as well as to legal marriage. We could go on, but rather than give a laundry list from our own platform, we decided to throw another dinner party, and document the resulting Third Wave conversation to demonstrate how feminism invigorates our lives.

We tackled the personal *and* the political on August 5, 1999, when we cooked dinner at Amy's apartment for six of our women friends—some new, some old, all of whom we thought needed to meet one another. Obviously, this random sample of friends (who live in New York City and mostly work in the media) can't represent all women. But this group of feminists who are observing and reporting on their generation, combined with conversations we have with young women across the country—women who write to Ask Amy or reach out to the Third Wave Foundation or respond to Jennifer's articles—gave us an idea of what a present-day political movement must tackle.

THE PARTY

At 8 p.m., the doorbell rang and Amaryllis Léon, a thirty-six-year-old executive assistant and serious student of belly dancing, arrived, sangria in hand. We hadn't seen Amaryllis much since she stopped working at *Ms.* two years ago, but since then she had separated from her husband and taken up bicycling, flamenco dancing, and smoking. Dancing, she told us, had become a way to express the rage she felt toward her dependent husband, her emotionally manipulative ex-lover, and herself for continuing to let these men lead when they were capable only of following. Becky Michaels arrived on her bicycle from her job at the book publisher Little, Brown and Company. Flopping into a chair, she informed us that she had just been promoted (literally an hour before) to assistant director of advertising and promotion. Becky has had two stepfathers, has one stepmother, and five siblings, only one of whom is biologically related to her. From chaos, Becky is committed to creating order. Married to a musician, she is the stable moneymaker. She also runs a support group for battered women at Victim Services. Our next guest to arrive was Hagar Scher, twenty-seven, clad in one of her trademark *Charlie's Angels* outfits. Hagar, originally from Israel, had been an intern at *Ms.* and is now a popular magazine writer. On the night of our party, she was coming off a hard six months since she and her husband had separated and she had recently begun dating a couple of other men. Elizabeth Wurtzel, a thirty-two-year-old author of two books (*Prozac Nation* and *Bitch*), attained early notoriety as a talented and exhibitionistic writer. Having just graduated from a successful rehab program in the city, Elizabeth was reorganizing her life as a sober and single person. Workaholic Farai Chideya showed up, informing us that she would have to leave a bit early due to her 5 a.m. call at *Good Morning America*, where she was a correspondent. (Soon after our dinner, Farai became a host of *Pure Oxygen*, a morning show on Oxygen, the new women's network.) Forever a non-monogamous worker, Farai also has a column in *Vibe*, has written two books about race, hosts her own Web site called Pop and Politics, and is a syndicated political columnist. On this night, she was full of tales of the first dates she had gone on recently. Finally, Sabrina Margarita Alcantara-Tan, the twenty-nine-year-old creator of the feminist zine *Bamboo Girl*, arrived. She was running late from her job at Women Make Movies. (Soon after our dinner, she quit her job.) Both of Sabrina's arms and her entire back are fully tattooed. She is a political, omnisexual (a term she prefers to the "too-limiting" *bisexual*), punk-rock feminist who is also proficient in Filipino martial arts. She recently married a traditional Filipino man.

The conversation covered plenty of ground:

"I can't stand the way Bruce Springsteen is misunderstood as some sort of eighties mall phenomenon when he's actually darker than Kurt Cobain. 'Born in the U.S.A.' was actually a very anti-American song. He left that sort of model-actress he was married to for Patti Scialfa from his band, the woman he should have been with in the first place . . ."

"When I got out of college, I started feeling all the rage I had been repressing as a good Catholic Filipina growing up in an entirely white suburb. My parents were abusive, and suddenly I fought back—if a guy would even look at me, I'd lash out. I felt out of control, but there was no way to stop my anger and aggression . . ."

"I think the missionary position is underrated. There has been a backlash against it in women's magazines for all the wrong reasons . . ."

"Sometimes I think about dating women because the men I've met are so emotionally retarded. If I can get the emotional needs met by women, why not let the sexual part grow? . . ."

"When I think that a man is seriously trying to get into my pants, I feel like I'm being judged—I don't want them to come at me directly . . ."

"I want men to be afraid of my intellect, I want some of the upper hand . . ."

"I feel much more comfortable flirting now that I'm married, as long as it's very clear that I *am* married . . ."

"What's interesting about sexual attraction is that there's always some element of stereotype. I think being with a white guy is so sexy . . ."

"I think if you're bisexual, there just has to come a day when you choose one or the other—and, face it, it's easier to be straight . . ."

"Sexuality isn't contingent on the person you sleep with—it's in you . . ."

"The whole bisexuality thing seems so normal and natural to me, and I think I've repressed feelings that would lead me more toward women. There is this one friend of mine who I know I could be married to and have kids with and live with the rest of our lives. We have this connection—sexual as well as emotional . . ."

"I put so many more expectations on my women friends, on women in general . . ."

"I can see my boyfriend as part of the rest of my life, but there is so much else I want to do, and these things seem attached to other people or, at least, to freedom . . ."

"There can't be one of us in this room who thinks that being with the same person forever means being the same forever . . ."

Every issue we discussed spiraled into our personal lives, and personal stories inevitably led to their political implications and strategies. A conversation about choosing our sexuality gave way to the prejudice we would face for having made the choice to be with a woman; flirting while married became a discussion about why and when we feel safe with men, as well as how our boundaries collide with a need to be nice. A comment about how Robert De Niro is dating every black woman in New York City became an analysis of fetishizing race in a racist culture, and how that differs from authentic attraction. And, as with many feminist conversations we have witnessed, all threads eventually led back to food, sex, and hair.

WOMEN PAY MORE FOR SEX

At our dinner party, Elizabeth recounted the story of her recent abortion—an experience that was altogether horrific. "Anyone who wants to take away abortion should just be shot," she said. "They just don't understand anything, because no one would choose that experience." Knocked out by general anesthesia, Elizabeth awoke on a gurney, with no curtained partition, and surrounded by a roomful of women who were also waking up. All of the women were scared and crying and disoriented, and Elizabeth felt totally alienated from them. The scene was more reminiscent of *M*A*S*H*—triage at the battlefront—than of a routine medical procedure. In terms of seriousness, a first-trimester abortion falls somewhere between having one's wisdom teeth removed and getting a biopsy. (Many women choose to go under because they fear the pain and trauma of the five-minute surgical procedure. General anesthesia, however, makes what is a very safe few minutes more dangerous, and the recovery longer.)

Elizabeth's factory experience is not what feminists meant when they fought for the right to a safe and legal abortion. They envisioned and invented counseling procedures in which each woman was paired with a birthing or lay companion, for example, and freestanding clinics where women could wake up privately, or to the gentle comfort of a nurse or a friend. But many of the independent clinics have turned into time-crunched, impersonal "abortion service centers," marginalized from the rest of medicine, and easy targets for anti-abortion terrorism.

As we continued talking, Amy revealed that she had had an entirely more pleasant and respectful trip to the abortionist, an experience that she shares with as many women as possible so that they will know what they can expect and so the shame and stigma can begin to dissipate:

I was nineteen, my boyfriend accompanied me, and I went to a women's clinic in Portland, Oregon. A friend of mine who had just had an abortion at the same place explained the logistics. Based on her advice, I chose Valium and a shot of Novocain rather than general anesthesia, and I was conscious throughout the procedure. A really nice nurse—who must have gone through the procedure herself, because she could anticipate every cramp and pull and twinge—talked me through the procedure. I was filled with fear that it was going to hurt. I imagined that an abortion had to be punishing, and that my insides would be sucked out roughly. They did use suction, which literally sounded like a vacuum cleaner, but the entire procedure lasted about two minutes, and the feeling was more of an awkward discomfort—the pain equivalent of fingernails on the chalkboard. I didn't stay in the recovery room for long because it was so unprivate. My boyfriend was waiting, and he took me home to recover there, supportive of me throughout it all. I had to wear pads and take it easy for a couple of days (and promise I wouldn't have intercourse for ten days to two weeks), but the hardest part for me was the shame I felt about having been knocked up. I harbored these feelings mostly because, since I had grown up a working-class kid, an unplanned pregnancy at age nineteen seemed expected—par for the course. Knowing that friends whom I idolized as the perfect upper-middle-class girls had also had abortions made it possible for me to talk about mine without feeling dirty and cheap. Though I wouldn't project those feelings onto another woman who had an abortion—working-class or upper-middle-class—I couldn't avoid the stigmas that, let's face it, are out there.

Earlier that evening while we were getting ready for our dinner, Jennifer received a call from Leona, a twenty-five-year-old friend of a friend. Leona has herpes, which she got from her boyfriend during oral sex, and she knew that Jennifer had had a similar experience when she was twenty-six. Leona was horrified to have an incurable sexually transmitted disease (STD), and traumatized because her boyfriend not only refused to learn anything about the virus and its transmission but broke up with her after he got an outbreak on his genitals. Leona called that night, panicked, because she was going to spend the weekend with a new guy whom she really liked. She wanted to sleep with him, and needed advice about when and how to tell this new flame about her virus. She wondered, too, if she should just keep mum and celibate, since the thought of telling him seemed so daunting. So far, the advice she had gotten from non-herpes sources ranged from "Don't tell him—the rejection is too much to risk" to "Just realize that you probably won't have another boyfriend." (That last was from her mother.) This convinced Leona that other people would think she was repulsive. But Jennifer, speaking from experience rather than conjecture, was able to impart her own anti-trauma to Leona and help calm her down:

I'm really open about having herpes—partly because I want to demystify the disease, but also because I refuse to be ashamed by it. Although giving the herpes speech to a new squeeze always makes me feel completely unsexy, I have never had anyone react badly. In fact, it's so intimate that it can be a leap of faith that you take together. When I first detected that I had herpes, I was pretty depressed. I had strep throat and shooting pains in my pleasure parts and was wracked with fear about my future love life. My friends were helpful—a guy friend told me that his ex had herpes and they worked around it by using a condom when an outbreak seemed imminent. He was obviously not bothered and also spoke of her as a sexpot. (I was feeling like a diseased eunuch at the time, so I was excessively grateful for the information.) My parents struck a balance between extreme concern about me and downplaying the seriousness of herpes, especially my dad. He's a doctor and had to deal with my three calls per day describing my vulva in intricate detail. The first thing my dad said to me was that herpes was one of the least serious medical conditions I would ever have. That's true, and it's also what I tell everyone I meet who has it.

The stories of the authors' abortion and STD are not meant to claim victimhood or bombard you, the reader, with personal details you don't want to hear. We simply want to demonstrate the difference between being paralyzed by silence, shame, and self-blame, and realizing that not only is a girl with an STD or an unintended pregnancy not alone, she is one of millions. It's this acknowledgment that turns the political wheel. Even if people don't judge a woman who has a sexually transmitted disease—or one who is depressed, bulimic, has been raped or sexually molested, chooses to sleep with a lot of people, ends an unwanted pregnancy, or brings a child into this world despite her poverty—that woman is still certain that the rest of the human race will condemn her. That's why women have long been radicalized by telling their secrets to each other. In fact, we have noticed that if you tell someone you have an STD or have had an abortion, she usually reveals some "horrible" secret from her life. We now know that most of our partners and friends have had crabs, abortions, or genital warts. (Keep *that* in mind when you're gearing up to reveal your own shameful secret. Your friend will probably be grateful that you initiated the conversation.) An ethic of silence keeps women isolated from one another, but, most of all, it keeps us from realizing the political issues at the root of our travails. That same silence hangs over men's heads, and in their case there may be even less encouragement to break it. However, doing so is necessary, not just for men's liberation but for ours.

Speaking of men, there is much feminist work that guys have yet to do. Most men certainly respect the women in their lives and, therefore, need to share in women's burdens, responsibilities, and privileges. Beyond dividing housework equally, there are many new creative ways in which men can aid in building a pro-feminist world. If married, a liberated man can make sure that his wife's name lives on with as much energy as his by either taking her name or by agreeing to let the children have her name. Doing the dishes can be a revolutionary act, as can picking up one's own socks. On the sexual front, men can come to grips with the fact that a vasectomy is the safest, the easiest to reverse, and the cheapest semipermanent birth control for a couple to use. It involves no hormones, is a onetime procedure, and is practically foolproof protection from unintended pregnancy. Single, sexually active guys aren't lining up at the urologist's office, however, because birth control is still viewed as a female problem. Taking male responsibility in sex a step further, a vasectomized sixteen-year old can freeze his sperm indefinitely until he is ready to bring a child into the world. The possibilities are endless. The point is that men's participation is necessary for full equality.

While we bonded over abortions and STDs, our dinner conversation went on to expose some of the gaps in sexual freedom. One big gap can be described, as we hinted above, in two words: male accountability. Not enough people are owning up to their sexual responsibilities, and those who are tend to be female. In Jennifer's and Leona's cases, their former boyfriends (who also happened to be the herpes carriers) took no responsibility for figuring out when it was safe to have sex, or even for finding out how they had passed on the disease without knowing they had it. It was as if it were an Immaculate Transmission (and all of this immaculate sex adds up to women holding the bag). This irresponsibility is not totally the guys' fault: women rarely expect—or voice their expectations of—equality in the game of love and its health-related consequences. Part of our empowerment is learning how to do things for ourselves—including asking the right questions—and part is learning how not to do them on behalf of others.

The facts: STDs are by all counts an epidemic. As many as one in two people will contract herpes, human papilloma virus (HPV)—which can manifest itself as genital warts—or some other booty-related disease at some point in their lifetime.[11] Thirty years ago, when there wasn't much popular knowledge about what perilous microbes awaited your pleasure parts, the job of the women's movement was education and teaching ladies how to protect themselves. The Third Wave is in a position to move from women-centered remedies to fighting for male accountability—meaning that we have *Our Bodies, Ourselves* on our bookshelves *and* versions of Washington Heights' Young Men's Health Clinic (a health center where boys actually have annual exams and learn about their sexual health) across the country. As feminists, we need to talk about living with STDs and raise consciousness that men should be worried about what happens when they have sex, too. The Third Wave manifesta means bringing down the sexual-health double standard, which will require better sex education, distribution of free contraception, and elimination of the potential shame and embarrassment associated with the consequences of sexual freedom. And men and women alike are able to free themselves from any false perception of immortality, and immunity from diseases and unplanned pregnancies.

On the abortion front, there is plenty to revolutionize. While Amy was frustrated that women have to deal with shame and men don't, Elizabeth was upset that she was denied privacy after having such an intimate and traumatic experience. One way to deal with Elizabeth's problem, at least, is by supporting access to medical (nonsurgical) abortion, such as the abortion pill formerly known as RU 486, so that the procedure can eventually be performed in the privacy of our own homes. As of 2000, RU 486 has almost been made available in the United States, but it's confronting an enormous threat from anti-abortion extremists. (RU 486 is now marketed as Mifeprex, which is a combination of two drugs: mifepristone and misoprostol.) Feminists should champion mainstreaming abortions into regular health care so that 86 percent of U.S. counties don't have to be without a provider.

Given that most medical schools don't offer training in the procedure, doctors trained in the past twenty years are unlikely to know how to perform an abortion. The prevalence of clinic terrorism—the murders of Dr. David Gunn and Dr. Barnett Slepian and the clinic staffs in Birmingham, Alabama, and Brookline, Massachusetts, among other examples—also helps to keep the pool of doctors who are willing to perform the procedure scant. Medical Students for Choice, an organization that has successfully fought to include abortion-training procedures in medical schools, was founded in 1993 by a University of California medical student named Jody Steinauer. That year, an anti-choice group did a mass mailing of a zine called *Bottom Feeder* (their parlance for abortion providers) to all of the nation's medical students. Steinauer was incensed by the scare tactics and threats she found in the pamphlet. She decided to provide students with the ability to change the curricula at their own schools, and raise awareness that providing abortions is inherent in women's full range of health care. The first wave of the four thousand doctors trained by Medical Students for Choice will be setting up shop over the next couple of years. (More than three-quarters of these future abortion providers are female.) This should foster a new climate, one in which doctors who perform abortions aren't uniformly approaching retirement age, or treated with disdain by their apolitical, fearful, or anti-choice peers.

In many ways, the movement for choice is as embattled and, therefore, necessary as it was before *Roe v. Wade* (the 1973 Supreme Court decision that guaranteed women the right to an abortion as part of a citizen's constitutional right to privacy). The pro-choice contingency has sheer numbers on our side, but the anti-choice fringe is more activist, organized, and better funded. The right-to-life movement successfully promotes itself as pro-child and pro-family. In actuality, it's anti-child, anti-woman, and anti-family. For example, Jean Schroedel, an associate professor at Claremont Graduate University, examined states with pro-choice policies (those that uphold *Roe v. Wade*) and those with anti-choice policies (those that implement restrictions such as parental-consent laws, waiting periods of up to forty-eight hours, spousal consent, and the like). She compared these policies with the amount of money committed to adoptions, foster care, and total spending on poor children. Surprisingly—or not surprisingly—the most anti-choice states spend the least amount of money on children's services. The opposite was also true: states that were pro-choice were the most pro-children. This anti-choice tactic punishes children and women who aren't seeking abortions, as do the anti-choice efforts to condemn dilation and extraction (D&X), a medical procedure that is performed on women for reasons other than to end a pregnancy—for instance, to save their lives.

The irony of the attacks on abortion rights is that 43 percent of all women under forty-five have had an abortion, in equal numbers from pro-choice and anti-choice groups, from Pagans to Catholics. In fact, although only 25 percent of U.S. women are Catholic, 33 percent of the women getting abortions are Catholic, and one-sixth are born-again or Evangelical Christians.[12] There are also annoying examples of anti-choice women who weren't anti enough to deny themselves the right to the procedure. For example, Susan Carpenter-McMillan (Paula Jones's fairy godmother) had two abortions before she used her wealth to become a staunch anti-choice activist.

Another way that the reproductive rights movement is attacked is by labeling it a "white woman's issue." True, for instance, Native American women often have a different orientation toward abortion because of their history with genocide. But it's important to remember that it's not feminism's goal to control any woman's fertility, only to free each woman to control her own. Mainstream pro-choice groups should continue to make sure that their agenda reflects all women, because as long as abortion rights remain cast as a white, middle-class priority and sterilization as an issue for people of color and the poor, reproductive freedom will continue to be divided by the racist intentions of those who oppose any woman's having control over her body. In the Second Wave, fighting against coerced sterilization came with and often before the fight for safe and legal abortion. The bottom line is that women need to be free agents of their own destinies, which includes having control over their own bodies, whether this means choosing to have a child or choosing not to do so. Reproductive rights are inherently a multiracial issue.

Issues of sexual health have always been a rallying point for young women. In response to the 1989 *Webster v. Reproductive Health Services* decision (which granted states the option of parental-consent laws, waiting periods, and further restrictions on abortion), 600,000 people, many of whom were female college students, flooded the Washington Mall to demonstrate for choice. Three years later, they did it again. Today, campuses don't appear to be awash in "keep your laws off my body" rhetoric, yet under this surface of passivity, nuances of this issue and many others are percolating.

Judging from the informal survey of the five thousand or so questioners who visited Ask Amy in 1999—approximately 80 percent of whom are younger than thirty-five—young women also care about sex discrimination (*and* harassment, the subject with which discrimination is frequently merged), pay inequities, custody and divorce laws, access to adoption and custody for lesbian parents, as well as the prevention of rape and incest. We don't have the ERA[13] (yet) or a pro-woman female candidate for president (yet) or the fight for the vote to gather around, but individual women, like our dinner guests, are out there slamming up against sexism and fighting it wherever they find it.

The Fault Lines: Work and Family

Only one of our dinner guests worked as a feminist—that is, made money in a company that is directly related to the women's movement—Sabrina Margarita Alcantara-Tan of Women Make Movies, a film distributor based in New York City. She, too, was the only one of our guests who explicitly did feminist organizing as we do. Sabrina co-founded Kilawin Kolektibo, a sociopolitical collective of queer Filipinas based in New York City. But everyone at the table was a feminist at her job or in her writing, and everyone had brought the ideals of female autonomy to her married or single life. The freedom to have careers or keep our names is assumed with Third Wave women. (Although three-fourths of married women do take their husband's name, we're hopeful that this is by choice.) A woman can seek out basically any career and be a feminist in it, it's true, but limitations do exist, even if our friends or much of the Third Wave hasn't recognized or run up against them yet. (Bearing this out, "approximately 33 percent of [young college women] reported they had never experienced discrimination based on gender" according to a recent poll of college communities discussed in the feminist journal *Labyrinth*.) The barrier often isn't the *first* job anymore; it comes later, higher up the ladder, when women are vying for promotions, or trying to combine salaried work with parenthood, or at retirement. Generally speaking, the poorer you are, the earlier you face discrimination. Class and gender biases are so intertwined that when feminists fight for women's rights in the workplace, they are fighting for access to both corporate jobs and realistic welfare-to-work programs, including those that consider parenting to be a job. Mothers taken off welfare because caring for children isn't a "job" are being discriminated against as women just as much as they are for being poor. This problem is usually cast in terms of classism, not sexism—even though job skills and a college degree may not keep you off welfare if you are a mother with young children.

Still, it's representative of our generation's political potential that so many of our friends are feminists at their regular jobs rather than having volunteer or paid jobs being feminists. After all, there are only so many positions at the National Organization for Women or in women's studies departments, but every profession could use someone on the inside agitating for egalitarian principles. Without making too much of a parallel between monotheism and women's liberation, being a feminist is not unlike being a Christian—not everyone is going to be a pastor, but everyone in the church is directed to lead a Christian life.

Our dinner-party guests are good examples of how this works. Becky was in a position to determine how books are marketed. When Katie Roiphe's first book, *The Morning After: Sex, Fear and Feminism on Campus*, came out, Becky, then a publicist, was in charge of promoting this controversial critique of the date-rape epidemic, one that lampooned activists such as Andrea Dworkin and Catharine MacKinnon. In addition to accomplishing her job, Becky drew from her feminist background, and turned media interviewers on to the Third Wave Foundation, *Ms.*, and a host of feminists who could comment knowledgeably on the prevalence of rape, as well as on the importance of women's sexual agency. Elizabeth has written about the extent to which depression is sexualized in women—from Marilyn Monroe to Sylvia Plath to Anne Sexton—and underscores how being so despondent that you can't find a reason to wash your hair or eat is the least sexy thing in the world. Her second book, *Bitch*, vindicated the infamous Lolitas our society has chosen to hate, from Delilah to Amy Fisher. (Elizabeth herself seems not to need approval, a liberated state for a woman.) Farai weaves political feminism into her writing about race and pop culture, and therefore helps bring to this generation the knowledge that sexism and racism are intertwined. Farai is also able to employ a strategy that is crucial to a forceful feminism: she transmits her message using mainstream outlets such as ABC News, *Vibe*, and now, *Oxygen*. For Amaryllis, there is a clear distinction between work and her talents. A day job on annoyingly masculinist Wall Street pays her bills, but her nights are spent practicing dance, writing a novel, and casting Wiccan spells.

So, whether casting spells or *Bitch*ing, it's a sign of the times that feminists today are more likely to be individuals quietly (or not so quietly) living self-determined lives than radicals on the ramparts. They are experts in their fields—media, politics, advertising, business—rather than expert feminists (though they are often that, too). Of course, the fact that no one in our generation is yet considered to be a feminist "queenpin" is a product of ageism in both the media and the movement; young women, apart from a few easy-to-control tokens, are not given credit for the leadership they are already showing. But it's also evidence that feminism is becoming mainstreamed via popular culture. This holds true for other social-justice movements, too. People talk about how hip-hop heroes such as Biggie Smalls and Tupac Shakur were advancing black power today in much the same way that Martin Luther King, Jr., and Malcolm X advanced civil rights and black power. As Mary J. Blige said, "They weren't up on a podium, but they were speaking truth in their rhymes." Rather than an activist hoisting a picket sign, or a suburban woman joining NOW, today, a typical young feminist might resemble Bridget Jones, the charmingly slaggy character created by British author Helen Fielding. Bridget's modern conflict goes something like this: "Is it hypocritical of me to be a feminist and still be concerned about my weight, to have credit-card debt from excessive shopping, and an overarching desire to become a 'smug married'?" Bridget, not unlike her televised American doppelgänger, Ally McBeal, wears an armor of egalitarian ideals pierced by pre-feminist concerns. These women are fictional, of course, but given the success of *Bridget Jones's Diary* (in the United Kingdom it was No. 1 on the bestseller list for thirty weeks, sold nearly one million copies, and is being made into a film) and the number of people who tune in weekly to *Ally McBeal*, many women relate to the desires and foibles of these (young, heterosexual, white, unmarried, urban, professional) women.

Some of our friends, we've noticed, bear similarities to Ally and Bridget. Four of our dinner guests were married, but two were separated; of the four unmarried women, two were in long-term monogamous relationships, one was dating, and one wasn't. Many had cohabited with partners without being married. Ally and Bridget are single feminist women, but not because they are trying to avoid the sexist traps of marriage, just like our single friends. Nowadays, marriage is less likely to be a compromise for women and more likely to be a choice. There is still incredible pressure to choose marriage, but it's fair to say that women and men now have a better chance of equality within the union. Women may keep their last names when they marry, maintain their careers, or have husbands who know how to wield the DustBuster like a pro—that is, like a woman. The reason women are less compromised by this state is that so many women and men have been reared by feminist parents or, at least, by mothers who were in some way influenced by the women's liberation movement. Most women expect and want to (not to mention have to) earn their keep outside the home; many men don't really expect to be waited on. In an ideal world, we would hope the sock issue—women who pick up *his* socks, men who don't notice that they leave their socks to be picked up—to become as anachronistic as eight-track tapes. However, we have to confess, observing our friends and listening to them complain has led us to believe that men's concepts of cleanliness and homemaking aren't yet on a par with women's. We know some untidy girls, but we don't know any guys who are picking up after them. Still, two independent people with somewhat similar expectations and roles are more likely to enter into the union, rather than a man who's burdened with supporting everyone and a woman who's undermined by the indignity of unpaid and largely invisible labor.

Back in Elizabeth Cady Stanton's day, marriage was the rule, not a choice. One exception to that rule was Susan B. Anthony, Stanton's collaborator, who remained single. Stanton (and Anthony as well as other suffragettes of the era) recognized the loss of personhood in marriage, and therefore fought for women to be able to divorce, preserve their own name, inherit money, keep their earnings, and own property.

In the Second Wave, two revolutionary approaches to marriage were added. On the one hand, there were women who reinvented the institution as a more egalitarian one. Alix Kates Shulman's "Marriage Agreement," published everywhere from *Ms.* to *Life* and *Redbook*, divided up child care and housework equitably, and valued the wife's work equally with the husband's, regardless of who brought home more bacon.[14] Writer Jane O'Reilly coined the "click," the term she used to describe epiphanies about sexism after watching her family walk around a pile of clean laundry on the couch for a week rather than put away their damn clothes themselves. Her essay, printed in the preview issue of *Ms.*, vaulted the term into popular use.[15] Analyzing the "politics of housework"—as the famous essay by Pat Mainardi is called—raised cultural consciousness about women's rights within marriage.[16]

Casting the division of labor within the house as political allowed feminists to transform the institution. There was a distinct interest in making marriage work, especially since so many women who were becoming radicalized already had husbands. On the other hand, there were women who eschewed the marital bond altogether, at least partly in order to avoid the compromises that seemed inherent in being a wife. Even if they eventually married, these pioneers for single girls, famously Helen Gurley Brown and Gloria Steinem (and, in their TV personas, Marlo Thomas as "That Girl" and Mary Tyler Moore as Mary Richards), defended being a single woman as a legitimate and liberating state. Jokingly, Steinem said that she wouldn't get married unless the ERA passed, indicating the bare minimum of social protection she would need to consider the institution. But whether marriage was revolutionized or avoided like the plague, the lines were clear: marriage was a sullied state from a feminist perspective. The energy it might take to reform a recalcitrant hubby and lazy kids might be too much to bear. Not to mention the loss of independence and identity.

Given that singlehood and living together have been largely destigmatized, why do so many feminists still bother to get married? (And, in an odd paradox, why do many feminists today have to justify both why they are single and why they get married?) For one thing, feminists have fought for and gained more equal marriage laws. And, like everyone else, they do it for stability, comfort, to publicly honor a private commitment, for security, romantic dreams, health care, better apartments (at least for urbanites), out of tradition, to please parents or in-laws, or because they want to have children. For one woman we interviewed, whose parents divorced (and then remarried often and not well), having a successful marriage remedied what felt like a painful failure in her sense of family. She's in love with her husband, but she's also had to grapple with their eight-year marriage, especially the conflicts that feel downright clichéd: a husband who doesn't carry his own weight emotionally or in terms of housework. "If I ask him to do the dishes, he'll do it," she says. "But I get so tired of asking."

This brings us to what hasn't changed about marriage, despite thirty years of feminism. According to a recent survey by Kelley Hall, a sociologist at DePauw University, 71 percent of straight couples agree that women end up doing 70 percent of the housework, regardless of whether they work outside the home. In addition, marriage still gives women a bum deal in other ways. Married couples who file tax returns jointly are taxed at the same rate, despite what are often gross inequities in income. (And, let's face it, it's still mostly women who make the lesser sum.) Single women have their own problems: they're taxed in their own bracket, but they suffer from wage gaps and receive less Social Security than they would if they were married and had access to their husbands' checks. (Not to mention that divorce and custody laws make the institution of marriage look positively pro-woman.)[17]

Marriage is also an institution that has so far excluded same-sex couples from its benefits, responsibilities, and pleasures; something no feminist should ignore. Indeed, a few straight feminists have refused to get legally married as a protest against this unfairness. Meanwhile, the debate about whether to keep one's name is far from over. Many women do hang on to their birth names, but they wouldn't dream of insisting that their children use them, too. Few men are willing to give up their identity so easily by taking their wife's name—or even to *consider* it, which underscores the absurdity of the tradition in the first place. Women may reconcile changing their patronymic if they hated their father, for example, but how many guys are there who gave up their name because of an abusive dad? More pointedly, how many guys sit at dinner with friends saying, "I don't know what to do. Part of me wants to take her name . . ."?

Sullied and unequal institution or not, the reality is that marriage, or a committed relationship that is acknowledged by society (and health-insurance companies), is what most people—not just Ally and Bridget—still want. A few months before we sat down to write this book, we ran into Debbie Stoller of the feminist zine *Bust* at a panel called "What Do Single Girls Want?" held at New York City's 92nd Street Y. The evening, moderated by the very funny writer Meg Wolitzer, capitalized on the publishing successes of two unmarried women who wrote about single *girls*: Helen Fielding (the author of *Bridget Jones's Diary*) and Melissa Bank (the author of *The Girls' Guide to Hunting and Fishing*). The consensus of the panel was that, while feminism had allowed women greater freedom to follow their ambitions and to support themselves, it hadn't done much by way of making the truly single woman (as opposed to the simply unmarried) less of a socially pathetic figure. Debbie Stoller thought that part of the problem lay in how feminists dealt with hetero relationships. "How a woman needs a man is not *anything* like how a fish needs a bicycle,"* she said, exasperated. That idea, she felt, failed to consider the impact of love and desire and basic human needs. "It made it seem, then, that if you did want a man you were betraying the feminist cause—a liberated woman needs *nobody*," Stoller said.

We argue that Stoller is misunderstanding the point behind the A Woman Needs a Man motto. The point is not that a woman shouldn't want a man or desire his companionship or his body or his kindnesses but that a woman shouldn't *have* to rely on a man in order to be valued or to survive economically. Although it analyzes how romance helps to socialize women into a subjugated role (as England's feminists put it, "You sink into his arms, and end up with your arms in his sink"), women's liberation doesn't exclude one human being's need for another; it just suggests a balance. Emotional need can be distinguished from financial or even social dependency. Amy's mother, Karen, for example, left Amy's father in 1969, while Amy was still in the womb, because Karen began to realize that her husband was mentally unstable and that she and Amy would be unsafe with him. Karen, age twenty, needed a man— or someone to help provide a house and food or, at least, free baby-sitting so that she could earn money—the way a fish needs water. So she got on welfare and moved back in with her parents, who helped baby-sit while she put herself through college. One woman we interviewed is an educator, a job she enjoys even though she makes only $16,000 a year after seventeen

---

*In this conversation, the slogan A Woman Needs a Man Like a Fish Needs a Bicycle was misattributed to Gloria Steinem, a common mistake. For the record, in 1970 an Australian woman named Irina Dunn wrote "A Woman Needs a Man Like a Fish Needs a Bicycle" on the wall of a University of Sydney public bathroom. Dunn, under the influence of Germaine Greer's *The Female Eunuch*, came up with the phrase by altering a line in a philosophy book she had just read: "A man needs God like a fish needs a bicycle." This is according to Dunn herself, who wrote a letter in response to Steinem's efforts to find the source of the slogan.

years of service. "If I didn't have a husband who made a decent wage, I would live in poverty," she says. The point is that there are still many things standing in the way of a woman's ability to have a life as freely chosen as a man's. This remains true along class lines. For example, many homeless women have children for whom they are responsible; most homeless men do not. Legislating the alchemy of hearts and bodies has never been the province of liberation movements. Striving toward equality in our homes, in our relationships, and in our abilities to earn a living *is*.

That said, love relationships can and do take on political connotations, especially in a climate of consciousness about sexism. It's become somewhat of a rite of passage for many budding young feminists, especially at college but also in high school, to pursue relationships with other women. Bisexuality, for lack of a better word, is often dismissed as a fad, a phase, or trivial—or, to some full-on lesbians, even cowardly and annoying. The reason some lesbians are critical of bisexuality is that it carries a lesser social penalty than lesbianism, and also preserves an escape route into heterosexual privilege. For example, a bisexual may choose to be with a woman only when being with men proves to be too frustrating. Yet there are many ways in which bisexuality serves a distinct purpose for women, especially as we come into consciousness. For example, loving another woman and finding out the secrets of her body is one way of learning about yourself. It's a way to resolve sexual competition—a very painful issue for young women struggling toward solidarity—by turning our gaze toward one another rather than vying for male attention. Because both parties walk through the world experiencing the prejudices and perks of being female, there is also the perception, at least, of a more equal relationship.

Many bisexual women eventually choose to identify as either gay or straight. And many straight-identified women think about bisexuality. At our dinner party, Farai talked about how she has always dated men, because it feels natural, but also because of heterosexual socialization. Because of this socialization, it wouldn't occur to her to explore desires she felt toward a woman who might, in other circumstances, just be her ideal mate. Meanwhile, Amaryllis was so frustrated with the men in her life that she wondered whether she should cultivate a sexual rapport with her women friends, who understand her emotionally. She hoped it could remedy some of the problems she had in her relationships with men. On the other hand, Sabrina, who is married to a man, identifies as omnisexual. This description includes her relationships with and connection to other women, and explains who she is, distinct from the gender of her partner.

Our friends' frustrations with the current state of male-female relationships are a barometer of what feminism still needs to change. In terms of equality, our married friends tell us that snags occur when couples have children. Many women enter marriage working right along with their husbands, ordering pizza when they are both too tired to cook, but all that changes when the baby comes. "I'll tell you where the barrier to equality lies," snaps Holly Peterson, an editor at large at *Talk* magazine, over dinner one night. "It's when you're thirty-two, have two kids, and, no matter what you do, it's not enough. You want to work, but your co-workers look at you with reproach when you leave at five—I can't blame them, I used to look at people the same way. So you stay longer, then come home to your kids' sad eyes, and you felt guilty for leaving them in the first place."

As for fathers, they have different, but still debilitating, pressures—even with parental leave that includes men, too, and all the promotion of the joys of fatherhood. Namely, just as they don't eat quiche, real men don't do flextime. Not only does sexism load the pressures of parenting on mom like a nasty girdle, but it makes fathers' roles more distant and rigid. There isn't yet a groundswell of revolutionary fathers looking to change the conventional family model. Given that men remain the majority of those in leadership positions, from *Fortune* 500 CEOs to legislators, if they really wanted things to change they could agitate to make that happen.

Many heterosexual couples wouldn't always choose to have the mother stay home, but the wage gap makes it more profitable for men to be the breadwinners, and women the caregivers. "I think my husband should kiss my toes every single day, and thank me for what I'm doing," says one friend who just gave birth to her first child, "because no matter what he does to help out, the inequalities are still so glaring." In addition to the physical strain pregnancy and birth exert on women's bodies, there is the limitation on one's schedule when one's breasts are in demand every few hours. The state of mothering, incredible as it may be, is still the opposite of liberation. You are bound to your body, to your baby, and to societal expectations in which motherhood means always having to say you are sorry. You are also unrewarded by a system that gives no economic value to rearing children and other tasks of human maintenance, even though such tasks represent about 40 percent of the productive labor in this and other developed countries.

"At the present time, for a woman to come out openly against motherhood on principle is physically dangerous. She can get away with it only if she adds that she is neurotic, abnormal, child hating and therefore 'unfit,' " wrote Shulamith Firestone in her 1970 best-seller, *The Dialectic of Sex: The Case for Feminist Revolution*. Firestone advocated procreation through technology, thereby eliminating any discrimination or resentment based on who has the baby. The biological determinism imposed by the wage gap, unequal parenting responsibilities, and men needing to learn how to do what women do, remain the same problems our generation faces. We have to agree with Firestone, even raising the subject of the family as a unit of oppression for women or a political argument against motherhood may still earn punishment.

The question is, Can we untie motherhood from womanhood without throwing childbirth out with the sexism? And, given that society still links some of a woman's power to her ability to reproduce, how do we want to challenge the mother-baby bond?

If feminists are to bring their own flesh and blood into the world without replicating the status quo, we may have a viable model in lesbian co-parenting. Feminists in Firestone's time seemed reluctant to embrace artificial reproduction so women could be free from the oppression associated with bearing and rearing kids. Feminists nowadays are slow to follow the lesson of lesbian parenting; that is, you can create your own rules.

Same-sex parents illustrate that biology is not destiny, and parenting is a job. As the gay-rights movement continues to pick up momentum, this understanding is likely to grow—with positive ramifications for all parents. Without romanticizing gay parents or ignoring the pressures of homophobia, other feminists can learn from them by observing how two mothers (or two fathers) divide child rearing and housework. In the case of Barbara and Kristen, two friends of ours, Barbara gave birth to both of their children, and was also the one with a full-time job outside the home that provided partner benefits. Kristen, a freelance writer, took care of the kids four days a week at home while telecommuting to what amounted to a forty-hour work-week. When Barbara came home from work, she helped with the cooking, cleaning, and child rearing, giving Kristen time to write. Recently, they changed places: Kristen became the director of a battered-women's shelter, and Barbara took on the stay-at-home parenting responsibilities for a while. One child is in preschool, and the baby has been in day care since he was four months old. For another couple we know, each woman has taken her turn at giving birth. The couple is biracial, and each mother used sperm from the race of the other mother so that their children would have the same racial mix. Another, single-race couple insisted on using different donors for each pregnancy so their family wouldn't be based on a biological relationship but, rather, on an emotional one. Their lives put a whole new, concrete spin on the nature-nurture debate. Obviously, heterosexual couples can and do base their family on the principal of love over biology, too.

Other lesbian couples may have a birth mother who goes back to work and a stay-at-home mother who has no biological tie to the baby, or a situation in which neither mother stays at home, or they might adopt and work out still another scenario. For another couple, Susan, the birth mother, works as a doctor, while her partner, Julie, stays home with toddler Laurie. Laurie sometimes calls Susan "Dad," an indication that biology may not be destiny, but "Dad" still equals the absent parent. Susan and Julie add credence to the idea that co-parenting doesn't always eliminate the role of the primary caregiver, but it does increase the likelihood that the arrangement will be chosen rather than predetermined. Susan says, "We talked about how we wanted to parent a child. We had the opportunity to look at the kids in Julie's classroom over the years she was a teacher, and we had pretty well established that, for some kids, to have both parents work full-time jobs is hard on the family."

The advantage of gay parenting is the lack of a rigid gender script. Gay parents are more likely to have the freedom to create "family" in a revolutionary way. Having two mothers puts the emphasis on parenting rather than on the roles of mothering and fathering, which too often translate as "nurturing" and "disciplining." Even on such small but powerful questions as naming, same-sex parents and their well-adjusted children provide ample evidence that hyphenating their child's last name is simply not a big deal for the kid.

Work outside the home can be revolutionized by a strike, a lawsuit, or a trip to the EEOC, but it's behind the closed doors of families that equality can be hardest to find. Consciousness-raising, which takes place behind those same closed doors, is the best thing we have to form more liberated households. "My husband should be kissing my toes" is a sop for a personal frustration born of sexism. The solution is to make more political changes that really do support women and children; universal day care and an attributed economic value for housework would be a start. How to get there on a practical and a political level is tackled in Chapter 8, "What Is Activism?" But we need to remember: equality starts at home.

THE FEMINIST DIASPORA

Relationships, marriage, bisexuality, STDs, abortion, and having children were the topics our friends were thinking about on the night of our dinner party. Among the subjects with which our dinner companions have also grappled were immigration problems, access to education, racism as manifest by white women befriending black women to get over their white guilt, taking care of an aging relative, credit-card debt, depression, and body image. Every woman's life touches many issues, some of which demand urgent attention at different times.

On every Third Wave Foundation membership card, for example, there is a place that asks, "My issues are . . . ?," and no two cards have ever listed the same answer. Among the responses provided, members list "Jewish progressive life," "war crimes," "student financial aid," "interracial dating," "issues of the South Asian Diaspora," "universal health care," "mothering as a teenager," "condom distribution," "chauvinistic fathers," "fat oppression," and "white and male supremacy." Those are just the tip of the iceberg of what young women are thinking about. And, when you scratch the surface of why someone cares about a certain issue, it's almost always because such issues have affected that person or someone he or she cares about. Whether it's a glance at the Third Wave Foundation's membership cards or at a plenary session of the Fourth World Conference on Women in Beijing, at an Honor the Earth board meeting or our dinner party, there is never one feminist issue that dwarfs all others. There will never be one platform for action that all women agree on. But that doesn't mean feminism is confused. What it does mean is that feminism is as various as the women it represents. What weaves a feminist movement together is consciousness of inequities and a commitment to changing them.

As two young women who believe in the importance of a political vision and have faith in our peers, we want to begin to articulate why a generation leading revolutionary lives is best known for saying, "I'm not a feminist, but . . ." Third Wave women have been seen as nonfeminist when they are actually living feminist lives. Some of this confusion is due to the fact that most young women don't get together to talk about "Feminism" with a capital F. We don't use terms like "the politics of housework" or "the gender gap" as much as we simply describe our lives and our expectations. To a degree, the lack of a Third Wave feminist terminology keeps us from building a potent movement, which is why we need to connect our pro-woman ethics to a political vision. And yet, even without the rip-roaring political culture that characterized the sixties and the seventies, Third Wave women are laying the groundwork for a movement of our own.

In the rest of this book, we describe what feminism is, what some of the stumbling blocks have been for Third Wave women, and what we need to do to make feminism a powerful, political movement. One such block has been that feminists from our generation who have begun to be famous as writers or leaders—those who could magnetize many of the feminist-minded young women out there—are either labeled too controversial or cast solely as antagonistic before their ideas have a chance to mature. Or, in a few cases, they themselves prefer to remain in a rebellious teenage-daughter mode. Other young women outside the media mecca *are* out there changing their worlds in small and large ways, and aren't recognized—by the media or by many older feminists. After all, it's pretty clear that feminists still haven't mastered the media, and therefore aren't able to wield its power to our organizing advantage. Meanwhile, everyday feminists abound, but it's the everyday anti-feminists on whom the media and other feminists focus with outrage.

Part of the problem stems from our generation's ignorance or confusion about what feminism is and has been. Some of it stems from the fact that the hubs of feminism—the groups and sub-groups that are active and visible—aren't really connected to one another. For instance, young, culturally driven Girlie feminists share few strategies with the old-school Second Wavers—and vice versa. (These Girlies are women in their late twenties and early thirties and are not the same as the girls in the girls' movement.) Some Second Wave women are leaping over the Third Wave altogether, and focusing instead on little girls (specifically their self-esteem) rather than tackling the challenge of working with young-adult women.

One recent example among many: At a January 2000 reading sponsored and attended by women in their twenties and thirties, Second Waver Susan Brownmiller, author of *Against Our Will*, insisted that young feminists existed—but "not in [Third Wave's] generation. It's the younger girls."

Manifesta is an attempt to open people's eyes to the power of everyday feminism right in front of our noses. We must see its reality if we are to corral that energy into attacking the inequalities that still exist.

Revolutions always start small. Our August 5 dinner party was everyday organizing in action. Yours could be, too. Every time women get together around a table and speak honestly, they are embarking on an education that they aren't getting elsewhere in our patriarchal society. And that's the best reason for a dinner party a feminist could hope for.

CHAPTER TWO

What Is Feminism?

A Concise History of the F Word

Feminism, *a word that describes a social-justice movement for gender equity and human liberation, is often treated as the other F word. Partly because it's a word of great power, it's nearly as unseemly as those other girl terms,* cunt *or* bitch. *This in part explains why by the time the two of us were at college, learning that we were indeed feminists, the term was dripping with qualifiers. "I'm a . . . power, postmodern, Girlie, pro-sex, Prada, academic, gender, radical, Marxist, equity, cyber, Chicana, cultural, eco, lesbian, Latina, womanist, animal rights, American Indian, Indian, international, diva, Jewish, Puerto Rican, working-class, Asian-American, philanthropic, bisexual, transsexual, lipstick, punk rock, young, old . . . feminist." All of these adjectives help women feel described rather than confined by a term that should simply connote an individual woman's human rights, and the possibility of liberating oneself from patriarchy.*

Some of the ideas behind this word were planted in Europe sometime before the late period of Western imperial expansion around A.D. 1400. In 1405, Christine de Pisan, a Parisian scholar, wrote The Book of the City of Ladies, *in which she argued that there have been women rulers in France throughout history who challenged the patriarchal structure. Henricus Cornelius Agrippa, a German philosopher, described such a structure in 1529: "By the excessive power of male tyranny which prevails against divine justice and the laws of nature, women's liberty is denied to them by law, suppressed to them by custom and usage, and eradicated by upbringing."*[18] *The word itself,* feminisme, *was being used to describe the activities of women like Hubertine Auclert, a French suffragist, in the late 1800s. Feminisme was a cool word, like calling someone hip or savvy. It denoted youth, psychology, sexiness, financial independence, and self.*[19] *By the nineteenth century, the term* feminisme *implied three evolving philosophies: the political belief that the sexes are culturally, not just biologically, created; the process of opposing male supremacy; and a woman's right and responsibility to realize her own potential. The F word was first recorded in America in a 1906 article about the European socialist and suffragist Madeleine Pelletier. Whether the word remained hip or had become tacky in France, its arrival on the shores of America elicited squeamishness and fear.*

At the beginning of the Second Wave, women's liberationist *was the favored term among radical women in the late sixties. But soon* feminism *gained common currency, uniting the radicals and the liberal women's movement under one umbrella term. Some felt that this merger compromised the revolutionary ideas of freedom and ushered in an empty prescription for social equality. In 1970, radical women's liberationist Ti-Grace Atkinson said "feminism is a theory but lesbianism is a practice," while Betty Friedan and the women of NOW were declaring that feminism meant gender parity, and had nothing to do with the person with whom one logged time in the water bed. By the time the Second Wave was drenching all America, the meaning of the word had become symbolic not of fairness* but, more aggressively, of social upheaval and a fear that female superiority was its ultimate goal. This was not unlike how white people felt about black nationalists, with their raised fists, as compared to civil-rights workers singing "We Shall Overcome" arm in arm with whites. In 1979, Barbara Smith wrote that "feminism is the political theory and practice to free all women. . . . Anything less than this is not feminism, but merely female self-aggrandizement." Although Smith's definition was both incontrovertible and in line with what feminism had always meant, fewer women were taking up the moniker to identify themselves. The term could be used against women, it seemed. Some thought, Better not to wrangle with it.

Just as the former slight suffragette doesn't sound any worse than the preferred term suffragist more than a generation later, bra-burner and its sister slight women's libber have lost their teeth as put-downs. Girl, bitch, slut, and cunt—all of which are titles of records and books by feminists of our generation—are no longer scary words we have to keep in the closet, in fear that they will become weapons to be deployed against us. Calling an adult woman "girl" was once insulting, like calling an adult black man "boy." But now that we can choose and use the word ourselves and not have it forced on us, "girl" is increasingly rehabilitated as a term of relaxed familiarity, comfy confidence, the female analogue to "guy"—and not a way of belittling adult women. More and more women own bitch (and what it means to be released from the "please like me" gene), cunt (both the complex, odiferous body part and the wise, badass woman), and slut (the girl whose sexuality is owned by no one but herself).

Thus it can't be far off that independent, self-respecting women begin to call themselves feminists—bravely, without qualifiers—owning the term rather than letting other people use feminism against women.

> **[Feminists are] just women who don't want to be treated like shit.**
>
> —SU,
> an Australian woman interviewed
> for the 1996 anthology *DIY Feminism*

In 1998, during the middle stages of Bill Clinton's personal "woman problem," Barbara Ehrenreich made a curious statement. In a *New York Times* op-ed entitled "Silence of the Beltway Feminists," the great leftist author lamented "The feminists didn't even give [Paula Jones] a hearing," and went on to say that "Paula Jones isn't the only woman betrayed by organized feminism." Ehrenreich is famous for dissecting sexual politics, feminizing the sexual revolution, and authoring books vindicating witches and abortionists, so it seemed odd that as long as she had the floor she—a self-proclaimed feminist—hadn't thought to give Jones that fair hearing, a hearing that the National Organization for Women (NOW) attempted to schedule with Jones on two occasions and each time was stood up by the famous plaintiff herself. So why didn't Ehrenreich stage her own defense of her maligned sister Paula? And if she thought she had, with that op-ed, or later, when she reported on Jones for the *Time* magazine piece "The Week Feminists Got Laryngitis," wasn't that a feminist defense?

Of course, Ehrenreich isn't alone in distancing herself from the movement. Other amnesia feminists—brilliant, usually prominently political women who forget that they are within the movement when launching a critique—include Katha Pollitt (columnist for *The Nation*) and Gwendolyn Mink (a professor of politics at the University of California at Santa Cruz). Mink criticized feminists' inactivity on welfare reform in the feminist monthly *Sojourner*, and, in *The New York Times*, attacked feminists for not taking up Jones's and Monica Lewinsky's cases as incidents of blatant sexual harassment. (The law disagreed with Mink's argument, which is why Jones's case was thrown out. As for Lewinsky, she never charged sexual harassment, and made it clear that she had initiated sexual relations with Clinton.) Shortly after the news broke about Clinton having an affair with an intern, Pollitt remarked in her *Nation* column that the "Feminists are hypocrites with a double standard," implying that these women, usually opinionated, were hypocritically unwilling to speak negatively about "their" President. The specter of these otherwise feminist women pointing their fingers at "the feminists" begs two questions: Who are the feminists? *and* What is feminism?

By feminists, *we* mean each and every politically and socially conscious woman or man who works for equality within or outside the movement, writes about feminism, or calls her- or himself a feminist in the name of furthering equality. In reality, there is no formal alliance of women we can call "the feminists." Although there are institutions and other forums under which women and men organize and rally, feminism isn't a monolith like communism or Scientology. It's a loose collection of individuals, like those women who were at our dinner party. There is one exception that we can think of. In the late sixties, there was an actual group of activists in New York City who called themselves The Feminists. Ti-Grace Atkinson, a Second Wave woman warrior who started off her career with the liberal gals at NOW but soon out-radicaled the radicals, was the most prominent of the group, but because they didn't subscribe to formal hierarchies, she was never the leader. Hard-core as hell, The Feminists were known for having the strictest membership rules: only one-third could be married or living with a man ("hostages," Atkinson called those ladies who socialized with possessors of the Y chromosome). At meetings, to promote a sort of communal conversation ethic, an equal number of poker chips was doled out to each woman. Whenever a member wanted to speak, she paid by tossing down a chip. Of course, some women chose to speak for twenty minutes with each toss, so it wasn't an incorruptible system. But, defunct since 1973, The Feminists are not who Ehrenreich, Mink, and Pollitt mean when they wonder where feminists are.

No, the organized feminists whom people seem to feel betrayed by are the leaders of feminist institutions and those anointed as "the feminists" by the media: most often Patricia Ireland and her company at NOW; Eleanor Smeal and the Feminist Majority Foundation; and Gloria Steinem of *Ms.* magazine and Voters for Choice, among other allegiances—women whose every statement is taken as representative of us all. For example, when the stories about Clinton groping Kathleen Willey *and* having an affair with Lewinsky broke in January 1998, the media, including Pollitt and Ehrenreich, devoted two months to asking, "Where are the feminists?" Then, on March 22, Gloria Steinem wrote an op-ed for *The New York Times* in which she argued that Clinton's behavior was gross and probably pathological but not sexual harassment and therefore not actionable. The next week, columns abounded: "Feminists Are Divided on the Clinton Scandal." It's a surefire sign of oppressed status when an entire group gets reduced to one, or even three, individuals.

At about the same time that the pro- and anti-woman media were hunting for feminists, we, two young feminists living in New York City, were reading Jennifer Pozner's criticisms of Clinton's behavior in *Sojourner*; we were attending Refuse and Resist's rallies that called for an end to the witch-hunts heading toward Clinton's impeachment; and we were writing our own thoughts on the subject, specifically "In Defense of Monica" for *The Nation*. This is only to say that we knew exactly where quite a few of the other feminists were. That said, feminists, too, are guilty of calling on the same triumvirate to opine rather than calling on ourselves. One feminist does not a movement make. In fact, the voices of many individuals are what give the movement its credibility.

Now for the second question. When the topic of feminism

tumbles out of anyone's mouth, whether it be the Vamp red-painted lips of lesbian film fatale Guin Turner asking, "What does feminism mean anymore, anyway?," the earnest jaws of your grandfather, or one of the seventy-five or so people who visit Ask Amy each week, the inevitable question arises: "What is it?"

In the most basic sense, feminism is exactly what the dictionary says it is: the movement for social, political, and economic equality of men and women. Public-opinion polls confirm that when women are given this definition, 71 percent say they agree with feminism, along with 61 percent of men. We prefer to add to that seemingly uncontroversial statement the following: Feminism means that women have the right to enough information to make informed choices about their lives. And because *women* is an all-encompassing term that includes middle-class white women, rich black lesbians, and working-class straight Asian women, an organic intertwining with movements for racial and economic equality, as well as gay rights, is inherent in the feminist mandate. Some sort of allegiance between women and men is also an important component of equality. After all, equality is a balance between the male and the female with the intention of liberating the individual.

Breaking down that one very basic definition, feminism has three components. It is a *movement*, meaning a group working to accomplish specific goals. Those goals are *social* and *political change*—implying that one must be engaged with the government and laws, as well as with social practices and beliefs. And implicit in these goals is *access* to sufficient information to enable women to make responsible choices.

The goals of feminism are carried out by everyday women themselves, a point that is often lost on the media. Maybe you aren't sure you need feminism, or you're not sure it needs you. You're sexy, a wallflower, you shop at Calvin Klein, you are a stay-at-home mom, a big Hollywood producer, a beautiful bride all in white, an ex-wife raising three kids, or you shave, pluck, *and* wax. In reality, feminism wants you to be whoever you are—but with a political consciousness. And vice versa: you want to be a feminist because you want to be exactly who you are. That may be someone patriarchal society doesn't value or allow—from a female cadet at the Citadel to a lesbian mother. Maybe you feel aligned with the self-determination and human rights implicit in feminism, but you also organize your life around race, religion, or class, rather than solely around gender. For instance, in *The Reader's Companion to U.S. Women's History*, the editors list seventeen prominent kinds of feminism based on identity, including American Indian, Arab-American, Asian-American, Jewish, Latina, lesbian, Marxist, Puerto Rican, and working-class. There are also womanists, which, as coined and defined by novelist and poet Alice Walker, designates a black feminist (womanists are rarely men) without having to "add a color to become visible." Womanism, as distinct from feminism's often white-centered history, is an alternative casting of the same basic beliefs about equality and freedom, and few womanists would deny the link to feminism. While each of these groups is magnetized by political equality, some additional aspect of their personhood needs to be emphasized because it affects their struggle for equality.

Using a qualifier in order to further define identity is very different from forgoing the feminist label altogether. For instance, women within other social-justice movements—environmental, peace, human rights, and hip-hop, for example—often opt for the term *humanist*. Although humanism includes men (and especially those who aren't white or otherwise privileged), in reality it is a retreat from feminism. Using *humanism* as a replacement for *feminism* is also a misuse of the term; theologically, humanism is a rejection of supernaturalism, not an embrace of equality between men and women. Feminism seeks to include *women* in human rights. Internationally, nearly twice as many women as men are illiterate, and it was only in 1998 that an international court denounced rape as a form of torture in prison, and as a war crime when conducted systematically by the military. Along those lines, gender-based persecution isn't recognized as grounds for asylum in the United States, which means that women who are likely to be killed by their husbands or sure to be genitally mutilated if they return to their countries are usually put on the next plane back, regardless of this potential danger. (Or, like Adelaide Abankwah and Fauziya Kassindja, they are imprisoned for years, and granted permanent residency, and later asylum, only after long campaigns conducted on their behalf by U.S. feminists.)

Most women come to feminism through personal experience, as we noted in "The Dinner Party," which is one of the reasons the core identity of feminism has to be so elastic. The term represents an incredible diversity of individual lives. Often, a woman who otherwise wouldn't align herself with feminism seeks it out when she is confronted with an abusive relationship, or if her boss is paying her less than her male counterparts are paid, or, on a positive note, if she needs credit to start her own beauty salon. Historically, who else besides feminists have been there to help women, whether they be Calvin Klein devotees or vegan Earth Mothers? Many women tap into or create feminist resources while not even knowing they are on a feminist path. On the work front, secretaries founded 9 to 5—a union for (mainly) pink-collar women workers—and feminists supported the National Committee on Pay Equity as well as microlending and the Equal Credit Opportunity Act, because no one else was interested in the problems of working women. Kris, a stylist who wrote in to Ask Amy, turned to feminist resources when she wanted to open her own salon. She didn't appeal to the Small Business Administration (SBA) because its process is complicated and full of red tape, when all she needed was a little money to tide her over as she built up her client base. Amy sent her to New York City's Women's Venture Fund, which makes microloans. Women even turn to feminism when they want to learn how to masturbate—vulvas were mapped out in Betty Dodson's video *Sex for One*, and orgasms expanded on in Susie Bright's 1990 *Susie Sexpert's Lesbian Sex World*. Most safe-sex shops were founded by feminists, from

Eve's Garden in New York City, opened by Dell Williams in 1974, and Good Vibrations, founded by sex therapist Joani Blank in San Francisco in 1977, to newer sex shops like Toys in Babeland in New York City and Seattle.

Clearly, the only people who are actively paving the paths to women's equality are feminists. Eventually, most women seeking to expand or change their lives find feminism. This makes it sound as if the movement is a huge force of conscious feminists constantly fortified by new recruits. Actually, though, diminishing "enrollment" is a problem in the movement, largely due to political co-optation. The moment a concern pioneered and promoted by feminists—such as domestic violence, microenterprise, the fight for affordable health care, and day care—becomes mainstream or at all successful, it is no longer seen as a women's issue but simply as a newsworthy issue. It becomes depoliticized, taken out of the hands of the grass roots, and divorced from the very process that was necessary to its success.

The most recognizable example of feminist issues being co-opted is the movement against domestic violence. Before feminism, there was no word for battered women or domestic violence, no legal argument of self-defense for women who killed their abusers, and no shelter system. In the seventies and eighties, shelters, funded by grassroots feminist groups and fledgling foundations (like the early Ms. Foundation for Women), proliferated, but the government, the police, and the media outlets still paid very little attention to violence inside the home. For example, the first shelter for women in the United States was started in California in 1964. (This was out of pure need, not because feminists were franchising.) Now, there is an organized battered women's movement of shelters, awareness campaigns, reformed laws and police practices, and legislative strategies. October is Domestic Violence Awareness month, and 1994 saw the passage of the Violence Against Women Act, which set the precedent for prosecuting abusers who cross state lines, and a mandate for nationwide enforcement of protection orders. Nonetheless, in 1994, when Nicole

Brown Simpson was murdered and her hulking football-hero ex-husband was accused of the crime, domestic violence was launched into the mainstream—"professionalized," according to one young activist—and divorced by the media from the grassroots organizations that had named its reality and pioneered its treatment. What this means is that a woman like GE executive Sam Allison can now be on the board of the Women's Center in Milwaukee and claim that she's not a feminist but simply an "advocate to end violence against women."

Similarly, in 1991 entrepreneur Melissa Bradley broke ground in the field of women's economic development without connecting it to the feminist legacy of this work—for example, the pioneering work done by Connie Evans, who started the Women's Self-Employment Project a dozen years earlier. By 1998, Evans had dispensed more than $1.3 million in six hundred short-term microloans, establishing the largest small-business fund for low-income women—all undertaken by her as feminist work. Bradley, who is the founder of the Entrepreneurial Development Institute and worked for the federal government's Office of Thrift and Supervision, where she advised on and critiqued welfare-to-work programs, until recently didn't consider her work to be feminist.

This could be construed as assimilation, and in some ways it is our goal. After all, as long as Women's History and African-American History are independent curricula, history itself will still be a white man's story. In that same way, the women's rights movement will have been successful when we no longer have to advocate separately for half the population's human rights. On the other hand, ideally women's egos would be more invested in their work. You can't continue change if you don't know the process that got you this far. If feminists first exposed domestic violence as a reality in many women's lives, funded the first women's shelters, and drafted and fought for legislation that is now working to end violence against women, then an "advocate to end violence against women" (Sam Allison's term for herself) is just another term for *femi-*

nist. Issues divorced from their feminist roots eventually become depoliticized, and the resulting social programs are reduced to treating the symptoms rather than curing—or preventing—the disease. In order to have a robust movement, domestic violence and economic development need to be reidentified as feminist issues and victories. And people like Allison and Bradley need to be outed as feminists.

FEARING FEMINISM

Now, let's discuss what a feminist isn't. T-shirt and button slogans such as a feminist is the "opposite of a doormat" and "not a masochist" have outworn their usefulness in bringing clarity to the subject. Feminism is more often described by what it isn't than by what it is, which creates some confusion (and is the reason that we defined it before going into all this). The inadvertently humorous descriptions by right-wing ideologues like Pat Robertson don't help, either: "Feminists encourage women to leave their husbands, kill their children, practice witchcraft, become lesbians, and destroy capitalism." Of course, that definition is not so much wrong as hyperbolic. To a fundamentalist, that's just a description of no-fault divorce laws, abortion rights, rejection of God as the Father, acceptance of female sexuality, and a commitment to workers.

Nonetheless, women far to the left of Robertson still fear feminism. The fact that the feminist movement has developed networks to help women who are victimized is one reason that women fear the word. Identifying ourselves as feminists means addressing uncomfortable topics: the humiliation of being discriminated against, the fact that we are vulnerable when we walk home late at night or even in our homes, or the sadness of discovering that the sons in our families are treated altogether differently from the daughters. Injustice and oppression are hard to face, a fact that is evident in the number of rape and sexual-harassment charges that emerge years, even decades, after the event actually happened. To use one example, Juanita Broaddrick waited twenty years to accuse Bill Clinton of forcing her into sex in a hotel room. This was during a time when forced sex among acquaintances—what is now called date rape—was excused as relatively inevitable, certainly not criminal, male behavior. Feminists fought for a realistic legal definition of rape that acknowledged degrees of sexual assault (and protected male rape victims, too), a minimum one-year statute of limitations, rape shield laws that prohibit using a victim's sexual history against her (or him), and the training of emergency-room and police personnel to gather evidence, including a so-called rape kit, when a victim comes into their hospitals or precincts. Had the incident happened today, feminism would mean being there for Broaddrick—utilizing the legal system and social-service institutions—the second she could get out of the hotel room to press charges. To take it one step further, the goal of feminism is to create a climate in which Clinton couldn't possibly have raped Broaddrick, or anyone, without knowing that "no means no" and a prison sentence was imminent.

Even at the beginning of the Second Wave, women were resistant to acknowledging discrimination. The results of the 1972 Virginia Slims poll (the first one that recognized women's issues) found that men observed discrimination against women more often than women did. As we said, consciousness is everything. Even now, acknowledging inequality begs one to do something about it—and that is a daunting, albeit righteous, responsibility.

More things feminism is not: Feminism's philosophy certainly isn't narrow-minded enough to be solely about our sexuality or our paychecks, and is certainly not about man-hating or chivalry. (In our opinion, whoever gets to the door first should be responsible for opening it.) Still, some people choose to stay away from feminism because they don't want to be associated with spooky stereotypes about feminists and their freaky excesses. You know this rap: *some feminists think all sex is rape, all men are evil, you have to be a lesbian to be a feminist, you can't wear Girlie clothes or makeup, married women are lame, et cetera.* This conversation is usually baiting and can ride the force of homophobia or internalized phallophilia (socialized glorification of the male principle and men). Women who love lipstick and also love standing up for themselves, but are not politicized, are especially vulnerable to being conned into distancing themselves from the feminist movement.

A good example of this is the evolution of Lilith Fair. Canadian chanteuse Sarah McLachlan put together a historic mothership of ladies. Most of the Lilithites were stars who had topped the music charts, and McLachlan trotted them across America to make the point that not only are female rock stars achieving a critical mass but that women rake in the audiences. The tour earned more than $16.4 million in the first year alone and drew more than 70-percent female audiences during all three years of its existence. To make it even more stunning, the Lilith management gave checks averaging $20,000 to a battered women's shelter or grassroots social-service agency in every locale in which the lavender Lilith backdrop undulated. But what happened when McLachlan was asked about women and politics? "The tour isn't a soapbox for extremist feminism," she said in a New York *Newsday* interview during the first tour. "This is not at all about dissing men." There are certain assurances we just shouldn't have to make, especially when a majority of the backup band members are male, as is the vast majority of the stage crew, sound people, bus drivers, talent management, and the male-owned companies that underwrote the tour. Besides, as a friend of ours pointed out, even if there weren't a male presence behind the front women at Lilith, there is no need for the disclaimer. After all, an all-black tour of hip-hop musicians wouldn't feel obligated to assure people that they're not dissing whites.

Furthermore, if Sarah McLachlan had brushed up on her feminist history, she would have been aware of Olivia Records, Redwood Recordings, Ladyslipper distribution, and Michigan Womyn's Music Festival. Then she could have built upon that separatist womyn's music movement (which flourished in the seventies and still exists) as her foundation, a movement that created a network of producers, labels, and festivals entirely outside the mainstream. Shining a light on the long line of women who continue to transform the male-run music industry would have gotten Lilith closer to its implied goal of equal treatment for women. Happily, McLachlan didn't remain fearful of the feminist implications of her tour. According to Amy Ray of the Indigo Girls, an artist who performed on all three Lilith tours, after a few years of being immersed in this experience, McLachlan changed her tune and proudly called the tour feminist. "I think Sarah always had the same vision for Lilith," says Ray. "But she became much more confident about standing up for the idea that women—audiences and musicians—need an all-female tour, they want it, and they're going to take it without apology."

Most of those Ladyslipper/Michigan/Olivia feminists are womyn-loving-womyn, an association that Lilith and many other women in rock tend to fear. "The idea that all feminists are lesbians is scary enough for some women to stay away from the feminist label and movement, even when their beliefs are basically feminist," wrote Barbara Findlen, then *Ms.* magazine's executive editor, in her pioneering anthology *Listen Up: Voices from the Next Feminist Generation*. Rooting homophobia out of the movement is as essential as rooting out racism. To eschew calling yourself a feminist because you don't want to be called a "dyke" is like not joining the civil-rights movement because you don't want to be called a "nigger" or a "nigger lover." Besides, regardless of one's sexuality, everyone has a vested interest in reclaiming the inherent dignity of the terms *lesbian*, *gay*, and *queer*, since straight women who refuse a subservient role (and straight men who refuse to dominate) are likely to be called gay. Findlen also points out the odd way that some straight women reconcile themselves with this threat: by arguing that feminists aren't *all* dykes. (Which implies, among other ignorant assumptions, that all gay women are inherently feminist.) Rather than challenge the homophobia—and misogyny—head-on, this tactic sidesteps the issue, allowing women to embrace a limited feminism without disavowing dyke-baiting.

In truth, the movement is made up of women from all points on the sexual spectrum. And, because they may be more able to risk male disapproval, lesbian and bisexual women have had a particularly creative and strong history in the women's movement, from founding the aforementioned womyn's music scene to writing world-changing books such as *Sexual Politics* (Kate Millett), *Sister Outsider* (Audre Lorde), and *Sisterhood Is Powerful* (Robin Morgan) and being the most iconic activists (Barbara Smith, Angela Davis, and Rita Mae Brown). It's interesting to note that homophobes never attack feminist critic Camille Paglia for being of the Sapphic persuasion—proof that dyke-baiting is employed only in the service of feminist-bashing. As Kaia Wilson, formerly the guitarist for lesbian supergroup Team Dresch and currently for The Butchies, puts it, "There can be really good reasons for not wanting to call yourself a feminist, but most of the time it's due to misogyny."

Even when the winds of misogyny and homophobia aren't blowing feminism's house down, women can be their own big bad wolves. Injudicious niceness, which is a socialized disease, often explains why women tend not to demand equality. It also may be why feminist women feel it's necessary to answer questions that are hostile to feminism, regardless of how silly or offensive they are. Conversely, when a woman is politically oriented and knowledgeable about history, she knows the burden of proof should be on the questioner and is less likely to have a misguided sense of politeness. When someone asks, "Why is it that all feminists think they're better than men?" (or insert any weird generalization involving lesbians, matriarchies, and hatred of sex), one should respond with something along the lines of "Who are you referring to?" Imagine the organizing and theorizing that has not happened because we have allowed ourselves to be delayed by these distractions. In the case of the mythical statement "Andrea Dworkin says that all sex is rape," recommend actually reading her book *Intercourse* (the salient chapter is called "Occupation/Collaboration"), and starting the conversation from there.[20] To give you a taste, Dworkin writes pungently: "Women lie about life by not demanding to understand the meaning of entry, penetration, occupation, having boundaries crossed over, having lesser privacy: by avoiding the difficult, perhaps impossible (but how will we ever know?) questions of female freedom." Clearly, she is making a much more subtle, disturbing, and ultimately liberating point than an easy generalization could convey. If you want more clarity, you could do what the *Hungry Mind Review*, now called *The Ruminator Review*, did, and ask Dworkin directly what she thinks sex is. "I think of sexual contact and sexual intimacy as pleasure," she told them. "And as a way of experiencing freedom."

Feminism is often mistaken as being an enabler, a "sop" discouraging women from taking action in their lives, the genesis of the victim culture that critics like Katie Roiphe and Christina Hoff Sommers so despise. Even women who rely on and are seeking feminist resources can mistake feminism for the equivalent of a Knight in Shining Armor to save them from their woes. In fact, the urge to protect women is part of the problem feminists fight. As Susan Faludi (famed author of *Backlash* and, more recently, *Stiffed*) and others have noted, protection starts out polite—women and children first off the sinking ship and so forth—and ends up justifying why women can't be naval captains or firefighters or subjects for medical research. Women can't ride this antiquated stereotype and at the same time fight for independence. In reality, feminism requires action and taking responsibility for oneself.

Take job discrimination as a case in point. A clerk at Wal-Mart, sensing that she was getting a raw deal, recently wrote to Ask Amy. For the last five of her ten years at the store, her salary had stayed the same, while male cashiers were given annual raises. Other feminists had done their part by creating laws against sex discrimination, trainings for implementation of these laws, and organizations to help women through the process. Amy's Web site informed her of her legal rights but also pointed out that now the Wal-Mart clerk must do her part: document the discrimination and file a complaint.

To sum up, feminism is helped by a working knowledge of history, and requires a willingness to act on behalf of yourself, and to stand up for all women in the face of everything from misogyny to a social mandate that says "be *nice*."

THE STORY UP TILL NOW

"It's our memory that connects us," says the poet Sonia Sanchez. She understands that, when women feel disconnected or put off by feminism, it's important to go back to the roots of the movement—whether it's in books or in our mothers' and grandmothers' lives—and find out what the struggle for equality has meant and could mean. And it's especially critical to excavate this history if you are working within the feminist movement, whether at NOW, as an individual activist, or as a women's studies major. Sadly, the women's movement too often misses the essential tool of collective memory. (The unmaliciously ignorant early meanderings of the Lilithites is a case in point.) Our history has been kept out of the mainstream, diverted to a stagnant pool that all but the most intrepid historian would miss. The books that sparked our foremothers' rebellion are out of print, and histories of the women who fought before us are just barely becoming archived. This isn't a new problem. Most of the American women who fought for the vote didn't know that they had a French forebear in Christine de Pisan or an example of living feminism in Native American women sharing their same piece of land; nor did they have much access to the work of Mary Wollstonecraft, author of the early manifesta *The Vindication of the Rights of Woman*, until after they had begun their campaigns. Most college students in the sixties didn't study Simone de Beauvoir's *The Second Sex*, although they probably studied her much-archived lover Sartre, and knew only a limited amount about the suffragists. (Among the things they learned was that these women were *all* white, reformist, racist, and ridiculous in their bloomers and blue-stockings—none of which is true, except perhaps the mild humorousness of their garb.)

Today, young women rarely learn about Victoria Woodhull, who, in the 1872 election, was the first woman to run for president, and was also the first female stockbroker on Wall Street. Nor do many of us know about seventies radicals Carol Downer and Lorraine Rothman, who invented the Del-Em, the first menstrual extraction device, even though this safe, do-it-yourself early-abortion technique might be a smart thing to know about as our right to choose is increasingly restricted. (In 1970, Carol Downer performed a self-exam at a California women's bookstore, and became the first person ever to be arrested for teaching women how to see their own cervixes. She was charged with practicing medicine without a license.) Nor do we learn that the activism of women of color was feminist activism; for example, that Fannie Lou Hamer campaigned against coerced sterilization and was a founder of the National Women's Political Caucus, that Aileen Hernandez was the first head of the EEOC, or that Shirley Chisholm, who ran for president in 1972, said it was harder to be a woman in politics than to be black. But Second Wave women are beginning to document their history and to retell their stories via women's studies courses, millennium wrap-ups, memoirs, histories, and PBS documentaries, all of which concretize women's contribution to history (if still not fully the contribution of women of color). As a result, it is possible that future generations of women won't have to excavate their history but simply learn it as they do "Dewey Defeats Truman" or "Neil Armstrong Walks on the Moon." Pragmatically, recounting the stories of feminism shows older women that the next generation is aware of their struggles, and shows younger women that their rebellion has a precedent. Having our history might keep feminists from having to reinvent the wheel every fifty years or so. Therefore our own revisiting of it in this chapter is incentive to build on this legacy rather than to have to rebuild.

For the sake of historical convenience, many scholars and historians have broken feminism down into the First Wave (the seventy-five years beginning in 1848 and winding down in the mid-1920s) and the Second Wave (which we're about thirty years into). Each wave has brought a swelling of momentum that has carried us closer to women's equality. Many young feminists today are choosing to call themselves the Third Wave in order to herald the future.

For most historians, feminism began in the United States sometime just before an 1848 meeting in Seneca Falls, New York, where female abolitionists began pondering why they could work their asses off in a movement to gain the rights of citizenship for a group of disenfranchised men when they themselves didn't have those rights. (At the time, the mid-1800s, women had fewer rights than a man deemed insane.) Empowered to think they could affect change via their own activism on behalf of American slaves, these women and at least a few men, including ex-slave and American icon Frederick Douglass, launched the women's suffrage movement by ratifying the Declaration of Sentiments at that 1848 meeting.

Although this is the first example of American feminism noted by white historians, sexual equality on this continent dates back before Columbus's chance arrival, to a time when there were five hundred thriving American Indian tribes, most of them offering a model of a much more egalitarian society than Europeans had ever witnessed. In the Iroquois and Cherokee traditions, for example, clan mothers decided who the chiefs would be and made many significant decisions, from food allocation to war strategy. Equal education was guaranteed to boys and girls, and divorce and women's control over their fertility, and their children, were basic rights. Matilda Joslyn Gage, the great First Wave leader and writer, *did* recognize the organic feminism of Native Americans. In historian Sally Roesch Wagner's authoritative pamphlet on Gage, she writes that the suffragist was so committed to the local Mohawk nation that she was adopted into the wolf clan in 1893. Having been tried that same year for voting in a school-board election, her role as a Mohawk—where she was being considered for full voting rights—must have struck her with a bitter irony. But worse than Gage's conflict is not knowing that equality is possible because equality was part of the not so distant past. "Feminists too often believe that no one has ever experienced the kind of society that empowered women and made that empowerment the basis of rules and civilization," wrote poet and novelist Paula Gunn Allen in *The Sacred Hoop: Recovering the Feminine in American Indian Traditions*. "The price the feminist community must pay because it is not aware of the recent presence of gynarchical societies on this continent is necessary confusion, division, and much lost time."

Now that we have acknowledged the "red roots of white feminism," in Gunn Allen's term, we can turn our attention to the "Seneca Falls Five," the aforementioned abolitionists who became incensed by their own disfranchised state. They were Jane Hunt, Mary Ann McClintock, Lucretia Mott, Elizabeth Cady Stanton—the grande dame and intellectual heavyweight of First Wave feminism—and Martha Wright. The Declaration of Sentiments, which they drafted at that Seneca Falls meeting, was modeled on the Declaration of Independence—but included women. "[T]he speedy success of our cause depends upon the zealous and untiring efforts of both men and women, for the overthrow of the monopoly of the pulpit, and for the securing to woman an equal participation with men in the various trades, professions, and commerce," they wrote in that document. Susan B. Anthony, Matilda Joslyn Gage, and Sojourner Truth joined these women after the 1848 meeting. Truth, a former slave, was instrumental in clarifying the true moral—and collaborative—nature of the struggle. Acknowledging that the forces working against both women and blacks were white men, she also made visible the frequently ignored civil-rights plight of the *woman* who is also *black* and advised against the efforts of white male abolitionists to award citizenship to black men but to deny it to women of any race. The inaccuracies persist today. For example, at the historic site of Lucretia Mott's birthplace on Nantucket Island, Massachusetts, a plaque identifies her as the first female abolitionist when she was merely one of the first *white* females to agitate against slavery.

In 1920, seventy-two years after this charter convention, radical tactics borrowed from the suffragettes in England (and a soft-pedaling of other radical goals) helped women attain passage of the Nineteenth Amendment. It states: "The right of citizens of the United States to vote shall not be denied or abridged by the United States or by any state on account of sex." Because of racist poll taxes and other means to disfranchise black citizens, black men and women, particularly those in Southern states, didn't really enjoy suffrage until the Civil Rights Act of 1964, which banned race discrimination. Although the Seneca Falls Five, Truth, Gage, and Anthony all died without seeing women across the nation win the right to vote, these First Wavers earned women many other basic rights as they fought for suffrage. Besides helping to attain the Thirteenth Amendment, which abolished slavery in 1865, feminists won the right to divorce, to own property, to claim their inheritance, and to keep their own names (as Lucy Stone did when she married Henry Blackwell in 1855). Stone, an abolitionist and a somewhat conservative feminist, was one of the first women to rewrite marriage vows omitting the word *obey*. She was also the first woman from New England to graduate from college—graduating in 1847 from Oberlin, the first college to admit women, just as it had been the first to admit blacks. Her life was so inspiring that her name became synonymous with independent women. In Stone's day, instead of being called a bitch or a women's libber, a spunky woman was called a "Lucy Stoner," as well as an "unnatural woman" and other epithets.

Although at least two generations came between the Seneca Falls Five and its twentieth-century descendant, the National Woman's Party, the two groups are both thought of as the First Wave, a demarcation based on the goal of suffrage and not on the culture or strategies of the women involved. Around the turn of the century, young women began infusing the First Wave—they were the new Lucy Stoners, replete with radical ideas and brave claims on freedom. For example, Emma Goldman pioneered her free-love movement, the women of the Harlem Renaissance, such as Zora Neale Hurston, began documenting black culture, and radical suffragist Alice Paul founded the National Woman's Party as a protest against her more complacent and conservative colleagues and some foremothers. (Stanton and Gage were as radical as they come, but Anthony ultimately caved in to conservatism—or pragmatism—and her foothold in history was much stronger than that of the more hard-core women.) Paul, the most instrumental activist in the final push for the Nineteenth Amendment, saw the vote as a baby step. She thought women needed the Lucretia Mott Amendment, also known as the Equal Rights Amendment, which Paul wrote. First introduced in 1923, the passage of the ERA was, to Paul, the only way that women could have any real claim to equality.

First steps or not, the women of the nineteenth century did enough for female emancipation that twentieth-century women were able to begin organizing in their own independent fields. In 1903, labor organizer Mary Harris ("Mother") Jones took children who were forced to work in Philadelphia's textile factories to President Theodore Roosevelt's Long Island home to demand the abolition of child exploitation. Jones's leadership led to state and federal child-labor laws, as did the work of other female reformers such as Jane Addams. Sparked by the 1911 Triangle Shirtwaist Fire, in which more than a hundred immigrant women workers (and many men) perished because their employer locked them inside their workplace, Rose Schneiderman organized against hideous labor practices as the head of the International Ladies' Garment Workers Union. Mary McLeod Bethune founded the National Council of Negro Women, and Mabel Keaton Staupers desegregated the U.S. Army Nurse Corps during World War II. Meanwhile, nurse

Margaret Sanger (creator of an early zine called *The Woman Rebel*) realized that women should no longer suffer injury, disease, death, and curtailed sexual freedom from numerous pregnancies, and thus began her crusade for legalized birth control. These women were breaking fertile ground and planting seeds for the further advancement of women's rights, but despite these breakthroughs women still confronted "fifty years of ridicule," as Second Wave author Shulamith Firestone called the backlash between the vote and the surge of Second Wave radical feminism.[21]

The modern women's liberation movement, or the Second Wave, percolated from at least two sources. One was political women working in the civil-rights and anti-war movements. They were often women from Northern universities who went down South in the summer to participate in literacy training and voter education, volunteering for such groups as the Southern Christian Leadership Conference and the Student Nonviolent Coordinating Committee, as well as Southern community activists. Well-trained organizers like the abolitionists a century earlier, these women eventually turned their raised consciousness to their own oppression, fighting their pigeonholed status as coffeemakers and sex providers for the New Left male leaders. The second source was composed of awakening white middle-class women who were fleeing their houses and "the feminine mystique" (as described by Betty Friedan in her 1963 watershed book) to find meaningful work, as well as the individual stalwarts who had begun looking for equality in Eleanor Roosevelt's day and never stopped. (And perhaps many women were jazzed by Helen Gurley Brown's 1962 tale of the glamorous working girl's life, *Sex and the Single Girl*.)

Simultaneously, the Black Power movement had replaced the more egalitarian and racially integrated civil-rights movement, which meant not only that whites were kicked out but that, generally speaking, black women were demoted from being organizers to simply being "nation-builders" (mothers). Black women who didn't buy that line created their own feminist groups, and some, such as Fannie Lou Hamer, Florynce Kennedy, Pauli Murray, and Aileen Hernandez, partnered with or helped to found mainstream feminist groups such as NOW (founded in 1966 by Betty Friedan and twenty-nine other women) and, later, the Women's Action Alliance (founded in 1970 by Brenda Feigen, Jane Galvin Lewis, Gloria Steinem, and Dorothy Pitman Hughes), and the National Women's Political Caucus (founded in 1972 by Bella Abzug, Betty Friedan, Fannie Lou Hamer, and Gloria Steinem, among others).

So the organizing began. Women's liberation groups sprouted up in cities: in Boston, Cell 16; Washington, D.C., Chicago, and Gainesville, Florida, had groups called Women's Liberation; in Seattle, Women's Liberation, Radical Women, and the Majority Union; and in New York, New York Radical Women, New York Radical Feminists, the Feminists, and Redstockings. The new-guard feminists, many of whom came out of the male left, devised and deployed such strategies as consciousness-raising, zap-action demonstrations, and speak-outs. By 1970, the women's health movement, also known as the women's self-help movement, was confirmed with the publication of *Our Bodies, Ourselves*, which demystified women's bodies and the doctor-patient relationship. The philosophies of women's liberation and women's political equality were delivered to suburbia and the rest of America in 1972, when the monthly feminist glossy called *Ms.* magazine hit the stands, the first feminist magazine to be available cross-country on newsstands and by subscription.

Some of these Second Wavers began where Alice Paul left off, fighting for an Equal Rights Amendment that would constitutionally guarantee women equality under the law. (And others didn't think it was radical enough to fight for.) In 1972, the ERA suddenly swept handily through Congress, thanks largely to the liberal (NOW) faction of the Second Wave and the few women in Congress, and was sent to the states for ratification. Within a year, thirty of the thirty-eight states needed for ratification had signed on. By 1975, five more states had signed on, and by 1977 what would have been the Twenty-seventh

Amendment needed just three more in order to become the law of the land. But a cold and sinister backlash against equality was already sweeping through the country. When Alice Paul heard that the ratification deadline was just seven years, she predicted that the ERA would not pass. She knew firsthand the conservatism of state legislatures. By 1982—the deadline—women were still the same damn three states short of the necessary supermajority. The amendment did have a majority in simple terms: three-quarters of the women who were polled about the ERA were *for* it. But the most visible opposition was, annoyingly, also female. Most famous among the enemies of equality were Phyllis Schlafly and Beverly LaHaye, who made jet-set careers for themselves telling other women to stay home. In 1982, the ERA went into hibernation, where it remains, awaiting a kiss from twenty-first century feminist leaders. (Some states are puckering up: in 1998, Iowa and Florida initiated state ERAs, proving that, despite confusion about the efficacy of the ERA, women do want constitutional equality. In 1998, trying to improve upon the brand name, the Feminist Majority Foundation and more than 110 other organizations introduced the National Women's Equality Act, a much more comprehensive and inclusive omnibus bill that sets up the wish list of an updated ERA.)

We don't have an ERA, and, to Phyllis Schlafly's relief, public rest rooms are still separate and, judging by the long lines at the ladies' room, still unequal. (Actually, rest-room allocation isn't covered in any version of the ERA.) Even without the ERA, the seventies feminists have succeeded much more than they have failed. The Second Wave has integrated the Little League, police departments, and help-wanted ads; it named and achieved legal redress for domestic violence, sexual harassment, sexual assault, displaced homemakers, child sexual abuse, lesbian custody rights, homophobia and gay bashing, and the right to be a single mother by choice. Women can be in combat, too, without the ERA, as the Gulf War proved. What feminists do have to worry about without the ERA is that any legislative body can make new laws based on gender—and they have to be challenged one at a time, since laws based on gender are constitutionally lawful. To give you some examples of how this plays out, in some states a father may be able to give permission for a child's medical treatment, but the mother cannot do so without also having permission from the father. In rural states, a farm wife may have to pay inheritance tax on her land if her husband dies; but the farm husband doesn't have to if he is widowed. He is seen as the owner of the land, she as the passive recipient, even though they are equally integral to running the farm.

Many Second Wave feminists do not consider the ERA to be the defining issue of the seventies and eighties. Certainly, some of us developed an interest in the ERA simply because the campaign loomed large in our eyes as kids. Whether or not Second Wavers believed in the importance of the battle for an Equal Rights Amendment, it's clear that the bulk of their legacy has at its heart formal and legal equality. They drafted and successfully lobbied for the Equal Credit Opportunity Act, Title IX (which guarantees equal allocation of money for boys and girls in schools that receive federal funding), the right to have an abortion (and thus equal ownership of our bodies), and so much more. Most significant, the Second Wave created an awareness of sexism through such innovations as the click, consciousness-raising, and by analyzing the politics of everything from hierarchical decision making versus leaderless groups to the politics of the clitoral orgasm and hysterectomy. There now exists an organized movement, with institutions and associations that sustain themselves, such as the National Black Women's Health Project, the National Women's Health Network, 9 to 5, and the National Women's Studies Association.

The Second Wave ushered in an era of feminist historians and other documentarians of the women's movement here and abroad. In fact, since the seventies, one can actually make a living as a feminist intellectual. Women's studies busted open the canon—uniformly white and male—and African-American studies, Native American studies, Chicano studies, Asian-American studies, and queer studies set up equivalent academic disciplines to fill out the histories we learn in school. From the beginning, women of color have been publishing important feminist texts, such as the National Black Feminist Organization's statement of purpose, which was circulated widely at the start of the Second Wave, the anthology *The Black Woman* by Toni Cade Bambara, as well as the work of Celestine Ware. Later came Michele Wallace's *Black Macho and the Myth of the Superwoman*, Gloria Anzaldúa and Cherríe Moraga's *This Bridge Called My Back*, Patricia Bell Scott, Gloria Hull, and Barbara Smith's *All the Women Are White, All the Blacks Are Men, but Some of Us Are Brave: Black Women's Studies*, and bell hooks's *Ain't I a Woman: Black Women and Feminism*. The Third Wave was born into the diversity realized by the latter part of the Second Wave. Furthermore, we came of age politically amid the backlash.

The early nineties also gave birth to contemporary Alice Pauls—young women who felt ignored by the women's organizations founded by another generation. Some of these young women felt that Second Wave tactics didn't speak to their media-savvy, culture-driven generation. Others weren't necessarily consciously feminist but simply living feminist lives, honoring the dignity and independence that were, in effect, their birthright. These young feminists appeared on this nation's radar in 1991 when Naomi Wolf, who *is* consciously political, called for a rekindling of feminism in her best-selling book *The Beauty Myth*. In early 1992, Rebecca Walker responded to *The New York Times*'s effort to declare an era of postfeminism. She wrote in *Ms.* magazine, "I am not a postfeminism feminist. I am the Third Wave."

"I beg[a]n to realize that I owe it to myself," Walker said, ". . . to push beyond my rage and articulate an agenda . . . My anger and awareness must translate into tangible action . . . To be a feminist is to join in my sisterhood with women when often we are divided . . ." The media attention on Wolf and

Walker was a belated recognition of a generation that was already galvanizing.

In 1989, and again in 1992, hundreds of thousands of people flooded the Washington Mall to demonstrate support for reproductive freedom. In the early nineties, a loose network of young punk feminists in Washington, D.C., and Olympia, Washington, who called themselves Riot Grrrls, pioneered a feminist voice that was both political and distinctly new. These pro-toradicals, teenagers and women in their early twenties, reclaimed and defanged epithets that kept young women in line, such as "slut" and "fuck no fat chicks," by scrawling these words on their bodies. Whether or not they knew that their mother's generation had marched with buttons that read "cunt power" and banners that proclaimed, "We are the women our parents warned us against," it didn't matter. Riot Grrrls were finding their own voices. In February 1991, seven hundred high-school and college-age young women attended NOW's Young Feminist Conference in Akron, Ohio. These were young women who had already been awed by or were working in Second Wave organizations. Earlier that year, Students Organizing Students (SOS), founded in 1989 to agitate for reproductive rights, effectively organized a boycott of Domino's because of the pizza giant's financial support of pro-life organizations. In April 1992, Hunter College in New York City was the site of a conference entitled "I Believe Anita Hill," which featured a panel on Third Wave feminism. That summer, Third Wave Direct Action undertook a voter-registration drive in the spirit of the freedom rides of the civil-rights movement in the early 1960s, taking 120 young people to 21 under-registered communities across the U.S. and registering more than 20,000 new voters. Books were written—*Listen Up*, *Third Wave Agenda*, *Don't Believe the Hype*, and *To Be Real*—and magazines and newspapers began to take an interest in this new crop of feminists. In 1994, *Newsweek* ran a story on Gen Xers, profiling Girlie sex writer Anka Radakovich and feminist critic Katie Roiphe; later Cincinnati's *The Beacon Journal* asked, "Riding a

New Wave?"; in 1995, in *The New York Times*, Wendy Kaminer wondered, "What Do Young Women Want?"; and *The Boston Globe* targeted cultural agendas, rather than politics, as the new feminist domain in a 1997 feature called "The Third Wave: Rebels with a Cause."

As great as it was to have some representation, two snafus were evident in the mainstream media attention for this younger movement. One, the coverage focused on analyzing the word *feminism* as if it were an autonomous construct rather than on understanding what the term represents—which is women's lives—and thus it was riddled with terms like "post-feminist" and "pro-sex feminist," not to mention "selfish," "apolitical," and "apathetic." And, two, feminist action was reduced to a few star-studded examples, just as the media had often misrepresented the Second Wave as consisting of only a few well-known white women writers in New York. This time it meant that the movement was portrayed as cultural events starring feminists—for example, the all-star performance of playwright Eve Ensler's *The Vagina Monologues* or Courtney Love acting up at a Ms. Foundation event. This superficial assessment was swallowed despite the fact that what got young women moving in the first place was pushing voter registration, organizing against date rape, becoming women in rock, blowing the whistle on sexual harassment, publishing zines, and fighting for young women's reproductive rights. Young women were using their personal lives as a launchpad to a women's movement of their own.

The Third Wave of the movement doesn't have an easily identifiable presence but, if you're looking, you can't help running into the hubs that are unique to this generation. Besides the aforementioned Riot Grrrls, there are legions of young feminist activists, such as the five thousand members of Third Wave Foundation, the women who work with the San Francisco–based Young Women's Work Project, and the Girlies, epitomized by the writers in zines like *Bust* and *Bitch*. All are expanding feminism, and reclaiming the word *girl*, but in very different ways. Riot Grrrls, who are mainly women in their teens and early twenties, breathe new life into feminism by marrying it with their own milieu, the youth movement known as punk rock. Girlies are girls in their twenties or thirties who are reacting to an antifeminine, antijoy emphasis that they perceive as the legacy of Second Wave seriousness. Girlies have reclaimed girl culture, which is made up of such formerly disparaged girl things as knitting, the color pink, nail polish, and fun. They also claim their right to a cultural space once deemed the province of men; for example, rock 'n' roll (although some Second Wavers were claiming the domain of rock music, too), porn, and judgment-free pleasure and sex. There are new politicos, women in such activist groups as Third Wave Foundation or Medical Students for Choice, who are the most likely to build on such Second Wave tactics as founding campus NOW chapters, emphasizing voting, and influencing (or challenging) the existing political system. There is also a thriving "girls' movement," which is distinct from Girlie and from the Third Wave. It was born of the Second Wave and counts as its beneficiaries girls aged nine to fifteen. Underneath all of these names and agendas is the same old feminism. All share a struggle for justice and equality, rather than paternalism or protection (or domination and violence). And all have their roots in fertile soil. It's up to us to continue this feminist work.

GETTING TO EQUALITY

"It's not surprising that we haven't achieved equality," observes critic-of-all-things Wendy Kaminer, writing in *The Atlantic Monthly*. "We haven't even defined it." Our need for feminism in the privileged United States is manifest in the fact that women still make only seventy-four cents, on average, to the male dollar; that only 5.7 percent of the nation's philanthropic dollars go to programs benefiting women and girls; and that only 9 percent of U.S. senators are women. These examples prove that even the most basic bean-counting parity is far from reality.

How would feminism's goal of a roughly fifty-fifty balance

between men and women (of all races, classes, ethnicities, religions, abilities, and sexualities) in all manner of public and private life be attained? A false assumption about equality is that it means inserting some women into traditional men's roles and vice versa. Therefore women could break the glass ceiling and men would therefore have to be relegated to the sticky floors of low-wage jobs. Men could become homemakers and women the Wednesday golfers. But this would replace one set of inequalities with another and not change the system at all—which, of course, is not equality. This is where feminism, for all its simplicity of definition, becomes much more complicated and revolutionary in its implications. After all, if we could simply tag every man as "bad" and every woman as "good," the trip to equality would be that much shorter. Likewise, if feminism were only about improving women's lives and leaving men to stay the same, creating a separatist state might be a better plan.

We could take a page from the environmental novel *Ecotopia*, which proposed that Northern California, Oregon, and Washington secede from the United States to create an environmentally sound country. Building on *Ecotopia* and a wish list proposed by radical feminist philosopher Mary Daly, perhaps Maine, New Hampshire, and Vermont could be seized to create Femitopia. Separatism, as annual week-long Michigan Womyn's Music Festival has proved, can be great in the short term—and for many feminists it's necessary to achieving certain kinds of consciousness, security, and possibilities that can be strong enough to transform the mainstream. The goal of liberation, however, is a radical restructuring of society, one that women can't achieve from the margins—even though they use this perspective to gain a clear vision of the center.

The separatist option may be only a stage leading to equality, but we can point to some concrete examples of what we mean by that goal of equality. Sometimes equality is as simple as numbers. Betty Friedan's *The Front Page Report*, for example, counted the number of male and female bylines in twenty major newspapers (and always revealed women to be doing worse than we think). For women to write 51 percent of the front-page stories would mean that jobs in journalism reflected the pool of writers and the readership more accurately. But equality also implies that the same level of respect and interest be paid to women and their issues of concern as the papers do to men and their issues. Therefore "women's issues," topics that affect women preponderantly—such as exposing the inequities of welfare reform, writing zealously about subsidized day-care programs, and using female subjects and doctors when writing a "Science Times" piece about lung cancer—would receive coverage as serious as do "gender neutral" mergers and acquisitions. To use a Third Wave example, women students have finally surpassed parity in enrollment numbers (61 percent) as undergraduates in liberal-arts colleges—in part because of the large number of returning older women students. However, one of the reasons liberal-arts schools traditionally had value is that this type of education was seen as the best preparation for future professionals and for earning potential. Indeed, blue-collar men with a high-school education have usually averaged more income than white- or pink-collar women with a college education.[22] Now, many men are eschewing college to start up or join tech companies where they can make more money and avoid the debt of four years of college. Tech jobs are going to be the most influential and lucrative occupations in the twenty-first century.

While our own liberal-arts educations appear to have furthered us in our own professions and were even the sites of our feminist awakenings, we think that women should be pioneering the tech world along with men, not simply going after those liberal-arts degrees. Equality means social transformation. It means raising the floor.

CONFIDENCE VS. CONSCIOUSNESS

Fundamentally, feminism is a political movement organized for the purpose of getting women out from under subordination, but, as we asserted in Chapter 1, its soul is consciousness. Vivian Gornick, a writer who chronicled Second Wave feminism for *The Village Voice*, described it this way back in the seventies: "For me feminism is, more than any other single thing, not a movement, not a cause, not a revolution, but rather a profoundly new way of interpreting human experience. It is a vital piece of information at the center of a new point of reference from which one both reinterprets the past and predicts the future."

Born with feminism simply in the water, the Third Wave is buoyed by the confidence of having more opportunities and less sexism. *Free to Be . . . You and Me* and the mantra "Girls can do anything boys can" protected us from the early decay (of their sense of possibility) to which our mothers' generation was vulnerable, and this political fluoride prepared us to expect equality. Unfortunately, our expectation exceeded reality and did not always indicate how gender fairness could be achieved. For that, we need a consciousness of women's place in society and of how the battles already won were achieved. The chasm between this generation's belief in basic feminism (equality) and its feminist consciousness (knowledge of what one is doing and why one is doing it) explains why, according to a 1998 *Time*/CNN poll, more than 50 percent of women between eighteen and thirty-four say they are simpatico with feminist values but do not necessarily call themselves feminists. Lack of consciousness is one reason that the movement is stalled: our mothers and foremothers gained their click that something was terribly unfair about doing all of the housework or having to resort to a coat hanger in order to avoid bearing an unwanted child. They changed those rules. We started where they left off, but often we spin our wheels at the starting gate.

"I think many women my age who consider themselves feminists are on automatic pilot, moving along according to directions set by women who came before us, but toward ends that have been determined more by the era of Reagan opportunism than by feminism," said former *Ms.* editor Gayle Kirshenbaum in 1991 when she participated in a roundtable on feminism for the magazine. In other words, radical times—the ones that provoked one hundred representatives of New York Radical Women to toss their bras, girdles, and *Cosmo*s into a "freedom trash can" at the Miss America Pageant Protest of 1968—aren't a hallmark for those 50 percent of eighteen- to thirty-four-year-olds who espouse equality. (And, just to set the record straight, no bras were burned in those early years of protests and priming for the revolution, but only because the protesters were unable to secure a burning permit on the Atlantic City Boardwalk.) Many young women are pre-consciousness and haven't yet had the opportunity to examine the politics of their own lives. They are pre-click, or maybe even pre-sexism in their own lives.

In addition to history and political consciousness, the Third Wave reputedly lacks a leader. It seems that everyone in this generation is looking for those very visible doyennes—as if we don't have feminism if we can't point to the "next" Gloria, Angela, Betty, or Alice (none of whom, incidentally, were famous in their twenties, either). Some might say that Ani DiFranco magnetized girls toward feminism with her one-woman record label and incredibly loyal grassroots following. Rebecca Walker, one of the founders of the Third Wave Foundation, is a popular speaker at colleges and for young feminists. Others would cite Naomi Wolf for attempting to politicize ambitious women with her books, the now defunct Culture Babes[23] in the early nineties, and later co-founding the Woodhull Institute for Ethical Leadership, but generally the current movement seems to lack those clear-cut icons. And yet that's not necessarily a sign of dissolution for feminism.

"[T]he public heroines of one generation are the private heroines of the next," wrote Alice Rossi in the *The Feminist Papers*, meaning that people who do big things for one era are replicated on the local level for the next. Therefore perhaps we should be looking for our feminist leaders in less famous packages. There are countless young women who fit this profile. For example, when Gina Amaro was twenty-one she co-founded Muevete, an annual Puerto Rican youth conference, which brought together more than a thousand young people in New York City. Samantha Gellar fought back at the age of seventeen when her Charlotte, North Carolina, high school refused to produce her prizewinning one-act play because it featured a lesbian romance. Hilary Russian agitated for "crip rights," especially the right for people with disabilities to have dates and sex and organized sex workers' art shows in Seattle, Washington. At twenty-three, Crystal Echohawk was living in Chiapas, organizing on behalf of the Zapatistas, and then went on to do this from the El Paso, Texas, office of the National Commission for Democracy in Mexico. This small sampling points to the reality of young feminist leaders. The dearth of easily identified, media-anointed stars means very little in light of how many younger feminists are simply out there building on the work of the Second Wave, doing things that their mothers never dreamed of doing.

So when you work with or meet women like Gina, Hilary, Samantha, and Crystal every day—as we do—imagine how annoying it is to hear from anyone (including the media and especially Second Wave feminists) that young women aren't continuing the work of the Second Wave, that young women are apathetic or "just don't get it." We've heard this repeatedly, and reacted by scrambling to be better feminists and frantically letting these women know how much we look up to them. Finally, though, we have refused to accept this myth.

The larger invisibility of young feminists is why one moment in 1995 is significant enough to recount to you here. An editor friend called us to say that she saw a book proposal by a well-established Second Wave feminist being shopped around. The writer was addressing her frustration with young women for abandoning, rather than preserving, the rights and the movement her generation had worked to secure. We both cringed at the idea. The book sounded preachy, and we disagree with her premise that young women are fleeing feminism. But the biggest reason for our cringe was that any message to stir young feminists, the pro-choice-but-passive ones, should come from young women themselves. If a Third Wave rallying cry were to be authentic and organic, then the author would have to lead by example. The book in question, *Letters to a Young Feminist*, by Phyllis Chesler, author of the Second Wave classic *Women and Madness*, was published by a small press in 1997. Chesler drew inspiration both from Rainer Maria Rilke's *Letters to a Young Poet*, and from Virginia Woolf's *A Room of One's Own*.

"I was one of the first to speak in a mother's voice," Chesler said when we asked her what she believes she accomplished with the book. "Many women of my generation, including the feminists, often continue to think and speak in their 'daughter-voice,' not in their mother voice." She continued, "In *Letters*, I tried to speak in a voice that embraced those much younger—and older—than myself." Though a maternal tone may have been necessary for her message to resonate with her generation, a "to-do" (and what not to do) list from a "mother" is a recipe for resistance from a younger generation already fluent in feminism. She offered insights from her experiences but forgot the essential ingredient that made *Letters to a Young Poet* so valuable: Rilke was responding to an actual person; Chesler was lecturing to her idea of a young woman.

Of course, once a real conversation has begun, talk of feminism goes only so far without the walk of activism. As Katha Pollitt—this time wearing her feminist hat—and others have pointed out, the problem with feminism nowadays isn't so much that women don't identify with its goals as that "a grassroots, militant, political movement" is not sufficiently in evidence. And what does exist is rarely reflected back by the media.

CHAPTER THREE

Feminists Want to Know:
Is the Media Dead?

Ms.topia

When Ms. *was born in January 1972, her peers were* Ladies'
Home Journal, Good Housekeeping, Cosmopolitan, Glamour,
and Vogue. *These glossies, well fed with ads, rested on every
coffee table and at every doctor's office, grocery store, and
beauty parlor in America. On the margins, there was a crop of
skinny, ugly-but-exciting feminist zines. These independents
were ad-free, with confrontational names like* off our backs, Up
from Under, Lilith, Aphra, Notes, *and* No More Fun and
Games.

Ms. *was almost named* Sister, Sojourner, Bimbo, *or even the
inclusive-but-snoozy* Everywoman. *But* Ms., *a fresh word, signaled equality and a break with the old, and it was perfect for
this brand-new beast: a mainstream feminist magazine. The
new community of feminist readers awaited their copies ea-
gerly—especially in rural or suburban regions, where* Ms. *was
often the only radical news in town. Having* Ms. *on one's coffee table signaled a certain kind of home—one in which
"Stories for Free Children," acknowledgment of all kinds of*

sexuality, and even debates about the politics of housework were part of the furniture.

At first, Ms. was pretty well liked across the board, and was always being called "the first" or "the only" when people were discussing her coverage of women's issues or the way she went about reporting on these issues. She was the first magazine to have a female ad-sales staff, and the first magazine to write supportively about abortion and being gay, to name a couple of revolutionary moments. She broke new, controversial stories and gave name to such tacitly accepted atrocities as domestic abuse, sexual harassment, and date rape. Once Ms. let the cat out of the bag, other glossies followed up with their own stories—but the pieces weren't detailed or political enough to scare off too many of their advertising suitors.

Ms.'s offices were loose, filled with kids, food, and idealists who maybe didn't have magazine experience but believed in the cause and so were put to work. Some of the radical feminists who had ignited the women's movement weren't so impressed with Ms.'s revolutionary spirit (mainstream? ads?). But left-wing journalists generally viewed it as an oasis. Finally, there might be a place to run the stories they really wanted to write.

But the flip side to being so singular and commonly liked is that Ms. attracted disappointment and criticism, like the lone girl at the Citadel. Some of her less famous peers, such as off our backs and On the Issues, resented her for her success. They were out there trying to be political general-interest magazines for women, too, and felt that Ms. got all the attention. Robin Morgan stormed the offices in protest (she and her cadre thought the magazine was too accommodating and wasn't radical enough) and was offered a chance to write for and, eventually, edit Ms.

Meanwhile, Ms. continued to be a litmus test for women and their relationship to the movement. In Middle America, Ms. meant radical feminist—abortion rallies, women with hairy legs, people waving speculums. In cities with thriving radical communities, reading Ms. meant not being feminist enough. To many, the magazine equaled feel-good, reformist politics, and to others it was dull.

By the time Ms. was in her teens, the magazine had become worse for wear. Because of the pro-woman content, advertisers, unwilling to give feminists an economic foothold, fled. Struggling to survive, the Ms. creators got mighty creative. For a few years Ms. was a nonprofit foundation, then, for one year, it was owned by Australian feminists, who added fashion coverage, celebrity covers, and an infusion of cash. After that year, Ms. was sold to Dale Lang.[24] Initially, he wanted her for her valuable subscriber list (he also owned Working Woman and Working Mother, both of which could use the readership boost), but he agreed to have her reborn as an ad-free bimonthly. A bold move, but one that, unfortunately, further marginalized the increasingly out-of-fashion feminist publication. During this time, the neglectful Lang and his successor, Jay MacDonald, treated Ms. like a wife. Her low-wage staff provided labor for next to nothing, and a little cash in pocket for the owners, but they didn't feel they had to invest in her. At the turn of the century, after years of frustration, Ms. is skinny, ad-free, pushing-thirty and owned by a group of committed (and rich) feminists.

Today Marcia Gillespie is editor in chief—the first black woman to edit a general-audience magazine. Ms. is still the first—and only—ad-free, 100-percent-reader-supported general-interest magazine. In an ocean of mega-media corporation-controlled publishing, Ms. remains an island of independence. On the Issues and many other feminist-minded magazines have quit publishing. She is dwarfed by the big magazines targeted for women, such as Ladies' Home Journal, Good Housekeeping, Cosmopolitan, Glamour, and Vogue. And there is, as there was in 1972, a thriving feminist zine community, with names like Chick Factor, Bitch, Rockrgrl, and Bamboo Girl.

Ms. is a survivor. And yet one of the questions most frequently heard when her name is mentioned is, "Oh, is Ms. still around? I haven't seen it in years."

[The media] is much better at transmitting failure
than success.

—FARAI CHIDEYA,
television journalist and author

In a November 19, 1990, *Newsweek* story, "The Failure of
Feminism," writer Kay Ebeling detailed how the women's
movement had done nothing to improve women's lives. She argued that what was meant to be women's liberation had actually freed up men by absolving them of the responsibility for
supporting their families—at least that was how it seemed to
play out in her own life. Men were liberated, and the women
who bought feminism's lie were overworked, underpaid, and
doomed to loneliness. Kathleen Hanna, then a college student
in Olympia, Washington, remembers reading that piece:

> I was sitting on the bus going to school from downtown, cry-
> ing. I had been hanging out with Tammy Rae Carland, a friend
> who had turned me on to so many things and changed my life.
> She introduced me to Fright Wig, the Breeders, and Opal—all
> this different music I had never heard of. We were in a band
> together called Amy Carter, and Tammy Rae told me about
> [the feminist avant-garde writer] Kathy Acker. I remember be-
> ing on the bus and thinking that I had just looked into
> Tammy's eyes, and we were so excited about everything that
> we were going to do. Then I read that *Newsweek* issue, which
> said feminism is dead, it failed. I was like, "It's not dead, I just
> saw it in [Tammy's] face." And I felt like I had to go get a bull-
> horn and tell everyone, because what about all of these
> fourteen-year-old girls all over the country who believe that it's
> over? What if they believe that it's already happened?

Kathleen and Tammy Rae, two activists and photographers,
were running a feminist gallery space called Rekomuse and

studying at Evergreen College. Both worked at the local battered women's shelter. Tammy Rae had grown up poor; Kathleen had worked as an exotic dancer in order to earn money to pay for school; and both had begun to see their own experiences in the larger picture of sexism.

A few months after the *Newsweek* story, Kathleen moved to Washington, D.C., with her band, Bikini Kill, and began canvassing local punk clubs. Clipboard in hand, she organized girls and women to attend an all-female meeting at the Positive Force house. Still in existence, Positive Force was a group of independent fans and musicians who combined youth empowerment and education with radical social change, including direct action. The meeting's agenda: to discuss sexism in the women's punk-rock community, in their homes, their relationships, their towns, and the world.

Two years later, this group organized a grassroots feminist meeting called the Riot Grrrl Convention in Washington, D.C. Though only a dozen or so women were expected, more than a hundred girls between the ages of seventeen and twenty-five attended. This success—as well as the fact that Bikini Kill, Huggy Bear, and other Riot Grrrl bands were breaking indie sales records—forced mainstream media to recognize the existence of young feminists. The conference title had come from Molly Newman and Alison Wolfson, of Bratmobile. They had a fanzine called *Riot Grrrl*, which provided the media with a name for these brave new radicals. After the term appeared in a few stories, the girls themselves began using the moniker, as did thousands of young women across the country who identified with Riot Grrrls' anger and energy. They were righteous and intent on challenging all forms of oppression: hatred of punks and kids who looked different, classism, the marginalization of sex workers, as well as sexism, racism, ableism, and homophobia. Riot Grrrls throughout the U.S. began hosting teach-ins, skills-sharing workshops ("I'll teach you to play guitar and you teach me self-defense"), and insisted on girls-only mosh pits. Riot Grrrls didn't need the punk boys' playhouse anymore; they had their own.

Meanwhile, Tammy Rae moved to California to attend art school and started a zine, *I (heart) Amy Carter*, which revised the geekish reign of America's former first daughter as one that was inarguably cool. (And she did it just as Chelsea Clinton was facing the barrage of media scrutiny and "ugly" jokes that accompany being the President's daughter.) The zine began as a sort of group letter to Tammy Rae's much-missed friends but became widely circulated in the burgeoning do-it-yourself publishing world, where it inspired people who were looking for confirmation that girls are good. Tammy Rae and Kathleen were taking what they knew from women's studies, their community activism, and their own lives to infiltrate and transform what had become a macho counterculture. In revolutionizing their own scene, they ended up influencing the mainstream, too. Thus, with its annoying and inaccurate death knell, *Newsweek* had inadvertently helped spark a new wave of feminism.

Nearly a decade later, most of Riot Grrrl had died down, but the media were at it again. In June 1998, *Time* magazine ran a (new! improved! news-breaking!) version of the 1990 *Newsweek* story, asking, "Is Feminism Dead?" Perplexingly, the cover featured disembodied head shots of Susan B. Anthony, Betty Friedan, Gloria Steinem, and . . . Calista Flockhart of Ally McBeal fame. The cover use was as much of a shock to Calista Flockhart, who considers herself a feminist, as it was to feminists around the country. Flockhart's publicist hadn't been told that the daylong photo shoot was held so that Flockhart could represent the decline of feminism. Writer Ginia Bellafante, whose first cover story this was, argued that the women's movement was dying under the weight of the lip gloss and self-obsessed sexual solipsism of young women. Instead of the usual accusation that the movement was for white women only, *Time* just excluded women of color altogether—except for photos of celebrities Scary Spice and Whoopie Goldberg. To demonstrate the so-called death of feminism, the article focused almost solely on celebrity actors and musicians, completely ignoring activists, academics, writers, politicians, and the everyday women who form the bulk of the feminist ranks. (This premature eulogy for feminism was as traditional a media tactic as dyke-baiting or calling women "bra-burners" or "bluestockings"—all ways of belittling the necessity of social justice for women. In a 1998 piece for *The New York Observer*, Erica Jong noted that *Time* has claimed feminism was dead at least 119 times since 1969. Coincidentally, the press started covering that story religiously just as the women's movement began to gain momentum.)

Just as Kathleen and Tammy Rae had done eight years earlier, feminists across the country looked into their friends' eyes and said some version of "This isn't true. This is not what I see." After all, any woman who is a member of Iowa City NOW or an editor at *Jane* magazine or a volunteer at an abortion clinic in Austin doesn't spend much time wondering if feminism is dead. Rather than starting a riot, however, women wrote angry letters to *Time*, so many that the article rose to the top-three spot *ever* in garnering responses. (First place went to the cover story entitled "Is God Dead?") Feminists were offended by the ridiculous, reductionist approach to the movement. A few angry women—Erica Jong, Judy Mann, Marcia Gillespie, Jennifer Pozner, and Janelle Brown—wrote editorials that countered *Time*'s argument. But these respected feminist writers made the same mistake Bellafante did. They wrote furious articles about the article, casting *Time* as historically and presently anti-feminist, but didn't describe the everyday activism that proves feminism is alive. In other words, feminists fought *Time*'s negativity about feminism with negativity about *Time*. And, although feminists got to respond, *Time* had the last word simply by dint of its ability to launch its point of view into the brains of most of America via the magazine's mammoth presence. Whether through subscriptions or at the dentist's office or at the grocery checkout, *Time* plainly had the farthest reach, and, therefore, impact.

It's clear that women get a bum deal in the mainstream media. But women have to realize that we have untapped potential in sheer numbers and collective consciousness. For example, anytime you find yourself sitting in your own home saying "Wait a minute," it's very likely that thousands of other women are doing the same. The trick is to use this disconnect between what the media say and what feminists know to galvanize women toward greater activism, as Kathleen and Tammy Rae did. Instead of screaming back at the Big Daddy media outlets that tune out individual critiques—and returning to business as usual—we need to transform our reactions into action. If you want to become a media revolutionary, and we hope that you do, the first step is to become media-literate. You have to be able to sniff out the sexism, racism, heterosexism, and classism—all of which are interconnected and fill the stories of the mainstream media. Looking at the daily news *as if women mattered* helps clarify what needs to change in order to make the media accurate.

As evidenced by the examples from *Time* and *Newsweek*, national newsmagazines rarely use the word *feminism* except to run negative stories about how weak the women's movement is or, in a contradictory spin, how powerfully detrimental it is to women's lives. This is especially troublesome considering that the majority of women and men rely on the mainstream media for information and news. Even in serious general-interest magazines, such as *The New Yorker* or *Newsweek*, women are tokenized in an annual "special" issue in the vein of other special issues such as those featuring Travel, the Home, Health, and Fiction. (Special women's health issues abound, but they are rarely drawn from feminist wells. In fact, they are more often produced for their ability to garner pharmaceutical ads.) Females can count on being fully represented in the annual women's roundups, but we can't expect to come close to equal time the other 11 months, 51 weeks, or 364 days of the year. For example, the May 16, 1999, *New York Times Sunday Magazine* special issue on women featured thirteen female-oriented articles, eleven of which were written by women. Three weeks later, the Adventure issue featured one story by a woman—and thirteen by men. Thus women are special from time to time, but men remain generic; they're the standard.

At the same time, the feminist issues that have improved women's lives—day care, microenterprise, anti-violence organizing, and much more—are covered but aren't identified as feminist issues in the pages of mainstream news outlets. In some sense, the lack of an adjective before the issue keeps women's rights from being marginalized, but in a larger sense it depoliticizes—and literally masks—the true nature of the work and who is doing it. For instance, teachers and children who read a *Time for Kids* (the youth supplement of *Time* magazine) feature about keeping Kenyan girls in school learned that this is a way of helping girls not to have children too early. They did not learn that this is, in fact, a program that was organized by feminists. In another example, the United States–organized protests against the Taliban's lethal anti-woman campaign in Afghanistan were reported on in *Time*. But this was done without mentioning the words *feminism* or *feminist activism*, which were responsible for the uproar and the level of consciousness. Women who belonged to women's rights groups such as the Feminist Majority Foundation and the Office on Women at the U.S. State Department were the only people who organized to condemn these human-rights abuses. Refusing to attribute this kind of everyday, newsworthy work to the women's movement gives readers the impression that feminism is about something else—usually something they can't relate to.

What to do? Well, first of all, we have to stop believing our own bad press. The Girlie zine *Bust*'s exhortation to embrace the chick label in the name of girl culture is one response to women's scapegoating. ("Yeah, goddamn it! *Bridget Jones is* a chick book! Hole *is* a chick band!" as co-editor Debbie Stoller says.) Indeed, a "chicks rock!" attitude is a strategy that works well with the pro-woman line developed by Redstockings in the late sixties. "We said that a woman acted out of necessity rather than choice," said Ellen Willis, one of the architects of the pro-woman line. "We wanted to counter the prevailing 'anti-woman' line." Therefore women weren't passively brainwashed by the patriarchy into marrying or looking as pretty as possible; they were actively making the best choice they could, given the circumstances of sexism. The reality was, and still is, that married women had some economic and social protections that single women didn't have; and attractive women *could* get better jobs than their mousy sisters. Willis and the Redstockings argued that women would make different choices in a nonsexist world, but the point of a pro-woman line is to acknowledge the barriers around which women must maneuver rather than to blame the women themselves.

The pro-woman (and pro-girl) line could stand to be applied to any arena in the media created with a female audience in mind: the style pages, the arts, the gossip columns, newsmagazines, newspapers, and the women's magazines. The conservative male ownership of the media might be the reason we find women-oriented media so lite. The daytime (and nighttime) talk shows fronted by Rosie, Roseanne, Oprah, Leeza, and Sally (and Dave, Jay, Conan, and Charlie) are all territory we need to claim. When we do, arenas that are feminine or soft won't be seen as incomplete, retrograde, or marginal. And arenas that are brash won't be seen as the domain of men. Comedy is still seen as a male thing, as evidenced by "Shouts & Murmurs," the *New Yorker* humor page, which went almost a year without a female-written column.

Using the pro-woman line on the media produces a few shifts in perspective. For instance, the pro-woman story about Monica Lewinsky would not have demonized her for using her White House connections to get a job—who doesn't use connections to get a job? Instead, the story would critique the fact that sex is still a successful way for women to get a job. Lewinsky wouldn't be condemned as either a victim or a whore (and women wouldn't have had to flounder around trying to figure out if they were on her side or Hillary's); instead, she'd be a young, ambitious woman in charge of her own libido and accountable for her own mistakes. Similarly, the "prom-mom" cases, teenage girls who gave birth and then killed their babies, are ripe for some feminist empathy. The pro-woman line would ask why the girls didn't feel that they could get abortions or even tell anyone they were pregnant. In other words, *"Where have all the choices gone?"* is the question a pro-feminist media should be asking, rather than "Can we go for the death penalty?"

The thing is, once you do apply a pro-woman or a gender lens to your view of the media, it becomes glaringly obvious that sexism permeates every corner, from *Crossfire* to *Elle*. For example, amid the end-of-the-millennium list-making, readers of the *American Journalism Review* were asked to choose the top-ten stories of the last century for the Freedom Forum's Newseum. Of the one hundred stories nominated by journalists nationwide, only seven had anything to do with women. "Babe Ruth Hits Sixty Homers" made the cut, but Title IX, which empowered entire generations of women to crack open the "male" sports world, didn't.

Same concept, different perspective: as long as compassion, emotionalism, and attention to the details are considered the domain of women, these human characteristics won't be woven into our definition of "hard news." For example, the economic inconvenience of paying women to stay at home to take care of their kids (a.k.a. being on welfare) is reported on, but we don't get to read any stories about how hard it is to be a mother raising a child on so little money and under so much scrutiny. Or how about a story on how welfare has made a positive change in women's lives, allowing them to stay at home to raise their children or to pursue their education?

Our everyday sexist examples so far have been drawn from the mainstream media, but lefty magazines such as *Mother Jones, The Nation, Z, Out,* and *The Advocate* don't fare much better. These magazines often fall into the trap of assuming that women can write only about "women's issues," not understanding that every issue is a women's issue—drugs, gun violence, *and* contraceptive coverage. *The Nation*'s special

September 1999 package on the drug war featured thirteen writers, only two of whom were women, and there was no analysis of the biggest increase in the prison population—women who are locked up for drug possession. In some ways, these lefty magazines do women a greater disservice than the mainstream magazines. They should know about sexism and its interconnectedness to such issues as environmentalism, economic justice, gay rights, workers' rights, and the prison industrial complex. But they don't. And feminists often let the left off the hook because, as an enemy of the right, it is assumed to be on feminism's side. Another example: in 1998, *The Nation* (which isn't the worst offender, it just publishes the most frequently) did a searing investigative cover story on the scattered state of progressive philanthropy, yet it didn't analyze or even mention the fact that programs for women and girls annually get only 5.7 percent of philanthropic dollars. Why is the lefty media so half-assed on women's issues? A former staffer at *Mother Jones* characterized the situation at that progressive magazine:

> There's a real fear of "earnestness" at *Mother Jones*. So when the magazine does address feminist issues, it's often through this skeptical, naysaying lens—like with Karen Lehrman's exposé of women's studies programs ["Off Course," September/October 1993]. Obviously, these critiques have their place, but the picture of feminism becomes distorted if you're always making the exceptions into the rule. More often than not, though, *MoJo* just ignores feminism. Probably the only thing the magazine is less interested in covering is the gay-rights movement.

Unfortunately, there is nothing new in women's being overlooked by the left, or in our antagonistic relationship to *Time* and *Newsweek* stories about feminism. The women's movement has had an undeniable impact on the media, yet it's still hard to find feminism—as in a consciousness of women's political rights, a clear vision of what is still needed, and a plan of action—on-screen, in print, over the airwaves, or electronically.[25] In fact, *Time*'s "Is Feminism Dead?" query, with its implied affirmative answer, points to a harsh truth: the media doesn't know how to deal with feminism, and feminists haven't mastered the media.

Given that women have never owned the majority of the media, we have long had to get our stories to other women via alternative sources. This included Susan B. Anthony and Elizabeth Cady Stanton's feminist paper *The Revolution* in the nineteenth century, as well as Margaret Sanger's self-published *The Woman Rebel* in the early twentieth century, which brought birth-control information to women who were dying from too many pregnancies and botched abortions. Decades later, during the 1992 and 1996 Democratic conventions, Jane O'Reilly and a group of women journalists published and distributed *The Getting It Gazette* to alert candidates to the positions and demands of the female half of their constituencies. In the seventies, *Ms.*, *Essence*, *Sage*, *off our backs*, *Sojourner*, *Lilith*, *The Furies*, and hundreds of women's newsletters and pamphlets were born just to get the word out that the women's movement was shaking things up. These publications laid the foundation for the hundreds of feminist zines, webzines, and magazines, such as *Bamboo Girl*, *Bust*, *I'm So Fucking Beautiful*, *Maxi*, and *Jane*, that proliferate today.[26]

These magazines provide vital new perspectives for their readers, and their success has also spurred the mainstream media to become more feminist in their editorial content. For example, essays like "Why I Want a Wife," from a radical feminist broadsheet, appeared in an early issue of *Ms.*, as did a list of well-known American women who publicly admitted to having had abortions. Eventually, mainstream magazines, trying to catch up with *Ms.*, began incorporating a few articles on birth control, and, later, domestic violence and rape, as well as good-news articles on female astronauts, lady governors, and stay-at-home dads.

———

So the mainstream ignores feminism except to announce rumors of its death. The lefty magazines are smug but still a boys' club. The indies are inspiring—if you can find them—but can't compete with the mighty mainstream. And mythic *Ms.*, that lonely unicorn of publishing, is persevering—but under more and more rarefied circumstances and limited distribution.

It is in this flawed press environment that we, Jennifer and Amy, work, live, socialize, and gossip. As organizers, we try to get media attention for our work; as magazine writers (mostly for the lefty publications but also for the mainstream) we pitch stories, wrangle with editors, watch our writing get changed by editors to make it less feminist, more heterosexual, or more consistent with the magazine's voice; as editors, we also alter other people's work to fit a page or a style; and as media critics we discuss the politics of what makes some news fit to print—and pay attention to what isn't. In other words, we participate in the behind-the-scenes machinations of the media that we all love to hate. Meanwhile, we constantly talk to women (and men) who *aren't* in the media, and who feel appalled, frustrated, and disempowered when they read the paper or turn on the TV. To comfort them and ourselves, we began naming the daily deadly sins the media commits against feminism. We detail some of them here. But remember, they are barriers only until we see them for what they are and fight back.

SEVEN DEADLY MEDIA SINS AGAINST WOMEN

1. The Byline Boys' Club

To properly illustrate this first deadly sin, we decided as we were writing this in the fall of 1999 to do a *Harper's*-style index of the editorial departments at the major general-interest magazines.[27] Here's what we found: *Rolling Stone*: 12 of the 13 top spots are occupied by men; 27 of 28 contributing editors are men; and a majority of the record reviews are done by men. *Spin*: men claim 7 of the 11 top spots. *Vanity Fair*: 9 out of 11 top editorial positions are held by men, and 31 of 53 contributing editors are men. *Harper's* magazine: of 30 contributing editors, 25 are men. *Time*: 8 male senior editors (of 11) and 20 male senior writers (of 22). *Newsweek*: the male senior editors number 19 (of 25), and there are 13 male senior writers (of 16).

Newer magazines do a bit better. At *Wired*, the editor in chief is a woman; after her there are 6 male and 2 female editors. At *Talk*, Tina Brown's latest venture, 5 of the top 13 spots are occupied by women. *Brill's Content* is the only magazine that has relative parity: 7 men and 9 women. All of the above publications are totally or majority owned and published by men. And from the mastheads alone, it is difficult to determine the racial identity and sexuality of each writer and editor, but we think it's a safe bet that people of color and gay people of either gender and any race fare no better at general-interest magazines than do women in general.

Bylines, the sign-off or acknowledgment that credits the author, are biased toward men in even greater proportions than the mastheads. In the June 14, 1999, issue of *The New Yorker*, for example, out of 14 bylines only 2, a book review and a theater review, were women's. The week before there were 5 features by women, 10 by men. Among illustrators, women are even rarer. In the January 31, 2000, issue of *The Nation*, which featured the "Global Agenda," all 16 articles were done by men, as were all of the illustrations.

"Byline biology" is destiny not just for writers but for readers, since who writes the story influences its placement and, therefore, who will read the story. When the purveyors of opinion are linked to Y chromosomes, it tends to ensure that women's tastes and artistry stay second-class. For instance, take *Rolling Stone* editor Jann Wenner's unspoken fatwa on Joni Mitchell. A genius who has influenced artists from Courtney Love to Prince to the Indigo Girls, Mitchell was profiled by *Rolling Stone* only twice in her thirty-year career. It's hard to imagine a similar blacklisting of a headstrong visionary man. By contrast, troublemakers like Bob Dylan, Michael Stipe, and Prince are bad and loved for it in *RS*'s pages. (Not to mention artists of relatively minor accomplishment—Lyle Lovett or Huey Lewis and the News—who have seen themselves glorified in *RS*'s pages.)

Okay, we'll stop loading on the bad news and offer some sunshine. Not so long ago, there were even fewer—almost no—female writers and editors at major magazines. Women were researchers and never got a chance to sign off on their own story or make a name for themselves. Class-action suits—against *Newsweek* in 1970, for one—began to right this wrong. Given the sorry state of unequally represented media, perhaps writers and editors need to revisit this tactic. Readers can employ other age-old tactics, such as writing letters to the editor, boycotting the magazines, and choosing, instead, to read or create zines. And if you don't see yourself represented in the media, recognize that it's probably because the media are wrong, not you.

2. *Cosmo*-Girl Myopia

Her breasts, two scoops of (almost always white) flesh, are pushed up, and her eyes are vacuous. She's scantily clad, voluminously coiffed, and is being used to sell everything from Palm Pilots to Pepsi. Her unspoken message to guys is: "Don't you want me? I want you." And to girls: "Don't you want to *be* me? I don't want to be you." You know the drill: a woman's body is used to sell products that are unrelated to sex, which is one way the patriarchy shows its fundamental disrespect of women.

But wait, before you slap a "This Hurts Women" sticker on another Calvin Klein advertisement, consider the following: Objectification is no longer our biggest problem. Historically, women's bodies in ads have always been conflated with the product, something that feminists worked hard to identify and critique. For example, part of what was so hideous about the Fly Me ads for National Airlines in the late sixties was that flight attendants were vulnerable to literal interpretations of this slogan. In that cultural climate, "Fly me" might as well have been "Fuck me" or "Rape me," or "Pinch my ass while I bring you your fourth Scotch, sir." But consciousness of sexist imagery has changed for the better, as have the rights of women (including the rights of female flight attendants). Whether or not you believe, as Camille Paglia and others do, that showing herself in sexual ways makes a woman feel powerful and men powerless, there are positive examples of women's "subjectification." These women aren't objects, because they hold the power. The obvious "subjectifier" is Madonna, but there is also hip-hop diva Missy Elliott, soccer pinup Brandi Chastain, and TV star Roseanne. All have parlayed their sexual selves into power in feminist ways. These women aren't exploited. They are whole women—both confident *and* conscious.

Feminists should not cease to critique the propensity to make women seen but not heard, but a feminist argument can't be limited to cries of "objectification!" First of all, critiquing ads is not critiquing the media but only going after something that is already "reader beware," because it is labeled "advertising." It is the editorial content that needs to be read and analyzed with a gender lens. Furthermore, censorship and intimidation from advertisers to make editorial changes is where the corporate patriarchy *really* shows its fundamental disrespect for women. So the real problem isn't the chick in the bikini used to sell sunscreen; it's the cosmetics manufacturer in the suit (Leonard Lauder comes to mind), silencing the voices we most need to hear.

3. The Scare Strategy

In *Backlash*, Susan Faludi revealed the stealth strategy of the right: to prove that the rights women have gained for themselves through the feminist movement are causing their lives to fall apart. Among other things, she recalled a famous 1986 *Newsweek* story that said a single woman in her mid-thirties with delusions of meeting a partner ought to be very frightened. It seems that women were more likely to be killed by a terrorist than to get married after the age of thirty-five. Faludi discovered that the story was no more than "a parable masquerading as a numbers report." In fact, it was an offhand remark made by a reporter, which was then taken seriously by a stringer in New York, who spun it into Spinstergate for *Newsweek*.

The media like to keep women in a state of anxiety or punishment about their choices, from cosmetic decisions to family planning. *Backlash* empowered its readers to question that agenda. However, in the eight years since its publication, the press has continued to feature stories that frighten women out of wanting their rights. A few samples: in the mid-nineties, the fear of breast cancer was whipped up to such a frenzied pitch that women began electing to have preventative mastectomies on healthy breasts.[28] (Imagine men having healthy testicles removed for fear of testicular cancer.) A 1988 report estimating that 375,000 drug-exposed infants are born every year got parlayed into a nationwide outcry, but instead of leading to a positive solution it was used to criminalize mothers, especially if they were black and young. According to Dorothy Roberts's authoritative book *Killing the Black Body*, much of the crack-baby hype was a way to justify state intervention in poor women's bodies and fertility. Many black and young women are put in jail to protect their fetuses, although jail means poor nutrition, little prenatal care, and easy access to drugs. Many more black and young women have had their babies placed in foster care on the basis of a single drug test.[29] Roberts writes: "Of course, the state should remove babies from drug-addicted mothers when they are at risk from harm. But it is also harmful to children to be wrongfully taken from their mothers on insufficient evidence of unfitness, often to be cast into a more perilous foster care system."

Men, too, can be victims in the Scare Strategy—in her recent book, *Stiffed*, Susan Faludi analyzes how scare tactics work against working-class men—but usually they're used to make the point that feminism has gone too far. Nancy Updike, writing in the May/June 1999 issue of *Mother Jones*, conjectured about a domestic-violence study ("Findings About Partner Violence," undertaken by New Zealand's National Institute of Justice), which reportedly found that wives hit their husbands at least as often as husbands hit their wives. From this statistic, Updike concluded that focusing on women as victims of domestic violence was outdated. On the other hand, the last U.S. Department of Justice study, from March 1998, concluded that women are five to eight times more likely than men to be victims of assault by an intimate. All partner abuse is inherently bad, but the important information left out of Updike's tale was this: First, women are much more likely to suffer injuries from domestic violence (thus the quantity of blows may be the same, but the quality is not). Second, the study was a snapshot of New Zealanders born between April 1, 1972, and March 31, 1973, not one that focused on violent partners. In fact, respondents were questioned about hitting their partners only once, when the respondents were twenty-one years old.

When the media paint women's claims as exaggerated, or when they represent men's victimhood as being at the hands of women rather than their fellow men, women are scared away from telling their stories and seeking justice. They fear that they won't be believed.

4. Unequal Time

Perhaps you've noticed that there are only a handful of leaders whom the media regularly recognize as feminists: Susan Faludi, Patricia Ireland, Eleanor Smeal, Gloria Steinem, and Naomi Wolf. The reasoning goes, if you're not white or not straight (-looking), you can't be an expert on the condition of all women. This is not a new problem. In the seventies, when Steinem toured the country speaking with activist Dorothy Pitman Hughes, lawyer Florynce Kennedy, or writer Margaret Sloan, the press would often report that "Miss Steinem," the one white woman of the group, was galvanizing women across the country and treat her partner as an add-on. (In addition, Steinem recalls that almost all questions about feminism were directed to her; Pitman Hughes, Kennedy, and Sloan were each always asked about civil rights. This pattern would continue until the duo speaking named and stopped it.) Similarly, members of the Women's Political Council, a feminist group active during the civil-rights struggle, were allowed to be spokespeople only for black rights, never for women's equality. The forced choice between racial and gender identity keeps social-justice movements separate and ignores the double oppression of women of color.

But even the chosen white women are kept in a narrow box. "Eleanor Smeal is only invited onto prime time to defend feminism against absurd attacks," says Colleen Dermody, the former press coordinator for the Feminist Majority Foundation, which Smeal heads. "She's never allowed to define the debate." And if the spokesmodels don't show up, feminists are left out of the debate altogether. When Smeal or Steinem refuses an invitation to talk about date rape, the wage gap, or environmental pollutants and breast cancer—and suggest, instead, other leaders of the women's movement, such as Susan Brownmiller, Ellen Bravo, or Winona LaDuke—the producers rarely follow up, despite the fact that Brownmiller is more of an expert on rape, Bravo on work issues, and LaDuke on the environment than the "famous feminists."

5. Internet Incontinence

While Internet magazines may look and read like their comrades in the professional print world (*Time*, *Brill's Content*, or *George*), they don't play by the same rules of journalism. They don't have big (or any) fact-checking departments and are under enormous pressure to provide fresh stories constantly. As a result, on-line information is often riddled with factual errors, and readers are too nomadic to hold the magazine accountable for them. In one small but salient example, a June 18, 1999, *Salon.com* review of feminist zines by media columnist Jenn Shreve misidentified *Ms.* magazine as a zine along with *Bust*, *Bitch*, and the brochure-size *Moxie*, and described it as having been ad-free for twenty-six years when the accurate number was ten. *Bust*'s writers were called "first wave feminism's rebellious daughters"; and Shreve completely missed the point when criticizing *Bitch*, which is subtitled "A Feminist Response to Pop Culture." "*Bitch* isn't concerned with real women," Shreve wrote, "just the fake ones in TV shows, movies, books and other publications." Any of these mistakes could have been clarified with a single phone call or even a visit to the magazines' Web sites (or by looking up *popular culture* in the dictionary).

Janelle Brown, the technology writer-editor for *Salon.com*, who also has her own feminist webzine, *Maxi*, had this to say about the ethic of this brave new media:

> The fact-checking, triple-read editorial process is an old magazine thing. Fact checking is relevant to *Salon*, but for certain kinds of pieces. We do long investigative magazine-type features that we fact-check from Timbuktu and back. We also do short, newsy pieces on a tight turnaround, as well as personal essay pieces, that we don't fact-check—much like many other media companies, on-line and off. These personal essays— more entertainment than investigative reporting—are something unique to the Web that we are helping to pioneer.

The big issue with the brave new world of the Internet is that it provides a limitless arena for diverse thoughts, new writers, quirky takes, and random hostility. So far, publications on-line have been more sexist, racist, homophobic, and generally hostile than those in the off-line world. *Salon.com*, for example, ran an op-ed about conservative pundit Ann Coulter in which the male writer of the piece accused Coulter of being a bitch, a racist, and anorexic. He advised her to quit injecting herself with horse urine and to get a less stiff hairstyle. (Wow—is this the future of political analysis?) With the prospect of offending people as a deterrent, a person is unlikely to make a bigoted joke in three-dimensional company. After all, even in the very conservative *Washington Times*, the arguments against rights for gays, women, and people of color are just that—arguments, not frothing ad hominem attacks. By contrast, the Internet thrives on connection, but not on human contact—it truly is a cave of one's own. With no one watching, one's inner diatribes and prejudices can be let loose. Therefore women who already face antagonism and prejudice can look forward to more of the same in the on-line world—if not from writers, then from readers who quickly post back. For example, at *Nerve.com*, an on-line sex and literature magazine, Joanne Kagan critiqued the coverage of the Women's World Cup, pointing out the homophobia implied by how psyched people were by the fact that the players "love men" and were pretty. The posted responses amounted to calling Kagan a "jealous dyke." A full third of the responses were deemed too hostile even to be posted (as if "jealous dyke" weren't hostile).

If the Internet is the future, and *Salon.com* is *The New Yorker* of 2010, we should be able to expect some adherence to basic standards of journalism. Readers deserve a distinction between fact and opinion. According to Joe Lelyveld, the executive editor of *The New York Times*, "The Internet . . . is a wonderful place to collect raw data. But it's not, so far, a wonderful place to find reliable and original reporting [or] real news, except where it has been siphoned off the old." An "old" that is not pro-feminism.

6. Only Über-Victims Need Apply

Women's magazines often run and even win awards for investigative stories featuring real women, and for highlighting issues pioneered by feminists: custody battles, domestic abuse, HIV, workplace discrimination, and sexual assault. Underneath this good journalistic cause lies a litany of rules dispensed to the writer to ensure the correct victim. She must be good-looking in order to be photographed and appear in the magazine without scaring off advertisers or otherwise lowering the beauty quotient, and the victim's story must meet certain requirements of hideousness.

This, then, is the über-victim, a woman (or man) who has

truly been victimized but whose story has been cosmetically enhanced for the magazine, or selected for maximum shock value with the idea that readers are unable to identify with cases that are too grubby or too complex; in other words, too real. The problem with the demand for über-victims is that it doesn't let readers relate to the real victim.

Marie Claire, a women's magazine owned by Hearst, for example, recently asked Jennifer to write a story about middle-class women and domestic violence. The original assignment was simply to find a woman to profile who had her own career while she was with her abuser, so that financial fears could be removed from the list of her reasons for staying. Soon, however, new requirements were added:

One woman I tracked down was too old at age fifty. Two women in their late twenties weren't married to their abusers, so the editors feared that readers wouldn't take the relationships as seriously. They maintained this even though one woman lived with her abusive beau for five years, the other had a child with hers, and this magazine targets readers who are single. One married victim, who remained with her abuser for nineteen years, worried the editors, too—she seemed "too pathetic" and, therefore, not "relateable." Many of the women were taken out of the running because they never called the police or went to the hospital, even though, as one woman put it, she was always too terrified to dial 911 when he had a knife to her throat. It seemed that not one of these real women was the right type of victim.

After the appropriate über-victim has been discovered, she can't just be photographed as herself, whether she favors Lycra or Lands' End. Instead, she must be remade into a neutrally stylish Condé Nast drone who resembles the women modeling clothes in the pages of its magazine. This Calvin Klein/J. Crew transmogrification obscures the real-life human being the magazine professes to profile. For example, Lisa Tiger, a Native

American AIDS activist, was photographed for a 1999 article in *Glamour* about women with HIV. Wearing a sleek gray sweater and demure skirt with pumps and shiny manicured nails, Tiger was made to look exactly like the half-dozen other women with whom she was photographed. Normally, Tiger wears running shoes and jeans. The editors could argue that they were simply dressing everyone formally and using a stylist so that the pictures looked beautiful. But there is a difference between enhancing a subject in order to bring out her personality and organic beauty and *making over* a subject in order to assimilate her into the culture of the magazine. The implication of the Lisa Tiger makeover seems to be that a more casual-looking Indian girl with HIV wouldn't be taken as seriously or deserve our sympathy as much as the Ann Taylor version. In fact, what's probably behind the scenario is the advertisers, who don't want to be near (or even in the same issue as) anything depressing or political.

7. The Magazines Everyone Loves to Hate

Since the 1970 sit-in at *Ladies' Home Journal* by radical feminists protesting John Mack Carter's editorship, and the male-directed content, the messengers behind women's magazines have changed.[30] Now, there is not a single women's magazine edited by a man, yet the male ownership hasn't changed and the advertisers' influence has increased. In short, female leadership has changed only magazines' mastheads; the content still must meet ad demands for "a fashion and beauty atmosphere" full of noncontroversial celebrities.

Women's magazines—from *Cosmo* to *Glamour* to *Vogue* and *Good Housekeeping*—hire and write about women, but few people take these cash-cow catalogs seriously because their content is compromised by the advertisers' influence. Less than a third of their pages are devoted to articles, and of that, most are required to provide a product-supporting atmosphere.[31] Because the articles aren't taken as seriously as the ad pages, the women who write for these magazines see the gig as retrograde, initiating a cycle of internalized misogyny. Christina Kelly, for example, a senior editor and writer at *Jane*, profiled *X-Files* star Gillian Anderson for a 1998 cover story. In order to get some dimension on her subject, Kelly attempted to make the standard round of secondary interviews—in this case, with David Duchovny and Chris Carter. But their PR people called back to say that Anderson's co-star and director didn't have time. "If I need secondary interviews for *Rolling Stone*," Kelly continues, "the same people that I called for this Gillian Anderson story are on the phone in two seconds." You see the cycle? When the writer does attempt to take her assignment seriously, she is unable to get the quotes, research time, or space in the magazine that would make her piece a heavy hitter. "People always complain about how fluffy and vapid women's magazines are, but you can't do a deeper story if no one calls you back," says Kelly. "A friend of mine at *Entertainment Weekly* tried to put in a good word for me as I was doing the *Jane* story. The Fox publicist came right out and said we don't bother because it's *Jane*. Read: just a women's magazine."

Which brings us to revising the common feminist position on *Elle* and the gang. Let's stop thinking these magazines are lame. They have the ability to bring crucial information to women and are being wasted if we deem them too inane and fluffy to bother with. Therefore we have to demand that what readers want—even what we, the producers, want—is more important than what advertisers want.

Women's magazines can be our friends. They aren't hostile or condescending to feminism, the way the mainstream media often are. However, they have shown little resistance to sexism—either in their pages or in pay scales. *Glamour*, to take one example, has long been considered the most feminist of the women's glossies. That was before Bonnie Fuller, ex-editor of *Cosmo*, took over as editor in 1998 and ditched the magazine's only political column in favor of horoscopes. Feminists were quick to criticize this bait-and-switch, but couldn't *Glamour* have a horoscope—some fun—*and* a political column?

Behind the scenes, *Glamour*'s mostly female writers make on average $1.50 a word; the (male) writers we spoke with who wrote for *GQ* made on average $2 a word. Yet with *Glamour*'s 2.2 million subscribers versus *GQ*'s 700,000, we know that ad rates and revenues are much higher at *Glamour*. Therefore women make more money *for* Condé Nast, the family- and male-controlled company that directs both magazines, but men make more money *from* Condé Nast. A politicized women's magazine would recognize this personal wage gap as part of the inequality of women and organize to change it. It's not fair to place all the blame on the underpaid staff and writers, but it is fair to put pressure on the male publisher and owner to raise his consciousness about equal pay for work that's of equal value.

Most women's magazines are proud of their health coverage and, indeed, women (who use the health system much more than men do, primarily because we are the reproducers) get much of their medical information from the media. But these health pieces amount to personal tips if they don't simultaneously agitate for universal health care or link the preponderance of STD-related infertility in women with the lack of STD screening in men. It's essential to have politics in women's magazines because improving oneself can't go very far in a sexist culture. The idea of "change yourself, and then there will be no discrimination" places prejudice and violence on the shoulders of the victim rather than placing responsibility on those who make the laws that support these injustices in our culture.

THE NEW PRO-WOMAN LINE

Given the magazines we were reading, we could have thought of more deadly sins, and so could you, but the point is that we have to approach the media with a pro-woman attitude. We need to expect and encourage more resistance to sexism within magazines, and a commitment to feminism in the media. Feminists need to grab hold of any forums that speak to women, wherever we find them. The glossies—or at least the women who work at them—have accomplished radical acts in the past, such as when thirty of the major women's magazines were successfully pressured by feminists to run positive stories about the ERA in 1976 and again in 1979. Or when a handful of researchers at *Newsweek* brought a sex-discrimination suit against the magazine. Or when women at *The New York Times* followed suit.

But why do smart women editors and writers continue to take the lesser pay, the tarnished prestige, the tight corset of advertising control, and the chopped-up, embarrassingly fluffy stories in the first place? Why do mainstream magazines continue to cover feminism poorly, if at all? And why hasn't there been a revolt? The main reason might be that *Ms.* has been there to pick up the slack. So let's apply our pro-woman line to that trouper of a women's magazine. *Ms.* was created in 1972 as a onetime test magazine by a group of women writers and editors, including Gloria Steinem, then writing "The City Politic" column for *New York* magazine, and Patricia Carbine, formerly of *Look* magazine, then new editor of *McCall's*, and easily one of the most influential women in the industry. Since its founding, *Ms.* has been a feminist forum that assumed women's full humanity and published the diverse voices of those who are trying to achieve it. Back in the early seventies, women around the country read *Ms.*'s first issue, recognized some part of their own experience within its pages, and suddenly felt connected to the movement—or realized that their kitchen-table organizing was a part of something larger. As the only national feminist publication available on newsstands, *Ms.* brought feminism to women in their own cities, towns, and communities, and helped spawn bookstores, consciousness-raising groups, and battered women's shelters. *Ms.*'s editorial mission expressly teased out the pro-woman angle on political issues.

Essentially, *Ms.* linked the disparate activists and everyday feminism that were going on around the country. Even today, *Ms.* remains the only magazine that's controlled by women, much less by feminists or a woman-friendly company. And, since the height of Second Wave organizing, *Ms.* has been there, countering all the aforementioned sins against women—and has also served as a punching bag. Here's how *Ms.* stacks up against the seven deadly sins:

- One, The Byline Boys' Club: Virtually all of *Ms.*'s bylines were women's, nourishing the careers of Mary Peacock, Letty Cottin Pogrebin, Ellen Willis, and Alice Walker. Naomi Wolf was an intern, Rebecca Walker became one of the youngest contributing editors, and Susan Faludi wrote one of her earliest pieces for the "Gazette" section of the magazine. Marcia Gillespie, the current editor in chief, is the first African-American to edit a magazine that isn't solely for African-Americans.

- Two, *Cosmo*-Girl Myopia: *Ms.* pilloried sexist ads simply by reprinting them in its "No Comment" section, but, more important, it provided companies with market research proving that women were the decision-making consumers for nearly every product, not just for eyeliner and floor wax. They even broke into ad categories—cars and an occasional consumer-electronics ad, for example—that had never advertised to women before, and thus the advertisers were willing to leave the editorial content alone. Even when there was pressure from advertisers to change its editorial content, *Ms.* held strong and lost ads instead of capitulating. For example, an exclusive cover story on Russian women who had been exiled for their underground feminist activity in the U.S.S.R. provoked Revlon to cancel ads it had agreed to run, all because the Soviet women weren't wearing makeup in their photos.

- Three, The Scare Strategy: As much as *Ms.* reported on the everyday violence women encountered, its message wasn't "Stay in your house" but, rather, "Get out, change the laws, and press charges."

- Four, Unequal Time: *Ms.* was dedicated to running diverse opinions within feminism. (And the magazine never pretended to be neutral on women's equality the way *Crossfire* or *Time* does; the views of feminism's opponents got enough play elsewhere.)[32]

- Five, Internet Incontinence: *Ms.* aspired to the highest standards of research and reporting. Besides, critics were quick to jump on the magazine for any mistakes; nor could it afford to lose a libel suit, so it couldn't run the un-fact-checked opinion bombs that the Internet media now produces.

- Six, Only Über-Victims Need Apply: *Ms.* rarely used models, even on its covers, and no one in editorial ever asked if the story subjects were attractive.[33]

- Seven, The Magazines Everyone Loves to Hate: The mere existence of *Ms.*—an explicitly feminist magazine—established a new parameter and allowed traditional magazines to move a little bit, too. *Ms.* also became a kind of unpaid research service for the rest of the media, both in its pages and as a result of its editors' willingness to help other editors, TV researchers, and the like.

As resilient and unique as *Ms.* was, it could never be all things to all feminists—or even come close. "[*Ms.*] proved to be slick, conservative, philistine . . . ," wrote feminist Vivian Gornick in *The Village Voice* in 1975, three years after *Ms.* debuted. "Its intellectual level is very low, its sense of the women 'out there' patronizing, its feminist politics arrested at the undergraduate level. For many of us the magazine was a great disappointment. For others, disappointment escalated into anger."

Twenty-five years hasn't helped *Ms.*'s reputation with feminist thinkers much. "I did a few book reviews for *Ms.* when I was starting out as a writer," says Katha Pollitt, the author of *Reasonable Creatures* and star columnist at *The Nation*, "and I found that the editors always seemed to remove the most interesting parts. The editorial process encouraged blandness—everybody's difficulties and issues having to be catered to, plus the general spirit of boosterism, the tendency to put a positive spin on whatever women do." "I try to read *Ms.*, but it drives me crazy. There's something reductive about the way they analyze and frame their politics—it seems committed to really outdated notions of *power* and *equality*," says Elisabeth Subrin, a thirty-four-year-old professor at Mount Holyoke College and feminist video maker. "At this moment, I don't really care about how many women are in the Senate as much as I care about how women communicate with each other, politically, socially, psychologically, intimately," Subrin continued. "The *Ms.* in our heads is the dream magazine," says thirty-year-old *Time* reporter and former *Ms.* research director Sandy Fernandez. "The *Ms.* that exists has absolutely no surprises—whatever the story is, it will be earnest and well reported and never, ever offer a whole new way of thinking about things." Debbie Stoller, the co-editor of *Bust*, explains, "I *want* to read it, but it's always so boring. They don't keep up with new developments." In 1998, when *Ms.* relaunched, aiming for a younger audience, Katie Roiphe told *The New York Observer*, "*Ms.* has outlived its relevance. It's become a dry, humorless, dogmatic rag, and it has failed to take up the complexities of modern feminism and to engage with broader points of view." A top youngish editor at a prominent Condé Nast magazine told us in 1998, "It's my dream to someday edit *Ms.* I would do [more] investigative health pieces."

On and on, feminists have problems with *Ms.* Radical

women bitch that it's too mainstream and cowardly, Betty Friedan thinks it's disrespectful of her role in the women's movement and of NOW, and mainstream women accuse it of being too pro-lesbian and too anti-family. Of course, many feminists consider it a lifeline, and sanity-saving—especially in communities that are more hostile to feminism than New York City.

The point is, *Ms.* is always in the defensive position, rarely setting the tone of a debate, even on issues that were pioneered in its pages. Pornography, S/M, and even marriage are issues *Ms.* editors do forums on rather than hard-hitting pieces about because there isn't a consensus on whether they're "good" or "bad." Not content to stop at its own low self-esteem, *Ms.* inadvertently promotes the superfeminist, who can never do enough. A typical headline runs along the lines of "Raped Feminist Activists from East Timor Flee Sexual Abuse, Turned Away from U.N." Even when it's not reporting on hideous international crimes against women (because readers look to it as the only source of information about women in other countries), *Ms.* is unable to let its hair down because it's so afraid of being fluffy (in its editorial, not its hair). A 1995 issue on sex called "Hot, Unscripted Sex"—which reads like an assumption that sex is usually scripted—featured very little sex, none of which was hot. There are too many "You go, girls," with forced jubilation, and *Ms.* has yet to be ironic—which means the old girl has something to learn from *Bridget Jones*. Because *Ms.* is so dedicated to nonsexist language, it always misses the boat on slang and will sacrifice the flow, ease, and punch line of a sentence in order to expunge potential sexism. (You can't spell *blond* "blonde," you can't use the phrase "the blind leading the blind," and so on.)

Some of these critiques of *Ms.* are in many ways accurate and insightful; certainly they come from a place of hope and expectations. Yet they are also a supreme cop-out. Everyone seems to think *Ms.* is disappointing, but the biggest disappointment of all is that these same people have allowed *Ms.* to be the best thing feminists have. Sole responsibility for feminist media cannot be shouldered by one magazine. We should have an entire feminist magazine for health, one for fiction and arts, one for kids, another for international news, a big rock-and-roll magazine, and on and on.

But, as for *Ms.*, the most revolutionary step this magazine could take would be to start to presume feminism. Realizing that many women have lived with the movement and its gains for more than thirty years (and that some younger women have never known a *Free to Be*–less world), the editors could trust that every article need not include the word *feminism*, accompanied by a detailed flow chart describing why the piece is important to feminists. In this realm of presumed feminism, we should have seen a great piece on Mia Hamm, the soccer star, four years ago, when she was just launching her campaign to start a professional women's soccer league. (This piece would have *shown* that Hamm was furthering the cause of women, not simply stated it.) The editors of *Ms.* have got to be confident—remember, the magazine's three hundred thousand premier issues sold in three days—and run stories without explaining to readers why Women's World Cup or cosmetic surgery is of interest to women.

"When it was founded, I thought *Ms.* was a really good idea," says Ellen Willis, who was a rock reporter at *The New Yorker* and a *Ms.* editor during the mid-seventies. "I never thought it would be radical, but it could be a great place to run the work of feminist journalists." *Ms.* should be a place where journalists can write personally or politically important pieces that they can't write for the other women's magazines; where they can cover stories that newsmagazines would have a man write or wouldn't cover at all. Presuming feminism might bring *Ms.* back to its original, rebellious mission as an oasis in the desert of the patriarchal press.

A feminist oasis is a valid raison d'être for a magazine, but it presents a problem, too. *Ms.* became a new kind of Knight in Shining Armor, expected to save women from the chauvinists in the media (that is, everyone else). Women wouldn't have to do much but escape to this better, collectively edited world and be "protected." Stories would not be killed, butts would never be grabbed, the coffee would make itself. Women's relationship to *Ms.* echoes that of women's relationship to feminism. In freeing themselves from the patriarchy, women became at least a little dependent on "feminism" to take care of them. This interpretation of *Ms.* helps to explain, at least on an emotional level, why so much anger, bitterness, and apathy have been directed toward it—especially by young women. Apathy is probably the operative word, since in our travels it seems that a majority of young women don't know about *Ms.*, or that it's still alive and kicking. "My mother used to read that" is a refrain we hear a lot.

Nearly thirty years after it was created, many young women turn to *Ms.* and both love and live by it. Others pick it up but feel no connection to its voice or its stories. It doesn't represent the issues they care about, so they put it down. Many other young feminists read it, but it feels like work—"homework," in the words of one thirty-something staffer at Planned Parenthood. And other politically minded, self-assured feminist women have their "guilt subscriptions" but aren't getting around to reading the magazine.

But as important as critiquing *Ms.* (and *Bust* and *Jane*) is, we can't let the mainstream media off the hook and turn all our criticism toward our own media. The only way to keep the women's media from being a ghetto is to keep the mainstream's feet to the fire. So let's return to *Time* magazine and their latest installment of the Dead Feminist Report.

HOW *TIME* COULD HAVE SEEN FEMINISM

Looking back on *Time*'s 1998 "Is Feminism Dead?" bombshell, we contend that the story *behind* that story could be the newsweeklies' next big splash—entitled "How the Media Killed Feminism." Since *Time* hasn't delivered on this exclusive, we will.

First, the atmosphere at *Time* was, as it has always been, a man's world. When the piece was published, the only feminist essayist, Barbara Ehrenreich, had just learned that her years-long contract wasn't going to be renewed. Out of a staff of eleven senior editors, three were women, and of twenty-two senior writers, only two were women. One was thirty-four-year-old Ginia Bellafante, the journalist who was responsible for the "Is Feminism Dead?" cover story but who was also very aware of her second-class status. After all, when *Time* celebrated its seventy-fifth anniversary earlier that year, its twenty male senior writers had A-list seating, rubbing shoulders with such heavy hitters as Tom Brokaw and Mike Wallace. Meanwhile, Bellafante was seated in the balcony with the Saturday secretaries, the copy editors, and the female researchers. (The other female senior writer, the well-known Margaret Carlson, got to sit downstairs with the A-list.) The weekend assistants deserve to be treated with as much respect as the writers of either gender, but the point is that there is a clear girl ghetto at *Time*. In the lap of the Byline Boys' Club, Bellafante surely considered herself lucky to be assigned her first cover story.

Playing it safe in hostile territory, Bellafante languished in the swamp of *Cosmo*-Girl Myopia, ignoring feminist activism and acknowledging only the Spice Girls and Ally McBeal. "Fashion spectacles, paparazzi-jammed galas, mindless sex talk—is this what the road map to greater female empowerment has become?" she worried. We would worry, too, except that *Bust*, the Spice Girls, and celebrity fund-raisers are actually part of a vast feminist diaspora, rather than the only party in town.

Bellafante's story was pieced together from gossip from the tabloids and women's magazines. A *Newsday* report about Courtney Love, for instance, and an *Elle* story about the star-studded anti-violence benefit performance of *The Vagina Monologues*. From these thin and disparate sources, Bellafante concluded that feminism today was "wed to the culture of celebrity and self-obsession," but was also elitist and just for intellectuals. If Bellafante had looked further than the culture of celebrity, she would have found a bigger picture. Instead, she herself fell victim to the starry hype she criticized. With no attempt at equal time, the interview subjects were all white, and mostly random celebrities caught in a feminist act, not feminist activists or leaders. Nancy Friday, for instance, an author best known for her Second Wave book about women's sexual fantasies, *My Secret Garden*, is quoted twice. Angela Davis, a hard-core activist who, during the time the piece was researched, was organizing a huge conference on women in prison, wasn't even mentioned. (And certainly there was no mention of the fact that Nancy Friday is married to Norman Pearlstine, the editor in chief of *Time*.)

Employing a pro-woman line, we might allow that Bellafante's ignorance and disavowal of the political activity relevant to the current feminist mandate is an occupational hazard (or requirement) when you work for *Time*. But she was hand-delivered evidence during her interviews that she, and her editors, chose to ignore. How do we know this? Well, months before this story was published, Ginia Bellafante had called Amy. *Time* wanted Bellafante to do a story about how older women and younger women viewed Monica Lewinsky. The angle Bellafante took was that Gen-X women, having grown up in a "victim culture," saw the first intern as incapable of having seduced the president because of the vast power difference between them. She posited that older feminists, by contrast, would probably think Monica was a retro hussy trying to sleep her way to the top. Amy's own informal conversations with younger and older women didn't support *Time*'s premise. Nor did Bellafante's subsequent research, apparently, since she recast her story into an analysis of the state of current feminism. Amy recalls:

The first time we spoke, I gave her reams of reports and names. I was shocked to read the piece and find Bellafante condemning NOW for not listing day care under its "Key Issues on its Web site," and blaming feminists generally for failing to solve the day-care shortage. Before I knew that day-care was going to be a big point—not just of her argument but of *Time*'s justification to the feminist critics—I recommended *repeatedly* that she call Theresa Funiciello. Funiciello is a long-time activist who has done a lot of work on welfare. She believes that compensation for caregiving could be as comprehensive and as much of an entitlement as Social Security is at present. While Ginia was researching, Funiciello was organizing a proposal for an innovative new child tax credit, an attempt to create a national savings account for caregiving that would function like the Social Security tax. (Imagine if *Time* had given this idea serious play.) I also sent her to the Massachusetts businesswoman and activist Anita Moeller, who trains in-home child-care workers, especially in immigrant communities. The employees of Acre Family Day Care, Moeller's company, earn salaries that far exceed the national average and are trained at a higher level than the state requires. Neither source was ever called.

Bellafante quipped, "Is Ally McBeal really progress? Perhaps if she lost her job and wound up a single mom, we could begin a movement again."[34] But Bellafante knew about the real working moms who have been helped by the feminist-organized economic-empowerment movement in this country. She was given the number of Connie Evans, one of the women who brought microenterprise programs to this country and was developing effective, humane welfare-to-work programs in Chicago. In fact, the most sincere programming to get women actually into work from welfare, as opposed to simply kicking them off the rolls, is being done almost exclusively by feminists.[35] Nonetheless, Bellafante scoured the gossip columns of the *New York Post* for references to Courtney Love. Bellafante's omissions are grievous. If you want to know how important microenterprise is to women's lives, consider this: small businesses employ more women than do the *Fortune* 500s. Not surprisingly, international feminism didn't merit a mention in the piece, simply because it wasn't covered in the few Third Wave zines profiled as the last word on feminism among young women. Of course, pop culture zines like *Bust* never made claims to covering international news in the first place. *Time* has no such excuse. Bellafante received a report on the Beijing Fourth World Conference on Women, which outlined the legislation to come out of the international meeting and what different countries were doing to follow up on the Platform for Action.[36] (For example, on its 1996 census, Canada included a question designed to document unpaid work. Counting women's work would increase the GDP by 40 percent.)

After the piece ran, *Time* set up specific Web content to throw a bone to the countless activists and feminists whom they ignored in the cover story. For days, angry women buzzed around the site, accusing Bellafante of treachery. But for all the intelligent women who wrote essays and letters and gave comment to refute *Time*'s argument—Katie Roiphe, Erica Jong, *Ms.*'s Marcia Gillespie, *Bust*'s Debbie Stoller, and *Salon.com*'s Janelle Brown—nothing changed at *Time*.

As for us, because we, too, work in the media, we had the privilege of knowing how this story was constructed—and we can also see the pro-woman line on the story behind the story. Bellafante didn't title, hire art for, or have veto power or spin control over that story. And the article also touched a nerve for the feminists who read it—namely, that various hubs of the movement were disconnected and divided. The Girlies *weren't* at the same table with the academics; bell hooks *wasn't* talking shop with Elizabeth Wurtzel. And as long as *Time* and the rest of the media resist changing the status-quo boys' club, insisting that feminism is dead will be part of their resistance. After all, they can't be accountable to women in their pages and on their mastheads without rethinking every molecule of their mission and modus operandi.

When we read the story "Is Feminism Dead?," and thought about the work we do every day, we knew feminism was alive. Jennifer is in contact with feminists of all ages on a daily basis, whether she is sniffing out stories that need to be written or listening to young and old women talk about wanting to take the next step in their feminist work. She is also working to get Second Wave classics back in print so that these works can be venerated as much as those of important male writers, and so that younger women can have access to their feminist history. Amy, through her work with the Third Wave Foundation, helps young women who want to have abortions get them, by providing money to cover a portion of the procedure and often the travel expenses. She is continually updated on the work of her fellow Third Wave members. Among them are Rozz Nash, Tomasia Kastner, and Imani Uzuri, who founded WERISE (Women Empowered Through Revolutionary Ideas Supporting Enterprise) to support artists in their artistic and activist endeavors; Rachel Timoner, who is currently at work on the Organizing Project, networking community activists in their own communities and those in other cities as well; and Gita Drury, who co-founded the Active Element Foundation to redirect money generated by hip-hop into underserved communities.

We also knew about Kathleen Hanna and Tammy Rae Carland, not just about their inspiring actions almost a decade ago but the fact that they still live and work by promoting their feminist convictions. Kathleen has made several more records, including a 1998 album called *Julie Ruin*, which blasts into the patriarchy via a power-suited alter ego, and a 1999 self-titled record with her new band, Le Tigre. Besides teaching art at the University of North Carolina in Chapel Hill, Tammy Rae cofounded Mr. Lady, a lesbian-feminist record label and video-distribution company in Durham, North Carolina, which put out a new women's music sampler and loads of other great records. Oh, you haven't read about any of these things? Well, the media still need revolutionizing—and, like it or not, feminism still needs the media.

Katha Pollitt admired Bellafante's verve in taking on her own generation, and we also appreciated her call for politics over Prada (or, at least, politics *and* Prada). In hindsight, though, her argument that style is sucking the life out of feminism is rather funny, given her recent job change to fashion writer for *The New York Times*.

Feminism's goal is change, and this requires that we take responsibility for our own lives and actions, but also that we come together with others in a shared purpose and create change beyond our personal spheres. It is likely that a movement of young women who believe in equality and have the confidence of Buffy and Missy Elliott and Mia Hamm is going to pick up momentum and the media will be forced to notice it. But first we have to ascertain that we are here. We have to locate the feminism and feminists who already exist, tucked into mainstream places and issues, everyday jobs, and a seemingly apolitical culture.

CHAPTER FOUR

Girl, You'll Be a Woman Soon

SEE JANE . . .

Jane Pratt grew up in Durham, North Carolina, the second old-est of four kids—two boys and two girls. Her mother and fa-ther were both university professors with the same professional responsibilities and the same educational background, yet her father was a full professor and made $30,000 a year, while her mother was an adjunct professor who made $8,000. When Jane was thirteen, her parents divorced and her mother decided that it was financially smarter to go on unemployment, receive food stamps, and get a paper route to support her children than it was to continue teaching at the university.

Mrs. Pratt had always told Jane, "You can be whatever you want to be." It was a message she hadn't gotten herself. At seven, Jane wanted to be an architect, so she began to sketch floor plans and study houses. A few teachers discouraged her from that path, though, reminding her that architecture re-quired excellent mathematical skills. Jane was great at math, but she trusted the teachers' implied message and curtailed her ambitions. She might be good at math now, they seemed to be

126

saying, but she wouldn't be at the higher levels. Dreams of architecture were scuttled.

At boarding school in the late seventies, Jane's only escape from the alienation and angst of high school was teen magazines. Though she didn't wear kilts or look clean-cut like the prissy models in Seventeen, *she pored over these magazines for reflections of herself. She revised her career plan and decided that she would start a magazine of her own someday.*

While at Oberlin College, the alma mater of Lucy Stone, Jane interned for a semester at Fairchild Publications in New York City, then returned later to intern at McCall's, Style, *and* Rolling Stone. *Her career break came when she was hired as second in command at a start-up called* Teenage. *There, she watched her boss closely and learned what it meant to be an editor in chief. By the time she was hired, at twenty-five, to helm a new teen magazine called* Sassy, *she knew what she would do to make it better than the ones she had read as a teenage girl—models that looked more weird, no messages that would send girls running for the Dexatrim, stories taken from the perspective of a girl rather than from an adult's lecture to a girl. She had a vision that she would be able to see a change in young women's voting patterns based on the founding of* Sassy.

Remembering how depressed she had been back at her New England boarding school, Jane wanted to reach girls in whatever time she had. She didn't worry about the next issue or about pleasing the advertisers and publishers. It felt that dire. Her emergency magazine for teenage girls went under in the mid-1990s, as a result of an advertiser boycott and right-wing mobilizing against Sassy *for speaking so frankly to girls. Battle-scarred, Pratt redirected her energy into a new venture,* Jane, *an older, wiser, more restrained sister to* Sassy.

"When I was a teenager, it was all of the girls pitted against each other in pursuit of the almighty guy," said Jane Pratt from the offices of Jane, *a year into her editorship of this new magazine for young women. "I didn't have any sense of group sup-*

port from other girls. *The most important thing is girls bonding together and banding together.*" Pratt hopes that Jane, *unlike Sassy, will be around for a long time. To please and attract advertisers, the pages for fashion and beauty are plentiful, the models are as thin as chives, and Pratt is more covert about infusing the magazine with her politics. Still, she believes that* "*we need to just keep feminism out there, letting girls know that it is their battle, too.*"

It's probably a fair assumption to say that "zigazig-ha" is not Spice shorthand for "subvert the dominant paradigm."

—JENNIFER L. POZNER,
Sojourner, 1998, about the Spice Girls'
version of Girl Power

One day in 1993, twenty-seven-year-old Lisa Silver took the Delta shuttle from New York to Washington, D.C., for a meeting of Second Wave feminists. The author and chronicler of male-female communication problems Deborah Tannen, CNN correspondent Judy Woodruff, inside-the-Beltway journalist Sally Quinn, political strategist Ann Lewis, and other luminaries had assembled to discuss the women's agenda for the Clinton era. "I walked into that room and was faced with all of these red blazers, brass buttons, and sensible high-heel shoes, and I was like, This is not me," Silver says, recalling the meeting in early 1999. "I thought, What am I doing here?"

Silver was working with Betty Friedan's Women, Men, and Media research group, which produced *The Front Page Report* that was mentioned in Chapter 2. As a graduate student in journalism at New York University, she had been thrilled to hook up with Friedan ("I mean *Betty Friedan!!*"), the "mother of the movement." She began as an assistant on a staff of three and soon moved up to program director, the No. 2 spot. Silver was excited to be in the thick of feminist journalism, exposing the still-unequal situation for women. She respected Friedan and the troop of glass-ceiling shatterers at the D.C. meeting, but she also felt alienated from them. Some of the disconnect was simply generational. At twenty-seven, she was working with women ranging in age from their fifties to their seventies. And some of it was aesthetics; a conflict about style, approach, or even emotion: "There I am, going to this meeting with all of these women who are highly successful, but where's the excitement? Where's the spark?"

The backbone of feminism isn't so different from one generation to the next. We want to distinguish ourselves from doormats, as early twentieth-century feminist Rebecca West and her cohorts did, and as Betty Friedan's generation did. And our values are similar, although our tactics and style often differ. (Suffragist Alice Paul was surely horrified when some early Second Wave feminists, including Shulamith Firestone, wanted to stage an action in D.C. to give *back* the vote as part of a 1969 Vietnam protest.) The difference between the First, Second, and Third Waves is our cultural DNA. Each generation has a drive to create something new, to find that distinctive spark that Silver couldn't locate that day in D.C.

The word "generation" is an apt pun here, because what distinguishes one era from the next is what we generate—whether it's music, institutions, or magazines—and how we use what has already been produced. Marlo Thomas grew up on Toni dolls and Nancy Drew stories. In her mid-thirties, she created one of the Third Wave's first glimpses of feminist culture, the 1973 book and record *Free to Be . . . You and Me*. When Thomas and Friends created this early manifesto of freedom, in which a football player sang about crying and girls wanted to be firemen, they couldn't have imagined the guys with earrings and girls with tattoos and shaved heads who would emerge a decade or two later—their former readers.

Thomas didn't choose to be influenced by Toni dolls any more than we chose to be influenced by *Free to Be*—or by

MTV. Our generation watched powerful, fashionable private detectives solve crimes and bond together in prime-time sisterhood on *Charlie's Angels* but couldn't help noticing that they did all the work while a male voice, always out of reach, told them what to do. We were a generation in which many girls grew up thinking that *Playboy* was for them, too, to sneak peeks at while Mom and Dad were occupied, or to lead tours of neighborhood kids out to the garage for the unveiling of an old copy featuring Miss November 1972. As girls, we saw the culture reflect a bit of our particular vernacular: Valley Girls who shop and register pronouncements about the relative grodiness or radness of all things. We were a generation that was forced to experience equality when it came to the newly coed gym classes, and reveled in Title IX's influence on sports for girls. These products of culture are mundane to us, simply the atmosphere in our temporal tank.

The fact that feminism is no longer limited to arenas where we expect to see it—NOW, *Ms.*, women's studies, and red-suited congresswomen—perhaps means that young women today have really reaped what feminism has sown. Raised after Title IX and "William Wants a Doll," young women emerged from college or high school or two years of marriage or their first job and began challenging some of the received wisdom of the past ten or twenty years of feminism. We're not doing feminism the same way that the seventies feminists did it; being liberated doesn't mean copying what came before but finding one's own way—a way that is genuine to one's own generation.

For the generation that reared the Third Wave, not only was feminism apparent in the politics of the time but politics was truly the culture of the time—Kennedy, the Vietnam War, civil rights, and women's rights. For the Third Wave, politics was superseded by culture—punk rock, hip-hop, zines, products, consumerism, and the Internet. Young women in the early nineties who were breaking out of the "established" movement weren't just rebelling; they were growing up and beginning to take responsibility for their lives and their feminism.

The following is a sampling of what the Third Wave grew up with.

- In 1984, Madonna came out with the album *Like a Virgin*. Lying on her back on the album's cover photo, elbows propped, looking sexy, bored, and tough as hell, she wore fluffy crinolines, black eyeliner, and a belt that said "Boy Toy." She was bad, and looked at you like she wanted it bad. *She* wanted it. Then there were the dozens of incarnations that followed for the material girl. The video identities: stripper, pregnant girl from the neighborhood, dominatrix, men's-suit-wearing activist for female sexuality (*C'mon girls! Do you believe in love?*), and a kick-ass version of the vulnerable, victimized Marilyn Monroe. (Which is why, no doubt, Madonna's fans were mostly young women, while Marilyn's were mostly men.) And Madonna's off-camera identities: strongest thighs in all pop music, bitch, best friend to all the fabulous lesbians, "serious" actress with affected English accent, beatific single mother, and most powerful performer in all the pop firmament. Throughout all this she was sending a message, teaching by example: Be what you want to be, then be something else that you want to be. (And earn a billion bucks while you're at it.)

- In 1988, when *Seventeen* had just been liberated from being run by an ex-nun, and *YM* still stood for *Young Miss* (rather than the current *Young & Modern*), a revolutionary new teen magazine debuted for girls. It was called *Sassy*, and it managed to put on makeup and fashion without prescribing it and created a camp aesthetic for girls. It took the pressure off beauty and fashion by turning away from *Go from So-So to Sexy!* and toward wardrobes donned simply because they were pleasurable: *Dye your hair with Jell-O! Dress like a mod from the sixties! Wear a little Catholic schoolgirl outfit with a down vest! Wear a furry hat with mouse ears! Wheeeee!* Writer Christina Kelly's two-page pastiche, called

"What Now" (essentially an archive of Kelly's taste), vaulted this teen fashion magazine into the counterculture. "What Now" profiled a zine of the month, legitimizing the DIY (do-it-yourself) publications at a time when zines were the only place where people who were too young, punk, or weird, such as Riot Grrrls, could publish. Bands like Jon Spencer Blues Explosion and Guided by Voices got their first teen or women's press in *Sassy*'s "Cute Band Alert." For once, a teen magazine was actually in touch with youth culture. But the salient point here is not so much that the *Sassy* creators were hip, although they were, as that they were hip to feminism. They told girls to get their own guitars, that it's okay to be a lesbian, and that it's even okay *not* to go to the prom. (*Ms.* may have believed this, too, but *Ms.* wasn't written with teenage girls in mind.) The *Sassy* editors were drawing from wells that were below the radar of *Ms.* and over the heads of nonfeminist competitors *Seventeen*, *Teen*, and *YM*.

- In 1991, twenty-eight-year-old Naomi Wolf published *The Beauty Myth*. This book analyzed body image and the consumer trappings of femininity—magazines and makeup and, by extension, porn—from the perspective of a new generation. Wolf was writing for us, about us, and she was one of us: a woman reared in the wake of the Second Wave. Gorgeous and articulate, she drew the reader in the way a fashion magazine did—with pretty pictures (at least, in the Scavullo portraits that accompanied interviews)—and then got you mad with her feminist research. Her critique was one that young women conversant in the coded language of eating disorders could recognize (six glasses of water and hard-boiled egg whites from the salad bar for every dinner equals anorexic masquerading as fitness fanatic; pointer fingers with scratches equals bulimic), as could the girls who felt hostile and ugly when they looked at magazines and porn. As one of the first itinerant feminists of the Third

Wave, Wolf traveled to college campuses across the United States, talking to young women. This touring led her to conclude that "girls are still understood more clearly as victims of culture and sexuality than as cultural and sexual creators," so she set out to change that assumption. Her next book, *Fire with Fire: How Power Feminism Will Change the 21st Century*, told women to embrace power, and *Promiscuities* recast the slut as a rebel.

- In 1991, a loose-knit group of punk-rock girls in Olympia, Washington, and Washington, D.C., rescued feminism from two hazards: one, the male-dominated punk-rock scene; and two, their own cohorts, women who didn't use the term *feminist*. Seizing radicalism and activism from the dump in which they thought it had slumped since the mid-seventies, Riot Grrrls weren't pushing a rational feminism. They scrawled *slut* on their stomachs, screamed from stages and pages of fanzines about incest, rape, being queer, and being in love. They mixed a childish aesthetic with all that is most threatening in a female adult: rage, bitterness, and political acuity. In bands such as Bikini Kill, Bratmobile, Huggy Bear, and Heavens to Betsy, these Grrrls shot up like flames, influencing countless girls and showing them feminism before dissipating, seemingly, around the mid-nineties.

- In 1993, a xerox-and-staple zine of fewer than twenty pages called *Bust* presented an embraceable, nourishing reflection of young women and their lives—and called it girl culture. "The Booty Myth" was a *Bust* story about black women's sexuality, "Elektra Woman and Dyna-Girl" was fiction about two young white girls who staged play–date rapes, "I Was a Teenage Mommy" was self-explanatory, as was "Blow Job Tips for Straight Women from a Gay Man." These articles were juxtaposed with buxom images from vintage soft-core porn, images now in the control of women. In *Bust*, porn was demystified, claimed for women, debated.

Vibrators tried and tried again. Childhood heroines revisited (Judy Blume! Farrah! Cynthia Plaster Caster!). Seventies artists and writers with varying degrees of credentials were recast as Second Wave she-roes (such as sex revolutionaries and authors Erica Jong and Nancy Friday). "We're not apologizing for the culture we've been raised with and not overvaluing masculine culture," said Debbie Stoller, the co-editor of *Bust*. "Barbies, for example, are seen by the main culture as kind of dumb, and playing with trucks is more important—but, in fact, when we played with Barbies it was complicated and interesting, and it's something we should tell the truth about." Rock critic Ann Powers codified Stoller's definition in the fall 1997 Girl issue of *Spin*: "Girl Culture girls have transformed what it means to be female in the nineties. Unlike conventional feminism, which focused on women's socially imposed weaknesses, Girl Culture assumes that women are free agents in the world, that they start out strong and that the odds are in their favor."

All of this Girlie culture, from Madonna to *Bust*, is different from the cultural feminism of the seventies. It promoted a gynefocal aesthetic (as a form of politics), too, but sometimes in the service of a "separate but equal" alternative world. (In keeping with the previously proposed Femitopia.) Cultural feminism put the *y* in *womyn* and brought us women-owned Diana publishing, the aforementioned Olivia Records, and all-ladies collectives such as the Michigan Womyn's Music Festival, which has been going strong annually since 1976 and allows males only under the age of six to grace "the Land" (as the nature preserve upon which everyone camps is always called, with reverence). But for this generation, having or loving our own culture isn't the same as cultural feminism—a separate ghetto (or utopia) for women—it's just feminism for a culture-driven generation. And if feminism aims to create a world where our standard of measurement doesn't start with a white-male heterosexual nucleus, then believing that feminine things are weak means that we're believing our own bad press. Girlies say, through actions and attitudes, that you don't have to make the feminine powerful by making it masculine or "natural"; it is a feminist statement to proudly claim things that are feminine, and the alternative can mean to deny what we are. *You were raised on Barbie* and *soccer? That's cool.* In a way, establishing a girl culture addresses what Gloria Steinem was trying to identify when she wrote *Revolution from Within*—the huge hole that grows in a woman who is trying to be equal but has internalized society's low estimation of women. "It was as if the female spirit were a garden that had grown beneath the shadows of barriers for so long," she wrote, "that it kept growing in the same pattern, even after some of the barriers were gone."

What does the Third Wave garden look like? Planted near Madonna, *Sassy*, Wolf, Riot Grrrls, and *Bust* are influential xerox-and-staple zines such as *I (heart) Amy Carter*, *Sister Nobody*, *I'm So Fucking Beautiful*, *Bamboo Girl*; the glossy-but-still-independent zines such as *HUES*, *Roller Derby*, *Bitch*, *Fresh and Tasty*, *WIG*; chickclick and estronet Web sites like Disgruntled Housewife, Girls On, gURL; webzines such as *Minx* and *Maxi*; feature films like *Clueless*, *Go Fish*, *All Over Me*, *The Incredibly True Adventure of Two Girls in Love*, *Welcome to the Dollhouse*, *High Art*; art films by Elisabeth Subrin, Sadie Benning, Pratibha Parmar, and Jocelyn Taylor; musicians such as Ani DiFranco, Brandy, Luscious Jackson, Courtney Love as the slatternly, snarly singer, Courtney Love as the creamy Versace model, Erykah Badu, Me'shell Ndege'ocello, Bikini Kill, Missy Elliott, the Spice Girls, Salt-N-Pepa, TLC, Gwen Stefani, Team Dresch, Foxy Brown, Queen Latifah, Indigo Girls, and all those ladies featured at Lilith Fair; products galore, Urban Decay, Hard Candy, MAC, Manic Panic; on the small screen, *Wonder Woman* (in comic-book form, too), *Buffy the Vampire Slayer*, *My So-Called Life*, *Xena*, *Felicity*, and Alicia Silverstone in Aerosmith videos; Chelsea Clinton; the New York club Meow Mix and other joints with female go-go dancers getting down for women; funny girls loving Janeane

Garofalo and Margaret Cho; angry women loving Hothead Paisan and *Dirty Plotte* comics; Jenny McCarthy, who somehow satirized being a pinup even as she was one; controversial books like *Backlash* and *The Morning After*; uncontroversial ones like *The* Bust *Guide to the New Girl Order* and *Listen Up*; the West Coast mutual-admiration society of sex writers Lisa Palac and Susie Bright; Monica Lewinsky; the Women's World Cup; the WNBA; and hundreds more films, bands, women, books, events, and zines.

We, and others, call this intersection of culture and feminism "Girlie." Girlie says we're not broken, and our desires aren't simply booby traps set by the patriarchy. Girlie encompasses the tabooed symbols of women's feminine enculturation—Barbie dolls, makeup, fashion magazines, high heels—and says using them isn't shorthand for "we've been duped." Using makeup isn't a sign of our sway to the marketplace and the male gaze; it can be sexy, campy, ironic, or simply decorating ourselves without the loaded issues (à la *dye your hair with Jell-O!*). Also, what we loved as girls was good and, because of feminism, we know how to make girl stuff work for us. Our Barbies had jobs and sex lives and friends. We weren't staring at their plastic figures and Dynel tresses hoping to someday attain their pneumatic measurements. Sticker collections were no more trivial than stamp collections; both pursuits cultivated the connoisseur in a young person.

While it's true that embracing the pink things of stereotypical girlhood isn't a radical gesture meant to overturn the way society is structured, it can be a confident gesture. When younger women wearing "Girls Rule" T-shirts and carrying Hello Kitty lunch boxes dust off the Le Sportsacs from junior high and fill them with black lipstick and green nail polish and campy sparkles, it is not as totems to an infantilized culture but as a nod to our joyous youth. Young women are emphasizing our real personal lives in contrast to what some feminist foremothers anticipated their lives would—or should—be: that the way to equality was to reject Barbie and all forms of pink-packaged femininity. In holding tight to that which once symbolized their oppression, Girlies' motivations are along the lines of gay men in Chelsea calling each other "queer" or black men and women using the term "nigga."

In creating a feminism of their own, though, Girlies are repeating a pattern as old as the patriarchy: rebelling against their mothers. For instance, Debbie Stoller, who was quoted calling Gloria Steinem a dinosaur in the dumb and now defunct Gen-X magazine *Swing* or Katie Roiphe writing books that seem to be a direct response to her seventies-feminist mother Anne Roiphe.[37] In the same way that Betty Friedan's insistence on professional seriousness was a response to every woman in an office being called a girl, this generation is predestined to fight against the equally rigid stereotype of being too serious, too political, and seemingly asexual. Girlie culture is a rebellion against the false impression that since women don't want to be sexually exploited, they don't want to be sexual; against the necessity of brass-buttoned, red-suited seriousness to infiltrate a man's world; against the anachronistic belief that because women could be dehumanized by porn (and we include erotica in our definition), they must be; and the idea that girls and power don't mix.

Although rebelling appears to be negative, we think it's natural—and the result leads to greater diversity and, in turn, produces a stronger feminist movement. For example, it's important that Andrea Dworkin identify herself as "a feminist, not the fun kind," but if it was ever implied that she was the *only* kind, the movement might feel a little Antioch, as in rigid.* Similarly, the Spice Girls make for a pretty thin definition of *feminist* because they are only the fun kind. And yet

---

*Antioch College is famous for a 1992 policy that required verbal consent for every step of a possible seduction; i.e., Do you want me to touch your breast?

preteen girls dancing around freely in their living rooms or at concerts singing "Wannabe," rock music made just for them, can be nothing short of empowering.

Girlie doesn't so much identify different issues for young women as say that this generation of feminists wants its own institutions and a right to its own attitudes and interpretations. Familiarity with porn, sexual aggressiveness, and remaining single and childless until pretty late in life play out in their take on issues such as censorship, date rape, and day care. The fact that most of the Girlies are white, straight, work outside the home, and belong to the consumer class provides some explanation for why they choose to promote certain issues. The Second Wave, our mothers, had *Ms.* (and *Sojourner* and *Lilith* and *Our Bodies, Ourselves*) and NOW and the fight for the ERA. We have *Bust* (and *Bitch* and the now defunct *HUES* and webzines and fanzines) and the Third Wave Foundation, Riot Grrrls and Queen Latifah and Lilith Fair and, well, we still have the fight for the ERA, and *Ms.*, *Sojourner*, and *Our Bodies, Ourselves*.

Where Girlie stops short of being the path to a forceful movement is that it mistakes politics for a Second Wave institution as well, rather than seeing it as inherent in feminism. This disconnect—politics versus culture—was on display at the 1997 Media and Democracy Forum, where Girlie debuted as a topic of conversation.

At a conference devoted to alternative journalism and leftist politics, "Girl Power: Progress . . . or the Selling of Feminism Lite?" was one of the few women-oriented panels. The panelists—Debbie Stoller of *Bust*, Ophira Edut of *HUES*, Erin Aubry of *L.A. Weekly*, Susan Douglas, the author of *Where the Girls Are* and *Listening In: Radio and the American Imagination* (and the token older feminist), and Tara Roberts, the former lifestyle editor of *Essence* and author of *Am I the Last Virgin?*—grappled with the meaning of Girlie before an auditorium filled half with earnest and frizzy old-school feminists and half with the pierced and tattooed new-girl feminists. To the audience, this panel of great women seemed scattered and oppositional. The confused debate that occurred produced three overarching conclusions. One, Girlie is pretty much an all-white phenomenon, and black women have never made such a big deal about the implications of wearing nail polish or makeup; two, the more you talk to Second Wave feminists about nail polish, the less they want to hear anything you're saying; and three, Girlie is both "progress" *and* the "selling of feminism lite."

Although she was asked to moderate this panel, twenty-nine-year-old Tara Roberts confessed that she didn't relate to Girlie per se. Nonetheless, she was able to draw some connections to her own experience. "Girl power—this tough, sexy woman who is speaking her mind—is not something that's new to black women," Roberts said. "When I was fourteen, Salt-N-Pepa rappers were definitely out there saying, 'I'm a sexual being, and I'm not gonna be taken advantage of.' The people in my high school that had the juice, the props, the respect, were the girls who were tough, who were sexy, who had their hair fly, their nails done, but you didn't mess with them." Bringing up the nearly opposite point, Erin Aubry asserted that black women's bodies, specifically their butts, have been seen only as sex machines and workhorses to such a profane degree that the simple act of trying to buy a pair of jeans becomes a metaphor for not fitting into the white patriarchy and its notions of feminine bodies.

In an effort to reclaim her booty and her body, Aubry had written an article called "The Butt" for *L.A. Weekly* and had her posterior photographed for the cover in a pair of tight blue jeans. Many in the black community were outraged. The butt was associated with the racist sexual objectifying of black women into hungry, haveable pieces of ass, and there she was promoting the stereotype. "It's like we've already decided what sexual images are in our community: bad," Aubry said. "They *are* bad. But, I'm trying to argue, part of me is me as a woman. But [the woman side and the black woman side] almost don't coexist."

In a racist and sexist society, Aubry is divided against herself in at least two ways. American culture has a history of slave rape and forced (on black women) miscegenation coursing through it like the white blood of the slave owners. During the plantation era, white women often did—or could do—little to protect female slaves from the unwanted advances of the master. It's true that some white wives left their husbands or joined the abolition underground. It is also true that some mistresses were threatened by the attention—albeit unwanted—that black women received, and were sometimes more punishing and cruel than the masters. This history is one of the reasons that black women sometimes feel more betrayed by white women than by white men. This was a betrayal that happened again, but in reverse, during the civil-rights movement, when some black male leaders began sleeping with white women, thus nudging out black women as sexual beings. The complex relationship continues, as Roberts pointed out with her Salt-N-Pepa comment—white Girlies appear to be borrowing, consciously or not, from black women in popular culture when they talk about femininity and strength. Think of actress Pam Grier, activist Faye Wattleton, or radical Angela Davis. (Of course, the "strong black woman" is a stereotype, too, and black women aren't hardwired to be powerhouses or to never let the black male forget that he's a man. But black women have more pop culture examples of sexy women who are also tough.)

Moments later, Debbie Stoller took the conversation in a different direction, vociferously arguing that painting one's nails is a feminist act because it expands the notions of what a feminist is allowed to do or how she may look. "Maybe we *should* be painting our nails in the boardroom," she concluded, in order to bring our Girlie-ness into male-defined spaces. In other words, not being allowed to wear a miniskirt is the same as being forced to wear a miniskirt. A Second Waver in the audience, outraged, countered that her generation fought to free women from the traps of femininity. While everything that Stoller said is true, the implication of painting one's nails in the boardroom is, best-case scenario, that you are claiming that space as your own. (Another implication is that you aren't quite ready for a job and are, therefore, unlikely to be in the boardroom in the first place.) Compared to the act of owning one's body as a black woman, nail-polish activism seems very silly. Or at least apolitical. Even with varying holds on the reins of political consciousness, what drove each woman on the panel was the same key issue—being able to claim that we are sexual ladies as feminists, as black women, or as whoever we happen to be.

The point is that the cultural and social weapons that had been identified (rightly so) in the Second Wave as instruments of oppression—women as sex objects, fascist fashion, pornographic materials—are no longer being exclusively wielded against women and are sometimes wielded by women. Girlie presumes that women can handle the tools of patriarchy and don't need to be shielded from them. Protective labor laws that were part of the original ERA limited the jobs women could do. They were changed by seventies feminists to promote egalitarian labor laws, which presumed that women could really do the police, car-assembly, and late-night work that men could do. Similarly, Girlie is replacing protective cultural "rules" with a kind of equality. "These days putting out one's pretty power, one's pussy power, one's sexual energy for popular consumption no longer makes you a bimbo," wrote Elizabeth Wurtzel in her 1998 glory rant *Bitch*. "It makes you smart." Madonna is in control of her sexual power, rather than a victim of it; she wields it the way she could a gun or a paintbrush or some other power tool that is usually the province of men. And she *is* enjoying it, which is her luxury and her strength. When Riot Grrrls screamed versions of *IlovefuckingIhatedanger* from rock clubs and fanzines and song lyrics in the early nineties, or when women rappers like Lil' Kim "objectified" men's bodies right down to their dicks, they presumed some sort of strength in the social arena. But where did that strength come from?

THE STUFF THAT GIRLS ARE MADE OF

Some cultural objects that girls consumed/read/loved contained feminism simply because of the political atmosphere in which they were created. The feminism was organic. Such was the way with the first feministy teen magazine.

Sassy was conceived in 1987, when Sandra Yates, an Australian feminist (she had been secretary of the Women's Electoral Lobby in Brisbane) decided to launch an American version of *Dolly*, which was already a successful teen magazine in Australia. Yates and her business partner, Anne Summers, who had headed Australia's Office of the Status of Women and had written a landmark book on Aussie feminism, also bought the wilting *Ms.* magazine from its original owners to play big sister to the new teen magazine. They hoped that an influx of cash could convince advertisers to buy ad pages in the beleaguered feminist monthly.

"I don't know that the idea was 'Let's do a feminist teen magazine,' " says Christina Kelly, who began with *Sassy* as a writer and was an editor throughout the period the magazine was owned by Dale Lang and at the time of its sale to Petersen Publishing in 1994. "I think it was more like, 'Let's do a magazine that speaks to teenagers in their own voice and that they can relate to, and let's have it be really fun and irreverent.' " Jane Pratt, who had recently graduated from college, where she had majored in communications and dance, came to *Sassy* by way of an ill-fated precursor called *Teenage*. ("It took teenagers seriously—a little *too* seriously," says Kelly, referring to the fact that the magazine never quite took off.)

Pratt—cute-faced and Ally Sheedy–like—showed up for her *Sassy* interview costumed for the new girl regime: big, black, clompy Polish workman's boots, a polka-dot skirt, and a vintage top. She was the only applicant who didn't interview decked out in corporate drag (a suit and heels), which Summers and Yates took as a sign that she "got it."[38] They hired her, and whisked her off to Australia for training.

Soon, a half Australian–half American staff was assembled. In early 1988, *Sassy* hit America. The first issue ran a story about a teenage girl's decision to lose her virginity, and had Pratt's feministy edicts about sex and no dieting already in place. "I was like, 'Alright! Yeah!'" says Kelly of Pratt's early editorial vision. "I hate those [dieting] articles." Kelly had suffered from an eating disorder as a teenager, and she was convinced that such articles contributed to it. "I came across an old issue of *Seventeen* recently from the time when I would have been reading it—the seventies. It was all like: *this* has this many calories and *that* has that many calories, so make sure that you don't eat *that* if you want to stay skinny."

Kelly carved out a wry, feminist-inflected writing style that was witty and free of the sort of earnestness that plagued most writing for teenage girls. In a typical story, she went to Stringfellow's, a famously macho high-end Manhattan strip club, and interviewed the dancers. She also deflated Miss America after spending a day observing her highness's vapid reign; she loved Claire Danes, and she demystified celebrities for teenage girls. (If Marky Mark was a dick, *Sassy* let you know.) Most editors of teenage magazines will tell you that what the readers want is tips on boys, beauty, crushes, and plenty of celebrity photos. Instead of giving them what they supposedly wanted, *Sassy* gave them what they needed. Since the editors themselves had just graduated to young adulthood, they had a unique perspective. They were young enough to relate to teenagers without being preachy, yet old enough to be able to impart some relevant wisdom. "A lot of the stuff we wrote about was stuff that we were interested in, and it wasn't concentrating so much on what the readership wanted," says Kelly. "We were just setting out to do a magazine that we thought was cool."

As it turned out, *Sassy* was a hit with girls who were ready for the feminist upgrade. (The first issue had a 250,000 circulation, which went up to 400,000 within the first year, making it one of the most successful launches in women's magazine history.) The content was real, and such a success with girls that a cabal of right-wing and religious fundamentalist groups, spearheaded by a Southern group called Women Aglow, launched a boycott of *Sassy*'s advertisers. Most of this was a direct response to articles that acknowledged that girls have sex. As much as this spoke volumes about *Sassy*'s sincerity in being responsible to a realistic treatment of girls' lives, it spelled death for a teen magazine that relied on advertisers, who pulled or threatened to pull ads—for example, Maybelline, Noxzema, and Cover Girl. Dale Lang, *Sassy*'s owner since 1989, exercised veto power on the kinds of stories that could run in order to appease the advertisers. But, as teens are wont to do, *Sassy* rebelled.

While Jane Pratt and crew were forced to put the panties back on frank discussions of sex and pleasure (though they still had a refreshingly confident yet blasé approach to gay teens) a subversive element began poking through their conservative swaddling. *Sassy* began reporting on the underground and culture-makers, and the underground began reading *Sassy*. Notorious Baltimore filmmaker John Waters read it. Thurston Moore and Kim Gordon of the band Sonic Youth read it. Chloë Sevigny, future "it" girl and star of *Kids* and *Boys Don't Cry*, became an intern after one of the fashion staff saw her and asked to photograph her for a style page. Courtney Love and Kurt Cobain (looking gorgeous in dyed magenta hair) did the April 1992 cover. The drag queens at the downtown New York couturier Patricia Field *loved* it; they called it *Sissy*.

"The thing about *Sassy* was that no one knows when or why people who were grownups began picking it up," recalls Mary Clarke, who began as a beauty editor with the very first issue and eventually became the magazine's creative director. Clarke remembers a friend of hers promising to translate from German a very serious poststructuralist discussion of *Sassy* in an art magazine. It's fair to say that *Sassy* was the only teen magazine so hip it was postmodern—and to Germans even. Nomy Lamm, writing about the punk-mythic town of Olympia, Washington, encapsulates what *Sassy* began to represent as an arbiter of trends. "I have lived here my entire life," she writes. "And it never seemed cool to me until I read about it in *Sassy*."

In a unique confluence, *Sassy* affected not only teen magazines but adult magazines such as *Allure* and *Ms.*, which took a page from it as well. Nomy Lamm became a favorite "young feminist" staple at *Ms.* after Christina Kelly received Lamm's zine, *I'm So Fucking Beautiful*, for possible inclusion in Kelly's column "What Now" and brought it to a *Ms.* editor's attention. *Sassy* reported on Riot Grrrls in 1991, but it wasn't until a 1994 feature called "50 Ways to Be a Feminist" that *Ms.* wrote about Kathleen Hanna, who is closely associated with the birth of the Riot Grrrl movement. *Sassy* loosened up *Seventeen* and *YM* a great deal, a fact *Seventeen*'s former editor Caroline Miller has admitted. Now the other teen mags are likely to include birth-control information and stories about having sex—though still nothing that might offend advertisers.

In 1991, Tali Edut, an eighteen-year-old University of Michigan student, applied to be art director on the second reader-produced issue of *Sassy* magazine. Chosen, she spent the summer in Manhattan, at the 230 Park Avenue office, putting the issue together. Stories included "These Skinheads Aren't Racist" (about anti-racist skinheads, obviously) and a piece on the importance of female friendships. Once she was back at UMich with her identical twin, Ophira, and her best friend, Dyann Logwood, and having been inspired by her summer at the fresh teen magazine, Tali decided to put together a magazine for her introductory women's studies class. They named it *HUES*, the acronym for Hear Us Emerging Sisters, which also signaled its multicultural mission. "We incorporated all of the stuff we talked about among ourselves and got our friends in the dorm to write," Ophira says. "So the first issue featured vending-machine snacks and late-night philosophical discussions." Because they themselves were the publishers and they weren't tied to any advertisers, the three would not have to conform to any less-than-cool compromises. (For instance, women of color weren't on many *Sassy* covers. The staff had to fight with the publisher when the girl who won the magazine's Sassiest Girl in America contest happened to be black—horror, according to myth, for the newsstand bottom line.) Furthermore, *HUES* wouldn't emulate *Sassy*'s ultraskinny model requirements (also advertiser-imposed, and thus required by its money-hungry publisher). A fashion story might be called "PMS Fashion." The bathing-suit issue featured size 10 and up.

HUES debuted in April 1992, and self-published eight issues over the next five years. This multi-culti independent women's magazine started off with such a bang that, upon graduating, Ophira Edut took out a $30,000 loan and attempted to expand the magazine. (By 1997, it proved to be too much work to keep going, so the Edut sisters and Dyann Logwood began looking for a buyer. *New Moon*, the Duluth-based girls-empowerment magazine, purchased *HUES* that same year. It was unable to make *HUES* profitable enough to keep it going, however, and published only five more issues before putting the magazine to sleep in early 1999.)

At the same time that Tali was interning at *Sassy*, Debbie Stoller and Marcelle Karp, both in their late twenties, were working at boring jobs for Nickelodeon, the cable-television channel for children. They met and soon realized they were both interested in "woman stuff and we both read *Sassy*," Karp recalls. They bonded over their infatuation with this teen magazine and its creators, women who were from their generation and who were doing what they wanted to do; namely, making a cultural product to which they could relate. They both thought that what was great about *Sassy* was that the staff talked to their female readership the way they talked to each other, not as if the reader was younger or less sophisticated than they were. "I thought *Sassy* caught on that it wasn't just about giving girls a good role model, and it was not just about the negative things that need to be changed about being female in this society," Stoller says. "*Sassy* realized that you had to embrace the positive stuff, and that would go a long way toward empowering people. It made me laugh, and it made me like being a girl." But despite all its kudos and adult fans, *Sassy* was still a teen magazine. Unlike Karp and Stoller, the average reader was just a few years into menstruating and had to be home before midnight.

Karp and Stoller would talk about how odd it was that they read only *Details* and *Sassy*, and how they didn't read *Ms.*, even though they were big feminists. "I was disappointed in *Ms.* I didn't understand why the Riot Grrrls weren't on the cover of that magazine. Here this was a new wave of feminism and *Ms.* seemed so disconnected," said Stoller, who had graduated from Yale with a Ph.D. in the psychology of women and had as her goal the creation of new media for women. Stoller was a fabulous typist—long a mixed blessing for women. She began temping at Nickelodeon, hoping to get in on the ground floor of MTV, which was owned by the same company. "In my late twenties, I wasn't living a lifestyle so different from that of a teenage girl," says Stoller. "Most single girls were living in our own apartments and cooking our own food, but we were also buying records, finding cute boys—sort of a chronic teenagerhood."

Stoller and Karp talked about doing their own magazine, a sort of *Sassy* senior for girls like them who weren't on a mommy track or a career track but cared about sex and brains and rock 'n' roll and feminism. Walking to the subway one morning, Stoller had an epiphany: "There should be a magazine for us, and it should not suck and it should be cool and funny and smart and we should call it *Bust*." She liked the way this aggressive double entendre made you think of tits *and* of breaking through barriers. It reminded her of a Dutch women's magazine she read during a stay in the Netherlands called *Opzij*, which means both "step aside" and "about her." Karp had just been fired from her too-menial job as a production assistant at Nick, and thus was freed up to realize their dream. So, one freezing spring day in 1993, the two met in Tompkins Square Park and hammered out what *Bust* would be. Karp recalls:

> We were so organized. It's incredible to think about it because we didn't even know what we were doing. Next thing we knew, we were getting a P.O. Box and a *Bust* E-mail account, and a checking account for the two of us. I called up the zine bible god, *Fact Sheet Five*, and they sent us the computer guide, the printer guide, and the retail-store thing. In the first four issues, it was me doing money and business, and Debbie getting stories. We did the editors' letter together and she did the editing. We read submissions together, and laid it out together, and took copyediting classes together—we did it all together. Gradually, we were getting the hang of being *Bust* girls, of being women in charge of our own thing. For that first issue, we went to Debbie's office at night and xeroxed and stapled the issue ourselves. For the second issue, I had made so much money on a project that I bankrolled the whole thing, and we upgraded and went to newsprint, two color. It was forty-eight pages, and I was so excited. We got Laurie Henzel involved as designer. Somebody told me about advertising, because I didn't know that revenue could really be generated that way. And then someone else said you can get money up front if you put a subscription page in. With every issue, people would give publishing cues, and we would take their advice and implement it and figure stuff out.

Five years after *Bust* debuted as a xerox-and-staple zine, Karp, Stoller, and Henzel were doing print runs of 35,000. (To give you a sense of that accomplishment, *Bamboo Girl*, another successful glossy zine with ads, was printing about 2,000 with each issue.)

Meanwhile, after years of boycotts, losing ad money, losing

readership because of censorship by advertisers, and the cowardice of its corporate parent, *Sassy* died in 1995. Actually, it was sold to Petersen Publishing, which also published *Guns & Ammo*, moved to L.A., and was made over as a *YM* clone. Within a year, that pale substitute was put out of its misery. *Jane* debuted in 1997 with the same creative duo that was behind the iconic teen magazine: Christina Kelly and Jane Pratt. *Jane* is doing a lot of what *Sassy* did, except the ethos is the single independent woman rather than the single independent girl. The food column is called "Eat," and the editorial content is in marked contrast to *Cosmo*'s "big pyramid," where all articles lead to landing a man. The "What Now"–type column in *Jane* is called "Dish" and is edited by Kelly.

"*Jane* is feminist," says Pratt. The feminism is tucked into stories like going undercover at the Aryan Nation and profiling the female astronauts who should have gone up with John Glenn, a story done by *Ms.* two decades earlier. There are many other feministy stories that seemed to be recycled from *Ms.* (A reversal of *Ms.*'s old reliance on *Sassy*). It's also a fashion magazine that courts fashion ads. So, while the stylists incorporate cheap pieces from Kmart and secondhand shops, *Jane* doesn't critique the skinny models wearing expensive clothes, or the preponderance of editorial directly related to advertising. Pratt is aware that this may seem like a cop-out, but she wants her magazine to have more "mall appeal," as in girls who aren't urban hipsters. "I wouldn't have gotten *Bust* when I was in high school at Andover," says Pratt. "I like seducing people with something that looks like it might be one thing and then actually giving them something a lot harder, stronger, more empowering than they might have expected it to be." But by her own admission, there is no way that *Jane* could have the impact that the original *Sassy* had. "By the time you are in your twenties your relationship to a magazine is so different. You are never going to need it in the same way—it's never going to be your lifeline," says Pratt.

Of course, adult women's magazines can be just as much of a

lifeline if the content is honest and speaks to women beyond their wallets. *Ms.* magazine has been a connection to feminism for thousands of women (and still is, to some). Still, the original *Sassy* did something crucial for feminism that *Ms.* couldn't. Beyond treating girls with respect *Sassy* talked about women's rights and politics cloaked in culture, and inspired *Bust* and *HUES* to do the same. Together, they pushed feminist institutions to acknowledge the power of the next generation and its culture. These magazines recognized Girlie culture and promoted it. Concurrently, they provided new avenues into feminism for women who might not have found their way to a NOW meeting. For instance, a college student at the University of Michigan might pick up *Sassy* to make fun of Joey Lawrence but could end up reading about how racist it can be when you go car shopping.

The *Bust* and *HUES* girls saw a gaping hole in feminism; they felt connected to the movement, but they didn't relate to the existing institutions and saw an opportunity to create their own. They in turn sparked women such as San Francisco writer Lisa Miya-Jervis and Andi Zeisler to found *Bitch* as a xerox-and-staple journal of media criticism in 1995. In it, she declares: "This magazine is about thinking critically about every message the mass media sends; it's about loudly articulating what's wrong and what's right with what we see. This magazine is about speaking up. Will that make us bitchy? Yeah. *You wanna make somethin' of it?*" The next year in San Francisco, Janelle Brown, a twenty-two-year-old tech journalist for *Hotwired* (*Wired*'s on-line magazine), decided to start *Maxi*. "It grew out of an interest in fashion magazines—I always devoured them and hated them at the same time—and I was getting into feminist zines," she says. "I wanted to write something smart about women who are interested in feminism and politics and the personal day-to-day hazards of growing up female. There was nothing on-line for women at that point."

What these zines and culture-makers had in common was that they were proving that it was okay to speak one's mind and that they didn't have to depend on advertising and its attendant censorship and shaping of editorial content. Each drew its critique from their and their readers' own experiences. Even if they weren't liberated enough to change anything, they were liberated enough to complain, celebrate, and generally jump into the media fray.

Even those women who weren't reading *Sassy* or *Bust* were picking up the reverberations of a new feminist voice—the explosion of women in rock, or the success of TV shows such as *Ally McBeal*, *Buffy*, and *Living Single*, which featured women for whom feminism was just a part of life.

In some ways, these magazines and TV shows were presenting old feminism with a new spin, and the process that each of these culture-creators went through is a feminist one. The magazines were the result and a manifestation of a nineties version of consciousness raising—honest talk that spawns more feminism, making connections between women—kind of like a dinner party in print or on the Web.

STILL WORKING ON THE WHEEL

Did you know that Mae West was arrested in 1926 for the Broadway show *Sex* because the play's message about women's erotic power was deemed obscene? Or that in 1970, when Jane Pratt was eight years old and drawing floor plans, Susan Brownmiller, Nora Ephron, and Sally Kempton were shopping around a glossy feminist magazine called *Jane* to big media companies? No one invested.[39]

We've been here before. As historian Gerda Lerner has said, the only constant thread in women's history is that it is lost and rediscovered, lost and rediscovered. When the suffragists declared their rights, they knew next to nothing of the women before them. When the radical feminists of the Second Wave began organizing, they had to retrieve the history of their foremothers. As Shulamith Firestone put it in an article entitled "The Women's Rights Movement in the U.S.: A New View" (from the June 1969 self-published pamphlet *Notes from the First Year*):

What does the word "feminism" bring to mind? A granite-faced spinster obsessed with the vote? Or a George Sand in cigar and bloomers, a woman against nature? Chances are that whatever image you have, it is a negative one. To be called a feminist has become an insult, so much that a young woman intellectual, often radical in every other area, will deny vehemently that she is a feminist, will be ashamed to identify with it in any way . . . without knowing even the little that is circulated about it.

Girlie, like all strands of the women's movement, is hindered by a divorce from history: specifically, the history of other versions of Girlie that have existed, women who have reinvented the image of feminism and brought new life to the movement. But when the image change is complete, the inequality remains. And it is the inequality and injustice based on gender that feminism addresses. But, when we are separated from our political history, it is primarily the reinventions that continue, as if women's aesthetics were what we wanted to transform rather than women's rights. Much of the story of the Second Wave is fragmented, mythologized, or difficult to find. In some ways, Girlie can't be blamed for its shortsightedness; the story of women wasn't part of school when we were growing up. But it is our fault that we haven't sought out our history.

This fuzzy sense of where we've been plays out when something like *Bust* or Bikini Kill or the phrase "girl power" turns masses of females on to feminism—and then peters out after that first rush. Having no sense of how we got here condemns women to reinvent the wheel and often blocks us from creating a political strategy.

One of the ways we got here was through a groundbreaking book by an atypical woman who tapped into a typical plight: being a housewife in the postwar, boom economy of America. In 1963, Betty Friedan wrote in *The Feminine Mystique* that "for more than fifteen years there was no word of the yearning in the millions of words written about women, for women, in all the columns, books and articles by experts telling women their role was to seek fulfillment as wives and mothers." She was describing "the problem that has no name," that well-educated middle-class housewives were bored out of their minds in the suburbs with endlessly expanding, Sisyphean housework. Friedan has been credited with starting the Second Wave of feminism by naming that problem, and sparking women to demand political rights and flood the job market.

One year earlier, another atypical "typical" woman had written another earth-shattering book—this one not nearly so well respected by history. It was *Sex and the Single Girl*, by Helen Gurley Brown. Whether or not most feminists now see it as significant, with that little book, Brown, the *Cosmo* queen, resolved another clash between what we want (nookie and the bachelorette life) and what we're supposed to want (marriage and keeping house). And her philosophy sounds familiar to anyone who's conversant with Girlie.

Brown suggested that single women like sex, and don't need to be married to enjoy it, but are badgered into marriage by a conservative, misogynist culture. She championed the career girl at a time when the culture painted an ambitious woman, or a woman who simply had to work, as doomed to be lonely, and a sexually active woman as a slut. In a small, gossipy tome, Brown told it like it was for girls like her. She made visible the emerging independent and sexual working woman, and seemed almost to summon into being the urban, swinging singles scene. Liberation was key for both Friedan and Brown, but the routes differed greatly. Brown had always worked—not necessarily by choice—and she believed that a full sex life was an essential right for working stiffs. Today, women can be as serious as Friedan and as sexual (and single) as Gurley Brown is (and was). Girlie feminists, for their part, are creating an embraceable culture, one that acknowledges the realities of mostly single, mostly childless working girls' lives, with a healthy focus on sexuality. That said, a little brunette called Helen Gurley Brown seems to be at the root of platinum-blond Girlie feminism, as much as a suburban intellectual named Betty Friedan was at the root of housewives' rebellion.

WHO IS HELEN GURLEY BROWN?

Young Helen Gurley was born in 1923 in the Arkansas dust bowl, and reared in Little Rock. When she was ten, her father ("a chauvinist who voted against suffrage," she says) died, leaving Mrs. Gurley to eke out a living for young Helen and her sister, Mary, who had polio and couldn't walk. "I think my mother was a feminist," Brown says. "Her life was in some ways boring because my father wouldn't let her work after she was married. She had been a schoolteacher, and she was good—but at that time if a man's wife was working it meant that he couldn't support her, and the neighbors would talk."

The three Gurley women moved to Los Angeles in the late thirties. Mrs. Gurley went back to teaching, and Helen attended high school. Living vicariously through her younger daughter, Helen, Mrs. Gurley encouraged the slender adolescent in her studies and social life, and desperately wanted Helen to be popular, making all of her clothes and driving her to sorority meetings, drama rehearsals, and parties. In high school, Helen was president of the World Friendship Society, editor and gossip columnist for an award-winning school newspaper called the *Polyoptimist*, and winner of an oratory prize. Although she was class valedictorian, president of the scholarship society, and had a great scholastic record, she didn't get a scholarship anywhere. "Yes, I had a brain, but we couldn't afford to send me to college," says Brown. "I had to support the family. I had the work ethic very early on." So, in 1940, her best friends went off to college, and eighteen-year-old Helen went to work.

At twenty-five, Helen Gurley became a secretary for Don Belding, of the advertising agency Foote, Cone, and Belding. Ten years later, she was an award-winning ad writer, and making enough money to pay for her Mercedes convertible in cash. At thirty-seven, after two decades in the L.A. dating game, Gurley finally caught a big fish—her partner for life, Hollywood producer David Brown. The next year, pushing forty and married, she wrote *Sex and the Single Girl*. Riding the profound success of that book, the following year she became editor of the women's magazine *Cosmopolitan*, recasting it from a respectable family magazine to a "girls on top in the bedrooms and the boardrooms" women's glossy.

Helen had experienced the sexism and unfairness that was part of being born female, but she saw this unfairness as directed at single women for working and being independent. Brown said that women who weren't married didn't have to face the indignity of being presumed to be damaged goods, a sexless spinster, or otherwise pitiful or invisible. Her book's message was basic bootstrap (work hard, play your man-pleasing cards right, and you can have it all, *including* a boyfriend) sharing space with tips for decorating and recipes for cooking for bachelors. But her breakthrough was asserting that single women were sexually valuable, even if they were older than twenty five. Her pages on getting what you need out of an affair are snappy and confident, especially for 1962: "Once in bed, it's kind of silly to fake inexperience . . . the only man who might 'suffer' from your experience is the man who is no great shakes in bed himself. If you have no one to compare him with, he might get an 'A'!" Or this advice for women dating men with occasional hydraulic problems: "*Him* you don't need. . . . A married woman has every reason to help a semipotent male get back to normal, but you have no more incentive than a short-term tenant has in rebuilding [her] apartment." This was strong stuff, especially considering the women's magazine formula up to that time, even for fiction: if a woman has sex outside marriage, she has to come to a bad end.

In 1962, Letty Cottin Pogrebin was a twenty-two-year-old director of publicity at Bernard Geis and Associates, where *Sex and the Single Girl* was being published. "It pretty much blew me away," Pogrebin recalls of the advice book. "I felt I was suddenly hearing the truth." Pogrebin, a petite blonde with the body of a teenager and the voice of an eight-year-old, hadn't yet become the radicalized married feminist who would become one of the first editors of *Ms.* magazine, and instrumental in creating the book and record *Free to Be . . . You and Me.* "I was a different person then, not political," she says of her publicity days. "I was really into the sixties fun mode: I was a person with a motor scooter who went to jazz concerts and dated a lot of men. I felt [*Sex and the Single Girl*] was about me." Many other women felt that way, too. The book was on *The New York Times* best-seller list for twenty-six weeks, and was published in sixteen different languages.

"She was smart and unbelievably driven," recalled Suki Nishi, a high-school "chum" of Brown's at John H. Francis Polytechnic, in a 1997 interview for this book. Nishi believes that Brown had a sort of internal sense of justice based not on politics but on her own heart. One year, for instance, Brown sponsored Nishi to join an elite club that had never before accepted a person of color. In 1942, Nishi and many other Japanese-Americans were sent to internment camps. The American Civil Liberties Union (ACLU) waffled on the issue, but Brown wrote to her friend regularly at the relocation camp. She did good things because she had a good heart, not because she had a political vision. Illustrating this point, Gloria Steinem recalled that Brown always supported legal abortions, citing girlfriends of hers who had suffered illegal and dangerous ones. On the other hand, Brown also called Steinem in a panic in the seventies. "Your people are down in the lobby protesting!" she shrieked. Steinem's "people" were a bunch of women protesting the fact that *Cosmo*'s expert psychiatrist, who wrote an advice column, had been accused of sexually abusing many of his female patients (and was eventually found guilty). When Steinem explained the reason for the protest, Brown replied, "But he's such a nice man." Similarly, Brown infuriates people with her Forrest Gump–in-a-leopard-wrap-dress responses to welfare mothers ("One shouldn't have kids if you can't support them; I don't even have a *pet*, because I couldn't take care of it"), date rape ("highly overrated"), and Packwood ("*poor* Senator Packwood").

Just as Brown's lack of political maturity (buffered by a big heart) had roots in her young life, so did her iconic drive for physical self-improvement. "I am not beautiful, or even pretty," she wrote in the opening pages of *Sex and the Single Girl*. "I once had the world's worst case of acne. I am not bosomy or brilliant. I am an introvert." This belief that she didn't measure up to the beauty-queen ideal was perpetuated and anthologized in thirty years of *Cosmo*: the dieting, the frantic makeup tips, the pushed-up Scavullo girls, all of which were controversial among feminists. Brown's trumpeting of makeup, models, and manipulation was seen as traitorous, or at least terribly gauche. But the story behind her ceaseless cheerleading for self-improvement is actually poignant, and certainly common.

"It's very personal, and not too interesting, but one naughty thing that my mother did was to never convince me that I was pretty," said Brown, perched in her leopard-carpeted pink office at Hearst, the megacorp that owns *Cosmo*:

She thought that to get along in the world you had to be pretty. Yes, use your brain, but I think she made all of those gorgeous clothes for me so that I would measure up. Even after I was grown, she didn't want to go to the market with me unless I had my makeup on. That influenced me badly, in a way. Maybe no more than any other little girl is influenced, but I've always thought that looks were important. And I have done everything that you could to be good enough, because for a long time apparently I didn't think I was. Now, I look at pictures of me when I was sixteen, nineteen, twenty—I was a pretty little girl. I wasn't gorgeous, but I was pretty. Well, pretty enough, anyway.

Brown never agreed with feminists who prescribed playing down one's sexuality at any time, especially at work. In other words, she was always a Girlie, but without the necessary irony or natural feminism added by growing up with the radicalism and support of the Second Wave. Brown's honesty points to an obvious but often underplayed issue for feminists: one's looks, or lack thereof, affect how one experiences life as a woman. This is a feminist dilemma. For instance, in the seventies Gloria Steinem was a favorite feminist spokesperson not simply because of her rhetorical brilliance, political activism, and journalistic chops but because her gorgeousness and glamour spoke a million words in support of women choosing feminism out of dignity rather than desperation. Misogynist writers couldn't attack her for being ugly and bitter (in contrast to Betty Friedan, who was portrayed in always-unflattering photos) but, at the same time, Steinem couldn't exploit her attractiveness because it undermined one of the goals of feminism—valuing a woman for her skills, not just for her sex appeal. Brown could exploit her feminine virtues because she didn't call for a feminist revolution. In the final analysis, looks and men undermined each woman's success: Steinem supposedly succeeded through the powerful men who courted her, and Brown's work ethic was a result of her supposed inability to get a man.

Brown did her best to avoid the analyses of power imbalances and sexism at that time, and her hard-won confidence never translated into political consciousness. Her instincts never matured into a more sophisticated feminist analysis than "Single girls can and do have sex and great careers!" and, many years later, "Older women can and do have sex and great careers!"—the principle of her 1993 book *The Late Show*. All of which points to one of the dangers of Girlie thinking: it doesn't allow women to age, change, mature.

"I think that Helen is trapped in a time warp," says Letty Cottin Pogrebin. "For her, the most revolutionary thing to do, she already did. She survived that horrible childhood and became a self-sufficient person, and she pushed the envelope for sexual freedom. I think she feels she didn't have to do another thing but parlay what she knew for the rest of her life. She had every desire to count herself part of the women's movement, but it just wasn't in her. You can't make Clare Booth Luce into Madonna."*

But, as for the principles of Girlie, in which feminists pine for sexy images that don't present women as victims, Helen Gurley Brown feels that she got there a long time ago, and never, ever deviated from her convictions: "I said that a woman at age twenty-three or older takes on adult responsibilities, she maybe gets married, she is a member of the community, she is a grownup. She may have a serious career. She is a full-fledged woman. At the same time, she never stops being a girl. I was always criticized for calling her 'That Cosmopolitan Girl.' I don't know any woman who doesn't think of herself as a girl— I think everyone from Madeleine Albright all the way to Madonna [does]. The girlish part of you is playful, optimistic and fun-loving, and you don't want that tamped down. And you can be both at the same time."

That doesn't sound so crazy. Nor does it sound so far off from Naomi Wolf (with her power feminism and radical heterosexuality) and the women who create *Bust*, *Bitch*, and *Jane*—adjusted, of course, for very different theories about dieting and its relationship to eating disorders, what you should do for your boss, or in whose interest you are pushing up your breasts. But for all the similarities between Girlies and Gurley— pinkaphilia, nail-polish revolutions, belief in sex and the value of single women, and the use of the word *girl*—Helen Gurley Brown is not a heroine of the Girlies. In fact, a distaste for Helen is something feminists tend to share. In 1969, Redstockings named her an "Aunt Tom of the Month" in its premier broadsheet, *Notes from the First Year*. Disgust and distrust of

---

*Clare Booth Luce (1903–1987) was the kind of dame who could be married to Henry Luce, a man who reputedly didn't allow women to write in the pages of his magazine (*Time*), and still write the beautiful and bitchy play *The Women* in 1936. She became a Republican congresswoman in 1942 and delighted in tearing down the Democrats.

the *Cosmo* girl's miniskirted mother was also revealed by a *USA Today* poll that asked readers to identify the three least admired women in America. Brown told us about the poll, published in the mid-nineties, and that the winners were Tipper Gore (who before her stint as second lady, you'll recall, was renowned as the head of the Parents' Music Resource Center, which pioneered warning labels on records), Janet Reno (of Waco fame), and Helen Gurley Brown.

Helen Gurley Brown remains a mirror of how society really feels about women, and especially older women. In 1997, Brown was retired from her thirty-year post at *Cosmo* (where she was uniformly loved by her staff) to make way for the much younger Bonnie Fuller. (After only a year, Fuller left *Cosmo* to replace another much-loved older woman editor, *Glamour* editor in chief Ruth Whitney.) Brown became editor in chief of Cosmo International, opening up new editions all over the world—forty so far—and supervising their product. The same ageism that devalued Brown, or at least kept her from heading the magazine she made so successful, is probably what keeps Kate Millett from landing any full-time work as a professor despite her Ph.D. and laurels, and turns hot tomatoes like Michelle Pfeiffer or Meryl Streep into lumpen character roles at age forty, while Jack Nicholson and Sean Connery get older, fatter, balder and—*ahem*—sexier. Brown espousing pro-sex girlish wisdom strikes a nerve of Girlie's own internalized ageism. A Girlie at thirty-five is hot; at seventy-five, she's pathetic.

People can write Brown off as trivial because her politics are negligible, because she kowtows to men and *loves* the beauty myth, and doesn't question that life is easier if you are pretty. People laugh at her because she went for the face-lifts and the nose job, believes fervently in being thin, and, even though she's old, thinks women shouldn't stop having sex or love in their lives ("being part of the human race," as she puts it) just because our culture degrades older women's bodies. And who's to say that believing that on a personal level doesn't have profound implications? However, it won't solve the day-care problem.

Of course, as it stands now, Girlies aren't standing in line to solve the day-care problem, either. Brown beat Friedan to the best-seller list, meaning her book was either pre-feminism or protofeminist. But politics is what could make the difference between today's confident culture-makers and Helen Gurley Brown. Clearly, it's much easier to be a girl. And yet the thing about being only a girl, even a fierce one, is that it's a perishable power. At some point, every girl becomes a woman.

ARE YOU THERE, GIRLIES? IT'S ME, POLITICS.

As feminists, *we* love Girlie because it makes feminism relevant and fun and in the moment. Because we love it, we want to maximize its bloom, and see if it can thrive in a political context, one that was missing for Brown. A lot of what Girlie radiates is the luxury of self-expression that most Second Wavers didn't feel they could or should indulge in. Other women wouldn't choose the knitting, miniskirts, or Barbies, anyway. But Girlie culture can be a trap of conformity, just with a new style. "Culture is always tied to material movements; you are not going to create a revolution through culture," says Pam Warren of the band the Coup, responding to the depoliticization of hip-hop.

With Girlie, there is danger that Spice Girls Pencil Set Syndrome will settle in: girls buy products created by male-owned companies that capture the slogan of feminism, without the power. Kathleen Hanna describes it this way: "The thing that disturbs me now, with the commercialization, is I fear that young girls will be encouraged to stop there. That young girls will go buy their Spice Girls notebook and not go to the library or the gay or feminist bookstores. But, deep down, I think people are smarter than that and when they experience girl power in the real form, they'll get excited and seek out more information."

As Third Wave women who relate to Girlie, we want to

know the difference between saying we want equal pay and knowing how to go about getting it. Or realizing that *Jane* can try to bridge feminism for a new generation of regular girls at the mall, but the message itself is hard to get out when its editors had to fight to get a two-page political column (as they did for a year before the column debuted). As defiant or cool as Jane Pratt is, the fact remains that her expression of feminism was first in the hands of a conservative white guy (Patrick McCarthy, the original owner) who loves Henry Hyde, and now of Condé Nast (no bastion of feminism, rest assured), and both depend on editorially sucking up to advertisers to make profits. Her feminism is caged. In essence, each of these women needs feminism to keep going: Pratt needs to own the magazine, or the owner and advertisers need to raise their consciousness and ethical practices. Meanwhile, the Spice Girls might have fired their Svengali in 1997, and Ginger might have moved on to an autonomous career, but they still don't understand that trumpeting milk-snatcher Thatcher is like any woman or person of color cheering on Clarence Thomas—a man who voted against affirmative action any chance he got. (Politically, Margaret Thatcher was Reagan with ovaries. Women didn't gain much under her prime ministership in terms of equality. Everyone did get a dashing of stereotypes surrounding female leadership, which certainly counts for something.)

That said, the spirit of Girlie is crucial to sustain. Anastasia Higginbotham is a twenty-eight-year-old writer and feminist in New York City, who for many years was a writer for the advocacy organization Girls Incorporated. After the college rituals of feminist liberation (cutting off her big Wonder Woman pretty hair and trading in the teetery heels for chunky combat boots), she found that she still hungered for those very accoutrements she so distrusts. She says:

> Lately, I've been buying pictures of these very coquettish pinup women at antique shows, and putting them up on the wall. I feel like I am trying to reconnect with this part of myself. It's

totally personal, but it's something I have to do. I am so hyper-vigilant about what kind of signals I send out that might get the wrong response. I can't be that girl with the long hair and the sexy clothes that I would actually like to wear, because I have internalized the belief that if some rape or violent attack happened to me, I would deserve it. I know better. Welcome to the world, I'd think. . . . You can't look and act like a sexed-up little girl and think that people aren't gonna treat you like a child and infantilize you—and still wanna fuck you.

So what happens is, Higginbotham is divided against herself, worrying that her desire to wear sexy clothes or to have attention is the result of brainwashing and destined to set her up for punishment; but, deep down, she knows that her need for sexual expression is real and hungry. She shouldn't have to starve herself of these desires, but she does, in an attempt to be safe rather than sorry, and typically feminist rather than typically feminine. On the other hand, Joan Morgan has no problem choosing the Girlie persona, right down to the Helen Gurley Brown–style wiles. As she wrote in *When Chickenheads Come Home to Roost*:

[If violated] we're not afraid of lawsuits, boycotts, organized protests, or giving the deserving offender a good cussing out. But we also recognize that there are times when winning requires a lighter touch. And sometimes a short skirt and a bat of the eye is not only easier but infinitely more effective.

Some people—women who have been abused or against whom enforced infantilism has been used as a weapon—can't yet choose the Girlie-girl persona. "The Butt" author Erin Aubry, for example, shakes her own world when she dons a pair of tight jeans. For others, sexiness might not be a sign of freedom but of childhood sexual abuse that has trained them to believe they have only a sexual value. Like Higginbotham, some women who have a love-hate relationship with Girlie might be reacting to something that exists. Society isn't safe for women and girls, and *everybody* runs the risk, Girlie or not, of objectification or even rape. In fact, what you're wearing or how old you are has nothing to do with being picked as a victim.

So feminism needs Girlie and Girlie needs feminism. *Minx*, a Girlie webzine and Internet talk show at Pseudo.com in New York City, is staffed by women who have no problem promoting the Girlie-girl persona. Their voice is confident, sexually bold, and into having best girlfriends, lots of boyfriends, and respect. Melissa Huffsmith and Shannon O'Kelley White are both cute rocker-type girls, with leather pants and bangs and two-tone streaked hair like punked-out Pepe Le Pews. Both left female slackerdom as bartenders to join the hopping but nascent world of on-line media. Pioneers of women's webzines, they have been profiled in *The New York Times*, *San Francisco Weekly*, and *Ms.*

White described *Minx*'s relationship to feminism this way: "I don't like to put a big label on it, but I believe in being treated fairly and I think everybody should. I don't think feminists are really seen as hating men anymore." Of course, feminism never meant hating men, but White, like many younger feminists, has been as subject to media stereotype as the rest of us. "We like men," she continues. "We like women, we like ourselves, and we just want to be treated fairly for what we do and what we work hard for, and we want to say whatever we want to say and not be called, like, some bitchy feminist or a cranky bitch who feels mistreated. I mean, we do get mistreated, and things aren't fair. All you can do is make an effort to try to expose those things. And make an effort to change them."

Their confidence and ability to embrace the beauty of being a girl is inspiring and infectious but, apart from believing that "people should be treated fairly" and "making an effort" to change inequities, the *Minx* girls have no framework or strategy for transforming the sexism—"mistreatment"—they confront in their own lives. Instead of the kind of connections being made that could foster social change, *Minx* stops at the rant, a manifesto without the necessary tools to make it a plan of action. "We demand satisfaction," reads its Web site raison d'être. "Meaning: Don't waste our time. Stay true to your word. Equal pay for equal work. And make us come."

They agree that men and women should be treated the same, but how to achieve this is off their political radar. For instance, at the time the interview was conducted, the *Minx* girls had been given word that they were to hand their newly decorated office over to some guys who ran another show on Pseudo. Meanwhile, two other women who worked on *Minx* had been fired from Pseudo after complaining about the male-owned company's sexist atmosphere. Those two former Minxers took political action and have since filed sex-discrimination suits with the EEOC. Huffsmith says that she feels writing for *Minx* is more effective than getting behind a politician or going to a march. Indeed, it could be, if she were proposing a Day of Pay Equity, sort of like Take Our Daughters to Work Day, and reported the evidence of egregious sexism to the EEOC. Or, if she wrote about the politics of her personal situation. Without any action or comprehension of where action is called for, talk is cheap.

The mature Girlie feminist is somewhere between the woman who believes she must be grimly vigilant or she'll get screwed, and the bold *Minx/Bust/Jane* girls, who want it all but don't necessarily want to figure out how to change anything. If we're strong enough to handle sexy clothes and Barbie dolls, then we should be strong enough to read Andrea Dworkin and other analyses of power, and still feel in touch with why we love skinny rocker boys or false eyelashes. The feminist transformation comes from the political theory *and* the cultural confidence. We can't afford to overlook the real barriers to women's liberation.

"All of that Girlie stuff feels right to me," says Lisa Silver, the feminist and journalism professor at NYU who worked with Betty Friedan. She is more comfortable with the women who create *Bust* than with the red-suited businesswomen. Silver sees the "spark" in Girlie and believes that pro-sexy representations underscore that women have a sexuality and can be as lustful as men. "However, Girlie as an ideology," continues Silver, "is not a rallying point. It's something we can all connect on—but now what? What do we believe? With the old feminists, they had something to work toward, like the ERA with all of its problems. All of the pro-pornography, pro-strippers, that's all fine, but ultimately, to my mind, so *what*? Unless it leads to something else."

Without a body of politics, the nail polish is really going to waste.

CHAPTER FIVE

Barbie vs. the Menstrual Kit

To Be or Not to Be Ophelia

The redheaded and freckled adolescent Maybonne is the Ophelia whom everyone is trying to revive. She is a study in self-consciousness and humiliation. She loathes her hair, her face, her body, and her wacky younger sister, Marlys, who, despite being in the same boat as Maybonne, has the confidence of Pippi Longstocking. Their folks are divorced, and they live with their grandma because Mom is a deadbeat on a par with Dad. Maybonne cannot seem to find joy in doing the funky chicken or the "Guess what? What? Chicken butt?" joke anymore, both glorious pastimes of Marlys's. Instead, she engages in cruel truth sessions with the popular girls' circle she desperately wants to break into and makes out with a boy who makes it clear that he just wants to use her for getting to bases. She's annoying and funny, a passive slug and a smart cookie, amazingly self-obsessed and incredibly good-hearted.

Maybonne houses an inner child who occasionally tries to remind her of the lively girl she used to be. "I'm such a dog," says Maybonne on a typical day. "No, you are gorgeous," says her inner child. Back and forth they spar, young Maybonne bragging about her exploits, present-day Maybonne dragging her down.

"I liked bugs! Here, hold this bug," says young Maybonne. "You were a weirdo," replies present-day Maybonne. "Remember my great dancing?" asks her young self, getting down. "You looked so stupid. And you didn't care that you looked stupid," says present-day Maybonne. To which young Maybonne replies, "Because I actually looked great."

Unlike her once-confident self, Maybonne now pants frantically for approval from anyone and everyone. Maybonne is the girl that people mean when they say that, at around age eleven, girls confront a crisis in self-esteem. She is also a cartoon character created by Lynda Barry.

GILLIGAN'S ISLE

Just sit right back and you'll hear a tale, a tale of a girl's grim
  fate
That started in her youthful bloom
Around the age of eight.
The girl was a mighty androgyne: intelligent, brave, and
  strong.
Until she met with puberty
And everything went wrong.
Mathematics started getting tough, when questioned, she went
  mute.
But then came the studies that revealed her plight,
And bore such telling fruit.
And bore such telling fruit.
The concept grew from one insight but launched an industry,
  composed of Gilligan.
New Moon, too.
Foundations
Of all kinds

All that could be seen, was failing self-esteem.
It's here! On Gilligan's Isle!

—JENNIFER BAUMGARDNER AND ANASTASIA HIGGINBOTHAM
a 1995 moment of clarity during Take Our Daughters to Work Day

"I'm never not my true self," says Jackie, age thirteen, in one of the breakout groups on Take Our Daughters to Work Day 1999 at the United Nations. She has braces on her teeth and silver sparkles on her eyes, and she wants to be a professional soccer player. "I always say what's on my mind, because if people don't like it, that's their problem." Heads nod.

It's April 22, 1999. Three hundred girls of diverse racial and ethnic backgrounds dot the pastel leather seats of the General Assembly, their feet barely grazing the floor, and teeny plastic butterfly clips scattered across the tops of their heads. Of the 188 ambassadors who normally fill this room, only 10 are women, which accounts for the single bathroom stall for females in the hall outside of the auditorium. Although the girls are giddily excited about seeing the actress Marlo Thomas, actress-model Isabella Rossellini, model-actress–Swedish goodwill ambassador Vendela, and the lawyer wife of the secretary general Nane Annan talk about their work and economic independence, the real topic for the day is self-esteem and girls' lack of it.

"I'm Andrea Johnston, I'm fifty-four, and I'm white," says a flustered-looking older woman with a New York accent to the group of mainly young women serving as mentors for the day. Johnston is the creator of Girls Speak Out, one of the original programs of the girls' movement. This project was designed to address females' failing self-esteem by teaching girls prepatriarchal history, and *Girls Speak Out* is also the title of Johnston's book. In 1994, Johnston, a former public-school teacher and journalist in California, began doing Talks for Girls (which was renamed Girls Speak Out preceding her book's publication), inspired by her desire to get women's history off the college campus and into girls' lives. A popular organizer in the wake of the girls' movement, she makes a point of always including girls themselves in her programs and public appearances. "I'll be walking around with the Swedish goodwill ambassador," says Johnston, who is the moderator for today's festivities. "Another white woman, so that sucks."

She passes the discussion topics out to the mentors, each of whom will be leading groups of twenty-five girls. Many of the girls are international students at the UN school; some are kids from public schools in New York City. Once they've been divided into groups, the mentors are supposed to keep their eyes peeled for two girls who can address the whole group at the end. "Two girls from each group or two girls in all?" asks a young woman from UNIFEM (United Nations Development Fund for Women). "*Two in all*. If it were two from each group, that'd be forty girls up there talking, and we'd all die of boredom," replies the woman whose career is based on making girls heard. "Anything you ask the girls, you should be prepared to answer," warns Johnston, using a lifeguard ("No Running by the Pool!") tone of voice. "Now, somebody tell me about a time when you couldn't be yourself." None of the twenty or so mentors offer a story. "See? Nobody could come up with anything spontaneous," she says, and offers her own story about not feeling as if she belonged when she was a girl.

The mentors then break off with their groups and begin to talk to the girls. The following are among the suggested questions: "Tell us about a time when you felt you could be yourself," "When do you feel pressure to be different from your true self?" and the supremely hypothetical, "How would girls' lives be different if they could hold on to their true selves all their lives?" The girls look at Johnston as if she were speaking another language. Perhaps she is. She came of age in decidedly more oppressive times, experiencing a gender-segregated world without a glimmering that things could, or would, change. (Most terrible of all, one supposes, many Second Wavers went through this time without a sense that things *should* change.)

There are many unfortunate ironies on this particular girls' day. The main one is that Johnston can't even acknowledge the success of the present day—a roomful of three hundred girls and their twenty-something "mentors" saying that they've never lost their voice. This is a generational disconnect, and it's not only between girls and women but between younger women and older women. As the barriers of sexism recede, thanks to feminism, the length of time in which we are disconnected from our "true selves" shrinks. For instance, many of the young women whom we interviewed for this book described their late teens as the most troubling.

In some ways, Johnston surveying a roomful of beaming girls and focusing on unseen perils replicates what happened to Carol Gilligan's influential book *In a Different Voice*. Gilligan's work is thought by many to have inspired the girls' movement. "The least discussed parts of the book are still the two central chapters that are [about] women right after *Roe v. Wade*," said Gilligan in a 1999 interview with us for this book. She continues:

[The two chapters in question are about the moment] when the societal resonance shifts and women actually bring their voices, struggling with the question of really being present both in their personal lives and in public life. [The moment when a woman has] a decisive voice and doesn't call it selfish but calls it responsible. I think the focus on the one [eleven-year-old] girl in the book was a reluctance to deal with the implication of the women [in the chapters dealing with the abortion-decision study] saying that if you have no voice, you do not have a relationship. You aren't a participant.

By also focusing on this often mythical loss of girls' sense of self, Johnston is overlooking the successes of feminism—and the girls' movement—and not acknowledging that it is her own loss that she's concerned with. In other words, "When did you lose a part of yourself" is the wrong question for Take Our Daughters to Work Day, and perhaps in any conversation with girls today. To find a more appropriate question for young girls, we have to look at the birth and development of the girls' movement.

In 1982, Carol Gilligan, a former modern dancer with a bi-racial Cleveland troupe and, later, a tenured professor of psychology at Harvard, published *In a Different Voice*. It begins: "Over the past ten years, I have been listening to people talking about morality and about themselves." During her years in academia, Gilligan found that the lack of women's voices in the study of psychology rang out to her. She noticed that even when women were in what she thought of as the human conversation, it was still a male discourse. Her own classes were no different. Female students would ask insightful questions, and she would hear herself say, "That's a great question, but we're talking about . . . ," redirecting their comments to a topic deemed important by a prescribed male norm. Once Gilligan realized that she was helping to socialize women toward the patriarchy, she set out to make the conversation one in which women's and men's voices were equally valued.

With *In a Different Voice*, Gilligan was providing a psychological road map for bringing female interior monologues into the public domain. "The different voice I describe is characterized not by gender but by theme . . . ," she writes. "Clearly, these differences arise in a social context where factors of social status and power combine with reproductive biology to shape the experience of males and females. . . . My interest lies in the interaction of experience and thought, in different voices and the dialogues to which they give rise, in the way we listen to ourselves and to others, in the stories we tell about our lives." Gilligan elaborated on this idea of socialization and expression in our interview with her. "Female voices were breaking into a conversation that was itself political, but was being called objective," she said. Therefore a different voice is heard the minute women enter into the conversation—"the conversation shifts, because things that had been held inside of us as women came out and gave a different resonance, which changed the conversation for everyone." She considered the work she was doing with women to be political because, as she puts it, "If you don't have a voice, you don't have a choice."

Like consciousness-raising groups in the early seventies, paying attention to women's stories reinforces their experiences and distinguishes them from the white noise of the patriarchy. Listening to themselves and to each other, women in CR groups began to realize that they had more in common than not—from illegal abortions to the second shift for women (housework after out-of-the-house work). CR was revolutionary, sparking public and political participation. But over time CR became marginalized; these exchanges among women happened mostly in their own homes and women-only spaces. By contrast, Gilligan's work came out of the most sacred bastion for training elite men: Harvard. Creating an acoustical chamber of women's voices within those ivy-covered walls would seem to have broader repercussions—or, at least, more credibility—than it would in women's houses.

By 1982, when Gilligan's work hit the public, it was mid-backlash, and consciousness-raising was about as popular as phone booth–stuffing. Within the movement itself, CR remained a popular escape from the backlash—a place to confirm that progress still needed to be made—and it began to exist in other forms, such as networking groups, book clubs, and covens. The ERA had just slipped into a coma: this simple amendment had been successfully misrepresented as asserting that women were the *same* as men and former debutantes would be forced to pee in urinals while male construction workers made quiche. But *In a Different Voice* managed to squeak through during this anti-feminist time. Perhaps this was because, in the face of the painful defeats of the late seventies and eighties, Gilligan's work could be construed as comforting, a salve. No Shulamith Firestonesque call for technology to take over childbirth, no Kate Millett–like withering of the phallocracy; instead, Gilligan's work called for the appreciation of women's voices, their different values and views.

Gilligan politicized women's "different" voices as being in opposition to the patriarchy, but even though her book was widely read and praised by feminists, it wasn't initially used to break out of the masculinist patterns that she analyzed. (Masculinism is the assumption that male ideas and values are natural and neutral, as opposed to learned and loaded. The related idea is that anything female is superfluous.) Bearing this out, the two chapters she said posed a challenge to masculinism— "Women's Rights and Women's Judgment" and "Crisis and Transition," which deal explicitly with the implications of *Roe v. Wade*—were overlooked by the same women who embraced the book. (But perhaps this was lucky. Given the anti-feminist tenor of the country at the time, the book might have been buried along with the ERA.) *In a Different Voice* affirmed that patriarchy had not receded enough to allow something so real as a constitutional acknowledgment of women's rights. In doing this, she took the pressure off burned-out Second Wavers who had busted their butts for the ERA and universal day care and gotten neither. Gilligan said to them, Free your voice, and your rights will follow.

Nearly a decade later, Gilligan built on the discovery of an untapped voice and turned her attention to preadolescent and adolescent girls. With co-authors Nona Lyons and Trudy Hanmer, she researched and wrote *Making Connections*, which linked the voices of girls and women at the Emma Willard School, an all-girls boarding school in Troy, New York. *Making Connections* was truly groundbreaking. Until this book came along only boys had been researched, so girls made no appearance in the *Handbook of Adolescent Psychology*, the *Gray's Anatomy* of teen behavior, and weren't part of even the most rudimentary study of human conditioning. "[Our] studies are designed to connect a psychology of women with girls' voices," Gilligan wrote. "[We] have come to begin a study of adolescence—to think about what 'development' means for girls coming of age in the late twentieth century." The book identified the time between ages eleven and sixteen as an "especially critical one in girls' lives," Gilligan noted. The crisis was one of relationship.

Taking a sort of "pro-girl line," to adapt the Girlies' approach, Gilligan assumed that the girls who mute their voices à la Maybonne aren't doing it out of self-loathing so much as they are making the best decision—what she refers to as "brilliant but costly moves"—given their circumstances. Girls are actively making these moves to keep relationships intact, relationships that are part of their self-esteem, as opposed to simply springing a self-respect leak due to the wounds of sexism. Girls had to build a resistance to the patriarchy, in the organized-underground-fighting-against-a-dictator sense of that word—and she saw women as girls' natural allies. In fact, girls would inspire women to take on some of that preadolescent verve and firepower they used to have in order to make choices and have a decisive voice. Gilligan believed that speaking up for oneself was responsible rather than selfish. "I remember going to Marie [Wilson, president of the Ms. Foundation for Women] and saying that I can go into any school and amplify girls' voices and it wakes the women and they get involved in political action," Gilligan says. "I think the grassroots implications are amazing."

Her conclusion in both of these books was essentially that women would tap into their voices when they once again formed strong relationships with other women. She implied that it is those very relationships that are our most profound weapon against sexism. Only when women are sounding boards for one another, affirming those interior monologues and adding to a chorus of voices, will we have the confidence and centrality to eventually change what society values.

Yet many Girlies, girls and young women today, having grown up with feminism, never lost relationships with other women. In other ways, Gilligan's message is analogous to the "love what you got" credo of Girlie writers, unbeknownst to Girlies themselves or to Gilligan. In fact, before *Bust* and Jane Pratt and all the other young femmes raised their besparkled middle fingers to all of this "it sucks to be a girl" news, Gilligan was there saying "girl is good—hold on to it." In essence, her work shattered the idea that teaching girls to take on male values is any better or more authentic than forcing them into stereotypically female roles; in fact, it's the same hijacking of selfhood and autonomy. And when Girlies claim Barbies, pink, eye shadow, and knitting to be as valid as trucks, blue, combat boots, and sports, that's all part of the resistance, too. Both are attempting to put girls' "voices"—broadly defined as what girls like, think about, talk about, and what moves them—into the human conversation. (What girls like depends on the individual girl. Of course, some girls love "boy" things—and those preferences should be valued, too.)

Gilligan and her colleagues' findings in *Making Connections* were a match held to the Orlon shirt of the Reagan-Bush–inspired culture wars. Around the same time, small bands of feminist women calling themselves Lesbian Avengers, Women's Action Coalition, and Riot Grrrls were permeating communities across the United States, and the movement was experiencing a surge of activism by a new generation. Meanwhile, Gloria Steinem, whose profile had been the very picture of thin, tanned-yet-Gandhi-like confidence, wrote a book that included several anecdotes about her own struggles with liking herself, and generally tried to forge a link between inner and outer revolution. She put a political spin on the term *inner child*, and identified the attainment of self-esteem for an oppressed individual—a "revolution from within"—to be the source of strength for public victory. *Revolution from Within* was a best-seller, as was Susan Faludi's *Backlash*, which documented in exquisite detail and hard, cold facts the attempt to "roll back" American feminism—an ordeal that was as tough as anything we put the Communists through. In the face of roughly fifteen years of some tactical defeats, plus running very hard to stay in the same place, girls became the Trojan horse for the Second Wave's political repositioning.

Gilligan's work was ostensibly good news, yet the flurry of research it spawned tended to accentuate the negative aspects of *not* being a boy. And the study itself was primarily based on privileged white girls yet ended up being applied to all girls. Much like CR, a feminist tool with radical social implications that was sometimes reduced to a self-improvement meeting, girls' empowerment went from looking at what girls had to lamenting what they then "lost" as teenagers. Within the study of psychology, girls went from being invisible to being vulnerable. A group of women and women's organizations turned their gaze on adolescent girls, and gathered a body of evidence that linked retrograde treatment of females in school with lowered ambitions and self-esteem. First came a report by the National Council for Research on Women for the Ms. Foundation called "Risk, Resiliency, and Resistance: Current Research on Adolescent Girls." Then a more critical take on the status of girls: an American Association of University Women (AAUW) Educational Foundation report, "How Schools Shortchange Girls," which revealed among many things the high incidence of sexual harassment in schools, asserting that this abuse began as early as age nine and followed girls through the senior prom. This depressing news was followed by *Failing at Fairness*, a book by Myra and David Sadker, which reported that teachers were more likely to respond when boys called out than when girls did. Somehow, between Gilligan's theories of resistance through relationships and everyone else's catalog of what there was to resist, a girls' movement was born.

It was, however, the best-selling success of *Reviving Ophelia*, by therapist Mary Pipher, that truly nudged these ideas into the mainstream. Pipher's research came from her clients, adolescent girls with problems. *Reviving Ophelia* carried stories of teenage girls' desperation into suburbia and Girl Scout troop meetings, and secured a prominent placement in public libraries. Her book resonated, in part, because her audience, which was moms, dads, and other adults who cared about young girls, had already been warmed up to its ideas. Like most of the work that has come out of the girls' movement, *Reviving Ophelia* was *about* girls, but it was *for* adults.

Helping girls be "visible, valued, and heard" is part of the agenda of the Ms. Foundation. Girls Speak Out harbors a "healthy resilience." Girls Inc. wants to keep girls "strong, smart, and bold." And *New Moon* magazine is committed to "listening to girls and their dreams." Girls' initiatives spawned books and movies for and about girls in crisis, which in turn spawned magazines and games and more money allocated to girls' programming. At the Ms. Foundation, for example, programs for girls received $610,650 more in 1999 than they did in 1992, the year before the foundation launched its hugely successful Take Our Daughters to Work Day (TODTWD). In 1992, grants given to support girls' programming amounted to $42,500; in 1999, the funding amounted to $653,150—not including money raised and devoted to TODTWD.

"What [feminists] started in the sixties went underground for a while," Gilligan told us. "But now," at the cusp of the twenty-first century, "it is resurfacing, coming of age." The girls' movement has at its core inarguably and incontrovertibly positive goals. It even seeks to liberate boys from the pressures of masculinity through classroom curricula and by exposing boys to doing what girls can do. And it has been so successful in part because girls aren't threatening—to *anyone*. Including feminists. (Unless, of course, you are Christina Hoff Sommers or another more conservative or professional anti-feminist writer, and then you think of Take Our Daughters to Work Day and Company as part of a highly threatening campaign to neglect boys. She counters claims of girls' lagging science scores or high rate of suicide attempts with the fact that boys lag in reading and outscore girls in actual deaths by suicide. Boys, apparently, are better than girls even at suicide.)

To many young women the work of the girls' movement is important *and* infuriating. Infuriating because this attention on girls has meant, in part, that young women and their contributions to feminism have been overlooked. Some people have responded to this invisibility by saying "girls and young women," but the subject behind such a statement is still girls. After all, the issues young women must deal with are very different from those that girls experience.

Now, ten years after Carol Gilligan presented her paradigmatic research on what it means to be eleven, female, and dealing with the restrictions of an unchosen femininity that descends on you, a veritable cottage industry has been forced out of the fertile soil of girls' failing self-esteem. Similar to the early women's movement, the emphasis on girls has been profoundly successful, especially in terms of launching a feminist idea into the mainstream.

GIRLS! GIRLS! GIRLS!

On February 2, 1992, a thirty-nine-year-old communications strategist named Nell Merlino pitched a five-page proposal to the Ms. Foundation. Ms. wanted to use the bleak research about girls' self-esteem to launch a strategy that would goose the successful but semiobscure twenty-year-old foundation and boost its National Girls Initiative, a small program that had been in existence since 1989. They also hoped to expand the children's programs that had been funded by the proceeds from *Free to Be . . . You and Me* since 1975.

Merlino likes to think big. She came to PR strategizing from union organizing in the sixties, and worked on political campaigns for Michael Dukakis, among others. She had already collaborated on a highly successful New York City–based AIDS-awareness campaign, and managed to get one million people into Central Park for Earth Day. Having worked on huge campaigns for controversial and really quite dismal subjects, she knew that the depressing statistics the foundation had asked her to publicize were exactly what news agencies ignored. She was flummoxed about how she would get the word out on girls without making it a recommendation for subsidized therapy in grade school. Loss, she decided, was not going to be the focus of her proposal.

Coincidentally, a few days before the proposal was due, Merlino found herself at a retirement party for her father, a longtime Democratic New Jersey state senator. "I was seeing his entire life at this dinner," says Merlino, now the president and CEO of Strategy Communication Action, a public-relations firm in New York. "There were neighbors, colleagues from every job he'd ever had, other officeholders. Seeing his whole life made me realize how much of it was connected to work." In that moment, Merlino knew "that the *workplace* was the place for girls to begin to hold on to their sense of identity and power."

She sat down the next day and wrote:

As you requested, I have developed a strategy that would focus unprecedented public and press attention on the National Girls Initiative while integrating your goals to educate the public and change the image of girls in the media. In turn, the National Girls Initiative strategy I recommend will also focus greater attention on the Ms. Foundation's overall activities, thereby gaining wider media exposure and public credibility.

She went on to describe a phenomenon that has become a theme, of sorts, of the girls' movement:

The emotional and moral content of the National Girls Initiative is overwhelming and inspiring. Every woman I have spoken to about the project has expressed a deep and familiar response. Women remember when authenticity left them, when they lost their voice, when they abandoned their true selves.

Merlino's vision was, of course, Take Our Daughters to Work Day, and the loss she described is women's. Merlino's own relationship with her father was indicative of the time before feminism, when it was absolutely normal to hand out cigars when "It's a Boy!" and smile wanly when a daughter is born. In Merlino's case, her father handed out cigars at her birth—as he did for all of his kids—but he had been mistakenly told that she *was* a boy. Furthermore, her mother, an accomplished amateur painter who displayed Donna Reed–era devotion to her husband, ran for office after Mr. Merlino was defeated, but Nell recalls that her mother bristled at the old-boys network, or hardball, side of politics. With this familiar example in mind, Merlino wanted people to come to terms with how much more present women were going to be in every walk of life and chose to do so by "literally flooding subway cars" with as many girls as there were adults. "I wanted America to have that image in their minds so that they could see that, five or ten years from now, there were going to be that many of us doing *everything*." She tells a story of one girl that embodies why TODTWD is revolutionary:

A principal named Pat Black said a company that needed an entry-level person in computers called her. Pat said that a senior girl who lived somewhere on the Lower East Side [of New York City] and who was the top of her class in computers was just the person. The girl gets all hooked up. The day comes. The girl does not show up at the interview. Pat is very concerned because she's seen the girl's record. She calls the girl's teacher, speaks to the girl, and finds out that the girl had never been out of the Lower East Side. She did not know how to get to this place, she got too scared, and she just didn't go. So the teacher gives her a map to the subway, they talk about how she's gonna get there and, again, she does not go. Pat now has her home number. She calls her. "What the hell happened this time?" "I got the number of that place," said the girl. "But the office was so big, I've never seen anything like that." Anyway, the third time, the girl's teacher actually went with her. And she got the job. But the issue of exposure and experience for girls is critical.

Still, when Merlino pitched her idea, women on the Ms. Foundation's board criticized the program as being insufficiently sensitive to homeless mothers, women on welfare, and others for whom the workplace wasn't a positive image. In fact, the first question that the then president of the board asked Merlino, hands on hips, was "And are the daughters of prostitutes going to go to work with their mothers?" This question prompted the proposal in question to be changed from "your" daughters to "our," in order to broaden beyond the biological bond. The Ms. Foundation's president, Marie Wilson, went for the idea, albeit with reservations, as a pilot program for girls in New York City. But after the event was announced in *Parade* magazine,[40] the letters from homeless women, women on welfare, and women whose lives weren't what they wanted for their daughters sounded a message that was poignant and clear: even if they couldn't take their daughter to work, they sincerely wanted *someone* to.

The Ms. Foundation had never before had a program that garnered as much media attention as TODTWD. More than one million people participated that first year—from as far away as Fargo, North Dakota, and Tokyo—and most were left to create their own ad hoc activities, since the foundation hadn't anticipated the huge success of the program. A mere two years into the event, its circle of corporate sponsors, many of which were new to funding feminist causes, was impressive: Merrill Lynch, Deloitte & Touche, New York Life, the Limited, NYNEX, *The New York Times*, Amoco, Morgan Stanley, IBM, Ortho Pharmaceutical, and *People*. By 1999, fifty-six million adults had participated in Take Our Daughters to Work Day, then in its sixth year, and more than nineteen million girls had personally gone to work. After the first year, the program got so large that the Ms. Foundation lost control of it, and the political message—that the workplace had to change in order to prepare for all the future women workers who would expect to be equally valued and successful—was sometimes watered down. This is surely one reason that right-wing women, like Texas senator Kay Bailey Hutchison, visibly supported the day.

Furthermore, participation hardly meant that everyone was ready for the consciousness change that was supposed to go along with the day. For example, an emergency room in North Carolina brought in a group of girls, and instead of showing them what it was like to be a doctor or a paramedic, the hospital staff provided the girls with makeup and hair rollers. Gaffes on that scale were rare, but more common was giving the girls goody bags filled with fun, corporate-endorsed products at the end of the day, instead of a real workplace experience. On a related note, actresses and models were often used as mentors, making the day more about getting autographs than about girls being visible—and certainly not a first step in a likely occupation. To cite just one example, in 1995, MTV brought in Tyra Banks to talk about being a supermodel. There is no doubt that Banks is incredibly successful, but hers is a career aspiration that hardly needs to be reinforced as the domain of women. (And, to paraphrase the much-discredited *Newsweek* story about a thirty-five-year-old woman's chances of getting married, a girl is more likely to be killed in a terrorist attack than to attain famous-modeldom.)

Anastasia Higginbotham, an outspoken advocate for girls, who escorted a group of girls from East Harlem to a big company on the big day, is instructive about the program. "It's not just an opportunity for your company to pose for photos with 'hard-luck' girls or to load them up with a lot of products featuring your logo," she says. "You have to prepare for it." Higginbotham values what Take Our Daughters to Work Day can accomplish, but she insists that success depends upon the adults' willingness to take the time to engage the girls in something worthwhile.

Even when the company gets it and prepares for the day, the workplace hasn't changed enough to maximize taking our daughters to work. Although she eventually praised the program, Katha Pollitt initially raised the concern that most mothers who have jobs outside the home work in traditional female "pink-collar" professions, and young girls hardly needed to be introduced to the low-pay, low-respect ghetto that awaited them. Many girls go to corporate offices and see that women are the secretaries and men are the executives. Or, if they go with their parents, it may mean going to work with Dad because Mom works at home or her work just isn't as "important." (With that in mind, perhaps there should be a Take Our Sons Home Day, which is what Gloria Steinem says boys need, a semi-serious suggestion on her part.)

Imperfections aside, there is no doubt that Take Our Daughters to Work Day *does* educate the public, and did officially spawn a wave of attention to girls, which supported the beginning of a girls' movement. In South Carolina, there is Wings, a girls' empowerment group; in New York there is Sista II Sista, and more places to hang out, like the Lower Eastside Girls' Club; on-line, there are thousands of Web sites for girls, many of which are girl-operated, as well as companies such as Girl Tech, Girl Games, Smart Girl (the largest Web site for girls on the Internet, which, unfortunately, doubles as a market-research firm); there is Girls' Pages, Girl to Girl, Girls' Place, *Girls Like Us* (which is the title of both a book of adult women writing about their girlhood and an unrelated documentary about five teenage girls living in South Philadelphia), Girl's Project, Healthy Girls/Healthy Women, the Girls Advisory Board of the Empower Program, Young Sisters of Justice, and the First Moon Passage to Womanhood Ceremony.

Even the head of Health and Human Services got into the girl action: In 1997, Donna Shalala poured millions into Girl Power, a program designed to help keep young females "healthy, smart, and strong"—the first girl-centered public-health initiative. After magazines like *New Moon, Blue Jean, Teen Voices, XX Empowered: The Magazine for Young Females* (which lasted about three issues), there was an explosion of books geared toward girls (*Brave New Girls, Girls and Women Leading the Way, Daughters of the Moon, Sisters of the Sun*), which parents gobbled up like chicken soup for Ophelia's soul.

All of the successful girls' movement "products," such as

New Moon and the 1999 book *Ophelia Speaks*, have the *desire* to be girl-centered and -inspired at their heart. But what did this proliferation of media and programming add up to for girls? On the one hand, it provided a space for girls to celebrate their girlhood. On the other, it produced high visibility of girls as victims of society.

That rap plays out this way: one of the goals of the Ms. Foundation is to help girls be "free from victimhood," presuming that girls *are* victims—of society's contempt, of boys, and of the patriarchy. The money came in for Ms. to cure girls of low self-esteem. The problem is not that we can't simultaneously acknowledge girls' strength and sexism; it is that girls are being labeled victims of society and, by implication, passive dupes—whether or not they themselves feel this way. Just as women deserve feminism not to protect them from men or porn but to afford them the same protections men enjoy in the eyes of the law, girls primarily deserve the same access to opportunities that boys have. Or, if there is a need for remedial treatment, given the perils of sexism, the call for it should come from the girls themselves.

With regard to a girls' movement, it's genuine only if we truly listen to girls, even when they reveal that they actually like Barbie and boy- and beauty-crazy teen magazines and giggle during the menarche celebrations. Which is to say, even when they like things we don't want them to like. As such, the women in the girls' movement need to take a page from Girlie; feminists who work with girls need to tap into girl culture instead of setting up a narrow "feminist" straw girl to replace the pink and frilly ideal (leaving room, of course, for the girl who wants to wear Toughskins or play with dump trucks). We need to listen to girls instead of lecturing them.

If you go back to the genesis of any program, book, or magazine that now comprises the girls' empowerment movement, you'll probably find a woman who is revisiting the ghosts of her childhood. This movement is not just *led* by adult women, in the tradition of Scout leaders and Brownie troop mothers; it is, in many ways, *for* adult women. Tangled in the Second Wave's dedication to the girls' movement—and the frequent implication that it's a selfless movement for our daughters—is the harsh fact that the shelf life of older women is short, many years shorter than that of men. Feminist women, therefore, may be masking their ambitions—which are considered unseemly or aggressive or threatening by a gynephobic society—by filtering them through girls. They also employ this tactic as an excuse to overlook the young women who are making strides right beside them. Likewise, Gilligan's work is presumed to be *for* girls, but if you look at it more closely or talk to her, it's more accurate to say that *Making Connections* is based on girls' lives but is *for* women to read, just as *In a Different Voice* was for women. Gilligan acknowledges again and again that the primary constituency of studying girls and girls' self-esteem is women. "It became essential in this work [for the adult women researchers, including Gilligan] to work through our own stuff as well," she writes.

Having a women's agenda at the root of the girls' movement is not bad or wrong or even particularly exploitative; clearly, the movement leaders are investing in the future and are committed to providing infrastructure to support girls with the clubs and resources they themselves lacked. But if the beneficiary is, in essence, changed from girls to women, some of the messages get skewed. Which is ultimately why a feministy girl-game company like Purple Moon has to shut down because of a lack of interest from girls, while Mattel makes another million dollars off Barbie. "Listening to girls" becomes telling girls what the mothers wished they could do. A day about exposing girls to the workplace—and exposing the workplace to girls—comes to be about how a previous generation lost their voices. The fact that the adult women's role in all of this isn't described accurately is largely the reason the girls' movement feels, at times, artificial—and, um, gross.

New Moon: A Magazine for Girls and Their [Parents'] Dreams

One day in 1992, Nancy Gruver was driving home to Duluth, Minnesota, from Michigan with her husband, Joe Kelly. They had gone away for the weekend specifically to rethink her career. (She had been working on a health-insurance pilot program for the state.) Gruver and Kelly had twin daughters, Nia Kelly and Mavis Gruver,[41] who were approaching the age Gruver was when she turned away from her mother. Anxious about their impending adolescence and intent on not repeating the same pattern, Gruver turned to the Gilligan and AAUW research about girls. Building on the idea of becoming allies of girls and helping them resist the patriarchy, Gruver had a sudden brainstorm: she would start a magazine with her daughters and other girls. If the whole family was working on a project together, they could hardly grow apart.

> [The magazine] really came out of my own personal needs and experiences, thinking about growing up myself as a girl. As I got older and was an adult, I realized how much of myself I had buried during my adolescence. I stopped communicating with my mother at that age—when I was about twelve. The concept that I had, and the thing that was important to me, is that it would be run by girls, that it wouldn't be my idea of what a feminist magazine for girls should be, it should be what they want it to be.

But, almost immediately, it became apparent that giving up the power to the girls was more easily said than done. The first evidence of differing perspectives came when they needed to name their new magazine. Gruver decided that the magazine should be called *Artemis*, as in the Greek goddess of the hunt and the moon, and wanted the concept of the magazine to be connected to the cycles of the moon and the cycles of women (that common experience that girls and women have). Her daughters predicted that the name wouldn't work. "We were all like no way!" says Mavis. "No girl will pick up a magazine called *Artemis*!" After six weeks of battling, *Artemis* became *New Moon: The Magazine for Girls and Their Dreams*, which debuted in March 1993. Seven years later, it's still going strong, with a worldwide circulation of 25,000, and has won many prestigious awards, including the Parents' Choice Award for best children's magazine on three separate occasions.

The meetings, publishing, and distribution take place in a sprawling old brick house on the outskirts of Duluth. At one such meeting in August 1998, eight or nine girls ranging in age from eight to fifteen are chatting and giggling as they pass around name tags and agendas for a 9:30 a.m. summertime editorial meeting. Adults at the meetings are given a strict "Guideline for Adult Observers at Girls Editorial Board Meetings," which states: "Ask questions only on breaks, share your opinion, but only if we ask, help us exercise our innate power and creativity, kids set the vision." The racial breakdown of the room is diverse in a Noah's Ark sort of way: two black girls, two Asian girls, two white girls. An eight-year-old flops on a teenager's lap. The mood is one of bubbly chaos, while each girl goes around the room naming her favorite animal and CD and offering up random stories that are chronically misheard and then restated amid giggles.

Welcome to the Girls Editorial Board meeting of *New Moon*. Molly McKinnon is a talkative redhead. She is fourteen and a half and a gymnast. (In the tradition of the Latin pop group Menudo, the girls have to retire from this gig when they are fifteen.) Alyza Bohbot is a shy, serious twelve-year-old with curly dark hair. Rachel Ostovich, thirteen, is sweet and wears two poufs of hair on top of her head. She has been on the board since *New Moon* began.

"We have a section in the magazine called 'How Aggravating!' " says McKinnon. "Girls write in about how girls are being treated unfairly. The biggest response we've had is that gym teachers are teaching their students unfairly. Like, my gym teacher tells girls to just hang on the high bar, but the boys have to do ten pull-ups. That is unfair. And we have to do push-ups on our knees, which are called 'girl push-ups,' and boys have to do them on their feet. My gym teacher also says that if it's girls against boys, it wouldn't be fair because the boys would always win and that certain boys throw like girls, and the list goes on and on and on." Bohbot says her gym teacher is sexist, too, but against boys. "She prefers girls, and if we do something wrong, she says 'Oh, that's okay.' But if a boy does it, she kicks him out or starts screaming or something," Bohbot says.

What is striking about most of the conversations is how similar the actual girls in the girls' movement are to the girls who read *Teen*. Having been reared in the wake of Second Wave feminism, they have a heightened sensitivity to inequities in gym or academics. However, a morning spent with them reveals that they *are* still talking about what affects their world: boys, worrying about how they look, feeling unpopular, competition among friends, being there as an emotional sounding board for guys, and cultivating girlfriends.

The girls are reputedly in charge of all creative content at *New Moon*. (Experience has shown, however, that girls aren't allowed to do all they want. *Minnesota Monthly* reported on a meeting where girls on the board were eager to submit cover art but were told by their twenty-seven-year-old managing editor that it wouldn't be properly sharing the fun stuff, since cover art is typically selected from submissions sent by the readers.) But where girls really don't set the vision is on the business or circulation side of the magazine. Down in the basement, a troop of adults, including the owners of the house, Kelly and Gruver, take orders for *New Moon* and associated products: *New Moon Parenting Guide*, girls' movement books, and, at that time, *HUES* magazine. Girls aren't trained or exposed to this critical—and historically male—aspect of publishing.

It is up for debate whether a magazine started in response to adults' needs can meet girls' desires. For example, the fitting-in drama, which is the staple of mainstream teen magazines, gives way to much more parent-approved girl stories. As their board-meeting conversation indicated, each of the *New Moon* girls really wants to address all the typical anxieties about popularity. Instead, their stories include international first-person narratives from girls living in Bosnia or China, and a character called Luna, who functions as a kind of mascot of the ideal feminist girl, who is, if anything, less real than Linda Barry's Maybonne. Bohbot mentions that her friends don't really read *New Moon*, preferring *Seventeen, Teen,* or *YM,* and most of the members of the editorial board admit that they like to read the teen magazines, too.

A few months after writing this chapter, we ran into Elizabeth Sprout, a Girls Editorial Board alumna, who is now a second-year student at Wellesley College, and asked her what she thought of the magazine. "I loved being part of the founding of *New Moon*," she said with obvious pride. But, she also noted her sense of the alternative magazine's accomplishment came from having been a part of a recognized element of the women's movement, and less so from reading a magazine that more truly represented her. It wasn't the product that spoke to this now adult feminist at Wellesley; it was the process she learned.

In truth, *New Moon* isn't solely an alternative to teen magazines, and the consciousness about how teen magazines hurt self-esteem is almost entirely on the part of the adults. The girls' movement definition of a girl is often the opposite of the feisty, self-empowered reclaimer of feminine culture and objects that Girlie advocates. Girlie takes the feminine and drains the weakness and inferiority from it; in the girls' movement, and specifically *New Moon*, being a girl is still a socialized weaker condition. This plays out by telling the ambitious members of the Girls Editorial Board that wanting to submit art is wanting *too much*. Girls should be encouraged to act on their own desires rather than to overdevelop the capacity to be selfless.

Barbie vs. the Menstrual Kit

Reading the literature of the so-called girls' movement presents nagging questions: Who are these books and magazines for? Who is slapping down good money for them? The answer to both questions is adult women (and maybe a few men).

Even though there is feminist consciousness tucked in these tomes (always adorned in the Modess-pad box colors of purple and pink), they don't address many of the negative messages purportedly given by teen magazines. They are still chock-full of workbook things you can do to improve yourself—in much the same way that the maligned teen magazines are—and they all start from the supposition that girls need fixing. The literature of the girls' movement might not be saying "you're not thin enough or pretty enough," but it is saying "you're not strong enough or confident enough." The dilemma, at least for feminists, is how can we support a flourishing movement of alternative girls' products—magazines, books, and menstrual-celebration kits, all of which are linked to the women's movement—and simultaneously respect the existing ones to which girls are already drawn? And how can we support girls without overlooking young women in the process?

If a girls' empowerment movement is to have any credibility at all, we have to look at what girls like and take it seriously. One of *Seventeen* magazine's most popular sections is entitled "Trauma-rama," where readers write in with absurd tales of bodily dysfunction and mortification. (Actually, *YM* pioneered this sort of column, but *Seventeen*, with its 2.4 million readers, is often more representative of what girls want.) For example, one girl wrote in about standing in a store when her bloody pad fell onto her shoe just as a cute boy—a hottie—walked in. Other tales include accidentally farting in class, bleeding through a pink skirt, and having a boyfriend diss a girlfriend for her halitosis.

Leaving aside the dubious physics of the first girl's story for a moment, why is "Trauma-rama" a favorite section? According to one fourteen-year-old we know, it's because girls really want to hear that they are not alone, that they are not the only ones who feel a sense of foreboding that their social ambitions, indeed their entire identity, can be derailed by their bodily anarchy. It's not too much of a stretch to say that girls reading these magazines first learn that they are not alone in much the same way that women sitting around a kitchen table doing CR did. The honest pages that address real life in teen magazines exist, it must be said, right next to the crappy sexist ads and articles that stereotype teen girls' concerns. But failing to acknowledge what speaks to girls in these magazines is done at our own peril.

The reason "Trauma-rama" carries so much weight with girls is that the confidences come from the girls themselves, rather than from the adult editors and writers, and are meant for other girls who are dealing with body hair and smells and sex for the first time—just like them. To older people checking out the department, it is a bit of a mystery why these girls are rushing to expose the most humiliating things that ever happened to them. But that's the point: we don't get it because it's not for us.

The feminist prescription to girls is to say that looks shouldn't matter (but do), to love your own unique and miraculous bodies, to nurture your self-esteem and the rest will follow. Let's face the facts: girls do care about their looks, and shouldn't be made to feel guilty about that in the context of a feminist movement—just helped to celebrate them, whatever the aesthetic. But the teen-magazine allure is more than photos of Johnny Depp and prom-dress spreads. Girls aren't just learning what's wrong with them; they're reveling in the creative possibilities of adornment, a genuine interest and concern about their appearance, and shared news about their social interactions. The good news is that these teen magazines have even been politicized. *Seventeen* (due, in no small measure, to *Sassy*) runs meaty features on racism and hate crimes to go along with the six-page spreads on the current hairstyles of stars like Daisy Fuentes and Gwyneth Paltrow. Consciousness-raising moments can happen in the pages of *Seventeen* in ways that may be impossible in a "first-blood" ritual.

In fact, let's contrast the teen-magazine *CR* with the first-blood ceremony, a restoration of pre-patriarchal ritual by older feminists in the hope of exorcising societal shaming of women's bodies. In the recent spate of books for the girls' movement, first-menstruation celebrations are as frequent as "Trauma-rama"–type columns are in the teen magazines. The rituals vary, but the First Moon Passage to Womanhood Ceremony kit, marketed by the Brooke Company in San Francisco, gives the general gist of what these celebrations are all about. The ceremony kit consists of three large tapered candles in white, red, and black to represent the maiden (girl), the menstruating woman, and the crone; a gray stone to pass around when speaking (to ensure that each participant has a chance to be heard); a bloodred cloth (to represent the first blood) and a hot-pink ribbon (no description given); a cassette with instructions and background music; and invitations, so that the girl who just got her period can invite her friends over to discuss and celebrate it with their mothers and other menstruating women in the community. Although the ritual is steeped in Wiccan traditions and is clearly pro-feminist, it often misses one crucial element: girls' points of view. Sarah Reid, a twenty-four-year-old who lives in a commune in Amherst, Massachusetts, writing in *Ms.* magazine, talked about her community's attempt to put together a ritual for teenagers:

> Of 84 people, there are 31 kids under the age of 15, and the adults wanted a ritual to bring the teenagers into our circle. Having lived in the community since I was 19 . . . I've often felt I span the gap between teenagers and adults. . . . Our first step was to ask the three girls who had come of age (13 or older and menstruating) what they wanted. Their response: no talk of periods and go light on the spirituality. Nor did they

want the spotlight directly on them. Mark the passage, not the girl, allow them to bring a boom box, and they would—reluctantly—join us.

In *Girls to Women, Women to Girls*, by Bunny McCune and Deb Traunstein, Chapter 6 is entitled "What's the Big Deal? The Meaning of Menstruation." The adult authors recount talking to girls and women about menstruation and, in a voice that would send anyone running for her *Seventeen*, write: "[W]e still have a long way to go to educate ourselves about the biological, emotional, and spiritual aspects of menstruating. Sometimes the very things that are messy, uncomfortable, and painful can also bring meaning, connection, and new life to this world. Let's remind each other that menstruation is one of the awesome and unique parts of being a woman." In the same book, the girls report that menstruating means "really bad cramps . . . being moody . . . something else to worry about . . . a mess . . ." Understandably, women going through menopause may be saddened about all the time they spent feeling ashamed and want girls to appreciate their time of the month before they lose it. However, as two women who just hit thirty and who are facing at least two more decades of generously supporting Tambrands and some ibuprofen company, we don't think we need to say too much about why girls complain about their monthly blood rite, or how complaints might be a signal of something other than self-loathing. Girls do bond over their periods, but probably not often over the cleansing and fertility aspects.

The menstrual-reaction schism is a symbol of the way women and girls (and mothers and daughters) often "turn away from each other," in Gilligan's words, and don't listen at crucial moments—even as a whole movement is created out of a feminist desire to connect girls to women and vice versa. This cultural disconnect between the women who lead the girls' movement and its supposed beneficiaries is made manifest in one controversial doll: Barbie.

For the first annual Girls' Congress, a gathering of the members of New York City–based girls' programs, the goody bags were looked over with consummate care by the board of the Lower Eastside Girls Club, the major sponsor of this event. Colorful T-shirts, three hundred copies of a girls' guide, and three hundred magnets forked over by Mattel, the toy company, featuring the platinum one's visage as well as a gorgeous brown, majestic doll called Cinnabar Barbie. The girls crowded the office as the organization's executive director unpacked the Mattel box and were thrilled by the prospect of winning Miss Cinnabar in the raffle at the Girls' Congress. The board, however, was adamant: no Barbie paraphernalia would be distributed at this event. Why? Was it because Mattel is a bad multinational, removing precious jobs from America to exploit cheap overseas labor in China, land of human-rights abuses? Because Barbies aren't biodegradable? Because Barbie's über-figure was actually modeled on a post–World War II porn doll imported from Germany? No. Barbie was banned because she's a bad role model—the same reason some girls in the past two decades have not been allowed to have a Barbie.

Barbie, it needs to be said, is not at the root of the girls' self-esteem problem, to the extent that there is a problem. When adults talk about Barbie, they aren't talking about the classic doll with sun-kissed flesh that many of us gripped as eight-year-olds; they're talking about "gender roles" and "white supremacy" and "body image" and "beauty myths"—none of which are acutely or perniciously symbolized by a little child's $20 beloved doll.

"My Barbie never affected my body image," said Lisi Grinberg, who was born in 1973. "She was just this form to put clothes on." Grinberg found the doll so inspiring that she went on to design fashions for Barbie, working for Mattel in New York. In fact, Barbie jives with Grinberg's style—she has pale-pink hair extensions and favors couture such as tight angora sweaters and carnation-colored vinyl miniskirts. Anastasia Higginbotham, the aforementioned writer and girls' advocate, used to make cuts in her Barbie and then fill in the gashes with red marker. In hindsight, Higginbotham remembers that her Barbie "needed to be hurt" so that she could take care of it. As an adult, she has enough to take care of that she no longer needs to mangle her toys. Amy has more pictures of her Barbie from when she was eight than exist of *her* during that time. (As she puts it, "Barbie was my rich friend. I wanted her town-house lifestyle.") And Jennifer's Malibu Barbie was surely the most coherent reflection of her burgeoning ideas about adulthood: Barbie was always getting ready to go out, managed to be single and in demand, *and* was often in need of an abortion. What we're suggesting here is that Barbie didn't so much influence us as that she was a blank screen on which to project what was happening in our heads.

Besides the lifestyle choices imposed on Barbie from her diverse, possibly perverse, owners, the forty-one-year-old doll has had some seventy-four careers, some of which broke occupational barriers that flesh-and-blood women are still just scratching at. She has been a dentist, a profession in which women make up only 10 percent, although 99 percent of hygienists are female; a firefighter (when in New York City there are only thirty-five female firefighters, of the eleven-thousand-strong force, and thirty-two of them were eligible for retirement in 2000); and an astronaut (when women make up only 23 percent of all astronauts). Barbie has these jobs because feminists pressured Mattel back in the seventies and eighties.

Many of our feminism-inspired mothers tried to get us to eschew Barbie, and twenty-five years later, pro-feminist mothers are still dissing this plastic doll. The Washington Feminist Faxnet's take is emblematic of the traditional feminist line. In response to a new product, a Barbie personal computer loaded with Barbie fashion-designer software and no room for educational software, the Faxnet writes: "We knew Barbie was dumb, but her maker, Mattel, is making her even dumber." Well, it's not making girls want her any less. In fact, Barbie stands as a symbol of the lack of understanding between the leaders of the girls' movement and the girls themselves: this is hotly contested territory. The traditional feminist distaste for Barbie has also kept many young women closeted about their dolly-loving past. They fear that loving Barbie will water down or jeopardize their feminism. Many of the young women we talked with for this chapter of *Manifesta* confessed that they loved Barbie; some still felt bitter at their mothers for not letting them play with her. Most of these young feminist women felt guilty about loving Barbie and were convinced that doing so would exclude them from feminism. Of course, some of the young women we talked with also had a genuine dislike for Barbie or never wanted to play with her.

Ironically, the one girls' organization that started in 1945 (pre-Barbie and pre-feminism), when the girls' movement leaders were just being born, is the one that has taken the first step into the Barbie abyss. Girls Incorporated was created to meet the needs of hundreds of teenage girls who had migrated from rural areas to work in the milltowns of New England and needed a place to hang out. Handwritten letters, addressed to the philanthropic women who ultimately founded Girls Inc., requested a girls' club for the new working class. One such letter read: "Us girls want you to do something for us. We would like you to open a Girls club. The reason for this is because we are always getting in troble [sic] because we have no place to play. We try to play ball in back of the police station, but the men chase us away. Us girls don't want to stay up in our houses like hermits. Please do something about this." The letter was signed by forty-three potential hermits.

With the exception of the Girl Scouts, Girls Inc. has the largest constituency of any organization in the girls' movement. The majority of its members are girls of color, and more than 70 percent are from families whose incomes are less than $25,000. The fifty-five-year-old organization delivers programs at more than 1,000 sites and reaches more than 350,000 young people each year. Depending on the location, programming ranges from the Oakland, California, branch, where girls literally pump iron and have a lesbian and bisexual group, to the branch in greater Atlanta, which has a Girls Under the Hood project that was designed by the girls themselves; the girls learn how to do an oil change and other car maintenance because their mentors want to expose them to careers in automotive maintenance *and* show them how to fix their own cars. In 1998, girls in central Alabama won an award for their Assertiveness, Self-Defense and Boxing group. Programming includes a Willpower/Won't Power template to help girls decide how and when they want to have sex. Girls Dig It takes girls on archaeological digs to help them uncover their own history.

In early 1999, Girls Inc. began working with Mattel, Inc., Snackwell, Nabisco's brand of fat-free crackers and cookies, and Condé Nast's *Self* magazine. Underlying these controversial collaborations (Barbies? Diet snacks? Fitness magazines?) was a recognition that Girls Inc. wasn't afraid of Barbie, just as girls weren't afraid of her. (Since two Barbies are bought every second, clearly Barbie is popular.) By aligning with Mattel, Girls Inc. is attempting to influence, rather than ban, the products that speak to its constituency, and perhaps continuing to change the center rather than creating a safe space for girls that remains on the margins.

But isn't Barbie the worst stereotype of feminine beauty? Maybe, but as young women who had Barbies post–Second Wave can attest, we didn't want to be our dolls; we just wanted to cut their hair, make them go out on dates, and swim in the Barbie pool with Skipper. Activists have already tried to change the face of Barbie, and nothing remained on the margins (or on the shelves of Toys "Я" Us) as much as Native American Barbie or a black woman firefighter. As utterly important as it is to have dolls that reflect different faces besides that of the Aryan goddess, the PC-inspired dolls were never quite as popular as the original. However, Mattel has begun changing its ads to acknowledge the range of girls—tomboys, brainiacs, girlie-girls—who play with this one doll. And the lessening of Barbiphobia finally acknowledges that most girls don't want to *be* Barbie; they want to use Barbie to explore what they can be (à la Lisi Grinberg, the Mattel fashion designer). In a pro-girl future, the Blond One won't be forced to reflect society's stereotype of girls, such as when she used to say, "Math is hard." But Barbie will remain a way to role-play about relationships. (And, as she did when we were prepubescents, Barbie, who spends most of her time naked and shorn, will always be a way for young girls to imagine fucking in numerous positions.)

Girls Inc. seems to be dealing with three steps forward, two steps back. The three steps forward is that the organization has broken the Barbie taboo. (Along with Mattel's new feministy ad campaign, the 1999 Working Woman Barbie comes with a CD ROM featuring Girls Inc. economic-literacy activities.) The two steps back is the fact that Girls Inc. hasn't radicalized Mattel much.

When we were writing this book, Jill Barad, then CEO of Mattel, made $4 million a year in salary and stock options—more than half of the operating budget of Girls Inc., which serves almost half a million girls. It will be five steps forward when Mattel is responsible to its constituency the way Girls Inc. is. Specifically, when the multinational gives $5 million of its $5.5 billion in annual revenues to Girls Inc., rather than the paltry $500,000 per year it has committed for three years (and makes sure it hires another female CEO as, alas, Barad, one of three women to head a *Fortune* 500 company, was fired months before this book was published). Although corporations do not have the same mission as advocacy organizations, it's high time Mattel recognized that it makes all of its Barbie revenue off girls, and gave back responsibly (not just by handing out products and not just to Girls Inc.) On the other end of the spectrum, the allegiance was not originally met with great kudos for Girls Inc. In fact, some of the affiliates and board members were enraged when they heard that a group for girls would prostitute itself to the doll we love to hate, no matter how much of a donation is involved.

But the five steps forward for the girls' movement can't just come after cues and money from corporate America. Women have got to start listening to what the girls want—and to what they already have.

OPHELIA APPEARS TO BE AWAKE

An appropriate question for the women in the girls' movement to address might be, Why is it still so hard to be adult women in this society? The answers are many. Carol Gilligan told us about a race retreat for black and white women that has met over the course of several years. Every time they came to a betrayal that was too painful to discuss with respect to their own lives, they looked to the future—to their daughters. Hope in the future is essential to any social-justice movement, but simply putting off the hard work or the critical questions, assuming innocence and uncomplicated sisterhood for the next generation, is naïve. Building on Gilligan's conclusions, women reforming relationships in the face of hurt and betrayal is what takes us from being an island in the sea of the patriarchy to being a movement—a wave. But if women are only looking to girls, and avoiding one another, then they condemn themselves to remaining isolated from one another as well as from authentic solutions. "The importance of women joining girls' resistance is that girls reawaken the *women's* resistance," Gilligan told us. "But what got reported when I wrote [*In a Different Voice*] was loss. Loss of voice, loss of self-esteem. We can talk about that, too. But the easiest place for us to go is to a place of loss and sadness. The hardest place to go with other women is to joy, strength, and energy, because to go there you are now standing on the other side of loss. I think the girls' movement has been an incredible turn in the women's movement. Now, are we going to be complacent?"

After all, girls and women (and men, too) learn mostly by example, not by lecture. If women are positive about their periods, their cellulite, and their strength and talents, they will no doubt enhance girls' lives and self-esteem—not to mention their own. Can we afford to look primarily to the future while feminism requires that women stand up for themselves today? As for girls at the 1999 UN Take Our Daughters to Work Day, they weren't talking about their "true selves." But maybe they were talking as them.

"It's sort of weird that all of the speakers are models or actresses," says Elin, age fifteen, a future scientist who is from Iceland and goes to the UN school. "They should have gotten Hillary Clinton or . . . Julie Andrews or something."

"Do you guys think prostitution should be legalized?" asks Carmen, moving the conversation in a feminist direction. She is fourteen, from a public school, and wants to be a neurosurgeon. "So that women who did do it could have it be more safe?"

"I don't think that should be treated like a regular job," says another fourteen-year-old girl with long black hair and nice nails. She wants to be a pediatrician. "You are not showing respect for yourself when you are a prostitute. There is *always* something else you can do."

"Yeah, but for some women they want to do it because they can make more money in a shorter period of time and maybe they want to spend time with their kids," says a white girl with braces and a brown bob. She wants to join the Peace Corps, and then be a marine biologist. "Shouldn't we make it better for them?"

CHAPTER SIX

Thou Shalt Not Become Thy Mother

YET ANOTHER MOTHER FOR PEACE

Carol Gilligan was raised on the Upper West Side of Manhattan in the 1940s. An only child, she was a girl who did "boy" things; she swam and ran and played baseball with her dad. Gilligan's mother came of age during the flapper era, a time when women were getting their first taste of independence in the form of jazz clubs and the workplace, cigarettes and sheath-like dresses that didn't require corsets and hours of time to don.

Her mother went by both Mabel Caminez and Mabel Friedman—her maiden and married names. In line with having these two formal identities, Gilligan says she got a double message from her arty, working mother. "She was liberated, she worked, and she always had very interesting women friends—some of whom didn't marry," says Gilligan. "But she also lived with my father in a very patriarchal world. My father was born in the back room of a dairy store, went to Cornell on scholarships, and then became a Wall Street lawyer. My mother became part of my father's projects. His helpmate. She ran the household and entertained."

Gilligan, who graduated from Swarthmore in the fifties, was

202

too young for The Feminine Mystique *and too old for the Red-stockings. In the sixties, she was radicalized by the Beats and put her politics to use canvassing for civil rights in Cleveland. Married by this time, she had three boys, and moved to Chicago, where she intersected with women's liberation just when it was exploding in the Windy City. She went to Harvard to teach, and ended up as one of the few tenured female professors. The lauded institutions of patriarchy were never her goal, however, and, sitting at the edge of the university pool with another of her rare breed of permanent female professors, watching the male faculty swim by in schools, the two women would ask themselves, "How did we get here?"*

It was in that stronghold of male privilege that Gilligan began her study of girls and girlhood. Running on the beach with a few of the girls from her study one day, she had a Proustian sensation: total recall of her own childhood voice and of being in her "body" in a way that she had forgotten. One of her first crucial insights—that girls might be experiencing a traumatic cleave from themselves at the time of adolescence—was drawn from an experience in her own life that came back to her suddenly. "I remembered going to camp when I was twelve and loving it—having girl friends, loving my counselor, and having a boyfriend. Then I remembered going back at fifteen and hating it—being miserable. During the time with the girls, I found letters I had written back and forth with my grandfather [about my time at camp], and I realized that this bad time was confused. I was really thirteen, though I had always remembered it as being when I was fifteen, two years later. In my time with the girls I started to straighten out my own story. In doing so, a lot of the compromises I had made living in a patriarchy were suddenly reopened. Watching the girls [struggling with remaining true to themselves] was like watching the tide come in—I saw the power of patriarchy."

In 1964, during the time that Carol Gilligan was in Cleveland with her babies doing voter-registration door-to-door, Elisabeth

Subrin was born. She lived in Newton, Massachusetts, the first of three daughters of a psychiatric social-worker mother and a law-professor dad. "I was the type of person who would declare 'Girls are equal, too!' and 'Free to be you and me.' Women's lib was completely part of my consciousness as I was growing up," Subrin says. "Later, I realized I was getting that as much from the culture as from my family; in many ways my parents were not feminist at all." Subrin's mother did have Ms. magazine around the house, but in the eighties would not march for abortion with her daughters in D.C.; she didn't want to offend people who had more conservative religious points of view. By the time Subrin's sisters were born, her mother wasn't working outside the home; instead, she organized the local school committee and nuclear-disarmament campaigns. Whether it was mothering, social work, or volunteer activism, helping others feel good was a significant and critical part of her identity.

"I remember collating leaflets for her and all of these political meetings at the house that seemed so activist and exciting," Subrin says. "In retrospect, I realize a lot of it was about parenting." Whether the inspiration came from good politics or being a good daughter, Subrin was an activist, too. In high school she started Massachusetts' first high-school nuclear-disarmament campaign, and acted as the youth liaison from Newton for the June 12, 1982, million person march in New York to protest Reagan's nuclear-arms policies.

By the time she attended college, at the University of Wisconsin at Madison, Subrin had turned her activist energy toward art. She began producing photographs, films, and videos as her politics turned inward, toward an investigation of the mythologies of her liberal suburban childhood. She had always seen her family as very progressive, but now began to realize that they actually had relatively safe, left-of-center politics. True, her mom had been an equal player in the household, and might even have been seen as aggressive by other mothers, but *aggressive in the way she fought to get her children the best teachers in the high school—not on her own behalf.*

Meanwhile, Subrin began thinking about her friends, other daughters of feministy moms: "I wanted to understand why, if women's liberation had informed my childhood, my generation was sticking their heads in the toilet in the eighties." Was women's liberation a myth, a bedtime story in a bright purple book, or was it a reality? She didn't so much answer this question as frame it with her 1995 film Swallow, *a thirty-minute video that centers on one girl who dies of anorexia. Her character is described with this ironic, increasingly angry refrain: "She wore brown corduroys and a blue sweater in the middle of July." Clearly, the girl didn't feel as warm or protected as the presence of the summer sun would imply. And why did no one explain this strange behavior, or recognize it as an urgent symptom? To Subrin, the girls in her childhood weren't with the* Free to Be *program; something was wrong in this atmosphere of purported freedom and equality.*

We think back through our mothers if we are women.
—VIRGINIA WOOLF

Many Third Wave feminists remember being little girls and being fascinated by their mothers—whether she was decked out in mod-sixties regalia or a dashiki or bell-bottom jeans—positive that she was the most beautiful woman in the world. Others might remember pretending not to see their mothers sitting in the stands at the basketball game or the band rehearsal, dressed down in a sweatshirt or fuchsia high-top Reeboks. As teenagers, did you bound out of the house, tears of frustration pricking your eyes, and fling yourself into your friend's car, yelling, "My mother is such a bitch!"? Or do you have permanent flashbacks of your mother's horrified glare at your choice of friends or profane vocabulary, or when your mother would use saliva and a Kleenex to modify the eyeliner application surrounding your flat, dispassionate gaze?

Mothers and daughters move through their lives observing each other, witnessing the times when being a woman is in season and when it is rancid. Both generations watch, but it is the daughters who are more likely to be shaped and influenced. We take cues from our mothers about what life has in store for us. We look at them and figure out what to do and what not to do.

Here's what some feminists remember about their mothers:

Isabel Carter Stewart: My mother, a divorcée in the forties when it wasn't cool, was a teacher for thirty-five years. She was very wary of having to work. And she brought me up to find a good husband and not have to work, because that would have been her dream in her generation. It was a logical message to find a profession, too, though—in order to have something to fall back on in case he doesn't do right.

Kathleen Hanna: My mom wasn't a housewife. She worked as hard, or harder, than my dad, and she made about an eighth of the money he made. But her sacrificing so much of her life for us, I don't see that as a good thing. It made me lazy, because I could always look to Mom: "Oh, Mom will fix my shirt, Mom will wash my clothes, Mom'll do this, Mom'll do that." I always loved her and cared for her, but she was Mom, not Barbara Hanna.

Dawn Martin: I've always thought of my mother's life by comparing it to the one she gave me. Hers seems like one of sacrifice, where she works forty hours a week and comes home every day to make dinner for my father, my brother, and me. She sent me to England for a semester because she had always wanted to go abroad but never did. In some ways I feel like I'm living her fantasy life. When I came out to her as a lesbian, I think she was most disappointed by the screeching halt that put on her dreams of fulfilling herself through me.

Lisa Silver: I was raised in a feminist household where my

dad would praise my mom's skills, and what a wonderful, loving person she was, and what a great meal she made, but he would praise us for getting As and for the books that we read and for awards that we got. It was a mixed message: that homemakers like my mother should be paid and their work is valuable, but he didn't want us to become homemakers.

Christina Kelly: I always thought that my mom wasn't happy when we were growing up. The way I processed it—she denies this—was that she didn't finish college, she had kids. So she didn't have the career she had planned on having. That was something I was never going to let happen.

Tanya Selvaratnam: My mother is my best friend and my biggest nemesis. She came from Sri Lanka a young and naïve bride, and she grew into a strong and formidable woman. She always pushes me to be better and to work harder, to be my own woman. She wants me to escape the hardships that she faced as a woman who was beaten and cheated on by her husband but was still dependent on him. But then every time we talk she asks me, "Tanya, when are you going to get married?"

Sandy Fernandez: My mother grew up in Nicaragua, where she very much felt limited by her life with her traditional family. My mom wanted to go to France for college. She was a French scholar, but my grandfather said "No way." And my mother felt how wrong this was. Because of her, I never doubted that I would have a career. What I did lose out on was any information or support about how to deal with a male partner. She would say "Have a career" and "Don't get pregnant"—I went to an all-girls school, so that was taken care of. Her message was only about maintaining your selfhood. But how do I deal with the personal stuff?

Nancy Gruver: I grew up with mixed messages: I should want to be President *and* Miss America. I feel like it was a reflection of the times, growing up in the early sixties. My parents gave me a lot of support for my personal ambition, but they wanted me to fit in as a woman.

Amy Richards: Now, I romanticize what it was like being

raised by a single mother—it is such a brave matrifocal tale, and freed me from witnessing any traditional family gender dynamics. The reality of my life felt much less heroic. In grade school, I was embarrassed about not knowing my father, and had to fight additional stereotypes that go with single mothering: the myth of the inadequate parent, that my two-person family couldn't be "enough," and my own fevered projections that because I didn't have a dad I was destined to be knocked up in the back of a pickup truck at the age of fourteen. I blamed my mother, not society, for giving me what I used to think of as a less than perfect upbringing.

Jane Pratt: My siblings and I thought of our parents as really equal in terms of their intelligence levels and their abilities as teachers and how they shared everything in the house. But there was this *thing* that Mom made no money compared to Dad, even though they had the same job. It was just funny to grow up and take for granted that a woman would make so much less for her work.

Many daughters are scared of falling prey to the indignities we witnessed our mothers suffer. This fear is a challenge to younger feminists. Young women should understand where that fear comes from, rather than simply avoiding it. Unwrapping motherhood from the swaddles of patriarchy means that we will no longer have to work so hard to be different from our mothers.

As it is, we are more likely to notice what our mothers are doing wrong than what they are doing right. We notice if Dad treats Mom like shit, if homemaking appears to be a fake job, or if Mom worked outside the home and was never there to ask us about our day. We may think that when Dad does "Mom's chores"—picking us up or doing the dishes or cooking—he's a hero. We notice if we look to Dad for decision making, and to Mom for love and comfort and mending. If the marriage falls apart, we notice if Mom doesn't know how to write checks, or dates jerks, or if her lifestyle becomes markedly poorer. We notice the passive-aggressive ways that she may work around powerlessness: the boyfriends she takes on to escape her unhappy marriage, the guilt trips, or the migraine headaches that befall her just before the guests arrived every holiday. Throughout our lives, we make mental notes, and swear on our mothers' lives not to let that happen to us or do what they did. This includes the most trivial sins: we'll never embarrass our kids, we'll never have our hair done every Friday at the same time, we'll never have a comfy-but-ugly outfit that we change into every day after work.

Our expectations of dads are so much lower than our expectations of moms that dads don't get such a bad rap from their daughters. We also let them off the hook because their lives appear more liberated—more like how daughters are told their lives should be.

"My dad is really amazing," says Katie Roiphe, whose mother is a successful Second Wave novelist. "He fought in World War II, and he wanted us to go to all-girls schools so that we would cultivate our minds and be outspoken. And my sisters and I *are* really outspoken." Vivien Labaton, the director of the Third Wave Foundation, was raised by her father after her mother moved out and essentially eschewed all the responsibilities of parenting. "When we were little," says Labaton, age twenty-six, "our dad would braid our hair to much praise from other adults—'It's so sweet that you do your daughters' hair!' I'm sure my mother wouldn't have gotten such kudos." Despite having a caring father and a live-in caretaker-grandmother figure, Labaton is still acutely aware of her mother's absence. "The relationship that I *don't* have with my mother has such power over me," she says. Meanwhile, Sabrina Margarita (one of the guests at our dinner party in Chapter 1) had an authoritarian and abusive father but still felt that she had more in common with him, a physician, than she did with her housewife mother. "I feel like he can relate to my activism more," she says.

Because women are rarely treated as well as men, young

women think they can avoid that bad treatment by being different from the woman they know most intimately. And so they rebel. Daughters often run in the other direction, and strive to be distinct from Mom. Part of running is also teenage rebellion, and part of it is a fear of losing oneself. On a political level, girls who reject their mothers are usually rejecting the roles cast for them by a patriarchal society.

To our mothers, this rejection must be sort of sickening and familiar. Not too long ago, they were fleeing the constraints of *their* mothers' lives. However, our mothers' rebellion was likely to be more absolute than ours, both because there wasn't really a feminist analysis of mother-hating (just a Freudian one), and because their mothers had fewer possibilities with which to create a life. This was certainly the case for many feminists of the Second Wave. Betty Friedan and Gloria Steinem, for example, saw no future in following their mothers. Instead, Friedan forged an identity based on her brain, not her social graces or looks—those were the province of her socialite mother. For her part, Steinem became utterly capable and optimistic, banishing the depression that deadened her mother's spirit, but continuing the caretaking she'd learned in looking after her. As the nurturer (a mother of sorts) for every progressive movement, Steinem made sure that her functioning was necessary to the world because her mother's functioning hadn't seemed to be.

In contrast, we have a generation of mothers who raised children with at least some hint of feminism in the air. Whether our mothers rejected, embraced, or stayed neutral on the women's movement, it was a force. When we were kids, many of our mothers awakened to new possibilities. Some relearned what it was to be a woman at the same time that their daughters were learning it. As Christina Baker Kline explained in the book she co-wrote with her mother, *The Conversation Begins: Mothers and Daughters Talk About Living Feminism*, "At times, it was scary to have a mother who was forming her identity at the same time I was forming mine." When the feminist movement showed up, our mothers' generation put their foot down about the politics of housework and risked their marriages. We then witnessed their ability to grab hold of their own lives, which had to have made the prospect of becoming one's mother less daunting than it was for our mothers.

Nonetheless, the relationship between mothers and daughters is one of the most basic to feminism, mainly because in dealing with our own mothers, many of us could be confronting our own misogyny—our dislike for the way women's power is forced to play out in a sexist society. Enter the Martyr Mom complex, an often invoked but still misunderstood female problem. Martyr Moms are passive-aggressive, making dinner for eight when they're exhausted, and then hating you later for it, essentially ceding their own lives in the thankless service of others. The selfless spirit that guides the Martyr Mom was also evident in the activism of mothers in the sixties and seventies. According to many of the women we interviewed, their activist mothers did work on behalf of children or the world at large, in groups such as Another Mother for Peace, and justified their activism because it was on behalf of others. (Protesting the Vietnam War—*Stop the killing of innocent children!*—is a larger version of agitating to make sure that one's kids have a free-milk program or the best teachers in the school.) A patriarchal society expects mothers to be totally giving and available, downplaying their own needs, ambitions, and desires, as well as fears and guilts.

Besides repressing natural ambitions, martyrdom can also send a negative message to the offspring of Martyr Moms. Girls who wage war on their bodies and starve themselves do so, perhaps, as a perverse way of expressing themselves and gaining control of something. If this is the case, they learned it partly by watching mothers who wore their own self-denial like a blue ribbon, or perhaps mothers whose womanly bodies only made them more vulnerable. Even though the trait is personified by the mother, it's a sexist society that is to blame. We should view the Martyr Mom's existence, as well as the cutter and the anorexic, as evidence that women's full liberation is still a thing of the future.

As much as we need our mothers to become women with their own lives so that we can respect them as individuals—and not just as mothers—daughters, too, send double messages. Philosophically, we want our mothers to be liberated—except, of course, when we want them to be home after school, making the meals, intuiting our pains and needs, and listening to our problems. In other words, we set our moms up to be martyrs, to sacrifice their own needs for ours. Unlike the role of daughter, which can be many things, "living for others" is the most basic definition of being a mom that we have. Children are, by definition, needy and time consuming. The answer isn't to give them less, but to divide the work more equitably between parents. Bringing wholeness to the identity of "mother" is a political challenge, especially in an era when the rights of an embryo are fast becoming greater than the rights of the woman who carries this tissue in her womb.

Even though autonomy is an overarching goal of feminism, people, including feminists, are very ambivalent about selfhood when it comes to mothers. In the mother-daughter interviews in *The Conversation Begins*, for example, many of the daughters said they sometimes felt abandoned by their feminist mothers, and frequently overshadowed. The mothers seemed uniformly shocked by this. They had tried so hard to raise their children in a revolutionary, healthy way.

Martyrdom puts pressure on daughters, too. Having given up so much, our mothers want us to achieve what they weren't able to achieve. At a certain point in an older woman's life, living through a daughter's campus achievements may be a more easily attainable goal than going to college herself when she's over forty or fifty. Jealousy is a natural response to the freedom daughters easily enjoy. A mother's main benefit may be in watching her daughter enjoy the fruits of her labor, and hearing a few words of thanks. But, ultimately, being a bystander to someone else's achievements isn't enough.

Revolutionizing the family, not just mothers and daughters, is necessary if we are to have any chance at women's liberation. After all, the home is still the most powerful and primal seat of patriarchy, housing and teaching the most basic inequalities between the sexes. Feminist researcher Shere Hite, whose latest book is about work, has observed that it's easier to "change the corporation than to change the family." For masses of Second Wave households, the rhetoric of women's rights was part of the dinner-table discussion. But the conversations didn't necessarily reflect what was going on inside the house—Dad never doing the laundry and Mom saying "Ask your father" when it came to finances. If it wasn't a feminist-informed household, it was likely to be more repressive inside the home in response to advances women were making in public.

Kathleen Hanna remembers her father needing to reinforce his man role at home, for example, lecturing her mother about what *The Feminine Mystique* meant. Elisabeth Subrin and Carol Gilligan, women from different generations, sensed this doubleness—what Subrin calls the "myth of liberation." The conflict between the feminist rhetoric in the culture and the resistance to it in private life is what Gilligan says resulted in girls "going underground." "[T]here is a lot of pressure on girls and women to turn away from one another," Gilligan explained in an interview for *Daughters of the Moon, Sisters of the Sun*, a book of exchanges between young women and their mentors about the transition to adulthood. She continued, "There is a kind of complicity in this turning away: 'If you don't look at me or say what you see or hear me doing, I won't look at you or speak about what I see or hear you doing.' And we began to ask the obvious question: Why don't girls and women turn toward each other at this point, instead of turning away?"

One True Thing, a Hollywood tearjerker based on a novel by Pulitzer Prize–winning writer Anna Quindlen, successfully analyzed this generational repulsion. In this 1998 film, Renée Zellweger portrayed an ambitious New York City journalist, Ellen Gulden, who returns to her suburban home to care for her terminally ill mother. "The one thing I never wanted to do was live my mother's life," Ellen says. "And there I was doing it." Meryl Streep, as Kate, zaftig and radiant in the housewife role, throws elaborate theme parties and makes a tabletop mosaic from her broken dishes. Creative and delightful as she is, Kate's domestic achievements are *nada* compared to the father's life as a sought-after English professor and would-be novelist (portrayed by William Hurt). After walking many miles (and scrubbing many toilets) in her mother's shoes, Ellen learns that her mother's accomplishments—her ability to bring the community together and make her family comfortable—far surpass her father's inflated dreams of his own literary importance.

"You spend all of your life thinking about what you don't have, and you have so much," Kate warns her puffy-eyed ungrateful daughter just before she dies. In that moment, any daughter might be shocked (as we were) into recognizing that we view our mothers in light of what we think they lack— youthful looks, brilliant careers, respectful husbands—not what they have. Finally, Ellen learns that her mother has actually chosen and fulfilled with joy the very life that Ellen had learned to disdain. The film isn't a call to join a kaffeeklatsch community group or bake up a storm as a one-way ticket to feminine authenticity. It's a warning to mothers and daughters to take a clear-eyed look at each other, rather than stealing glances and making notes about what not to do. *One True Thing* teases out a feminist challenge: to understand the choices our mothers made, knowing they were made in a context we will never experience. For mothers, the challenge is to realize that their daughters came of age in an entirely different era, one that makes their lives fundamentally different.

The latter underlies the basic problem of the girls' movement. Its agenda is based more on assumptions from older women's lives than on observations of girls' lives; more on what an individual mother didn't have than on what her daughter needs. As Third Wave women, we no longer have to measure our success by how far away we got from our mothers' lives. A feminist daughter who lives her life differently from her mom has really learned feminism, not just passively inherited it.

To do feminism differently from one's mother, to make choices that are our own, and not simply a reaction or a rejection, is the task of our generation. Robin Pogrebin, a culture reporter for *The New York Times*, grew up partly in the offices of *Ms.* magazine, the daughter of a superfeminist, Letty Cottin Pogrebin, and a labor lawyer, Bert Pogrebin. When Robin writes now of her generation's struggle "to free ourselves from the pressure to emulate or satisfy our mothers," she is trying to find a feminist voice that isn't rejecting her mother's feminism, or simply collapsing into it in an unconditional embrace, but that is truly her own. When science writer Polly Shulman wrote (in *The Conversation Begins*) about the downside of having a famous feminist mom, Alix Kates Shulman who wrote books and looked fabulously glam while dressing the kids in unisex jumpsuits and proffering a speculum for a toy, she was demonstrating that her own self is strong enough to differentiate from her mother's and even have a sense of humor about her upbringing.

Women who didn't have feminist moms don't have to reject their mothers, either. *Bust* creator Marcelle Karp, thirty-six, knew that she would never have the life her mother had. How could she? Her mother was a first-generation immigrant from Israel who worked as a cashier at a Roy Rogers restaurant and was married to a dictatorial man prone to rage. Karp is a smart and smart-ass girl who went to college, became a producer in such youth-oriented media ventures as Nickelodeon, HBO, and Oxygen, and dates cute younger men. Debbie Stoller, one of Karp's partners in the *Bust* venture, has a similar biography. She was the brainy first child of an immigrant mother from the Netherlands, who was at the beck and call of a controlling, angry husband. Stoller's mother was highly domestic, cooking dinner, knitting, and caring for the kids in the most traditional ways.

In Stoller and Karp's drive to create a very ambitious and

feminist future, they were able to maintain a connection to their mothers' lives and values. Central to Stoller's feminist theory, for instance, is the concept of reclaiming feminine culture from a misogynist society: valuing knitting, cooking, and dressing up. In Stoller's own words, "It's not as simple as everything Girlie is good; it's more that not everything Girlie is bad." As for Karp, in her vixen, "I won't make any excuses for my pleasure" mantra, she invokes her mother, whose flirtations with boyfriends and pleasure in driving a foxy red car compensated for an unhappy marriage.

If Third Wave women have the advantage of seeing our mothers in the context of a sexist society, we also often have the support of our fathers in our quest to be free and ambitious. As a visual aid, think of all the dads taking their daughters to the Women's World Cup or the WNBA games. They, too, want for their daughters what their mothers didn't have. But many of those same men don't easily support their wives in those pursuits because it requires greater sacrifice or, at least, uncomfortable changes.

Jennifer's pro-feminist father, David, impressed on his three daughters the importance of having their own money and autonomy—to the point of practically issuing an injunction against joint checking. And yet when Jennifer's mother, Cynthia, got her own bank account in 1999 because she wanted to start a business, David was surprisingly hurt, even offended. He felt that her independence was a way of shutting him out, because from the first moment of their marriage they had made all financial decisions together. (After a few hashing-it-out conversations, the shock of Cynthia's economic independence subsided.) Families may bristle when mothers strike out on their own, even as most acknowledge that it's women's lack of a legitimate place in the world that is the root of their oppression.

"Perhaps the biggest reason my mother was cared for but not helped for over twenty years was the simplest," wrote Gloria Steinem about her mother. "Her functioning was not that necessary to the world." In that essay, "Ruth's Song (Because She Could Not Sing It)," Steinem saw her mother partly as a casualty of the patriarchy. Politicizing our understanding of our own mothers helps us to understand and sympathize with them, and form an alliance against sexism. We actually can imagine changing the world to be more respectful to women who are mothers, rather than just changing our lives so as not to resemble theirs.

Ever since feminists began having daughters, they've been trying to resolve the mother-daughter conflict. There is a limit to what one generation can accomplish in this regard, and daughters need to continue the revolutionizing process that their mothers began. We no longer have an excuse not to transform this relationship. How do we respect those women who mother us, not just romanticize them? How can we both honor what women's bodies do—including in the literal sense of developing and nourishing a new life—and truly support the notion of individual liberty for women, just as we do for men?

For starters, we have to think back to our liberation primer, *Free to Be . . . You and Me.* One song on that album goes like this: "Mommies are people/people with children/When mommies were little/they used to be girls. . . ." In other words, we must first see mothers as individuals whose lives exist independently of their children's. Elisabeth Subrin can be an activist on behalf of herself (and her children and others), though her mother was respected for and confident of being an activist only on behalf of her children and others, not on behalf of herself. This evolution is key. It's only when women are valued—independently of their relationship to other human beings—that daughters will no longer be afraid of being like their mothers.

CAN YOU SAY *AUTOKEONONY*?

In the summer of 1983, a University of Chicago professor and seventies radical lesbian named Sarah Lucia Hoagland began writing a book exploring her theory on resolving the feminist conflict between independence and community. She took her book to four feminist publishers, all of whom wanted to publish it, but each press wanted to tailor the argument. Hoagland wouldn't compromise. With the help of $20,000 in loans from a bunch of sister lesbians (she agreed to pay them back within five years) and a friend's extra ISBN number, she self-published her book, *Lesbian Ethics: Toward New Value*, in 1988. In a single year, during which she toured to promote the book and engage lesbian communities, Hoagland sold more than five thousand copies, did two print runs, and paid off her loans; to date, seventeen thousand books have been sold. "The book's publication coincided with the Second International Feminist Book Fair, and the publishers there helped me enormously," Hoagland says. "It was as if the fair had been created for me. I toured to help organize and engage lesbian communities. And I worked with many activists in the United States and abroad, from Amber Katherine in the United States to the Irshin Collective and Orlanda Press in Germany." Hoagland's activist story of publishing this book mirrors the feminist theory that she has always tried to promote:

I mean to invoke a self who is terrified neither of solitude nor of gatherings, a self who is both elemental and related, who has a sense of herself making choices within a context created by community. I mean to invoke a self who is both separate and connected. So I create a word for what I mean: "autokeonony." Which I take from the Greek "auto" ("self") and "koinania" ("community or any group whose members have something in common"). What I mean by "autokeonony" is the self in community. The self in community involves each of us making choices; it involves each of us having a self-conscious sense of ourselves as moral agents in a community of other self-conscious moral agents. And this is not a matter of us controlling our environment but rather of our acting within it and being a part of it.

In this instance, Hoagland is invoking a lesbian feminist community. At a time when sisterhood relied on conformity to show its strength, Hoagland was defending her place as an individual within a community to which she was devoted and integral. This struggle for independence *and* connection is emblematic of the relationship between mothers and daughters. It also reflects the struggle between individual women and the feminist "Mother"—the movement that we plug into. Specifically, if Second Wave women created much of the movement called feminism that young women are connecting to now, how can Third Wave women negotiate their independence and still remain part of the family?

Third Wave's agenda has to include making "autokeonony" mainstream. We have to make it clear to our mothers, our foremothers, and ourselves that our actions are not a rebellion but a necessity of speaking our truths; they are not *against* but *for*. To illustrate, when *we* critiqued Take Our Daughters to Work Day and other components of the girls' movement in the previous chapter, our goal wasn't to suggest that this holiday should be relegated to the scrap heap. What we're doing is offering our observations in order to strengthen and fine-tune this important feminist concept.

The Third Wave began speaking for itself in the early nineties, just as Second Wavers began to pay attention to the girls' movement and to analyze how older women's voices had gone "underground." In the wake of the Reagan-Bush era's opposition to feminism, women of the Second Wave were coming back after a decade of running hard to stay in the same place. The clash between a new generation defining its voice and an older one remembering losing its voice makes the feminist movement feel as if it is at cross-purposes. To negotiate this tricky space, women have to scratch out common ground with our foremothers.

The two of us share some common ground with the Second Wave. We have both logged in a few hours as Ms. Young Feminist. We can attest to the heady perspective of access to Second

Wave heroes and history. In the eight years that we have worked at the roots of the Second Wave—at *Ms.* magazine and with the New York Women's Foundation, Voters for Choice, and Gloria Steinem among others—we have spent most of our time acting as intergenerational mediators: *"Gloria Steinem is really cool and interested in what younger feminists are up to. She's actually not a dinosaur." "Elizabeth Wurtzel's work is smart and original. She's not a solipsistic exhibitionist." "Ms. isn't just for asexual fifty-year-old women." "You should get Strawberry Saroyan (or Tara Roberts, Jennifer Gonnerman, Anastasia Higginbotham, Nomy Lamm, or Sandy Fernandez) to write that story." "There have* always *been black women in the movement—and the movement has* always *been more diverse than the mainstream."*

We've seen up close and personal that the biggest conflict between the generations is a lack of communication, mutual ignorance of each other's accomplishments, and sometimes suspicion about each other's motivations. Our good rapport with many leaders of the Second Wave has given us a chance to learn our history. Our constant interaction with the Second Wave has also revealed that many of its members weren't seeing the Third Wave.

Then again, we have seen young women put up a wall of ignorance about the Second Wave's achievements, not the least of which is that these older feminists didn't die with the ERA and have kept right on doing important work. Because of schools' failure to teach even recent women's history and because of generational tension, many young women are more likely to know the media's image of the movement than the women who actually lived it. This is the main reason we felt inspired to write this book. Lucky for us, important memoirs, biographies, and histories are beginning to archive the movement.[42] For Second Wavers, this archiving is evidence of what was and, for Third Wave women, it's also an indication of what is next. We can see in the 1970 *Ladies' Home Journal* sit-in the idea for a *Rolling Stone* takeover. Amid the victories, we learn the real stories behind the myths—the D.C. radical lesbian-feminist gang the Furies really *did* expect members to give up their boy children; many women of color really did feel alienated from the movement. These stories of mistakes, foibles, and triumphs invite us to sympathize and listen, not defend and reject. Perhaps this is the kind of honesty that we need with our mothers.

This mutual confusion was typified one evening in 1999. The occasion was a reading we, Jennifer and Amy, hosted to celebrate International Women's Day on March 8. It was a program of radical writings from the Second and Third Waves, read by feminists like Andrea Dworkin, performance artist Tanya Barfield, and comedian Wendy Shanker. Elizabeth Wurtzel, author of *Prozac Nation* and *Bitch*, was introducing her reading from Kate Millett's *Flying*, and having trouble being heard in a room packed with 170 feminists. When audience members asked her to project, she retorted *bitchily* that it might be okay if they didn't hear her, since *Flying* wasn't Millett's best work anyway. Older feminists in the audience gasped. Then, following up on a reference made to the Bobbitt marriage, Wurtzel alluded to Millett's complicated relationship to her former husband, Fumio. Millett, in attendance, stormed the stage and demanded to read the book herself, assuming that Wurtzel was implying that her marriage was abusive. (Wurtzel was probably referring to the fact that Millett had had quite a few female lovers during her ten-year marriage, which, to the reader, qualified as "complicated.")

Back in the audience, the split between old and new was made resoundingly clear: many of the young women yelled out that they were pissed that Millett took over when a younger woman had the floor. Most of the older feminists cheered their sister on for having stood up to a rude slight, assuming that the brash younger author was dismissing Millett's contribution to feminist writing. The irony was that Wurtzel may have been one of the few women of her generation who had actually read the lesser-known *Flying* as well as *Sexual Politics*. No small feat, given that, at the time of the reading, nearly all of Millett's books were out of print. It's not that older women didn't agree with Elizabeth; it was her tone that they found offensive. After all, another Second Waver in attendance that night said privately, "[Wurtzel] was right—*Flying* isn't Kate's best work."

In another example of intergenerational suspicion, womyn's music icon Alix Dobkin laments frequently (in conversation and in her column called "Minstrel Blood") the lack of radical gay youth. "You can imagine how depressing and aggravating it is to see disinterested, disconnected younger dykes distancing themselves from their foremothers as many seem to be doing," she wrote recently. At the same time, *The Nation* published an article on young gay activists, "Gay Teens Fight Back," that paints the opposite scenario. In fact, *The Nation* piece reports that "gay youths themselves often complain that there is a lack of support from the adult gay movement." For instance, nineteen-year-old Candice Clark explained it to *The Nation* this way: "A lot of the older gay community here is fearful of youth as jail bait, since so many [straight] people think that if you're gay you're a pedophile."

The tension between the Second and Third Waves of feminism is similar to the squeamishness and stress between mothers and daughters. Making matters more fraught, our intergenerational strife occasionally resembles a male-female relationship as well: young women get the coffee, make the copies, and wait to be discovered—or, at least, thanked—by their superiors. Young women have too few opportunities for leadership. Subconsciously or not, Second Wavers often deny that they could benefit from younger feminists' knowledge and experiences. Instead, they focus on little girls—sweet, young, and as unthreatening to the Second Wave way of doing things as possible—as a not so subtle way of avoiding and ignoring the generation of young-*adult* feminists. Young women are often overlooked even when the subject of the article, conference, or debate mainly affects them (such as abortion rights). When they are included, it's often just to give the appearance of being inclusive, not really to listen and learn from young women.

As a result, young women are like any other tokenized group invited on a panel to give the program some diversity. If we are invited, it is more likely to be a panel specifically about "young feminism" or to join in intergenerational dialogues, not to contribute our expertise on reproductive health, welfare, or the impact of budget cuts on student loans. (One common way of including young women without really including them is to have a young feminist introduce the speakers for a panel. Amy personally has fulfilled this duty on at least a dozen occasions. Each time, her responsibility was only to introduce or moderate the panel of older feminists, not to contribute her expertise on the given subject.)

For example, the Pro-Choice Public Education Project commissioned an ad campaign targeting young women and highlighting the fragile state of choice, yet it didn't ask a single young woman to be on its nine-person steering committee. Perhaps this explains why one of the Barbara Kruger–style ads, supposedly written in language for Gen Xers, had a preachy and presumptuous tone. It featured a pierced and tattooed twenty-something woman looking smugly into the camera. The text read, "Think you can do whatever you want with your body? Think again." The tactic of assuming that young women knew little about the issues surely undermined the goal of the ads. If 76 percent of the women getting abortions are under thirty, shouldn't they be involved in a discussion about the fragile state of choice? Many young women eager to join the movement find themselves repeatedly cast aside, and so jump ship.

One addendum to the "I'm not a feminist but . . ." could be "I would be if older women would recognize that I am." Second Wavers who don't see feminism unless it looks like their brand have created a phenomenon that Diane Elam, a professor of English and critical and cultural theory at the University of

Wales, in Cardiff, calls the "Dutiful Daughter Complex" or the "Blind Obedience Syndrome." In "Sisters Are Doing It to Themselves," an essay in *Generations: Academic Feminists in Dialogue*, she explains this phenomenon:

> This problem manifests itself when senior feminists insist that junior feminists be good daughters, defending the same kind of feminism their mothers advocated. Questions and criticism are allowed, but only if they proceed from the approved brand of feminism. Daughters are not allowed to invent new ways of thinking and doing feminism for themselves; feminists' politics should take the same shape that it has always assumed. New agendas are regarded at best with suspicion on the part of seniors, at worst with outright hostility. Daughters are regularly sacrificed if they step out of line.

Naomi Wolf was the good daughter, reaping accolades and the crown of Ms. Young Feminist in 1991, when her book, *The Beauty Myth*, critiqued the patriarchy's pressure on women to be beautiful. When she switched gears to challenging the old strategies of the movement and presented a pragmatic "power feminism," she was quickly demoted. (This was before she recommended, in *The New Republic*, that the pro-choice movement embrace guilt about abortion.)

Second Wave author Phyllis Chesler's 1997 book *Letters to a Young Feminist* was reviewed by a few younger feminists, as the title would seem to invite. A review in *Ms.* magazine was positive because, as we heard, the young writer was worried about alienating Chesler. The author, Winter Miller, a young feminist writer, activist, and actor, told us later that she also worried about the repercussions from older, practiced feminists thinking, Who's this young upstart, and what does she know anyway? "Women like Chesler have put a great deal of time and effort into a movement from which I've benefited," said Miller. "Although I found her book elementary, I didn't want to spit callously in her face and be perceived as unmindful of my foremothers." Less timid, Kim France gave *Letters* a mediocre review in *The New York Times Book Review*: "Part memoir, part manifesto, *Letters to a Young Feminist* is Chesler's attempt to pass on the kind of wisdom that she and so many of her generation were left to figure out as they went along. But she proceeds to share this information without considering the possibility that if the movement ever is resurrected, its goals and tactics might differ significantly from those of its earlier incarnation."

There's nothing too outrageous in those thoughts, even if France did give in to the media myth that the movement is dead, but Chesler reacted as if she had been set up by Rush Limbaugh. She enlisted another young writer, Leora Tanenbaum, to shoot off a letter to *The New York Times* on her behalf. (Curiously enough, this letter of defense managed *not* to praise the book.) As for her own credentials, France was a former *Sassy* writer and, while on staff at *New York* magazine, had written a very prescient piece connecting women rock musicians to current feminism ("Feminism Rocks," June 1996). At the time of the review, France was at work on a book about the origins of girl culture. In other words, she was and is a young feminist. A few weeks after the review, a contemporary of Chesler's called us with some gossip: Did we know that Kim France worked for Bob Guccione of *Penthouse* fame? This could have been proof of an anti-feminist plot behind the Chesler review, except that France was simply a contributor to *Spin*, formerly edited by Bob junior, the *Penthouse* king's estranged son. That the vitriol and rumors were this out of hand said a lot about this older feminist's skepticism and ambivalence about the next generation, as do the following scenes from the complicated world of intergenerational feminism:

- In 1994, the Sister Fund (which funds programs for women and girls) and the Women's Desk at FAIR (Fairness and Accuracy in Reporting) convened a strategy meeting. The urgent agenda: the right wing was training young people in anti-woman beliefs, and the left wing needed to gather its troops of young feminist leaders. Of the nineteen people in the room, only four were under thirty-five and most were over fifty. Far from being the keynote speakers at this meeting, the four young women hadn't even been invited. Because they worked with the Ms. Foundation for Women, where the meeting was being held, they had seen the invitation and came out of a personal interest in the topic. After the presentation by experts on the topic of the right wing, the Q and A session featured one burning question: "What are young women thinking?" Apparently, it was a rhetorical question. The four young women sat in the room with their hands up, and were never acknowledged.

• At the aforementioned intergenerational reading of radical women's writings where Wurtzel and Millett scuffled, Andrea Dworkin, in her trademark overalls and a soothing voice, read from young novelist Danzy Senna's *Caucasia*. She introduced the passage this way: "If any of you were afraid that there has been no good writing since the seventies, this book will make you happy. It is beautifully done." The many younger feminist writers in the room looked around with "thank you—or should I say *fuck* you" looks on their faces for what they took to be a condescending comment—while the older feminists nodded approvingly. Despite this gaffe, Dworkin's reading was characteristically moving, and she was interested enough in Third Wave women to have accepted this invitation in the first place.

Many young feminists have a horror story concerning mistreatment at the hands of a Second Waver, or at least being told that they haven't really done anything to rival their forebears. A self-fulfilling prophecy, after all, we are or have been their students, assistants, researchers, interns and fans—in other words, subordinates. Lisa Silver recalls meeting her new boss, Betty Friedan, for the first time. "It was almost as if I wasn't in the room," she says. "She was just 'Here, do this.' I was so sub, I was invisible—and I was stunned because at the time, I thought, Hey, we're all feminists!" One young woman, referring to her work with another prominent Second Wave feminist, said, "I began the job thinking that I had the potential to accomplish a bit of what she had accomplished. Before long, she had erased all of my confidence, even in my ability to do the simplest things." (Of course, both of these prominent Second Wave feminists are also divas, so they treat their colleagues much the same way.)

Even from afar, older feminists can send zingers that reduce Third Wavers with a single accusation of silliness. "These are not movement people, I don't know whom they're speaking for," Susan Brownmiller, author of *Against Our Will*, was quoted as saying in *Time* magazine about some younger feminists. "They seem to be making individual bids for stardom." These accusations of personal ambition aren't untrue, but they were also true of Brownmiller's generation. (In fact, Brownmiller herself was skewered by many activists for seeking to rise to fame on the back of the women's movement in 1971, something that we're sure she found both hurtful and laughable.)

Up close, Third Wave language and tactics are often viewed with misunderstanding and contempt. Sabrina Margarita, from our dinner party, used the word *girl*, well aware of its historical context *and* its contemporary usage, to refer to a new hire at Women Make Movies, the feminist-owned and -run film distributor where she was briefly office manager. Her boss, voice dripping with sarcasm and aggravation, replied, "I don't know about the new '*girl*,' I thought we hired an adult woman." If this woman had even known about Margarita's zine, *Bamboo Girl*, she would have gained some insight into what *girl* means to a new generation of feminists. It's hardly a term of disrespect in that context. Anastasia Higginbotham handed in a treatise for the twenty-fifth anniversary issue of *Ms.* about how Second Wave women bitch that younger women aren't flocking to the movement, and then ask young women who do come to stack the cups and make the copies. Her setting was a party, symbolizing the movement, and she interviewed dozens of women, letting younger activists talk about their frustrations in their own words. Her approach was redirected by the editors.

Of course, older women aren't the only feminists on this trip; the Third Wave brings its own baggage. Is the prospect of reaching out to older feminists simply too frightening for some of us? Are we afraid of what we'd learn? Can we avoid the pitfalls of becoming aging feminists ourselves? Are we too filled with twenty-something ambition and optimism and immortality to believe that we have anything to learn? Younger women certainly harbor a fear of being old ladies *(Thou Shalt Not Become Thy Foremothers)*. Perhaps we fear experiencing unrequited feminism, nagging the next generations about why there isn't any government-subsidized day care or, worse, running around in a leather mini and baby tee at seventy-seven, as Helen Gurley Brown does today.

You might be thinking, But young women can hardly be invited to be on as many panels as Gloria Steinem or other older feminists, who, given their age, are more experienced and therefore qualified. Or perhaps you think that younger women are unrealistic about older feminists, a surefire recipe for bitterness and disappointment. This may be partly true. But young women have been on the receiving end of this argument for too long without reciprocity. Take, for example, *Letters of Intent*, an intergenerational anthology edited by Anna Bondoc and Meg Daly in which we both have essays. The editors are two young feminists who began their anthology in the anticipation that it would be an exchange among colleagues. In the end, however, older women had the last word—with young women sending letters to their mentors, who then responded. In some instances, we're confident that the younger women could have responded to the older women's questions, signaling dialectic. Instead, the book contained many tributes to our "mentors," as if older women had nothing to learn from younger women.

(In the reviews, the young women were criticized for sounding namby-pamby, full of complaints, and bereft of ideas.)

In addition to younger women shedding the inferior role, it would have been interesting to have an essay acknowledging that seventies feminists fell on hard times during the eighties. Many who thought they saw the revolution around the next bend entered retirement age with no money in the bank, no guarantee that they would be remembered by history, and with their books out of print. As we write this book, three of the most important works of the Second Wave have been out of print for years: Shulamith Firestone's *The Dialectic of Sex*, Kate Millett's *Sexual Politics*, and Germaine Greer's *The Female Eunuch*. (Although *Sexual Politics* was reissued by the University of Illinois Press shortly thereafter.) Cindy Cisler devoted her life to archiving the reproductive-rights struggle and lost all of her work when, poverty-stricken, she was evicted from her apartment in the late nineties. A movement historian, she sees precious out-of-print books on the street, sold by ad hoc vendors, and opens the cover to discover her initials penned inside—but they are no longer her books, and she couldn't re-create her collection if she had all the money in the world. Millett and Firestone, two of the fiercest revolutionary thinkers of their time, essentially suffered great depressions and multiple "loony bin trips" that may have been a result of their pioneering troubles. Chronic fatigue syndrome felled both Naomi Weisstein and (temporarily) Phyllis Chesler, two dynamic speakers and writers. One reads the memoirs and histories coming out and recognizes that Cisler, Firestone, Millett, Weisstein, and Chesler were once young and strong and sane.

Even if we're not afraid of poverty and sacrifice, there are other perils of aging that fuel the generational strife. In another scenario, women are still pitted against one another in a depressing relay race, whereby the younger body wins out because it is more valued in a patriarchal society. In a sexist climate, women's development isn't respected. Their vitality and experiences are cheapened—and even erased—in a culture that believes that "men age, women rot."

Even feminists who are dedicated to appreciating women as more than sex objects presume that older women are, if not less valuable generally, less valuable sexually. We haven't quite mastered the art of believing in women's worth throughout their lives. At a reading sponsored by *Bust* in late 1998, for instance, the young performers—who, on any other day, would be only too happy to write frankly about being a "cocksucker" or incredibly horny—dissolved into embarrassed giggles at their own sexual frankness and apologized to the "parents" in the room. Alix Kates Shulman, who was in attendance, later said she wanted to cry out, "*We all did plenty of fucking to make you children!*" Why didn't the youngish writers see in sixty-something Shulman, who writes explicitly about sex, a sister blow-job queen? When younger feminists buy into the cultural myth that older women don't have sex (and that everything boils down to being young and nubile), we contribute to the same misogynist rules that will eventually smite us. As young women, we have the opportunity—and the responsibility—to change the rules about who is sexy while we're still young and sexy and have the power to attribute sexiness to women of every age. Sympathetically, at a panel for her book *The Feminist Memoir Project*, editor and Second Waver Ann Snitow offered this reason that her generation is always harping on us for not being feminist enough: "We, or at least I, feel so guilty that we didn't accomplish more." It has got to be painful to watch us struggle with the same issues they struggled with—the politics of housework, whose last name the children will get, sex discrimination, what to do about day care. Mother guilt—all of it.

Clearly, there is plenty of work to be done if we are to understand and respect one another. Some women are already moving toward rich intergenerational partnerships. We file Steinem under Second Wavers who get it. Whenever she is asked what young women are thinking, she says, "Ask a young woman," and she is Third Wave activism's most enthusiastic supporter. The health activist Barbara Seaman comes to many Third Wave gatherings, and acts as an activist fairy god-mother—making sure that young feminists in the media know one another and encouraging the two of us to write articles and books (including this one). bell hooks's primary audience is young women. Second Wave writer Mary Kay Blakely has hosted three intergenerational dinners for the Third Wave Foundation. Katha Pollitt has lobbied to get our editorials into *The Nation*, while *The Women's Room* author, Marilyn French, treats young women with as much respect as she does older fem-inists. Marlene Gerber Fried, the director of the Center for Re-productive Health and Policy at Hampshire College, is one of the forces behind Young Women's Day of Action, but she man-ages to keep young women front and center and in positions of power. In 1998, Fried launched a biannual networking meeting of young staff members from various pro-choice groups. Two years later, she began inviting a few older women to the meeting, which now calls itself New Leadership Networking Initiative, re-versing the usual process, and the usual ratio of young to old.

Some support comes in the simple form of faith that the torch has been passed. For instance, Alice Walker, a passionate, tireless activist, is relieved when she can write her books peace-fully in the privacy of her own home. She knows that others are fighting the good fight. These women are rewarded by young women's energy and accomplishments, not threatened. Beyond such individual relationships, women's foundations and femi-nist institutions are beginning to realize that they shouldn't *just* address the needs of girls; that young women are a distinct arm of the movement and can't be rendered invisible by the labels "women" and "girls."

We've noticed a difference between the good relationships and the bad. Steinem, Seaman, et al., go out of their way to forge connections with campus radicals, twenty-something writers, burgeoning activists, and the "peons" who answer the phones and read the slush manuscripts. *They* have reached out to *us*. Nonetheless, young women have to take their own initiative and create their own relationships.

The need for intergenerational communication brings us back to Phyllis Chesler's *Letters to a Young Feminist*, a Second Wave book directed at feminists between the ages of eighteen and thirty-five. Not really an attempt at dialogue, *Letters* was more of an owner's manual, a list of dos and don'ts from a worried mother. To anyone who has grown up in a feminist era, chapter headings such as "Principles, Not Popularity," "Self-Love and Team-Spirit," and "Being Direct Is the Best Defense" might appear a bit corny. These titles carried over into the book's tone—the voice of the archetypal embarrassing mother, the one who is supremely out of touch with her kids and doesn't even realize it. "Sex is not something that you only share with members of the opposite sex. Nor is it something that always results in genital orgasm," she writes in Letter 13, called "Sex and Humanity." Chesler was inspired to write *Letters* after a long illness. She understood how crucial it was to "pass the wisdom on before you die. I did not want younger feminists to have to continually reinvent the wheel." Chesler had noted that the most "radical and dazzling feminist work and history had, for twenty years, increasingly 'disappeared' from the High School, College, and Graduate School Canon." Many works, including her own, had gone out of print. "When young women came to see me who suffered from eating disorders, panic attacks, depression, fear of success, or who had been raped or battered, they had no feminist analysis of what their symptoms might mean."

In the chapter entitled "How to Develop a Strong Self in a 'Post'-Feminist Age" she writes: "I was flying solo, without an instructor or manual, doing a high wire act without a safety net." As two young feminists who are familiar with Chesler's large and wonderful contribution to the women's movement, the most shocking thing to us about her book and its aftermath is that she doesn't see her spunk, independence, and fearlessness in young women.

Even if her message amounted to "Listen to me, even though I'm not listening to you," Chesler did reach out and attempt to let us know what the movement looked like from her eyes. *Letters to a Young Feminist* begs for our perspective. Here goes:

LETTER TO AN OLDER FEMINIST[43]

Dear Older Feminist,

Because we, too, believe that women can't afford to have another generation's voices go underground, this letter is our way of talking to you above ground—rather than bitching about you behind your back.

If our message were to be boiled down to one bumper-sticker-size *pensée*, it would be: "You're not our mothers." We want to reprieve you from your mother guilt. You are officially off the hook for not having solved the day-care problem or made the world equal. You *did* make the world a better place, and you continue to do so. We have our national soccer teams and women's studies, legal abortion, and the right to commit *outrageous acts* and sue for *everyday* injustices. Although there is still much to be done, we've got words and laws for many of the abuses you called "life."

We let you off your mother trip. Now you have to stop treating us like daughters. You don't have the authority to treat us like babies or acolytes who need to be molded. You have inspired us from afar by doing your own work, and taught us by example by figuring out your own life. You wrote important books that we read and pioneered the ideas that we accept as givens. If you feel that you don't "get" what Third Wave women are thinking, you're responsible for raising your own consciousness. This might mean figuring out where Katie Roiphe *and* Rebecca Walker (two young women who believe in and write about feminism, albeit in slightly different ways) are coming from. Engaging with them rather than knocking them down will help them—and you—to clarify where they are. Their arguments might evolve into stronger assaults on the patriarchy rather than in-fights for the movement. When you want to broaden your constituency to include young women, make sure that women under thirty-five are part of the planning process. When you want to know what young women think about Monica Lewinsky, ask young women. When you want to know where the movement is, or where it needs to go in the next century, look to younger feminists for this answer. Ask women under thirty-five to write or speak about all feminist issues, not just about what it feels like to be young or to inherit your mantle. Introduce *us* at panels.

Before criticizing young women for their lack of feminism, or yourselves for what you think you didn't achieve, take a good look at what's out there. Read our books, buy our records (and read the lyrics), and support our organizations. Don't treat us as if we are competitive with you. Respect our different tactics in the service of shared goals. Realize that anything we create adds to the momentum of the movement. And when we are righteous, naïve, wide-eyed, annoying, or obsessed with, for example, recycling in the office rather than the welfare bill in Congress, think back to your first moments in the movement and the first issues that radicalized you.

If younger women and older women were really talking, we would be able to look at one another and see not the fabulous Amazon or the controlling parental figure, the Girlies who need to be spoon-fed feminism, or ingrates who ignore their forebears' accomplishments. Instead, we would see the real, everyday women who make up this movement. The characters—young and old—whose lives show us where the movement needs to go. In other words, we would see each other.

CHAPTER SEVEN

Who's Afraid of Katie Roiphe?

GROWING UP KATIE

Katie Roiphe was born into an upper-middle-class family on the Upper East Side of Manhattan in July 1968. At that time, radical feminists were organizing abortion speak-outs and moderate feminists, such as her mother, Anne Roiphe, were writing their first books. In 1969, Anne Roiphe wrote the novel Up the Sandbox, *and later she contributed to* Free to Be . . . You and Me. *Katie's father was a psychoanalyst who fought in World War II and did all of the cooking in their household of five daughters. In the seventies, Katie's grandfather gave her a Barbie Beauty Palace, which she loved. One day when she went to play with it, the toy was gone. Her mother told her it had been lost.*

Katie attended an all-girls school, Brearley, because her father wanted his daughters to cultivate their minds. Years later, as an undergraduate at Harvard, she sat at Take Back the Night marches, not expressing her first feminist activism but noting similarities between Victorians and nineties "victim" feminists. Then Katie went to graduate school at Princeton and wrote the book The Morning After. *Her second book,* Last

Night in Paradise, *about how AIDS has affected the sex lives of the members of her generation, was partly inspired by her older sister Emily Carter, a writer who is HIV-positive.*

"I call myself a feminist largely to connect myself to the past," says Katie Roiphe. "I have a sort of attachment to this political movement and the opportunities it brought about. I also believe that once it works well, feminism has got to contemplate its own extinction."

While everybody hopes for the day when feminism will no longer be necessary, Roiphe predicts that extinction will happen very soon.

Where's your activism? It would be nice to see some passion . . . even some rebelliousness. And I don't mean the phony rebelliousness of a Katie Roiphe or a Rene Denfeld, or a Naomi Wolf, who present themselves as daring iconoclasts even as they embrace the most shopworn conventional views.

—KATHA POLLITT,
to Emily Gordon in *Letters of Intent*

In 1992, Jim Silberman, an editor at Little, Brown and Company, handed a manuscript called *The Morning After: Sex, Fear and Feminism on Campus* to his twenty-something female assistant, who was the same age as the author, Katie Roiphe, and had attended the same college. The assistant found the book offensive, and Roiphe's argument—that the crisis of date rape on college campuses was greatly exaggerated—specious. Specifically, Roiphe described a campus climate in which feminists were clamoring to be part of a sisterhood of victims. The assistant told her boss that Roiphe was way off base, the book was not an accurate portrayal of Harvard feminists, and it made her sad and angry to read such crap from another woman. Silberman said good, then it will be controversial, thus going for heat instead of heeding his young assistant's opinion.

Silberman was no slouch when it came to sniffing out controversial or groundbreaking feminist books; he had edited works by both Betty Friedan and Marilyn French. He listened to his assistant's rage and went for its form over its content: young feminist Roiphe, the daughter of Manhattan privilege and a Second Wave writer, claims the women's rights movement is one big pity party, full of witch-hunts and definitions of rape that would get Mr. Rogers locked up. Roiphe was ambitious, smart, and her book was easily digestible—impressions of her Ivy League community and a simple, black-and-white argument about how to characterize the gray areas of sex. Her issue with date rape wasn't so much denying that blurry, befuddled, coercive sex happened as deciding what to call it. "People have asked me if I have ever been date-raped," writes Roiphe in *The Morning After*. "And thinking back on complicated nights, on too many glasses of wine, on strange and familiar beds, I would have to say yes." She didn't accept that pathetic label, however, and ergo she didn't have to be a victim. Jim Silberman was *convinced* that if enough women reacted as his assistant did, this book could get publicity.

The manuscript that so provoked the young assistant grew out of a media-nurtured and publicity-swaddled gestation, beginning with Roiphe's November 1991 op-ed in *The New York Times*, called "Date Rape Hysteria." The lively response to that op-ed encouraged the young scribe to expand her disdain of Harvard feminists into the 174-page tome-ette that Silberman edited and Little, Brown published in 1993. A big excerpt made the cover story of *The New York Times Sunday Magazine*. The incendiary cover line blared, "Rape Hype Betrays Feminism."

That line was important, almost more important than what was in the book. Often, it's this first media categorization that frames a book's future. And after that moment, many skip the book and just read the reviews. Furthermore, buzz has so much influence that when people do read a book after a media blitz it's read with an eye to confirming the rumors. As an aside, Becky Michaels, the publicist for Roiphe's book, also did marketing for George Stephanopoulos's 1999 memoir, *All Too Human*. Reading the book two months prior to its publication, Michaels loved his dissection of spin and admired the author's ability to write about the Clintons without betraying them. After the onslaught of reviews excoriating Stephanopoulos as the millennial Benedict Arnold, Michaels couldn't help wondering if people weren't reacting to what they heard about the book, forgoing actually reading it.

True to Silberman's instinct, the mainstream media embraced the book, making Roiphe very difficult to ignore. It eventually garnered over 350 book reviews, interviews, excerpts, and features; all of this buzz obscured the fact that the book sold approximately 13,000 copies during its initial hardcover run. For the average book, a figure like this is nothing to sneeze at, but in this case there's certainly a glaring disparity between Roiphe's record-setting media presence and the number of people who actually *read* her book. In fact, it's not a stretch to say that her constituency, as in people who claim to agree with the book, verged on few more than Camille Paglia, editors at *The New York Times*, and Helen Gurley Brown (who was the only women's magazine editor to run an excerpt, cheering, "Roiphe says this idea of putting women on the pedestal is wrong. We finally just got off the pedestal!"). This odd political triumvirate made it abundantly clear that this feminist spokesperson wasn't just not speaking to or for feminists; she wasn't speaking to or for much of anybody. (As a point of reference, even the small press–published anthology *Listen Up* sold 50,000 copies, while Roiphe has sold only about 30,000 books—hardcover and paperback combined. Another big book of Katie's era, Naomi Wolf's *The Beauty Myth*, has sold more than 200,000 copies in the United States alone.) Apart from *The Satanic Verses*, *The Morning After* looked to be the most talked-about book never read.

Back at Little, Brown in 1993, Silberman's editorial assistant had written an anguished letter to a confidante: "My problem with Roiphe's book is less with her argument than with the fact that I think her argument will be taken to support the unsophisticated anti-feminist sentiments swirling around our society today." In other words, what was so influential wasn't Roiphe's analysis but the fact that Rush Limbaugh was ascendant, Newt Gingrich was gearing up to put out a Contract with (or on, depending on your viewpoint) America, and Clinton's antiwoman welfare bill was pending. Roiphe's words added fuel to the fire, like cozying up to the invaders during wartime, and provided another opportunity in the pages of *The New York Times* for the old stale jeer "Look at feminism's excesses!" Roiphe's initial op-ed had coincided with the Clarence Thomas–Anita Hill hearings, the outcome of which also seemed to reinforce the right-wing attack on women's rights, and specifically on sexual-harassment law. The Little, Brown assistant thought the best way to deal with Roiphe was to ignore her. She encouraged other feminists to do so as well.

For the most part, feminists agreed and didn't take Roiphe on publicly. In private, however, many reacted strongly and defensively. (We recall the debates both at *Ms.* and at the Third Wave Foundation—they were intense and outraged. Jennifer remembers meeting her at a party hosted by some *Nation* interns in 1994 and feeling a rush of excitement, as if she had just met Phyllis Schlafly.) In June 1993, for example, the New York City chapter of the Women's Action Coalition (WAC) challenged Roiphe to a debate, but the debate never materialized. Soon after the book launched, *The Village Voice* writer and young feminist Jennifer Gonnerman took her on in *The Baffler*, positing that Roiphe was entirely media-constructed. In "The Making of Katie Roiphe," Gonnerman reported that the controversial writer was the beneficiary of serious nepotism—beginning with her mother's more than twenty-year connection to the *The New York Times*, which, Gonnerman implied, surely greased her entry into its vaunted op-ed pages. Roiphe also benefited from media that are always hungry for women antagonistic to feminism. In 1994, Katha Pollitt reviewed the book at length in *The New Yorker*, and concluded that *The Morning After* was a shoddily researched, rather embarrassing display of gossip disguised as journalism. In the spring of 1995, *Ms.* finally weighed in with a heavy-hitting piece about the "faux feminists" (subtitled "I'm Not a Feminist, but I Play One on TV") by Susan Faludi. The author of *Backlash* expertly foiled Roiphe's research but also lumped her together with women supported by the right wing. Failing to distinguish between Roiphe and the right wing, regardless of legitimate critiques of her work, is where feminists did themselves damage.

Christina Hoff Sommers was and continues to be chief among those conservative-kissing women. Sommers's 1995 book *Who Stole Feminism?* declared that domestic violence wasn't a big problem, and that it was boys, not girls, who were getting shortchanged at school. (Her latest book, *The War Against Boys*, appears to be a rehashing of these same points.) Her tactic was to use the occasional fault in individual authors' statistics as a way of dismissing the social problems feminists were addressing. For example, Joan Jacobs Brumberg, the author of *Fasting Girls*, wrote that 150,000 girls and women die of anorexia every year, a statistic that was reprinted in a book by Naomi Wolf and another by Gloria Steinem. As it turns out, the number is not as high as Brumberg believed, but it's not even close to being as low as Sommers's estimate of fewer than one hundred deaths per year (which shows that the critic's statistics are also fallible). In fact, there is no definitive number, because casualties of eating disorders are rarely listed as such on their death certificates. The cause of death is more accurately defined by some complication of the disease; for example, heart failure, malnutrition, or pneumonia. At any rate, Sommers was missing the point: even five girls dying per year from starving themselves is five too many.

Unlike Sommers's screed on feminists and their supposedly compulsive lying, much of Roiphe's destructive power came from the media's hype rather than from the content itself. And it came from the shock of a young woman's talking back to feminism so cavalierly, like an insolent daughter. Roiphe was one of the first Third Wave feminists to debut officially, and the shock waves hit women in the movement like a slap on the ass by a male secretary: offensive, disrespectful, and ungrateful. And damaging, too, because, like swatting a fly with a wrecking ball, she seemed to take down the structures of rape theory in adjusting for a small annoyance with her college feminist peers.

At the time of Roiphe's rebel yell in 1993, *we* felt more hostile toward her and her impact than we do at this writing. We were both working in the women's movement, Jennifer at *Ms.* and Amy with Gloria Steinem. We were shocked that a young feminist, a woman like us, was refuting and misunderstanding a staple of college activism, the Take Back the Night marches and rallies. We were also pissed that so much attention was directed at this one negative young woman when we knew so many other young feminists who were doing great activist work. In other words, focusing on Katie Roiphe became another way of ignoring young feminists generally. Apart from Rebecca Walker and Naomi Wolf, Roiphe was really the only younger woman whom some older feminists acknowledged and approached seriously (even though they regarded her as a serious idiot). As a consequence, *we* were in the position of distinguishing our views from this new feminist thorn at a time when Third Wave activism was poised to ascend. Students Organizing Students (SOS) was organizing itself, as was the Third Wave Foundation and the Young Women's Project. To us, Roiphe's critique was annoying, even insulting—as if the entire feminist movement could be discredited because of one woman's experiences at Harvard and Princeton. She was blithely knocking down essential feminist institutions that, even if she didn't need (and she probably really didn't), others did.

At that time—and still today—Amy received letters from girls on campuses who hadn't reported assaults and were struggling to deal with the aftermath alone. Both of us had many friends who had been taken advantage of while passed out or otherwise unable to give consent. But no one from the media, feminist or not, asked us what we thought of date-rape activism, women's sexual agency, and Take Back the Night marches. Only Roiphe was visible.

TAKE BACK THE TAKE BACK THE NIGHT

The object of Roiphe's derision, the Take Back the Night march and speak-out, began in 1978 with a national anti-pornography protest march in San Francisco led by Andrea Dworkin and the feminist group Women Against Pornography. The event gathered ten thousand people to protest pornography as a normalization of violence, primarily against women. This was a new and important critique. Porn had been banned in the past simply for being sexual and, therefore, prurient and immoral, a tactic that rendered the women in it vulnerable to society's contempt and also ignored pornography's deeper message of violence and hatred. Dworkin and others viewed much of sex work as a part of sexism—and wanted to blame the industry rather than individual women. The idea was to decriminalize the selling of one's own body, and to punish those who profiteered off other people's bodies. This gave feminists in particular a forum for protesting sexism without attacking sex workers.

Today, Take Back the Night is most associated with college campuses raising awareness around date rape and violent attacks. It's not clear when the meaning of the movement transferred from the red-light district to the blue lights* of the university campus, but by the time Roiphe was having too many glasses of wine at Harvard, Take Back the Night marches

---

*Blue lights were installed on many college campuses in the eighties as a security measure to illuminate emergency call boxes. In *The Morning After*, blue lights were shorthand for the excesses of the date-rape scare.

had become annual events at most schools. (And continue to be. Seven years after *The Morning After* came out, Take Back the Nights are still going strong. Jennifer Gottesman, a junior at Barnard College, confirmed that her college's Take Back the Night rally and march are the most important political events on campus.)

Take Back the Night is crucial for reasons Roiphe didn't explore. For many women of Generation X, these marches are our entry point to political consciousness—just as the student-based civil-rights, anti-war, and free-speech movements were for the Second Wave. The speak-out can be the click that first feeds a feminist awakening, and many women report first recognizing a humiliating experience as a violation or rape from hearing other women tell their stories at speak-outs. One reason Roiphe caused such anger was that she was, in effect, denying women their clicks of consciousness and understanding. When we were at college (in New York City and Appleton, Wisconsin, respectively), we witnessed the value of these marches as a tool of empowerment. For Amy at Barnard College, sitting on the lawn at her first speak-out, listening to women's stories of having nonconsensual sex and being labeled as sluts brought back a memory from junior high:

I was at a party, drank way too much, and passed out in a bedroom. The next morning I woke up with my pants down around my ankles. First I was just vaguely mortified, but without a sense of what to be mortified about. I later learned that while I was passed out a fellow eighth-grader had gone down on me—a part of sex that was pretty far away from my fourteen-year-old consciousness—and hearing of this violation made me feel more exposed and humiliated. Until that moment at the Take Back the Night march, I had written the event off as just something stupid I had done. But at the speak-out, I suddenly began to question why I was made to be ashamed of this when, with the exception of drinking too much and lying to my mother about staying over at a friend's house, I had done nothing wrong. Today, even with all my organizing around sexual assault, I hypocritically still don't identify my experience as rape. When I think about my rape, it suddenly conjures up "whore!" "slut!"—blame, I guess—as well as violence, ripped clothing, and bruises, none of which I had. It's embarrassing to be a "victim," which is why, personally, I doubt that women would lie about it. If someone as knowledgeable and comfortable with feminism as I am has trouble, imagine the shame involved for women who don't have such support networks.

These marches help women to realize that sex you feel obligated to have or weren't awake for is very different from sex you choose, not to mention all those who were coerced or forced in more obvious ways. In this context, going to a Take Back the Night might help you become safer, rather than sorry. Once a woman acknowledges that she has been raped, for example, she doesn't have to stay in the same psychic place forever as an angry or cowering rape victim. This is why "survivor," rather than "victim," is often a more accurate description. She has survived it and is moving on. Despite this distinction, the date-rape debate on campus is often confused and incendiary.

Jennifer attended college at Lawrence University, a small, politically conservative Midwestern college with a big, traditional Greek scene (the frat guys had the houses, the sorority girls planned the formals). The understanding of rape and the rules of sexual conduct were mystifying for both men and women:

My first year at Lawrence, a very brave freshman named Susan stole the minutes for the Sigma Phi Epsilon fraternity meeting in which they discussed their next event—a "rape-a-DG (Delta-Gamma)" party (a twist on their traditional "rape-a-Theta" party). The minutes were leaked to the press, presumably by Susan, the Sig-Eps were put on probation for one year (no parties) for perpetuating the "rape culture," and Susan was fully ostracized. "That fucking bitch!" was the consensus.

Everyone knew that the Sig-Eps weren't actually going to rape the DGs—"rape" was a metaphor for "sweep them off their meeting-having feet." Susan transferred to Smith the next year.

When I was a junior, and already a pretty well-known radical feminist on campus, I had a close, kinda foxy male friend who had "feelings for me" and with whom I flirted. One night he came into my room all drunk and got on top of me. He said, "You wanted this," and the thing was, I didn't want that—him on top of me, trying to scare me, possibly fucking me. But I did want him wanting me in less freaky circumstances. Before that happened, he used to tell me that guys would talk about wanting to "hate-fuck" me. So I had this sense that there was considerable potential violence and aggression behind the desire I had been courting. Therefore I took the hours he'd spent on top of me as a total violation, one step on a path that could lead to rape, and refused to be in the same room with him for about six months.

By the time my feminist organization participated in the local Take Back the Night march (sponsored by NOW), I knew many friends and relatives who had been raped. I loved marching down the streets of a Midwestern town with all of these other women and men who identified as feminists, and who would stand in solidarity with women who had survived an attack on body and soul. It wasn't a typical night.

In some ways, Roiphe's sense that something is off at these marches is right. Take Back the Nights gather their special magic from creating a situation where men, rather than women, feel off balance and uncomfortable. To someone who is observing this, it may be alarming to glimpse a space of concentrated female anger, no matter how briefly. But for a woman who *is* a participant, *is* inside that magic circle, suddenly it is she who is normalized. It's as if she had put on decoder glasses, and when a male friend mentions that he and the boys talk of hate-fucking her, she now has a context in which to place her unease, really her oppression. At a speak-out, a woman who has a shameful secret—such as an eighth-grade imposed-oral-sex session—could finally name her humiliation and renounce blame. The real power of speaking out is that women achieve the strength and clarity necessary to be neither victims nor victimizers but proud survivors.

Roiphe's conclusions about the exaggeration of date rape were not supported by her thin research, nor by the sound research Susan Brownmiller did for her 1975 book, *Against Our Will*, which, twenty-five years later, is still regarded as one of the definitive resources on rape. Nor is the argument supported by the annual FBI statistics. Notoriously conservative, the FBI reports that one in four girls, and one in seven boys, is sexually assaulted—which includes molestation by relatives, acquaintances, and strangers—before the age of eighteen.

As is always the case with violence statistics, the anecdotal evidence of date rape is even stronger. For instance, since 1993, when *The Morning After* came out, young women across the country have written or called the Third Wave Foundation with their stories of sexual assault: "I am eighteen years old and about four months ago I was raped by an old high-school teacher . . ."; "I am a freshman in college, and I was raped in my eighth-grade year . . ."; "I am twenty years old, and I was sexually assaulted when I was eighteen by a much older man. I had never even kissed a guy before this . . . I want to press charges but I'm scared." The testimonials go on and on: a stripper who was raped at a University of Florida frat house; a minor who wanted to press charges but was told (erroneously) that the police would have to tell her parents about the rape; a girl given the incapacitating drug Rohypnol (roofies) and raped, tied up, and then laughed at by the police because it sounded so "unbelievable." (A few weeks later, the assailant raped again, but this time he was caught and charged.) These real-life stories confirm what we already know: rape is more often overlooked than trumped-up, and the crime is so painful that a woman is more likely to keep it to herself than to report it. Therefore

Roiphe's main argument that date rape is exaggerated is easily refutable.

Still, there is something Roiphe did in *The Morning After* for which feminists, especially young feminists, should be grateful. She rejected the received wisdom of the women's movement and of college rhetoric, and struck out on her own. She observed her surroundings and refused to budge on her version of reality. In fact, Roiphe is just a critic, not an assassin, which she makes clear when speaking on panels with the real conservative women who are working to undermine feminism.

> I've traveled all over, and when I am in Utah or Ireland—places where some of my basic assumptions [about the importance of equality] aren't shared—I go back to scratch. In Ireland, for instance, I remember thinking: They just haven't come far enough to take on the criticisms [of feminism]. I was on a show with Emma Donoghue, the lesbian novelist. The host started insulting her, saying that she was going to go to hell. The things that I found myself saying were much closer to what I think of as older [ideas of feminism].

Instead of being dismissed and demonized, her book should be read and critiqued. What if feminists expanded on her work—rejecting "victim" status, analyzing the efficacy of handing a woman a rape whistle at freshman registration—and, rather than mounting a knee-jerk dismissal, listened to her complaints. (We think young feminists have a lot to gain from this exercise.) As a blurb on her own book jacket says, "Roiphe doesn't have the answer . . . but at least she has the nerve to raise the question." Answering Roiphe's questions could make feminism stronger.

First, Roiphe's concern that the definition of rape had become too confusing is important. It has—not legally but in other ways. The legal definition of rape in the first degree, according to the 1998 *Criminal Law Handbook*, is: a male who engages in sexual intercourse with a woman "by forcible compulsion," or "who is incapable of consent by reason of being physically helpless," or "who is less than 11 years old."[44] In *The Morning After*, Roiphe points to very broad characterizations of sexual abuse, which is the preferred term in the legal community, such as feminist legal scholar Catharine MacKinnon's statement: "Politically, I call it rape whenever a woman has sex and feels violated by it." Using the Andrea Dworkin rule, it behooves a feminist to go back to the source of this outrageous-sounding comment before casting judgment. On page 82 of *Feminism Unmodified*, MacKinnon discusses the reasons that women don't report rapes to the police. The most significant of these is that they fear they won't be believed because the legal understanding of violation is based on the woman's relationship to the assailant. Ergo if it's a stranger with a knife, it's rape. If it's your neighbor (with a fist or without), it's not; which discounts the vast majority of rapes. MacKinnon recommends changing the definition of rape to one that gets at the act being committed against the woman, independently of the actor. She wants to describe women's violation, not society's view of the mythical rapist—a pro-woman line if there ever was one.

Besides, the power of denial is enormous. A study at a Philadelphia hospital, for instance, surveyed more than 206 girls aged ten months to twelve years who were treated for rape and sexual abuse as children. In 1990–1991, twenty-five years later, 129 of these girls were tracked down. Thirty-eight percent of them did not remember being abused or did not admit to remembering it.[45] The definitive answer on rape is that you have as many people denying that a violation occurred as labeling sex undertaken by choice (even under creepy circumstances) as rape. Elizabeth Wurtzel characterized her own sketchy sex incident this way:

I went to visit this guy in his apartment in the afternoon. He was a junkie, just lying in bed. I was sitting on a chair next to the bed, sort of talking to him, but he didn't want to talk. Finally, he said, "Come here." And I think I realized that if I wanted to stay there, if I wanted to be in that room, we weren't just going to neck, it was going to be sex. And I didn't want to leave so . . . I did it. It was strange. I definitely had a choice, and it was nothing I would go to the police about. But if I had been five years younger when that happened, I might not have known that I had a choice.

Wurtzel's "gray" example, and the MacKinnon quote that Roiphe decontextualizes above, could help women articulate what happened to them during those times when it's not clear whether they had a choice. That clarification aside, Roiphe is right that a broad definition of feeling raped or violated can hardly translate into legislative policy. For instance, does feeling "used" because he doesn't call the next day qualify as rape? How about if a woman didn't push to use a condom and is now terrified about disease, to which, for reasons of biology, she is more vulnerable than her male partner? Obviously, these aren't instances of nonconsensual, coercive sex, and, therefore, aren't rape. Not even pro-Roiphe forces remain pure on not using the term *rape* to describe any old violation. "Katie Roiphe—who critiqued the theory that all intercourse is rape in *The Morning After*," writes Erica Jong, defending Roiphe after *Time* magazine's "Is Feminism Dead?" cover story, "is herself raped by Ms. Bellafante [the *Time* journalist who wrote this cover story] for appearing in a Coach ad." Clearly, rape used as a metaphor has nothing to do with a crime, but such glib references may still undermine the definition of rape in some people's minds.

Second, Roiphe believes that feminism was originally about sexual freedom. Therefore organizing most vividly around violations has some built-in limitations. Some women don't want to admit that they were sexually violated, which is their freedom, too. And women deep in denial aren't going to open the door marked Victimhood to get to feminism. Roiphe herself says that she considers some of her drunken one-night stands at college nonconsensual, but she doesn't consider them rape. She believes that her feminist friends, whom she describes as dancing joyfully with their shirts off at coed parties, and then marching with grim determination at Take Back the Night, are ceding responsibility for their bodies and their sexual actions. (Ergo the *brio* of topless dancing implies an ability to say "no," or an ability to knee coercers in the balls.)

Roiphe's instinct not to restrict sex is shared by many other young women, but she doesn't appear to understand that one can be both pro-sex *and* anti-rape. (Or isn't sufficiently sympathetic to the gray areas.) Celebrations of women's sexuality co-exist with stories of abuse in plenty of Third Wave zines. This is evidence that pro-sex and anti-rape is not a contradiction but, in each case, a support of the freedom to determine one's own fate.

Third, Roiphe argues that admitting victimhood is at cross-purposes with gaining empowerment. Women, and feminists especially, do feel compelled to offer their victim credentials—or, more often, their oppression credentials—as giving them authenticity to speak. It's important to name our experiences in the service of honesty, but not when exposing injustices is used as a quick way to rid yourself of guilt or your own complicity. Amy remembers break-out groups at the Beijing Women's Conference sometimes feeling like one long circle of introductions in which richer, whiter, Northern Hemisphere women tacked labels such as "working-class," "sexual abuse survivor," "bisexual," or "young" onto their identities. This compulsive labeling may have been a way of bridging the guilt they felt about their less privileged Southern sisters, or perhaps it was an attempt to make a connection. As two white-privileged women ourselves, we have sometimes felt a need to emphasize our rural and working-class upbringings. However, the inability to admit strength, or even privilege, thus becoming "unfeminine," is proof of the patriarchy's hold on women. Why else would we need to have a label that validates our opinions?

In the same way that Girlies are trying to make female culture as important as male culture, women who emphasize crimes against women are trying to make visible the invisible misogynist violence. As the word *victim* is bandied about, there are many "victims of a different kind" who are not even granted the dignity of that term, though they are certainly victims of sexism. We're thinking of unsympathetic women such as Monica Lewinsky, Tawana Brawley, or Amy Grossberg, who are called slut, liar, and baby-killer, respectively. Of course, Monica was called a victim by people who sought to exploit her, as evidenced by the fact that they ignored her when she said that, far from being a victim of sexual harassment, she was having an affair.

Finally, Roiphe complains about the feminist rule book. At most, this rule book is a vibe encouraging women to censor themselves as individuals, to remain connected to collective opinion. For example, in a *New York Times* op-ed, a former *Ms.* staffer admitted, "In the 1980s, when I was working at *Ms.* magazine, I heard an editor express concern about her politically incorrect sexual fantasies and was shocked by the Puritanism I saw creeping into the women's movement. More concerned with reality than fantasy, I came to this movement for sexual equity, not sexual purity." The rule-book vibe also keeps women from constructively debating one another for fear of appearing divided. But they can be divided. There is no rule, in fact, that a feminist can't have rape fantasies. Our fear, that there is a no-rape fantasy rule, is wrong.

"A vital movement needs to critique itself," said Roiphe in *Elle*, in an interview that was part of her 1993 media blitz. "You can't always worry that if you speak a certain kind of criticism, it will be used against the greater good. Otherwise you have a lifeless argument and that, to me, seems worse than the risk that the book may be misused." Her point is well made. No matter what you think of her argument, her book expanded feminism because Roiphe spoke up instead of censoring herself. This is true of Camille Paglia, too. Feminists would do well to look beyond Paglia's and Roiphe's cheap shots and test out their ideas. Pulling out of the conversation is what changes Roiphe's and Paglia's words from a critique to a turf war.

THE PERSONAL IS APOLITICAL

"The nuts and bolts of politics is not something I pay attention to," Katie Roiphe told us. This, more than anything, is where the confusion between her self-identity as a feminist and her reputation as an anti-feminist lies. She claims that feminism is a political movement, which she believes has no business in people's personal lives, and yet she disavows the very politics that lend credence to her complaint. Perhaps this is why she didn't put her observation that college feminists resembled Victorians into a larger political context of life for women at Harvard. For example, when she was an undergrad in the mid-eighties, there were at least two high-profile student cases involving rapes of young women by sons of Harvard legacy families. These cases were unjustly resolved pro-rapist, yet they didn't make it into Roiphe's book. Betsy Reed, a senior editor at *The Nation*, was Roiphe's roommate at Harvard for a year. She recalls that the future critic was not part of the burgeoning feminist movement there:

> I've heard that there were once thriving women-only organizations that sometimes, though by no means always, depicted male sexuality as predatory and female heterosexuality as vulnerable and/or compulsory, not chosen. But when I was there women's studies was tiny and embattled, the social scene was hostile to lesbianism, and there was lots of casual heterosexual sex. "Date rape" was only beginning to enter people's consciousness as a problem, while you'd often hear stories of sexual coercion in what I think of as preppy hell—men's "finals clubs." So she singles out a once-a-year Take Back the Night march to pick on?
>
> I remember thinking that the women, one or two years older than me, who led and spoke at those rallies were so brave and

inspiring to be defying the conventions of coolness at Harvard, which frowned on any activism but particularly the feminist kind. The leading feminists were self-confident and sexy and unapologetic—not hysterical and Victorian and judgmental. What she described in them (and us) just wasn't there. But, then again, I never saw her at the rallies. It's that limitation that Katie refuses to acknowledge—that her experience is hardly representative of anything.

Also, Carol Gilligan was a tenured professor at Harvard when Roiphe wrote *The Morning After*. "While she was writing that book, only 8.5 percent of the tenured faculty were women," says Gilligan. "What was astonishing was that she and the women students at that time didn't seem to think that was a problem. They weren't speaking out or anything. Now, 13 percent are women, which means that seven out of eight tenured faculty are men. They are the ones who are making the decisions, allocating the money, deciding the curricula." In a way, it all makes sense: what Roiphe learned at Harvard was that the path to success lies in opposing women and supporting men. The critique she saw most clearly was of feminists, and it is her right to pursue the argument. But to argue that we have achieved sexual freedom, which Roiphe does, presumes an atmosphere of equality. If this had been true, Roiphe's so-called Victorians would have stopped bitching, been able to take advantage of tenured professorships and high-ranking positions at the Harvard *Crimson* and the *Lampoon*, and commenced partying in the female-only "finals clubs." If the atmosphere during her college years was as over-the-top pro-woman as she believed, Radcliffe wouldn't have been absorbed by Harvard in 1999.

IF FEMINISM *IS* TO BE A VITAL MOVEMENT
"If feminism is to be a vital movement," Roiphe said in the introduction to the paperback edition of *The Morning After*, "then it is going to have to be able to sustain critique, not just

critiques like 'We should be able to wear lipstick,' but critiques that are unsettling, that shake us." Katie Roiphe sent feminists to recheck their rape research, and they found it basically sound. Still, Roiphe's story is instructive in other ways, and snidely dismissing her ends up only weakening feminism. She was used by the mainstream anti-feminist media for her controversial qualities, yet ignored or disparaged by most feminists. She remained a rebel always outside of the feminist cause, yet she wasn't rebellious (or self-defeating) enough to go sit at the picnic table with Laura Ingraham and the other Pink Ladies of conservative punditry, the ones who are actually undermining feminism.

There will always be another Katie Roiphe, a feminist who exists to get all the other feminists riled up. Other rebels within the cause (of varying repute) include Naomi Wolf, who was embraced after *The Beauty Myth* but shunned by some of her former fans when she wanted to endorse power feminism and pro-choice guilt in *Fire with Fire*. Ginia Bellafante's 1998 *Time* cover story entitled "Is Feminism Dead?" launched her into the ranks of those much-despised young feminists who write as if there weren't a movement, or history, just a current media image. Elizabeth Wurtzel graduated from her best-selling memoir, *Prozac Nation*, to write *Bitch*, a convincing defense of the women for whom almost no one has sympathy. Although there *was* a two-paragraph review of *Bitch* in *Ms.*, Wurtzel remains below most feminist radar. Rebecca Walker edited an anthology called *To Be Real: Telling the Truth and Changing the Face of Feminism*, which she intended as a response to the restrictive feminism she grew up with but ended up alienating some Second Wave women. Rene Denfeld wrote *The New Victorians: Why Young Women Are Abandoning the Women's Movement*, and Paula Kamen wrote *Feminist Fatale*, in which she polled a few hundred young women and discovered that they weren't "stupid, there were reasons why they weren't embracing the term *feminism*." The list goes on. Young women were trying to present feminism as they knew it, and it wasn't going over well.

These are Katie Roiphe's contemporaries, confronting head-on what they perceived they were being told to do as feminists. With the exception of Wolf and Walker, who toured the country, vivifying feminism and co-founding a young activist group, respectively, their primary interaction with feminist activism was through writing books—not actively participating in the movement. Although these writers are smart and talented, few of them ever bother to really define *feminism*. Perhaps they see feminism as the domain of their mothers. Perhaps they see it as journalists do, simply as an image. In any case, they critique this thing called feminism and skip over what feminism is composed of—women's lives.

Their "new" tactics and their rising star-ness was confirmed when Tad Friend penned a 1994 article for *Esquire* proclaiming a brand-new kind of feminism. "Yes," panted the men's magazine. "That's the message from a new generation of women thinkers, who are embracing sex (and men!). Call them 'do me' feminists." The article positioned this new guard in opposition to the "old" feminists—the Glorias, Andreas, Bettys—and their supposedly anti-sex ways. (Then again, in other articles published around this same time, Wolf gets her Gloria Jr. credits precisely because she is "making feminism sexy again." The anti-sex, pro-sex, virgin/whore dichotomy is certainly not what's new in terms of looking at feminism.) The response from the media had a purpose: to use young feminists primarily as antagonists to play out a catfight between this generation and its predecessors. The feminist response was clear as well: these women don't come from a movement background, and besides, they aren't serious, smart, insightful, or even feminist.

"It's 'babe feminism,'" snorted Anna Quindlen in her 1994 *New York Times* column, just after the "do me" article. "I've been a babe and I've been a sister. Sister lasts longer." In the *San Francisco Weekly*, L. A. Kaufman described these women as trumpeting "feminism for the few." Yvonne Abraham in *The Boston Phoenix* called these women "lipstick feminists," light on issues and heavy on vanity. They were criticized for focusing on sex to the exclusion of child care, women's ability to make a living, or to achieve domestic equality. Christine Stansell, writing in *The New Republic*, concurred: "Contemporary postfeminist writings—notably the recent books by Katie Roiphe, Karen Lehrman, Elizabeth Wurtzel—belong to the literature of adolescence rather than the literature of ideas. They confuse sex with life, as adolescents do. They are driven mainly by appearances. They are unable to grasp the requirements of the world, outside the self. They defend little and they build nothing. From these books the misogynists and the enemies of equality have nothing to fear."

But if the misogynists had nothing to fear from these silly girls, what, then, did the friends of equality, the gynophiles, have to fear from them? Was it just the pain of hearing women say anti-woman things? Were feminists eating their own, the way a few radical feminists did in the seventies? Back then, being successful was called being "male-identified" or "power-mad," and it was definitely a criticism. Anselma Dell'Olio, an actress and early NOW member (and a former roomie of Ti-Grace Atkinson), committed to paper her theory about why a part of the women's movement began to falter: "[Our] refusal to wash our dirty linen in public . . . to examine and thus politicize the new experience of (nonsexual) competition between/among women, brought us to an intellectual and emotional impasse." Other Second Wavers, including poet June Jordan, novelist Alix Kates Shulman, and cultural critic Ellen Willis, are now writing about some of their regrets for having towed a party line (or kept mum about their failed relationships) in order to achieve an appearance of unity.

The idea of eating one's own is at the root of much mythologizing and mudslinging and is really just the resurfacing of women's patriarchal training to support men and complete with other women. It is imperative that we address female competition as we slouch toward equality. It's not that women shouldn't criticize each other; it's just that we have to learn to criticize each other's acts without devaluing the whole person.

(By the way, this is not such a problem with Girlies. They often write about the reality of sexual and female competition in *Bust* articles rather than either promoting an amorphous vision of all-equal, all-nice sisterhood, or totally trashing each other.) In lieu of honesty about competition and jealousy, critical energy is diverted into passive aggression and misplaced righteousness.

How this plays out in the attitude toward so-called Do Mes is that, no matter what a young woman writes about, she—because of her age—is a threat to the old guard and, therefore, subject to an onslaught of skepticism. (*She's reinventing the wheel, she's making an individual bid for stardom, she must have issues with her mother.*) Whether their work was really about expanding women's lives is almost irrelevant, because the mainstream media (which has always been fuzzy to hostile on the concept of feminist politics) crowned them feminist spokespeople for their generation—an identity that alienated these women even more from the actual movement. Unlike Bella Abzug, or the countless women who came to feminism via the work they were already doing even before the Second Wave, these young writers believed they could write about the movement without logging time on the front lines. After all, their lives were spent living with feminism in the water, which gave them enough credibility to write about it. Movement women didn't know who these upstarts were, and felt affronted by their presumptuousness and lack of clear commitment to issues. The fight about who is entitled to speak for feminism is in many ways a generation gap.

The most potent critique launched against the Do Mes is that they aren't movement people. The Do Mes, with their lipstick and flip comments, are like Girlies (in fact, many of the Do Mes are the same women we call Girlies), but the Do Me label is entirely a media construct. And there are also the young women who work in the movement in traditional ways (us, for example), who have been no more visible or respected than the Do Mes. In fact, young movement women are, in some ways, more threatening than Roiphe, et al., because we *do* want to run the foundations, teach women's studies, and "compete" for the same stories and bylines as the older feminists—and we have the required movement credentials. But most young movement women aren't famous enough for TV, or to chair a panel at the UN. That remains the domain of the Do Mes and is one of the reasons that the state of politics is so intellectually bankrupt: we have begun conflating celebrity with expertise. She who gets the most attention is presumed to be the "leader," regardless of the content of her message or her character.

Meanwhile, Roiphe, Wurtzel, and Wolf, for example, clearly didn't write the perfect feminist book in their still-young careers. The bottom line is that they each wrote feminist books. If the movement is to gain some speed, we can't stop ourselves at each flaw—and there were certainly many flaws in each young writer's work—that tempts us to chuck the entire book. Nor can we be such "victims" of the mainstream media, allowing them to tell us who speaks for feminism or for a generation. We have to put down our relentless search for feminist purity and look at Katie Roiphe, Elizabeth Wurtzel, Naomi Wolf, and the rest of the emerging young women as what they are: feminists, the next generation, young women who are writers and thus may not represent other feminist occupations. Yes, all feminists deserve critique and debate, but save your political vitriol for the young babes who are right-wing and political.

THE RIGHT GIRLS
However annoying it is for women, young or old, to deal with the Do Mes (or the Girlies) who want to increase the moral guilt about abortion (Wolf), or talk about female responsibility without discussing male responsibility (Roiphe), or bitch about everyone (Wurtzel), substantively these gals aren't trying to take away your rights. Although it was unsettling to have Roiphe and Company call themselves feminists and simultaneously deride feminism, each says she just wants a different approach. Big book deals and fame came with their attempts to do so. Meanwhile, the women we should be afraid of are the

new right-wing babes, some of whom also call themselves feminists, command book deals, and pose for cheesy magazine spreads. The lipstick and selfishness critiques could be applied to them, to be sure. In fact, underneath the always-short skirts, suit jackets, and stilettos of the new Right Girls, there had better be a Versace chastity belt, or we'll really think they're hypocrites. The distinction between the Right Girls and the Do Mes is that the former *do* want to dismantle welfare, criminalize abortion, and make sure that domestic abuse is again "just life" rather than a crime. And, like Phyllis Schlafly before them, April Lassiter, Laura Ingraham, Amy Holmes, Danielle Crittenden, Kelleyanne Fitzpatrick, and Ann Coulter have high-paying and satisfying careers, while striving for other women to be 1950s hausfraus. Contrary to young feminist-movement women, these gals are embraced by *their* elders; indeed, they've been trained and financially supported by right-wing media groups, think tanks, and foundations. The mostly male right wing will keep throwing money their way as long as the girls keep trying to dismantle feminist social policy.

There is only a little evidence that Roiphe or any of the Do Mes gave fuel to right-wingers. They are not anti-choice or anti-sex enough to appeal to them. Indeed, their apolitical critiques are really the opposite of the right-wing strategy. So what this adds up to is that while we're dissing the Do Mes' critiques of feminism, right-wing women are dismantling feminism's gains. As Third Wave feminists, we would do well to align ourselves with the feminist thorns like Roiphe and focus our combined scrutiny and acerbic tongues on the right.

Here's what you need to know: Though *Heather Has Two Mommies*, the children's storybook about lesbian mothers, is a favorite target of the right wing, the conservative women's movement also has two mommies. They are Phyllis Schlafly, founder of the Eagle Forum, and Beverly LaHaye, founder of Concerned Women for America. The birth of both groups coincided with that of the current, post-McCarthy right-wing movement: the 1964 Barry Goldwater Presidential campaign heralding an attack on the liberalism of JFK's brief tenure.

The emergence of these two *conservativas* was, and continues to be, an indication of feminism's strength. The groups were created specifically to counter feminist progress. For instance, the Eagle Forum was founded in 1967, one year after NOW successfully harnessed the energy of educated housewives trying to escape their own lives. At that time, the Eagle Forum wanted to pass the Family Protection Act, to restore head-of-household thinking, just as it now wants to pass the Defense of Marriage Act in each state to counter the growing acceptance of gay marriage. (Talk about self-hating—Schlafly's son is gay.) In the eight years since Susan Faludi wrote about these women and their secretly progressive personal lives in *Backlash*, there has actually been a bigger backlash. The right wing is stronger than it was during the Reagan-Bush years, thanks in part to the growth of a new breed of conservative daughters. Eight years of Clinton in the White House has made these grassroots back-to-the-fifties groups more necessary; when Bush was in office, he was on the *conservativas'* side.

The 450-member Independent Women's Forum (IWF) was founded in 1992 to counter the swell of feminist energy after the Anita Hill–Clarence Thomas hearings. Its first act was to oppose opening the Virginia Military Institute to women, and it went on to attack the Violence Against Women Act, calling it "feminist pork." The Women's Freedom Network (WFN) and its newsletter, the catchy "Neither Victim Nor Enemy," was founded in 1993. It criticized sexual-harassment laws and advocated harsher treatment for victims of statutory rape. Both the IWF and the WFN are less conservative than traditional Christian women's groups on abortion and gay rights, but they are vehemently conservative on economic issues and funding for the arts, and are really anti–day care. And among this generation of conservatives, many actually call themselves feminists—a perverse sign of progress when you consider that Schlafly and LaHaye wouldn't dream of it. When some people have to pretend to be on your side in order to have credibility, you know you're winning.

Besides identifying as feminist, these women are proactive. Right Girls one-upped feminists by moving beyond reacting and making feminists react to them. Even though we speak to and have the support of a larger percentage of the population, they are much more efficient. They fund just a dozen or so leaders (such as the Ingraham gang that we see as commentators on MSNBC and PBS), rather than hundreds of specific groups with diverse agendas. Their think tanks target narrow issues, and prove that money can make a silk purse out of a sow's ear. For example, Paula Jones, who *never* had a sexual-harassment case to stand on, was nonetheless able to keep her suit alive for four years thanks to millions of dollars from The Rutherford Institute.

Other newcomers to the anti-feminist fray include the Clare Booth Luce Policy Institute, which conducts women's leadership-training sessions on college campuses, led by none other than Patrick Buchanan; the National Journalism Center, which trains hundreds of people to debate on camera and give sound-bite answers to the media; and the blandly named Leadership Institute, which trains conservatives in the techniques of influencing public policy.

As if that weren't enough investment in the next generation of conservatives, the Trent Lott Leadership Institute at the University of Mississippi (Lott's home state) is rolling in dough. Like other conservative think tanks, it is funded by multinationals such as Lockheed Martin and MCI Worldcom, Inc., companies that have been the beneficiaries of Lott's own leadership on deregulation. Tom Monaghan, the Domino's Pizza founder, whose company was picketed by Students Organizing Students for its support of anti-choice activities, has recently pledged $50 million for a new law school that will integrate the study of law with Catholic values and teachings.

Meanwhile, lest you think there is freedom of the press, or that universities are full of radicals, the Young America's Foundation has targeted college students with its guide "How to Start a Conservative Newspaper." In 1999 and 2000, the Independent Women's Forum launched such right-wing magazines for women as *The Guide: A Little Beige Book for Today's Miss G*, at Georgetown University, the "girls' answer to the *Dartmouth Review*" (the conservative newspaper popularized by Dinesh D'Souza); and clones of that at Smith and Yale. Clearly, the right knows to invest in young women and students. Who's afraid of Katie Roiphe? It's not conservative women. If anything, conservative women are probably happy that Roiphe detracts attention from them.

Despite Christina Hoff Sommers's assertion that feminists "are the ones getting most of the money, the professorships, and the well-paid (but vaguely defined) jobs inside the burgeoning new victim/bias industry," there are few professional feminists. Instead, feminists are simply women who live by example, free of charge. That's not the case for this bunch. Sommers earned $164,000 in grants from the right-wing Olin, Carthage, and Bradley foundations, plus a rumored six-figure advance from her publisher, Simon & Schuster, for her feminist-bashing book, *Who Stole Feminism?* (Furthermore, the buzz created around Sommers's book was instigated by the right wing's own media.) Roiphe did get an advance, but her research was done on her own time and it belongs to her.

Clearly, conservative women are effective in ways feminists just aren't right now. According to Ann Coulter, "We're using the courts to make law, just the way liberals used to." Laws against so-called partial-birth abortions and any sex that isn't intercourse (a.k.a. sodomy), which are sweeping through state legislatures, are two gleaming examples of this tactic. The right also understands the interconnectedness of issues, and the value of a vague name. This combination enables them to oppose funding for reproductive rights and AIDS research under the aegis of the Family Protection Act or the Teen Endangerment Act. Right-wing "feminists" would never say outright that they are anti-woman or anti-education, despite the fact that all of their work gets funneled in that direction. Instead, they support "Opportunity Scholarships," which divert money from public schools into religious academies, and a Social Security Trust Fund, which would privatize benefits right out of the hands of women. (Privatizing Social Security means taking the savings account or trust fund out of the hands of the government, where it is regulated, and handing it over to "private" Wall Street investment firms. This hurts women because, having earned less their entire lives because of the wage gap, they will have less money to invest.) Of course, the Republicans also have gained control of everything, from Congress in 1994 to local school boards, often through "stealth candidates"; that is, radical religious fundamentalists who have no voting record for the average voter to turn to.

Just as the right has borrowed a few tactics from the left, we are beginning to crib from them—with a few glitches. The Pro-Choice Public Education Project and many other pro-choice groups have created proactive media campaigns in order to shock young women about the fragile state of choice and, hopefully, mobilize them to go to the voting booths each November. So far this is banking on the assumption that these campaigns' messages will resonate with young women. The groups might have more success if they funneled this same amount of money into training young women to be spokespeople for their generation and to the media—going to young women rather than handing down to them. The left is also just beginning to form liberal think tanks, but most aren't women-centered. Therefore feminists are creating their own think tanks, such as Naomi Wolf and Margot Magowan's Woodhull Institute, Faye Wattleton's Center for Gender Equality, and the Policy Institute of the National Gay and Lesbian Task Force. To do so, we must compete for a fraction of the measly 5.7 percent of philanthropic dollars committed to programs for women and girls. Corporations are rarely our allies.

Conservatives often accuse feminism of being elitist, which is laughable. The few black people who attend the Republican

National Convention get a disproportionate amount of camera attention, but nothing is whiter than the right wing, and nowhere besides feminism does one find a social-justice movement that has such a proud history of multiculturalism and of visible lesbian activism.

The irony of the new, ambitious Right Girls is that a conservative woman leader will never be "man" enough to garner the support to really lead the right wing, just as black, Latino, Jewish, or gay conservatives will never be Waspy and straight enough to really represent right-wing values adequately. Conservative women are hindered by the sexism that they try to maintain. To wit: when Elizabeth Dole announced her exploratory candidacy in March 1999, a Republican at the press conference assured the *The New York Times*, "[I] don't believe a woman ought to be in that particular place of leadership. She would be a good helpmate. But, the Bible teaches us that women shouldn't have that authority over men." (*Sigh.*) Phyllis Schlafly has written five books on defense and foreign policy, but you wouldn't know it from her role in the movement. When she tries to get out of the kitchen of fighting against the ERA or gay marriage, her expertise is hardly welcomed. And it's clear that the Right Girls are facing the same barriers. "Reporters never want to ask me about substance," says April Lassiter, whom *Harper's Bazaar* dubbed the Alanis Morissette of the right. "They just want to talk about how I dress." Likewise, Virginia Postrel, a conservative editor and author (*The Future and Its Enemies*) profiled in the November 1999 issue of *Vanity Fair*, is "alarmingly well-informed" (according to Sam Tanenhaus, the piece's author) on many issues. Her husband, Steve, postulates that she isn't called on for her expertise on Silicon Valley or, well, *the future* because "she's a woman." Or, as comedian Bill Maher put it in his 1998 profile of Laura Ingraham for *Esquire*, "[She] is a strong, smart, beautiful woman—and except for the smart and strong part, that's exactly what men crave."

It's the same old sexism, but without a feminist argument

with which to fight it. Although the Right Girls don't share consciousness with feminists, they do share contentiousness within their own ranks—despite racial, economic, and heterosexual hegemony. Jean Hardisty, a philanthropist and expert on the right, noted in her book *Mobilizing Resentment*, "In 15 years of observation, I have never seen Phyllis Schlafly and Beverly LaHaye together in the same room. I have never heard or seen them refer to each other. I have never seen the Women's Freedom Network tell its members about either the Eagle Forum or Concerned Women for America." However, conservative women's long-term infighting remains behind closed doors, and the press doesn't pick up on it the way it did the long spat between Betty Friedan and lesbians. The former seem to dislike each other enough not to give each other props, but they don't attack each other. Or perhaps their catfights aren't of interest to the media in the same way that feminist ones are. Regardless, it's clear they are not at cross-purposes, and their ability to look beyond their differences is another reason we should be watching them closely. It's in distinct contrast to how the feminist movement treats women like Katie Roiphe.

While we watch the Right Girls in order to protect ourselves from attacks on our liberties, we should also get a load of their walking, talking contradictions. Danielle Crittenden, the former editor of IWF's magazine, *The Woman's Quarterly*, made the rounds—and probably the bucks—with her book *What Our Mothers Didn't Tell Us: Why Happiness Eludes the Modern Woman*. For Crittenden, happiness lies only in having a husband and children. Her book's premise is that feminism has "robbed women of a choice that belonged to every previous generation of women—the choice to care for their children and expect support from their husbands for doing so." In reality, it was feminism that made motherhood a "choice," not a must, and is still striving to attribute an economic value to parenthood and work in the home. Meanwhile, did Crittenden fail to notice that she herself is a working mother, and has kept her own name?

In the final analysis, feminists may underestimate the threat of the Right Girls because we assume they must have some sense of self-preservation. These women are ambitious and are drawn to the right because it is easier to rise to the top as a conservative woman. After all, they're promoting an agenda that strengthens male power; therefore right-wing men are comfortable promoting them. (Conversely, men on the left are in some ways more resistant, because women's equality imperils their unearned privilege.) Knowing, as we do, that very few female conservative leaders, from Schlafly to Fitzpatrick, really practice what they preach (full-time-high-powered-speaking-tour jobs that they have), it's hard to take their actions seriously. But we will realize that we have to when we can't download research in the library because the right wing has demanded "content filters," or when we go to a museum and learn that it's open only on Tuesdays from one to four because of budget cuts, or when an eighteen-year-old goes to refill her birth control and discovers that she needs parental notification.

Clearly, right-wing stars want what feminists want: independence and freedom. Therefore there is one thing to keep in mind about right-wing women: don't do as they say; do as they do.

CHAPTER EIGHT

What Is Activism?

FREE TO BE . . .

Amy:

When I was about eight years old I wanted desperately to go to Girl Scout camp. I was slightly too young, but my mother hinted that it might be a possibility. I made it impossible for her to say no: I won a free ride to camp by selling Girl Scout cookies to cover the cost. I was an entrepreneurial kid, so I confidently set out, going door-to-door, and approached anyone I could think of: teachers, the crossing guards, and strangers on the bus. I got to go to camp, and I was the top cookie salesgirl.

As proud as I am to have clear capitalist talent, I'd prefer to credit my early days in my brown uniform and beanie with nurturing the budding young activist in me. That experience certainly was a part of my early training. However, I think the real genesis of my instinct for activism and organizing is something that isn't tangible. It's an innate sense that anything is possible, that you should always take a chance on a stranger, and that the worst thing you can learn is never to try something again. I am not particularly fearless, but I am daring and I do have an independent spirit. (I'm an only child. I was reared by a single mother who said, "You can do and be anything," and I'm an Aquarius.) The reality is that I'm guided in part by a sense of shamelessness, so I do it rather than think about it.

Years ago, I wrongly believed that only those with "access" to people and power could successfully take on social change. But I had it all wrong. It's really about accessing what you do have. For instance, I didn't think that I knew people with money, but I saw friends spending $20 on dinner now and then, so I began leveraging that $20 as a contribution. I have musician friends who helped me contact other talent for benefit performances and obtain sound equipment for events, and graphic-designer friends who designed invitations or flyers. I also have a few friends who can make many long-distance calls on the dime of their mega-employers, a great resource for phone banking. Still other friends have tons of acquaintances and, therefore, can amass people power for forums and rallies. These connections, which come from my community, are the real power, especially when it comes to grassroots organizing.

The fact that I make my own luck explains, in part, why I am shocked by people's assumption that I was born with lots of access to power or that it came to me easily through my "connections." What access I do have, I have made happen. This misrepresentation no longer offends me, because I realize the problem isn't the signals I send out but a misunderstanding of what power is. I have always loved a quote by Alice Walker (so much so that I want it on my tombstone): "Wherever I have walked a path has appeared, whenever I have knocked a door has opened." I have shared this quote with other people, and often they wrongly interpret it as implying an easy ride. I believe it's about acting on instinct.

One of my instincts led me to Freedom Summer '92, the inaugural project of the Third Wave Foundation. When I first got involved in organizing Freedom Summer '92, my half-dozen co-organizers and I had big dreams: we wanted to mobilize one million young people from all fifty states to vote in the

1992 elections, with a focus on states where women were running for office. This would send a signal that young people were ready to claim their political power. Meanwhile, we didn't even have a name for the organization or the project, any money, or much experience. All we had was a core group of people who were ready to divvy up tasks.

To begin, we needed a framework for our project. It couldn't be so rigid that it would thwart us the minute something didn't go as planned, but it also couldn't be so loose that it would encourage confusion and duplications. The initial goal of Freedom Summer '92 (register one million voters in all fifty states) bore little resemblance to the final product.

Conversations along the way revealed what we needed to work on and what would remain a pipe dream. I volunteered to figure out how we were physically going to get all these potential riders across the country. I went to the Yellow Pages, looked up bus, and began dialing. I explained the basics of the project to each company and soon learned the possibilities. I'm sure that my naïve first calls were met with quite a few smirks on the part of the bus company: "Hi, I'm calling to inquire about renting buses to take five hundred people across the country in one month for almost no money." But with each call I began to fine-tune my questions: "Does that include the cost of gas?" "Is there a restriction on the number of hours or miles you can drive in one day?" "Do you have female bus drivers?" (To that one they almost always responded "No.")

I was intimidated about organizing a voter-registration drive. I had passion for the work and for making voting available to more people, but I had never registered anyone to vote in my life. As it turned out, my perception was so much more intimidating than the reality. I sought out my own continuing education. I called the Board of Elections, my mother, and someone I once worked with in Senator Ted Kennedy's office asking about voter registration. From these conversations I learned about Project Vote, a respected voting-rights organization, and volunteered to spend a few days registering with them.

One of the many things I learned during my two days with Project Vote was that our proposed goal of registering one million new voters was impossible to attain. In two twelve-hour days, I registered about twenty people on the streets of Philadelphia; we didn't have the people power or enough time for a million. Even fifty thousand was a big goal (twenty thousand was the number of people we eventually registered). I also learned that numbers don't really matter. If you register five voters who weren't previously registered, it's a success. Smaller constituencies also leave room for voter education and get-out-the-vote efforts. During this period of trial and error (a.k.a. research), I developed a commonsense approach: what did we want to accomplish, and how were we going to do that?

As idealistic young activists are wont to be, we began organizing with no concern about how we were going to pay for it. From reading pint containers of Ben & Jerry's ice cream, I knew that the company supported progressive endeavors. I had a faint memory of an environmentalist friend telling me how disturbed he was that Outward Bound had to throw away its sleeping bags each year because of sanitary restrictions. Before long, I found myself on the phone with Ben & Jerry's, asking it to donate money and ice cream, and begging Outward Bound to donate used sleeping bags for what promised to be a good cause. Next, I started flipping through my address book, looking for anyone I knew who might have money. I found old employers, friends' parents, and friends of my own. In this instance, my ignorance was bliss. I didn't ask for an amount but assumed that, at a minimum, if friends could afford $40 for a pair of Levi's, they could contribute something toward participatory democracy. I wrote long, passionate letters, followed up with a (timid) phone call or a second note, and I began to see results.

During this time, I also went to the library to read about the Freedom Rides of the sixties. Unfortunately, this was an important part of history that got minimized in my U.S. history course. From these books I learned about Bob Moses, who later founded the Algebra Project, James Farmer, one of the or-chestraters of Southern Christian Leadership Conference (SCLC), and Dorothy Zellner, a wonderful white civil-rights activist who was asked to step away from the movement when it became dominated by black power. I also learned about Matt Jones and the Freedom Singers. Again, acting before psyching myself out, I called information for these activists' phone num-bers. They were listed. So my education in civil-rights organiz-ing grew from reading books to listening to oral histories. I learned so much from these people's stories and was able to convince some of them to join our efforts when we were in their neighborhood. Matt Jones sang freedom songs at our pre-trip retreat, and James Farmer (who died in 1999) told me how much harder this work was today than it was when he was do-ing it. (He knew who his enemies were.)

The Third Wave Foundation, which dominates my activist time, came together in a way similar to Freedom Summer. I had worked in a variety of jobs—as an intern for Senator Ted Kennedy, a legal intern for a law firm specializing in domestic relations, a baby-sitter, and an ice-cream scooper. These differ-ent work environments prepared me for organizing an office, and a foundation. For instance, Third Wave's mail had piled up, so I used my Kennedy office skills to impose an alphabetical filing system. In the beginning, files seemed a little excessive, since each manila folder contained only one or two things, but those same files are still being used and they are full of infor-mation. I remember when we had enough members—fifty, I think—that I decided it was time to organize our membership cards. I went and bought a recipe-card box to hold them.

These little things are both hopeful and defeating. It's excit-ing when the pace starts picking up, but it was frustrating that the current five thousand members and $300,000 in annual fund-raising didn't come immediately. This range of emotions is so hard to translate to other people. Vivien Labaton, Third Wave's director, and I often speak in shorthand—not intention-ally but because we are simply doing activism rather than talk-

ing about it. After four years of working together, we share the minute joys of activism—such as recalling when someone sent a stamp as a donation or responding positively to a young immigrant woman's request for money for an abortion. These baby steps are the best part of organizing—and proof that things happen only when people make them happen.

These examples of my work with Third Wave are just a snippet of my activist work, perhaps the most tangible way to define how activism plays a part in my life. However, the same gene that fuels this work fuels my instinct for organizing dinner parties and friends' birthday parties and arranging flowers and exotic travel plans. This everydayness of activism is what I find most inspiring. Accomplishing things often just requires accessing the power that is right in front of you, rather than looking to create something that isn't within your purview. This doesn't mean you should reach beyond your limits but scrounge around within them. Look what I did with just some cookies and the desire to go to Hemlock Girl Scout Camp.

Jennifer:
At the age of six, I already knew that I was pro-choice. I wore a button with a little wire hanger stamped on it with one of those Ghostbusters symbols that mean "No more of this crap!" Later, I debated with my Lutheran Sunday-school teachers about the intrinsic morality of Planned Parenthood's Every Child a Wanted Child slogan. Somewhere after my Judy Blume phase and my Valley Girl stage, going to rallies and writing letters to the editor became as natural to me as playing baseball or music was to other kids. I liked to stand up for myself, loved helping the underdog, and I was a theater kid—exhibitionistic and dramatic. Political activism beckoned.

I think the thrill of righteous problem solving kicked into high gear when I was barely fifteen and my big sister was sixteen. It was the summer of 1985. We had just gone waterskiing and taken a few of those terrible wipeouts. Recovering and whispering in the bathroom of my boyfriend's family's lake cabin, Andrea told me she was pregnant. She was going to college the next year and in no way wanted to have a child—she didn't even want the guy she slept with to know what had happened—but she had no money. My parents are pro-choice and deeply into communication with their three daughters, but Andrea was the oldest, the smartest, the most rebellious, the first to have sex, and she didn't want to worry or disappoint them. (She was convinced that they would judge her: "If she's so brilliant, why did she get knocked up?") Hence my mission: to get enough money for Andrea to have an abortion without involving Mom and Dad or the hapless father of the growing blob of tissue.

Andrea, a minor living in a state with parental-consent laws, went to a judge toward the end of her twelfth week to bypass that restriction and get her files sealed. (She was a member of the National Honor Society, and if it had been known that she was a pregnant teen, she would have lost her status.) Meanwhile, I got on the phone and fund-raised. She needed $260 for the procedure and we needed it by Friday, because the one abortion clinic in the entire state of North Dakota did procedures only one day a week. If we missed that Friday's doctor, Andrea told me, her pregnancy would be past the first trimester and she would need a more expensive, more extensive abortion than the Fargo clinic could do. We would have to go to what we in Fargo call "the Cities"—Minneapolis/St. Paul.

I called my boyfriend, who said that he could give me most of the $50 that his parents had given him for his recent Presbyterian confirmation. Andrea had a little bit of money from her job at Burger King, but we needed another $200. I had no money: my allowance was $5 a week; my baby-sitting rate was $2 an hour, but there weren't enough hours left for me to make a dent in the abortion price tag. There weren't any abortion funds to help us with the cost (or, at least, we and the Fargo Women's Health Clinic had never heard of any) and they didn't do payment plans. It was Friday morning. How to raise the rest of the money?

I called a guy I knew from high-school musicals—let's call him Danny Zuko. He was a senior. I knew he was going to college the next fall, and paying for it himself. He had to have savings.

"Hello?"

"Hi, Danny. It's Jenny. I need to borrow $200 for an emergency."

He told me to come over and he'd lend it to me if I would pay him back in two weeks. Aces! I pedaled up on my ten-speed (mountain bikes weren't yet in vogue), but before handing over the dough he asked me what it was for. "Oh, um, it's for an abortion—for me," I half lied. "And I need to do it today." Unfortunately, Danny Zuko was Catholic, something I hadn't thought of or I would have come up with a less sacrilegious story—something like "I need it to buy a new Gunne Sax dress for the homecoming dance."

"I thought you needed it for something else, like a plane ticket to run away," he said, looking sheepish. Not pausing to ponder why there was no dictum that Catholics couldn't abet a minor to leave the state, I asked if he had any friends with savings accounts who were Protestant. "Yeah," he said. "I'll call my buddy."

Long story short: His buddy took me to the drive-through window at Northwest Savings, the local bank, and withdrew $200. I swore I'd pay it back in two weeks. I hopped back on my ten-speed and raced two miles to the normal-looking vinyl-sided house on Main Avenue that was home to the Fargo Women's Health Clinic with just moments to spare. The security person wouldn't let me in the door, but I was able to hand off the ten twenties. Andrea, waiting inside, was able to have her abortion. I felt very powerful.

Fast-forward to the early 1990s. I am a college student at Lawrence University, home for summer break, and the Lambs of Christ, an activist anti-choice group, have stormed my town in an attempt to close down the only abortion clinic for hundreds of miles. My little sister, her boyfriend, and I wake up early on Fridays and escort patients into the clinic for their abortions. *The streets in front of the little vinyl-sided house are oozing with protesters and escorts of all ages, security guards, police, and local media. The little kids of Lambs of Christ are positioned closest to the sidewalk leading to the clinic because minors can't be arrested for getting too close or for assaulting anyone. When a woman is led to the door of the clinic, with a blanket over her head and surrounded by a dozen or so escorts protecting her school-of-fish style, the kids scream, "Mommy, Mommy, please don't kill me! I promise I'll make my bed! I'll get straight As! I'll make cookies for you! I love you, MOMMY!" with glee and hysteria.*

It was the year of the big push from Operation Rescue to close down clinics, and the country was awash in anti-choice zealots. The landscape along the highways in the Midwest was dotted (as it still is) with billboards featuring teeny fetuses and big pro-life slogans: Abortion Stops a Beating Heart; Life, What a Beautiful Choice. My feminist group back at Lawrence used the last of our university-allotted money (around $600, as I recall) to purchase a billboard on College Avenue that said, If You Can't Trust Me with a Choice, How Can You Trust Me with a Child?

Since those early days of activism, I have worked on many campaigns. Some are odd, controversial, or theatrical. Like when my college guerrilla theater group dressed like terrorists (with fake guns and panty hose over our heads) and staged a siege of the commons on the eve of Operation Desert Storm to demonstrate the horrors of the Gulf War. We poured chocolate syrup from the sundae bar all over the floor before making our escape to the Amnesty International House. Other examples are more pragmatic—helping to call five hundred or so Third Wave members before elections to encourage them to vote, or helping to found an alternative (amateur lefty) paper, The Other, *at my college.*

My most recent campaigns require only that I get off my ass, as when I organize a reading with disparate feminist writers for the one women's bookstore in New York City or help land artists for a Voters for Choice concert. Often, it's just doing a full-court press on editors at Jane (or wherever) to cover the movement for the ERA or the fact that bisexuality exists and is serving some sort of crucial and liberating role in the lives of many young feminists. Or calling Shulamith Firestone to see if we can get The Dialectic of Sex *back in print. I think of myself as an activist, and when I do, I feel the way I did when I was fifteen: strong and in control of my destiny.*

Every time I move, I make a woman's movement.
—ANI DIFRANCO
"Hour Follows Hour"

Act 1, Scene 1: 1848. The Seneca Falls Convention, the first conference in this country held expressly to discuss women's rights, takes place. Here, on a Saturday in July, in the Wesleyan Chapel in the woods of upstate New York, two hundred women and forty men come together to approve the Declaration of Sentiments, a plan of action to grant women citizen's rights. "In entering upon the great work before us," the framers of that declaration wrote, "[W]e anticipate no small amount of misconception, misrepresentation, and ridicule; but we shall use every instrumentality within our power to effect our object. We shall employ agents, circulate tracts, petition the State and National legislatures, and endeavor to enlist the pulpit and the press in our behalf. We hope this Convention will be followed by a series of Conventions embracing every part of the country." A young mother named Elizabeth Cady Stanton, one of two main convention organizers, puts forth a plank—that women must have the right to vote—which her friend Lucretia Mott almost talks her out of, asserting that its radicalism would weaken public support for other goals. And, in fact, the right of women's suffrage is the only resolution of twelve in the Declaration of Sentiments that is not approved unanimously.

Act 1, Scene 2: 1923. Women may bob their hair, "reach for a Lucky instead of a sweet," and cast a ballot in all forty-eight states. A critical mass of women who had gotten a taste of the workplace within the past half decade are at home again, replaced by men returning from World War I. The service sector is providing new jobs—laundry workers, telephone operators, and secretaries. Alice Paul, the founder of the National Woman's Party (a radical offshoot of the National American Woman Suffrage Association), is young and full of vision. So much so that after spearheading the final successful push for the vote, she publicly states that it is only an opportunity to launch a much larger battle. On the seventy-fifth anniversary of the Seneca Falls Convention, Paul announces the fight for the Equal Rights Amendment, also known as the Lucretia Mott Amendment, which states: "Men and women shall have equal rights throughout the United States and every place subject to its jurisdiction."[46]

Act 1, Scene 3: 1998. It's sixteen years after the titanic campaign for the ERA came to a halt, the victim of a ratification time limit. That July, at the 150th anniversary commemoration of the Seneca Falls Convention in Seneca Falls, there are many needs, as there were before the First Wave ended with its focus mainly on the vote. Equal and comparable pay, reproductive freedom, eradicating violence against women—all these and more had been hammered out in a kind of Constitutional Convention for Women, the 1977 National Women's Conference in Houston, with delegates elected by every state and territory.

At this 1998 conference, however, there isn't any central campaign, agenda, activism, or feminist goal. Ellie Smeal of the Feminist Majority Foundation uses her one-hour time slot to explain the Women's Equality Act, an omnibus bill that articulates the exact arenas in which women are getting a raw deal. Getting the act into action doesn't appear to be the higher purpose of this event; sales and tourism are. A huge Barnes & Noble tent sells books about women's history; multigenerational packs of women, including Secretary of Health and Human

Services Donna Shalala (followed by Secret Service men trying to blend) and sixteen-year-old Tennessee Jane Watson walk the green lawns amid outdoor booths selling crafts by women. The convention is billed simply as Celebrate '98.

But celebrate what? The fact that the ERA didn't pass? That it took seventy-two years for women to get the vote? That the Violence Against Women Act II (the one that actually protects immigrant women) is currently stalled in Congress? Presenters from Hillary Clinton to Betsy McCoy Ross, who was then campaigning to be New York's next governor, make the point that there is still plenty to be done. So shouldn't the sesquicentennial have been called Activate '98 or Flay the Patriarchy '98?

Act 2, Scene 1: 1999. September in New York City, two women sit down to write in a studio apartment on Avenue B. The coffeemaker is on. It's late. Wafting up from the streets are the psychosis-inducing sounds of the Mister Softee truck playing "Music Box Dancer" while making its rounds. "When in the course of thirty years of uninterrupted feminism," one woman types, while the other leafs through pages of clips, notes, and correspondence, "it becomes evident that a single generation can only go so far, it behooves the next generation to pick up the reins and articulate the plot that will move their cause forward. The first two waves of feminism had clear political goals that involved holding the government accountable to its citizens, the majority of whom were getting an unequal deal. In order to have a government that responds to the Third Wave, rather than a society by the few for the few, we need a similar declaration of our sentiments. We need a Manifesta."

THIRD WAVE MANIFESTA:
A THIRTEEN-POINT AGENDA

1. To out unacknowledged feminists, specifically those who are younger, so that Generation X can become a visible movement and, further, a voting block of eighteen- to forty-year-olds.

2. To safeguard a woman's right to bear or not to bear a child, regardless of circumstances, including women who are younger than eighteen or impoverished. To preserve this right throughout her life and support the choice to be childless.

3. To make explicit that the fight for reproductive rights must include birth control; the right for poor women and lesbians to have children; partner adoption for gay couples; subsidized fertility treatments for all women who choose them; and freedom from sterilization abuse. Furthermore, to support the idea that sex can be—and usually is—for pleasure, not procreation.

4. To bring down the double standard in sex and sexual health, and foster male responsibility and assertiveness in the following areas: achieving freedom from STDs; more fairly dividing the burden of family planning as well as responsibilities such as child care; and eliminating violence against women.

5. To tap into and raise awareness of our revolutionary history, and the fact that almost all movements began as youth movements. To have access to our intellectual feminist legacy and women's history; for the classics of radical feminism, womanism, *mujeristas*, women's liberation, and all our roots to remain in print; and to have women's history taught to men as well as women as a part of all curricula.

6. To support and increase the visibility and power of lesbians and bisexual women in the feminist movement, in high schools, colleges, and the workplace. To recognize that queer women have always been at the forefront of the feminist movement, and that there is nothing to be gained—and much to be lost—by downplaying their history, whether inadvertently or actively.

7. To practice "autokeonony" ("self in community"): to see activism not as a choice between self and community but as a link between them that creates balance.

8. To have equal access to health care, regardless of income, which includes coverage equivalent to men's and keeping in mind that women use the system more often than men do because of our reproductive capacity.

9. For women who so desire to participate in all reaches of the military, including combat, and to enjoy all the benefits (loans, health care, pensions) offered to its members for as long as we continue to have an active military. The largest expenditure of our national budget goes toward maintaining this welfare system, and feminists have a duty to make sure women have access to every echelon.

10. To liberate adolescents from slut-bashing, listless educators, sexual harassment, and bullying at school, as well as violence in all walks of life, and the silence that hangs over adolescents' heads, often keeping them isolated, lonely, and indifferent to the world.

11. To make the workplace responsive to an individual's wants, needs, and talents. This includes valuing (monetarily) stay-at-home parents, aiding employees who want to spend more time with family and continue to work, equalizing pay for jobs of comparable worth, enacting a minimum wage that would bring a full-time worker with two children over the poverty line, and providing employee benefits for freelance and part-time workers.

12. To acknowledge that, although feminists may have disparate values, we share the same goal of equality, and of supporting one another in our efforts to gain the power to make our own choices.

13. To pass the Equal Rights Amendment so that we can have a constitutional foundation of righteousness and equality upon which future women's rights conventions will stand.

STANDING ON SHOULDERS

Kim Miltimore, a twenty-eight-year-old from Kent, Washington, sat down one night in the fall of 1999 and fired off an E-mail to feminist.com. "I cannot accept that insurance companies cover Viagra but won't cover infertility drugs such as Clomid," she wrote. "I want to help change this gross inequity—do you have any links to groups fighting for equality in medical coverage?"

At the same time, Jewish Women Watching, a group of feminists in New York City, sent out hundreds of cards in celebration of Yom Kippur, the Jewish New Year, which listed various excuses that institutions give for not being sympathetic to women's issues. The cards offered snappy retorts to sexist comments. For example, "We don't offer child care. If women want families, they are going to have to make career sacrifices." To which Jewish Women Watching responded: "This year, support working parents" and "Sexism Is a Sin."

In Australia, junior champion steer rider Peta Browne, age thirteen, and her friend Ayshea Clements, age fifteen, protested the fact that girls are banned from riding in the junior steer ride within the National Rodeo Association (NRA). The girls filed a complaint with the Human Rights Commission, but the HRC responded with twenty-four reasons that they and girls like them are not covered by Australia's Sexual Discrimination Act. Both have been reaching out via the Internet for support to appeal this sexist exclusion.

What all these feminists have in common is this: they saw an injustice and used their rage to become everyday activists. One can be an activist with one's voice, money, vote, creativity, privilege, or the fearlessness that comes from having nothing left to lose. Activists may work within the system—by voting, lobbying Congress, advocating at the United Nations, or monitoring a governmental agency set up to protect human rights and civil liberties. They may also work outside the system—by creating nongovernmental organizations (NGOs) to fill in the government's gaps, contributing to existing grassroots groups and foundations, organizing boycotts or protests, or doing something individual and agitpropesque, like walking from Pasadena to Washington, D.C., to demonstrate the need for campaign-finance reform. (That last is exactly what eighty-nine-year-old Doris Haddock did in anticipation of the 2000 Presidential race.) A regular woman becomes an activist when she rights some glaring human mistake, or recognizes a positive model of equality and takes the opportunity to build on it.

Webster's defines activism as "the doctrine or policy of taking positive, direct action to achieve an end." Regardless of how you define it, activism, like feminism, can be something organic to our lives, a natural reflex in the face of injustice and inequality. Also like feminism, activism is one of the most confused concepts we know.

Even among women who relate to the goal of equality and the necessity of achieving it, activism can be an alien idea. To most people, the image of an activist is someone who is out of the ordinary—someone who hoists picket signs in front of the Pakistani Embassy, marches on the Washington Mall demanding money for cancer research, or chains him- or herself to trees. Given these images, it's easy to imagine that activists are "other" people—weird or dauntingly benevolent. If news stories highlighted the real faces and sources of activism, activists would be much more mundane and familiar.

Though activism can be grand or all-consuming, it is also as common and short-term as saying "That's not funny" to a racist joke, "No" to the boss who asks only the "girls" in the office to make coffee, or calling your senator to protest the passage of the House's version of the Unborn Victims of Violence Act, which seeks to give an embryo separate legal rights, thus criminalizing women who abort or use drugs. (Needless to say, this would give embryos rights that the same right-wingers won't give gay people.) On those oddly feisty days, activism can also be organizing boycotts against Nestlé for pushing its expensive baby formula in developing countries where poor women lack the clean drinking water to mix it with and should be encouraged to breast-feed in the first place. In other words, activism is everyday acts of defiance. And these acts, taken together, make up a vital feminist movement.

It seems almost odd to have a separate chapter on activism. One of our goals for *Manifesta* was to make each page a call to action. This book is itself a response to the masses of people we have come across who were looking for tools to change their own lives.

THE MYTHS

Knowing there is feminist work to be done, and that the second most frequently asked question at Ask Amy is "What is activism?," it seemed necessary to lay out the nuts and bolts of personal activism—from radical-feminist Yom Kippur cards to general advice, incentive, and myth-busting.

The first myth is that activism will bring an immediate and decisive victory. In reality, the journey to justice is usually damn long. So while the click of consciousness brings immediate gratification in itself, social change, even on a small scale, is slow and arduous work.

One example of this (on the large scale) is the active call for birth control, begun by Margaret Sanger around 1916 in response to American women's overwhelming need and desire to control fertility. A nurse in New York City, Sanger witnessed firsthand the hideous conditions experienced by poor women on the Lower East Side. After a stream of pregnancies, these women were so exhausted by bearing and rearing children that they often met an early death. Sanger made and distributed pamphlets telling women how to avoid pregnancy, and also conducted teach-ins. For both, she was jailed, yet she eventually founded both the first birth-control clinic and the American Birth Control Association (the precursor to Planned Parenthood). She converted many eminent doctors and literally millions of citizens to her cause.

Despite this popular support and demonstrated need, birth control was not legalized in all states until 1964, when the Supreme Court decided in *Griswold v. Connecticut* that married couples had the right to seek contraception. Fifty years of agitating for birth control had to happen before that legal barrier fell. Even with that hard-earned triumph, it took the radical feminists of the seventies to extend the right of privacy won by *Griswold* to protect the rights of single men and women to seek birth control.

Another famous example: before Rosa Parks refused to give up her seat to a white man on December 1, 1955, the act that initiated the Montgomery Bus Boycott, she and others had spent years as activists. They had been trained at the Highlander Folk School, a progressive political training ground founded in 1932 in Tennessee. This one act, a black woman's refusal to stand up for a white man, symbolizes the civil-rights movement to modern audiences. Parks herself is often depicted as a spontaneous actor, almost an accidental activist. In actuality, her act was a conscious part of a campaign, and nearly ten more years of nonstop activism by Parks and thousands of others were necessary before the Civil Rights Act was passed in 1964.

Change doesn't occur overnight, and the expectation that it will is often what breaks the spirit and heart of many an impassioned idealist. *The Feminist Memoir Project*, an anthology by Rachel Blau du Plessis and Ann Snitow, chronicles the voices of some activists struggling with Second Wave letdown. Carol Hanisch, who is credited with coining the phrase "the personal is political," writes about how she wonders often if she has "blown" her life because she gave so much of her heart and time to the movement, and feels unsure of what was accomplished. Many suffragists died without seeing women enfranchised nationally. When Margaret Sanger died, birth control had been legal for only two years. If the push for the ERA picks up steam and passes sometime in the next decade or so, Alice Paul, who wrote it, and Bella Abzug, who lobbied for it tenaciously, will not have lived to see this triumph; nor will thousands of less famous women across the country who feverishly organized their state legislatures. Reproductive freedom, which most Second Wavers consider to be their major goal, is a campaign that we who call ourselves Third Wavers will probably be working on in this country and internationally all our lives.

The second myth about activism is that it has to be huge—*A Million March on Washington!* Thousands of men and women marched on Washington in August 1963 to hear Martin Luther King, Jr.'s "I Have a Dream" speech. However, that glistening moment of victory and grandeur was only one event in years of unexciting, tedious, utterly essential organizing—much of it, again, women's work. Splashy events get attention, but the work behind them doesn't. Activists might not even recognize themselves as part of this process.

The third myth is the importance of the superleader. *Gandhi organizes India! Gloria Steinem organizes American women! Martin Luther King, Jr. organizes black Americans! Cesar Chavez organizes farmworkers! Ralph Nader figures out what to boycott!* Or, in our own generation, *Rebecca Walker is the Third Wave! Katie Roiphe is the anti–Third Wave! Kathleen Hanna IS Riot Grrrl!* It is a myth that effective activism is the result of one person, or even a few. Using the example of the civil-rights movement, while you've heard of Rosa Parks and Martin Luther King, Jr., it is less likely that you know about the Women's Political Caucus, Jo Ann Gibson Robinson, Ella Baker (who trained the young Martin Luther King, Jr.), and all the other women whose organizing was responsible for the Montgomery Bus Boycott. Similarly, you know Mahatma Gandhi and Jawaharlal Nehru, but it's unlikely that you have heard about the Indian women's movement of the late nineteenth and early twentieth centuries, which pioneered nonviolent resistance and the strategy of going from community to community to organize the grass roots. Seeking independence from male colonization of their bodies and lives, they campaigned against child marriages and *sati* (widow burning). Gandhi not only borrowed their techniques but tapped into their already existing movement, which then became part of the drive toward independence from British rule. (Speaking of men creating historic events off the backs of women's organizing, the Boston Tea Party was precipitated by women who refused to buy tea that was taxed by England.)

The leader of a movement has an important but misunderstood role. Because of charisma and oratorical skills, leaders attract media and mass. They usually have a gift for inspiring hope by stating a possibility that could become real, thus raising consciousness and righteous anger. But they are just the tip of the iceberg, and would have no impact without the activists who form the foundation of the movement. They are the ones who fold and mail the flyers, answer the phones, and translate the agenda to and from the grass roots—whether there is any media attention at all.

At the beginning of a new century and a new millennium, Third Wave feminists shouldn't be discouraged that we don't have the equivalent of a Betty Friedan or a Rosa Parks—an icon that the whole movement can be reduced to at our rallies. And, even when we do, nothing will be accomplished without a truly aggressive Third Wave movement to push that iceberg's tip above sea level.

Although we may not yet have a critical mass of Third Wave activists, we need to dispel the fourth and final myth: that our generation is politically, um, impotent. Our purported lack of activism is usually chalked up to vague notions of apathy. We were reared by the boob tube, and made cynical by the cold-war politics and consumerism of the Reagan-Bush era. For a while, ad executives and media pundits conjectured that Generation X was simply lazy and irresponsible—fullfilling the slacker persona of the early nineties. The apathy rap has some truth when it comes to feminism. Some people do believe that everything is fine now, and that there is no need for feminism, either because they have low expectations or because they haven't been in the outside world long enough to experience the limitations brought on by sexism. Many younger women in general haven't yet smacked up against job discrimination by sex and race—though they have certainly, however subtly, faced it socially and culturally. But history tells us that for each big leap, for each crystal-clear moment in which people refused to give up their seats on the bus or at the lunch counter, there is a time of collecting energy and stating new visions—a time of pre-emergence. Understanding that change takes time will lead us to a redefinition of our generation politically.

In a 1999 *Atlantic Monthly* cover story, "A Politics for Generation X," Ted Halstead, the writer and the founding president of the New America Foundation, came up with much the same diagnosis of entitlement mixed with political disengagement. He asserted that "young Americans are reacting in a perfectly rational way to their circumstances," but he also observed, as the sociologist Karl Mannheim did, that "political generations have been thought to arise from the critical events that affect young people when they are most malleable."

Most movements are undertaken or, at least, swept along by young people in response to some galvanizing moment. The Tiananmen Square uprising began as an issue of free speech at a Beijing University newspaper. School integration, the lynching of Emmett Till, and ordering the police to turn fire hoses on peaceful marchers in Alabama by George Wallace and Bull Connor all swelled the ranks of the Student Nonviolent Coordinating Committee and the Southern Christian Leadership Conference. Many white students in the North were so outraged by these events that they went South, and soon it become a national issue, not just a community one. In turn, the chokehold that racism had on our nation was loosened. Young men's resistance to the draft for the Vietnam War sparked the antiwar and free-speech movements of the sixties. These movements, which were started on American college campuses by such organizations as Students for a Democratic Society, as well as the ongoing civil-rights struggle, spawned the radical women's movement, which then coalesced with the reformist women's movement already in progress.

So what are our circumstances? For the first time in American history, there is no war, not even the cold war, to mobilize and bond Americans. As desirable as this is, it also makes finding a collective identity more difficult. Culturally, the meteoric explosion of the Internet has been at least as drastic a change as the fall of Communism. There are no borders, a global extension of what *Generation X* author Douglas Coupland was getting at when he wrote about all the malls having exactly the same stores, with no regional character. Percolating below this formlessness, however, are critical events: Reagan was shot, the *Challenger* space shuttle blew up, Anita Hill testified against Clarence Thomas, and William Kennedy Smith went to trial for date rape. There was also the Gulf War, the Rodney King verdict, the O. J. Simpson trial, the Tailhook sexual-harassment scandal, clinic bombings and murders of abortion doctors, and Monica Lewinsky's affair with the President. Events like these add up to our generation's political DNA. These are the circumstances to which our generation is reacting, rationally and emotionally, but rarely politically.

The most infamous moment on that list is probably Monica Lewinsky's impeachment-provoking affair, about which everyone had an opinion. However, Lewinsky herself considered the affair to be entirely personal. Some young feminists mobilized in defense of her right to her own sexual choices, and Lewinsky herself resisted the right wing's attempt to make her into a victim of sexual harassment—a political act or, at least, one with political consequences. Her story, as it is, wasn't capable of propelling Third Wave feminism onto the national stage the way, say, the fight for legal abortion did for the Second Wave. Still, the Third Wave is not apathetic. It is more likely a still-growing political force.

Although we are still preemergent, young feminists are activists in their own individual ways in every tributary of the mainstream. And, just as our feminism looks different from that of the waves that came before us, the Third Wave's activism has produced its own tactics, style, and generational imprint. Feminists of various eras, including the nay-saying Wendy Kaminer and the yay-saying Naomi Wolf, have lamented the lack of cohesion among feminists. But just because this generation of feminism is a "disparate movement" doesn't mean that it's not on the path to becoming an active movement. A woman who is working for abortion rights may seem to be working on a separate track from the Vibrator Vixen who is fighting for women to have as much sexual freedom as men enjoy. Yet at some point they realize their tracks are parallel and are heading toward the same destination—in this case, women's right to control their own bodies. A bunch of individuals doing this work adds up to a movement, and it could also catch fire if the match of yet another critical event is struck. That could be a Republican victory in the 2000 election, and thus a President who would almost certainly appoint two conservative Supreme Court justices and overturn *Roe v. Wade*. If this occurred, the feminist response would be overwhelming and fierce.

Sea changes of consciousness do not happen unless events trigger them. Learning that Anita Hill had been sexually harassed by Clarence Thomas, and then watching her vilified by the Senate Judiciary Committee in the fall of 1991, produced one such galvanizing moment. Outraged women all across the country chose sides decisively: they called their representatives and senators, and donned "I believe Anita Hill" buttons. In a sign of sisterly allegiance, female members of Congress marched together to the hearings. We were college seniors at the time, and it ushered in a burst of radical energy and a sense that things had to change for us as well. This triumphant swell of action was the result of years of preparation—from naming sexual harassment to electing women.

Before that, the Guerrilla Girls were running around in gorilla masks, shaking the art world from its sexist perch. ACT-

UP was forcing America in general and the government specifi-cally to wake up to AIDS, and in 1987, 500,000 people marched on Washington for lesbian and gay rights. In 1989, Derrick Bell, then a law professor at Harvard, resigned to protest the absence of tenured women faculty of color at the law school. *Thelma and Louise* was putting a kick in women's steps all over the country, and Linda Hamilton's ripped body in *Terminator 2* brought a whole new vision of woman power to millions of summer moviegoers. In 1991, the *Rust v. Sullivan* decision allowed states to decide whether federally funded clinics could provide pregnant women with information about abortion—a.k.a. gag rules. The Women's Action Coali-tion (WAC), which had been sponsoring monthly meetings in Boston and New York, among other cities, began organizing in earnest, holding all-male bake sales to raise money and publish-ing *WACstats*, which documented injustices against women. In other words, all the feelings of self-preservation were out there bubbling and boiling, but watching the Thomas confirmation hearings—right in our own living rooms—got feminists all riled up simultaneously. The specter of Strom Thurmond wagging his pink finger in Hill's demure face spawned not only the Hol-lywood/media/Washington, D.C.–created event known as the 1992 Year of the Woman but real collective action.

Young women at this time had their own arc of feminist ac-tivity. In December 1989, feminists protested the misogynist murder of fourteen female engineering students at Montreal's École Polytechnique. That same year, feminists also protested the *Webster* decision granting states the right to restrict abor-tion; hundreds of thousands of activists gathered in D.C. to chant "George, get out of my Bush!" and "Free Barbara's Bush!" as slogans succinctly pronounced. While an undergrad-uate at Cornell University in 1989, Alexandra Stanton formed Students Organizing Students. By 1991, 175 schools partici-pated in SOS. Around the same time, the short-lived arts collective Fierce Pussy sponsored a festival in New York City's Tompkins Square Park. Women's Health Action Mobilization

(WHAM!) organized a new generation of women who knew their bodies and their rights. Novelist Sarah Schulman recruited for her agitprop group Lesbian Avengers while on her book tour for *Empathy*, spawning dozens of chapters. And in the summer of that same year, Third Wave's inaugural project, Freedom Summer '92, took 120 people, primarily young women, to twenty-three poor and urban locales off the radar of most politicians and pollsters to register voters and educate them on how and why they should cast their ballot.

A revolutionary movement will eventually emerge from what young people are starting today. When there are as many red suits as red ties at board meetings, we might look at the Jewish Women Watching mailing and see its cards as one of the first steps. Thirteen-year-old Peta Browne and fifteen-year-old Ayshea Clements could be the Shannon Faulkners of the rodeo: the ones who got the girls in. Someday we might look back on the E-mail fired off by Kim Miltimore, the incensed medical consumer, and realize that it was the first step toward a successful campaign in which fifty million women, *en masse*, boycotted their insurance companies to pressure them to cover not only infertility drugs but birth control, abortion, and STD treatments.

We have hundreds of examples of positive and innovative Third Wave activism that has not yet brought huge and sweeping change but is slowly and surely draining the power of the patriarchy. There are all the women we have so far mentioned in *Manifesta*, who are transforming medical schools, girl culture, and the women's media. In addition, there is Inga Muscio's and Eve Ensler's public reclaiming of women's private parts with the books *Cunt* and *The Vagina Monologues*, and their accompanying book tours, and the women musicians who started the Seattle-based Home Alive after the murder of the Gits' lead singer Mia Zapata, in an attempt to make the streets safe by teaching women to kick ass. There is Mary Chung, who in 1994, at the age of twenty-six, founded the National Asian Women's Health Organization because there were hardly any resources aimed at Asian women and their reproductive health. And Kory Johnson, who in 1988, at the age of nine, founded Children for a Safe Environment to mobilize the kids in her Maryvale, Arizona, neighborhood about its hazardous waste problem. Now, eleven years since that original act, Kory is a student at Arizona State University and is still organizing for the group. There is Nancy Lublin, who at twenty-four founded Dress for Success with a small inheritance of $5,000 she received from her great-grandfather. Then a student at New York University law school, Lublin noticed that women going from welfare to work often didn't have interview suits—something that seemed trivial to legislators passing welfare reform but is actually key to landing a job. In 1996, a week after receiving her inheritance, Lublin started Dress for Success by simply asking professional women to donate their gently used suits and getting the suits to women who needed them. (She networked with the social-service agencies that were helping women move from welfare to work.) Three years after the first suiting, Dress for Success has forty-eight chapters across the United States, one apiece in London and Vancouver, and has been profiled in mainstream media ranging from *60 Minutes* to the cover of *Working Woman*.

Meanwhile, as our radical foremothers predicted, young women keep getting together for conventions. Every few years, NOW or the Feminist Majority Foundation sponsors a young women's conference, where young women prepare themselves to inherit the reins of these venerable organizations. (For instance, in April 2000, the Feminist Majority Foundation sponsored Expo 2000, which drew six thousand women from around the world, including a large contingency of young women.) In 1995, three years before Celebrate '98 promoted a crafts fair more than a campaign for fairness, fifty thousand women converged on Huairou, China, for what's known as the Beijing Women's Conference. There was a large and encouraging contingency of young women and girls from around the world, who, for an hour every day, rode on old diesel buses from downtown Beijing to the muddy, Woodstock-style fields of the conference. Women in saris, veils, blue jeans, and boubous all came together to sign the "Platform for Action," a human-rights document that included planks about issues from poverty to education and training to the rights of the "girl child." From the Beijing conference, Amy learned about the ad hoc organization The Caritas Fund, which brought more than thirty young women from diverse countries to participate. She also met women from the United States, like Rinku Sen, who at that time was the co-director of the Oakland-based Center for Third World Organizing (which has, among other things, organized women living in a San Francisco welfare hotel to insist on habitable and affordable housing), and Daphne Scholinski, a young artist who spent her teenage years institutionalized for a trumped-up mental illness called gender identity disorder (a code word for pathologizing gay kids and girls who don't wear dresses. Haven't these shrinks and parents heard of *Free to Be . . . You and Me?*). Amy was inspired by these and many more young women who are living activist lives.

So was Jennifer when, the next summer in Olympia, Washington, a group of punk women ranging in age from sixteen to twenty-three, many of whom had their roots in Riot Grrrl, decided to throw a smaller-scale women's rights convention. It was called Foxfire, and more than sixty women, including Jennifer, attended. (Men were invited, and came, to some sessions.) Over the course of four days, there were twenty-five workshops and three meals a day, plus parties, dancing, and karaoke at night—all for between $10 and $40 for the entire conference. The workshops were led by women from the community and included a disability workshop, a striptease and lecture by a transgendered woman named Diana, a speak-out against violence, an S/M workshop led by a spunky girl with green hair who taught attendees how to "play" safely, a self-defense workshop (where girls practiced screaming "*no!*" and kicking a potential assailant), a body-image workshop, and a mental-health workshop. There were also workshops on race and class where the mostly white women discussed how they could become better allies to people of color, and also organize across and against gross disparities in wealth. In addition, there were zines for swap and purchase, work shifts to divvy up the food preparation and cleaning, fire-eating, and a useful, real-life demonstration of how to insert and remove a menstrual cup. Jennifer learned about the activism of Hilary Russian, who lost her legs while train-hopping and now fights for "crip rights," as Hilary terms them, and is becoming a sort of bisexual revolutionary in her town. Most of the Foxfire girls were activists every day. Val Jackson helped run the Olympia AIDS Project, and Nomy Lamm reinvented activism by co-writing a punk anti-corporation rock opera called *The Transfused*, which debuted at the Capitol Theater in Olympia in July 2000.

Other radical women's conventions similar to Foxfire are picking up steam around the country, especially in the Pacific Northwest, with names like Badass & Free and Art & Revolution. And there are mainstream women's rights conferences, too: Beijing Plus Five (to review what governments have done in response to the Beijing women's conference), and the twenty-second anniversary of the Houston Women's Conference (the first national women's rights conference of the Second Wave, and the only one with elected representatives from every state). On the rock 'n' roll front, July 2000 saw LadyFest, a radical women's music conference in Olympia, and in November, the Rockrgrl Conference will hold forth. As these examples and this book bear witness to, there is a lot of individual organizing going on.

GETTING TO ACTIVISM

Historically, many women have become feminist activists after logging time in other radical movements. Like their mothers, girls are often politicized about their own lives by first working on behalf of others—animal-rights advocates, environmentalists, and advocates for youths, male and female. The problem is that while feminism includes these issues, these movements don't necessarily include feminism; thus girls and young women are rarely radicalized around gender.

Still, their first step comes from saying they can do anything—as even the Spice Girls seem to convey—and, in doing so, they end up challenging the causes to apply a gender lens. For example, many young women have organized to support the activist and journalist Mumia Abu Jamal, who is on death row for allegedly killing a police officer. His plight has attracted a large youth movement, the focused energy of Refuse & Resist, and lots of rock-and-roll stars. The moment of feminist activism will come when the organizers make a connection between Mumia's plight and women who are also in prison. In fact, women are the fastest-growing segment of the prison population. Their number has increased threefold since 1985. Many of these women are serving time for petty drug crimes, while their children are left motherless.

A woman might start out by saying, "I'm not a feminist; I'm a humanist, I'm an animal liberationist, I'm a vegan." Before long, though, she realizes that women—their leadership and potential, as well as the impact of social injustices on them—aren't equally included in other groups. This click of understanding sparks the activist instinct to join or start a feminist group, or to radicalize the group she is in.

Once you embrace the idea that you can change your world, you begin looking for the tools with which to do so. Although activism can take forms ranging from picking up your phone and calling your congressperson to picketing your phone company for paying women less, some tools work better than others. Clear intention, a realistic plan, and an identifiable constituency distinguish political activism from random acts. The Internet, for example, is a phenomenally effective place to distribute information and raise awareness but not, so far, to take action. For example, you may have received either the Save NPR and PBS or the Stop the Taliban E-mail petitions. (We each received them about ten times.) The authors bade everyone to mass-distribute the information when they received it, with the fiftieth signatory sending it back to either the author or NPR/PBS. The intention behind these mass E-mails was to persuade the government to continue its funding of public broadcasting and to stop the Taliban's torture and domestic incarceration of women, respectively. Ironically, even though both petitions have circulated wildly, neither ever reached its target of Congress or the State Department, according to a March/April 1999 story in *Mother Jones*. (In fact, both mailboxes crashed early on, unable to handle the onslaught of petitions.) In general, Internet petitions tend to lack explicit agendas, a realistic plan, or accurate information. A spam E-mail decrying the use of asbestos in tampons is still circulating, for example, and is untrue according to *Jane* magazine. The Internet is, however, a truly essential organizing tool when it is used correctly, disseminating information about demonstrations and legislation without killing a single tree. It also provides instant networking. For example, Kim Miltimore wrote to feminist.com and immediately had a link to Planned Parenthood's campaign to pressure insurance companies to pay for birth-control and fertility treatments. Activism starts with the acknowledgment of injustice, but it doesn't stop with the rant, a declaration that something is rotten in the state of the patriarchy, or even with the manifesta.

Volunteering is another tool that could use some sharpening. Activist volunteering must be distinguished from the "charity" variety, which can support the status quo of unpaid women's labor, always for the sake of others—Martyr Moms, again. People expect women to volunteer, in the long, annoying tradition of unremunerated work—but we need to refrain from selling ourselves for free. Organizations with lots of volunteers, most of whom are likely to be women, often execute work that the government should be funding (such as the reliance on literacy volunteers rather than on federal reading programs; victim services staffed by volunteers rather than by paid aides; docents at museums instead of paid guides; candy stripers instead of nurse's aides; volunteers at voter-registration sites, homeless organizations, and soup kitchens instead of salaried positions and job creation). Selflessness and good works are important, beautiful, and even necessary at times. But in the context of women's rights, unpaid and selfless volunteer labor can be a misuse of a woman's energy, perpetuating the myth that women's issues are somehow less important. If we go for this, we are again buying our own bad press. (I.e., "No, *the government* shouldn't have to pay to keep women safe in their homes or on the streets. *We'll* pay for that. *You* build another highway!")

We should, however, volunteer for the revolution. Activist volunteering should be directed toward organizations that are too ahead of their time to be funded by the government. For example, thirty years ago in England the first battered women's shelter, Chiswick Family Rescue, was founded because the government didn't recognize the need or responsibility to protect women from violence inside their homes. Similarly, in this country now, child sexual abuse isn't recognized adequately by the government or the courts. Therefore truly activist volunteering can help the Mother's Alliance for the Rights of Children (MARC), which runs an underground railroad of sorts for women and children fleeing abusive dads and boyfriends who have been given custody by the courts. Rather than letting the government off the hook and reinforcing the idea that it's not responsible for basic services, we need to assume that our tax dollars should go toward the needs and securities that we vote for. Volunteering should be the icing on the cake of a basically just society.

Now for the tool of constituency building. For years, at the Astor Place subway station (*and* at Eighty-sixth Street *and* on Seventh Avenue in Brooklyn), New Yorkers have rushed by a lone woman with an info-table, a sign-up sheet, and a large placard that she waved in the air. The placard featured the *Hustler* cover that portrayed a nude woman being cranked through a meat grinder. This activist, who we're calling Amber, a representative of a group called Feminists Against Pornography, appears to be the organization's only member. She prompts a philosophical query not unlike the old standard If a tree falls in the forest and there is no one to hear it, does it make a sound? If someone agitates or protests without any constituency, is it activism? In a word, no. Activism implies a certain level of efficiency, accountability, and impact. Amber does raise consciousness, but she is mostly an example of (wasteful) action, not activism.

Are we being too harsh? Social change requires that a critical mass of people support a certain law or reform, deep down if not yet openly. Many people agree with Amber's anti-pornography stance, but they are repelled by her tactics—screaming at pedestrians, for example. In Amber's singular crusade, there is no point of entry for a like-minded person and therefore she can never build her constituency. Amber's tactics leave no room to challenge, question, or engage, which is probably why she is an organization of one—and has been for more than ten years.

Without a constituency, an activist with notoriety is at best a Valerie Solanas, whose *SCUM Manifesto* is funny and radical but who remains that lone nutcase who shot Andy Warhol. (Solanas, who died in 1984, came up with SCUM—Society for Cutting Up Men—her plan for women to take over the world in 1967, just before the radical women's movement took off. She was ahead of her time, yet unable to catch up.) In order to draw people into a collective movement, one has to develop rational and effective strategies. Amber's desire to eradicate porn needs to be broken down into a plan of action. Amber herself is unlikely to take this on, given that her placard of late features a terribly abused kitten, and her sign-up sheet says "Homeless Cats." But, despite her change of campaign, harried urbanites are still treated to the danger of being hit with her placard as they head toward the subway.

CREATIVE SOCIAL JUSTICE

We think of Amber as an example of "What not to do," but a lone radical woman with a passionate idea can accomplish a lot. Margaret Sanger began as a one-woman brigade. So did record-label owner and singer-songwriter Ani DiFranco. Julia "Butterfly" Hill lived in a giant redwood for two years and succeeded in getting logging companies to reduce their destruction of an endangered old-growth forest.

Although Amber isn't a movement builder, her strategy has worked to raise awareness. (In fact, she's something of an icon, having appeared in the book *Going Down*, by Third Wave writer Jennifer Belle, and in an article in *Playboy*, not to mention her place in *Manifesta*.) And there are certainly other strategies that are more effective. We brainstormed for a single afternoon and came up with a list of alternate methods—some old, some new—to attain seemingly uncontroversial goals:

- *Women remain excluded from 39 percent of the positions in the army.*

  Responding to the objection that redoing living arrangements to accommodate women will cost too much, activists should write to the Defense Department and make the point that the cost of one F-2 fighter plane is equivalent to retrofitting the living quarters of 850 submarines. As for being excluded from combat because of our delicacy, that has already been disproved by women's role in the Gulf War, not to mention the fact that women are in something of a combat arena in the streets and even in their own homes. If the letters don't work and you want to try something more radical, try a taxpayers' strike: refuse to pay the portion of your taxes that goes to the military, just as our mothers did in protest of the Vietnam War.

- *Refugees are given political asylum in the United States for persecution due to race, religion, nationality, political opinions, or membership in a social group. Gender persecution does not count. Therefore genital mutilation, domestic abuse, and bride-burnings are not yet considered serious crimes worthy of protection on U.S. soil.*

The United States is the only industrialized nation that hasn't signed on to the Convention for the Elimination of Discrimination Against Women (CEDAW), and therefore we join Iraq and Kuwait in our insensitivity to women's human rights. Lobbying the President to sign on is the first step in attaining equal protection for female refugees. After almost two years, Wild: Womens Institute for Leadership Development for Human Rights, a group in San Francisco, actually managed to lobby the mayor to pass an ordinance whereby the principles of CEDAW apply locally. Within San Francisco's city limits, there is a mandated gender analysis of employment and public services. Though women can already sue using Title VII in the workplace and Title IX in education, this San Francisco resolution extends to cases of human-rights abuses and to discrimination in the civil, political, economic, social, and cultural spheres.

- *The few movies that portray female sexual pleasure, as the 1999 teen movie* Coming Soon *did—even without nudity and certainly without violence—are still slapped with an NC-17 (just shy of X) rating, instead of R, thus drastically reducing the number of theaters that play these movies and the number of people who see them. By contrast, the 1999 summer blockbuster* American Pie *showed plenty of male pleasure and was granted only an R rating.*

  First, call for a picket and a press conference against the Motion Picture Association of America (MPAA), the body that determines the ratings. Then draw attention to the fact that there is only one woman on its twenty-member board. If you like to organize ambitious projects, spearhead a female consumer boycott of all movies for one month to drastically reduce profits and wield some consumer force in the industry.

- *Until 1999, there was a 1901 law on the books in Alabama which made interracial marriage illegal.*

Use this example to show your classmates, book club, union—whatever—how present racism is, and how pervasive it has been. To change similar racist laws, tell states you will not travel or hold any conventions there, or buy any of their products, until the law is changed. Also, network with the state-level National Association for the Advancement of Colored People, Southern Poverty Law Center, and the American Civil Liberties Union in order to challenge the constitutionality of these laws.

- *Georgia struck down its sodomy law in 1998 (based, interestingly enough, on the case of heterosexuals engaging in oral sex). Nonetheless, these backward laws persist in a dozen states.*

    In addition to using the educational and economic pressures above, heterosexual couples, especially "civic leaders," such as progressive clergy in these states, should turn themselves in at the police station for having violated the sodomy laws and hire a lawyer to launch a class action suit, therefore bypassing state-by-state remedies.

- *Very few women in prisons have ob-gyns (obstetrician-gynecologists) or any other reproductive health care available, largely because the prison health-care system was set up for men.*

    There is a two-pronged approach to this problem. One is through the courts, where it should be argued that women are suffering cruel and unusual punishment if they aren't receiving adequate health care. The other is recruiting public-spirited ob-gyns to go to prisons regularly and do exams, similar to the way progressive ob-gyns are organized to provide services at abortion clinics, or to rural and poor women.

- *When women retire, they receive, on average, $189 less in Social Security per month than do men.*

The aforementioned 1998 Women's Equality Act has a plank about this. Furthermore, because the current disparity in women's and men's Social Security benefits is rooted in the time women take off to raise kids, parental-leave policies in the workplace also need to attribute a value to child rearing that is comparable to staying in the out-of-home workforce. A comprehensive Fair and Equal Pay Act would close the gap in wages and, eventually, in Social Security, which is based on wages. In terms of reform, women should oppose privatization and, instead, focus on passing legislation that ensures equal payouts.

- *With government-subsidized insurance, ob-gyn services are reimbursed at a rate of 60 percent of their total cost; men's urological services are reimbursed at 91 percent.*

  Women have had some success in getting Congress to pass bills to prevent shortened hospital stays after mastectomies and childbirth and to include prescription contraceptive coverage in their plans. Now we need to lobby Congress to pass an Equality in Insurance Reimbursement Act so that comparable services are comparably paid.

- *The National Honor Society (NHS), a scholarship organization benefiting high-school students, denies membership to girls who are pregnant.*

  This most likely violates Title IX. Though this organization is not federally funded, all public schools are. In addition to legal action, enterprising high-school girls could compile a list of boys in the National Honor Society who have impregnated girls, and request that these boys also lose their membership in the interest of equality and moral continuity.

We can organize women's spaces, too; those long lines for the bathroom at movie theaters are a great place to pass petitions asking for more toilets; nurses' stations at hospitals are a good place to organize for pay that equals that of physician assistants; beauty shops in the African-American community have long been sites for activism. In the fifties and sixties, a Saturday hair appointment often doubled as a voter-education seminar—and that could continue, or blossom into other subjects. Hairdressers in Brooklyn have been trained to pass on information about breast self-exam and mammograms. A salon in Washington, D.C., offers HIV/AIDS education by providing their clients with ConPacts, which includes condoms and an HIV/AIDS–education pamphlet. A salon in Salisbury, Connecticut, has trained its stylists to detect signs of domestic violence among clients. This is brilliant, not just because the hairdresser-client rapport is one of the most regular and often open relationships women have but because here is someone who's physically close enough to notice carefully masked bruises, scratches, or anxiety. Based on those examples alone, there is an opportunity to organize in every job, town, or institution.

UNDERSTANDING RADICALISM

Activism requires thinking outside the box. Radicalism means going to the root. Social-justice work is the act of digging deep to the root of social problems.

Solving much of the concerns of current feminists involves acting on laws that already exist and fighting to make sure that these laws are enforced, rather than trying to create them. However, legislation by itself is clearly not enough, which is why we advocate activism on a very grassroots scale to support the formal structures for equality. For instance, abortion is legal, yet Michelle Lee, a twenty-six-year-old mother of two with cardiomyopathy and awaiting a heart transplant, was denied a medically necessary abortion by the state of Louisiana in 1998. Instead, she was sent by air ambulance to Houston, at great expense and only with the help of abortion-rights activists (including the Third Wave Foundation), to have the legal procedure that would save her life. Given some verdicts, it's also easy to forget that rape is illegal. Remember the famed

Glen Ridge rape case of 1989, where a seventeen-year-old mentally disabled woman with the emotional and intellectual maturity of an eight-year-old was said to have given her consent to sex with a gang of neighborhood boys, who used a baseball bat and a broomstick to molest her? And, even though Title IX has been in place for almost thirty years, in the early nineties gymnast Amy Cohen had to sue Brown University, where millions were spent on the football team and zero was spent on women's gymnastics.

Feminism is not concerned with Band-Aids but with a radical restructuring of society. Therefore feminist activism means figuring out how to change your life, each and every day, so that it represents your values. Here are radical, not reformist, approaches to women's oppression.

PRISONS AND CORPORATE WELFARE

Nearly 130,000 women are spending a portion of their lives locked up in prisons. The number of women in New York State prisons alone rose 148 percent in a recent five-year period. Women are outpacing men in prison-population growth, at a national rate that is double that of men. These women are consistently poor, and 50 percent are women of color, which is nearly twice the proportion in the population at large. Once there, they are often used as a cheap labor force for corporations from TWA (on reservation-booking lines) and MicroJet (as machinists) to Starbucks (which used prison labor for coffee roasting until recently).

For these reasons, the women's space known as women's prisons has to be organized. Jails must be made more woman-friendly—cleaner, safer, and more conducive to seeing one's children, and with therapy, job training, and other services. But improving prisons is just treating the symptom, not the disease, of women's oppression. The radical step is to prevent women from resorting to criminal behavior, and to keep their behavior from being criminalized.

First: "The crime problem can only be addressed ultimately

by the eradication of poverty, by the eradication of the circumstances that lead people to commit the kinds of crimes for which most people are sent to prison," Angela Davis, the University of California, Santa Cruz professor and famous radical, told *Ms.* magazine in 1998. Second, how we define what a criminal act is needs to be reevaluated. Davis points out the double standard. Drug trading is criminal, with sentences of up to fifteen years for even a few bags of marijuana. Illegally trading millions of dollars is a white-collar crime, with a sentence of as little as eighteen months. We must redefine crime according to how many people were hurt by the act. Then a woman arrested for possession of an ounce of crack or cocaine would receive a suspended sentence for her first conviction, rather than the fifteen years she currently serves under mandatory drug laws. Street crime costs us $3.8 billion a year, according to FBI statistics. Corporate white-collar crimes, contract fraud, environmental crimes, worker injuries due to company negligence, and the costs of dealing with dangerous consumer products total nearly $3 *trillion* each year, according to Ralph Estes, a professor at American University, in his 1998 book, *The Tyranny of the Bottom Line*. In addition, the federal government shells out $125 billion in tax breaks that are really corporate welfare. Meanwhile, the welfare given as temporary aid to needy families comes to a mere $16.5 billion annually. The tax breaks divert money that should be the government's (according to the tax laws that the little people have to obey) back to a private company. Therefore the government is passively subsidizing business and, at the same time, declining to collect tax revenue that could be used to fund social programs.

PAY INEQUALITY

Women make on average 33 percent less than men. So far we have been unable to raise women's wages because women are clustered in the kinds of jobs that don't pay much. The most effective implementation of equal pay has been in the public sector, because the federal government, which employs nearly 10 percent of all Americans in the workforce, can't help but conform to the Civil Rights Act and the Equal Pay Act. The standards that have been imposed on the public sector have to be imposed on the private sector, including small businesses, which have traditionally been exempt from government regulations due to the small number of employees. Jobs should be coded according to comparable worth.

Ellen Bravo, co-director of the pink-collar workers' organization 9 to 5, compared the 82-percent-female job of gift-shop salesclerk with the 81-percent-male job of car sales in the January 2000 issue of *Ms*. Both positions are in the same line of work—sales—and require the same skills (knowledge of the product and people skills). Gift-shop employees typically make minimum wage, while employees at car dealerships pull in a hefty base salary plus commissions. If these sales positions were coded for comparable worth—and at the same designation— we might see gift-shop work become a long-term, unisex career. Similarly, accountants are usually male and likely to be more highly educated than the usually female job of bookkeeper. Still, they have much the same skills and job requirement; therefore their universal designation should be the same. Players in the NBA and players in the WNBA require the same skills and should receive the same base compensation (at present, women start at $20,000, men at $90,000). Once you begin to pay equally, women's value is raised in every sense of the word. Higher salaries make a profession more desirable—for those who choose it and for those who observe it. Suddenly people begin to say, "Wow, Teresa Weatherspoon must be a great player. The WNBA must be worth watching." (This pay jump could be closer than we imagine. It took only two years for the WNBA to average ten thousand spectators per game. It took the NBA more than thirty years to secure this kind of audience.)

BODY IMAGE

For years, feminist groups have lamented the prevalence of skinny models and linked it to girls' low body image and the high incidence of eating disorders among them. The main solution has been to get girls to stop revering models rather than to change the models themselves. In 1999, the director of Spain's Salon Gaudi (an influential fashion show) announced that he would no longer accept women who were smaller than a size 40, which is the equivalent of a U.S. size 10. (The average size now is 6 or smaller.) This takes the onus off girls to stop admiring models and instead changes the role model.

LEGAL EQUALITY AND WORK

Scandinavian countries have a national system of child care, parental leave for both mothers and fathers, close to equal numbers of male and female governmental representatives, and a narrower pay gap than do other countries. Sweden's budget devotes 6.6 percent to defense and nearly 20 percent to education. Iceland has long had a feminist political party, and it gave this glacial isle its first female president decades ago. Countries such as Iceland and Sweden have created a climate in which inequality is less tolerated.[47] Meanwhile, in France in 1998, two resolutions were introduced to that country's governing body: one that required an equal number of men and women as candidates from each political party, and another that legally recognized homosexual couples. France also recently reduced the workweek from thirty-nine to thirty-five hours, with no loss in pay (which proves that the government can put limits on the workplace that will make the home, traditionally the female sector, as important as the work sector). And in Tokyo, the city government advances up to $4,300 to victims of domestic violence so they can press charges against their perpetrators. These are all strategies that feminists in other countries have pioneered and that we can learn from.

Knowing that these examples exist makes the possibility of changing our own unequal situation all the more imaginable.

But even in the United States, where capitalism is king, a few megacorporations are attempting creative solutions. The Xerox

Corporation offers its employees a $10,000 Life Cycle Assistance Program, money that can go toward day care, elder care, extended health care, or the down payment on a home. Meanwhile, the *Harvard Business Review* reported on different approaches to diversifying the workplace in its September/October 1996 issue. Authors David A. Thomas and Robin J. Ely found that the usual approach, which they called the "Discrimination and Fairness" model, consisted of hiring women and people of color purely for their numbers, and expecting that these hires wouldn't change the workplace. In that climate, people who were hired simply to make a white male company look diverse often did not advance.

The second model, "Access and Legitimacy," attempted to mentor women and people of color for decision-making roles. Good enough, but the problem was that these token leaders were then expected to marginalize their expertise—a black woman, for example, would handle an "urban" account, or a product designed primarily for black usage.

The emerging paradigm, the "Learning and Effectiveness" model, connects diversity to work perspectives. As the authors observed, "[I]t wasn't a commitment to window-dressing and continu[ing] programs as usual. The commitment was to become a diverse organization and radically move [the] program." This meant supporting the leadership style that was natural to a given employee, even if it means altering the protocols of how business is done. If a woman "became emotional" during a particularly heated board meeting, her expressiveness wouldn't be seen as evidence of her inability to handle her job but simply as her way of communicating an opinion. In a sales organization that had relied exclusively on aggressive cold calling, a saleswoman's ability to develop long-term relationships with clients would be recognized as valuable, even if she didn't have a lot of success with direct calls and with fishing for new clients. This would affect the work style of the entire office, and new employees would be trained in the *quality* as well as the *quantity* of sales.[48]

As the Thomas and Ely study illustrates, feminist inclusion in male worlds doesn't mean just adding women and stirring; nor does it mean including women simply to address "women's issues." Instead, previously male-defined companies can learn how to have a more effective and representative company. That concept can be applied to a country, foundation, family, bodega, radio station—*everything*.

We also have to take a hard look at how feminists are being bought off by business as usual. For instance, when women's groups, traditionally underfunded, are engaged with the corporate sector, the conflicts usually have to do with whether the money is dirty. Obvious bugaboos are tobacco money (such as Philip Morris), clothing manufacturers that use sweatshop labor (such as Nike), and sexploitative industries (such as Playboy Enterprises). Instead of making a choice between poverty and purity, women should presume power in the situation (other than the power to say "no" to much-needed financial support). Women's groups could form a pro-feminist cartel. The cartel's rules would be that any company that supported women's causes also had to support feminist values: equality on their boards and in their pay scales, good health care, and subsidized child care for starters. The power to enforce their rules would come from their own constituents and the consumer boycotts they could launch using their affiliations and mailing lists. Good companies would be rewarded and supported.

Similarly, grassroots activists, in their urgent belief in justice and their passion for their cause, eschew critical alliances not only with corporations but with people in positions of power. For example, in rape cases, activists could make it a priority to work with the county prosecutor's office, the hospital, and the police to raise consciousness about how to gather forensic evidence that would distinguish consensual sex from an assault.

Smoking is one of those things that, like everyone else, feminists love to hate—or, at least, hate to love. Our national ambivalence means that in the past fifteen years cigarette companies have been banned from more and more avenues of advertising, fined surreal amounts in class-action suits on behalf of cigarette addicts, and found that smokers' rights are an oxymoron. As part of an ongoing bid for popular support, to-bacco companies have turned to the groups that receive the least support from society: gay people, women, and people of color. The Kool Jazz Festival, the Virginia Slims Dueling Divas contest, and the Philip Morris–supported Doors of Hope domestic-violence initiative (part of the Family Violence Pre-vention Fund) are among tobacco money's progressive funding and philanthropy. In other words, the government and your own mother may hate you because you're gay, but the Marl-boro Man would like to be your special friend. Virginia Slims, owned by Philip Morris, demonstrated its commitment to women artists and community activists in Atlanta in 1999—as well as ten other cities—by giving $5,000 to one female band and up to $10,000 to a local AIDS charity in each locale. But, in Georgia alone, Philip Morris also gave more than $500,000 to Congress members who consistently voted against women's rights, gay rights, and even AIDS funding. Campaign-finance reform *is* a feminist issue.

Meanwhile, if Philip Morris is going to buy its way into women's, gay, and minority people's groups and souls, fine, but it should really pay. Therefore, rather than smile when an orga-nization such as Teach for America gets a $2,000 check from Philip Morris, the board members should write back: "Thanks, but your revenues were over $5 billion last year, much of which came from young women. We look forward to the other $48,000. Or you will pay the consequences: consumer boy-cotts, negative press about your hypocrisy, and, if we're lucky, even a penalty from the government."

If corporations were freed by campaign-finance reform from their prostitute-john relationship with elected officials, Philip Morris would have an extra half a million to give to community-development projects. Until that time (and until the government fulfills its responsibility to the citizens it repre-sents), progressive individuals are left to pick up the slack—which is where philanthropy comes in.

Almost all activism requires some money, whether it's the quarter to make the phone call, $20 to buy supplies for picket signs, or $10,000 to rent a bus to take forty people to Washington for a march. It's time to explain that the everyday philanthropist is not a Rockefeller. And that writing a check itself is a form of activism. Anyone who wants her checkbook or credit-card statements to reflect her values—understanding that if one can find the nine dollars to go to the movies once a week, one can probably find twenty bucks a month to donate to Hale House—is a philanthropist.

In the wake of government cutbacks, progressive projects are increasingly dependent on fund-raising from individual donors. The visibility and raw cash that stars bring to organizations is undeniable and essential. Increasingly, the only way grassroots activists can get their messages across in the media is by hooking up with a celebrity. Thus, a proposition: if every rock star would do two benefit concerts a year, the music world could provide the yearly budgets for many grassroots organizations. It's such a simple equation. A typical midsize organization—the Third Wave Foundation, for example—has an annual operating budget of $300,000. Pearl Jam can net $50,000 in profits on a single 3,000-seat benefit concert. Two shows of that magnitude per year, plus a couple of grants, and the Third Wave Foundation could devote itself to its programs—paying for young women's abortions and granting scholarships, for instance—rather than having to spend a majority of its time begging for money (which pays for mailings to beg for more money). But, given how important rock stars have become to the underfunded progressive groups, is the rock-politic alliance as conscious and effective as it could be?

The short answer is no. Here are a few examples of what often goes wrong and how to fix it. At the 1997 Pearl Jam concert benefiting Voters for Choice, Gloria Steinem addressed the audience, as she always does at events for the pro-choice political-action committee that she co-founded. Electricity was in the air, the show was sold out, and the sexy heroine of feminism was about to commune with three thousand people who had paid to support a woman's right to choose. She entered the stage; the audience booed. They had come for the music—or, at least, to hear Eddie Vedder's message, not Steinem's. Supposedly, this crowd didn't come because of the politics, nor did the majority of the crowd at the 1999 Rage Against the Machine/Beastie Boys show at the Meadowlands. The purpose of the concert was to raise money and awareness for the aforementioned Mumia Abu Jamal. The arena held 20,000 (mainly white male teen) fans. When the pro-Mumia activists took the stage to speak between sets, the crowd booed and some even screamed racist remarks such as "Kill him" and "Lynch him." Pearl Jam, Rage, and the Beastie Boys can't control who their audience is, but they can do a few things to make these concerts more conducive to consciousness-raising.

First, the activists, clearly vulnerable in the milieu of thousands of amped-up rock fans, should always be introduced by a member of the band, and that band member should stay onstage with the activist, lending support and respect. Two, the concert lineups need to be more diverse in order to draw the kind of crowd that is ready to hear the message of Mumia or women's rights. Rage/Beasties had neither a woman nor a black artist, glaring omissions given the issues at stake. Finally, the artists have to be activist enough to make these concerts politically credible atmospheres, which requires doing more than one-shot approaches to political issues. The politics musicians support should be a part of their everyday lives, not just their performances.

In 1999, the alternative-rock trio Smashing Pumpkins actually went one step beyond the typical rock activism of lending one's name or doing one benefit concert, the expenses of which are usually picked up by the benefiting foundation. Smashing Pumpkins underwrote its own fifteen-concert tour (to the tune of $1 million), and gave away the gross profits—another $1 million—to local children's programs such as Hale House, a New York City–based nonprofit organization that cares for children who were born addicted to drugs, alcohol, or tobacco, as well as children who were abandoned.

Most of us will never have a million dollars to give away, but truth be told, rock stars in general could probably *afford* to give away a lot more. But if you break down the Smashing Pumpkins' million dollars, it was composed of $25 concert tickets. That twenty-five bucks could have been given directly to Hale House by the concertgoers themselves, which would be philanthropy in action, or music lovers could buy a CD and give away the difference.

Raising the floor, thinking outside the box, every person is a philanthropist . . . these are all phrases that don't often speak to our generation. Underneath these clichés, though, are revolutionary strategies for making the world look a lot more feminist. In the beginning of this chapter, we said that Generation X is a pre-emergent political force. So what will our emergence bring? Given the activism that has preceded us, one enormous change appears to be in the territory of gay rights. In the next few years, critical masses of kids who have gay/lesbian/bisexual/straight alliances at their high schools—for example, GLSEN (Gay, Lesbian, and Straight Education Network) alone has more than eighty such alliances in high schools across the United States—will reach voting age. Add to that gay-rights momentum the fact that the first waves of children born to openly gay parents will come of age, never having known a time when gay people weren't on TV, in Congress, or on the cover of (not to mention owning) *Rolling Stone*. Someday the atmosphere in the United States won't tolerate anti-gay bigotry—and not just on paper but in fact.

A hundred years ago, not long before Freud asked a similar question, Elizabeth Cady Stanton turned to her friends and said, "What do you women want?" If the answer to this question, and to a similar question, "What do I want?," is "to be free, to be adults and not just girls, to have volition over and dignity within our lives," each person has to become an activist. The poet and activist June Jordan recalls listening to her hero Martin Luther King, Jr. speaking on the radio in the late sixties, and, for the first time, not agreeing with everything that he said. She realized right then that she had her own ideas; she knew what freedom meant to her. That powerful moment is the click of understanding that challenges you to do something about your ideas. When our generation begins to take ownership of our own ideas, and thus our activism, we will have drawn closer to a world of equality.

A Day with Feminism

Women and men are paid equal wages for work of comparable value, as is every race and ethnic group, co-parenting is a given, men lengthen their lives by crying and otherwise expressing emotion, and women say "I'm sorry" only when they truly should be. To the extent that we can imagine this even now, this is the equality feminists have been working for since that day in Seneca Falls in 1848. With each generation, the picture will get bigger and at the same time more finely detailed.

When Elizabeth Cady Stanton and her crew wrote the Declaration of Sentiments, they knew that this nation's Declaration of Independence would have no justice or power unless it included the female half of the country. For these women, equality was being full citizens who were able to own and inherit property, just as men were, to have the right to their own children, and the ability to vote. In 1923, Alice Paul had the vision to write the Equal Rights Amendment so that laws could not be made based on sex, any more than they could be made based on race, religion, or national origin. By the 1970s, Betty Friedan, Audre Lorde, Gloria Steinem, and Shirley Chisholm could imagine women's equality in the paid workforce, a new vision of family and sexuality, and legislative bodies that truly reflected the country. They could not have foreseen a twenty-three-year-old White House intern who owned her own libido and sexual prowess the way Monica Lewinsky did. (They certainly wouldn't have imagined that a woman with that much access to power would just want to blow it.)

Now, at the beginning of a new millennium, we have witnessed a woman running for President who has a chance of winning, a first lady who translates that unparalleled Washington experience into her own high-flying political ambitions, easily reversible male birth control, gay parenting, a women's soccer team that surpasses the popular appeal of men's, and parental leave for both parents. And we can imagine more: federally subsidized child-care centers for every child and legalized gay marriage in all fifty states. A number of leaps are still needed to bring us to a day of equality, but at least we can begin to picture what such a future might hold.

Whether children are born to a single mother, a single father, two mothers, two fathers, or a mother and a father, a family is defined by love, commitment, and support. A child who has two parents is just as likely to have a hyphenated last name, or choose a whole new name, as she or he is to have a father's or birth mother's name. Carrying on a lineage is an individual choice, not the province of the father or the state.

Men work in child-care centers and are paid at least as well as plumbers, sanitation workers, or firefighters. When kids sit down to their breakfast Wheaties, they are as likely to confront a tennis star like Venus Williams as a golf pro like Tiger Woods. On TV, the male and female newscasters are about the same age and, whether black or white, are as likely to report foreign policy as sports. In general, people on camera come in all shapes and sizes. If you are watching drama, women are just as likely to be the rescuers as the rescued, and men are just as likely to ask for help as to give it. Women are as valued for their sense of humor as men are for their sex appeal. On

Monday-night television, women's soccer or basketball is just as popular as men's basketball or football. Barbie no longer has feet too tiny to stand on or finds math hard; nor do girls. G.I. Joe, now a member of a peacekeeping force, likes to shop at the mall. In grade school, boys and girls decorate their bedrooms with posters of female athletes.

By the time girls hit junior high, they have already had the opportunity to play sports, from soccer to Little League, hockey to wrestling, and they share gymnastics and ballet classes with boys. Boys think ballet and gymnastics are cool. Kids hit puberty fully aware of how their bodies work: erections, nocturnal emissions, periods, cramps, masturbation, body hair—the works. These topics still cause giggling, curiosity, and excitement, but paralyzing shame and utter ignorance are things of the past. In fact, sweet-sixteen birthdays have given way to coming-of-age rituals for both genders, and don't assume that the birthday kid has never been kissed. Around the time that girls and boys are learning how to drive, both have mastered manual stimulation for their own sexual pleasure.

In high school, many varsity teams have coed cheerleaders, athletes all, but mostly cheering is left to the fans. Differences in girls' and boys' academic performance are as indistinguishable as differences in their athletic performance though they are very different as unique individuals. Some girls ask other girls to the prom, some boys ask boys, and that is as okay as going in as a mixed couple. Some go alone or not at all, and that's okay, too. Athletic scholarships have no more prestige or funding than arts scholarships.

Students take field trips to local museums where women are the creators of the art as often as they are its subjects. In preparation for this trip, students study art history from Artemisia Gentileschi to Mark Rothko, from Ndebele wall paintings to Yayoi Kusama. The museums themselves were designed by architects who may have been among the 11 percent of architects who were female in the 1990s. Military school is open to everyone and teaches peacekeeping as much as defense. Women's colleges no longer exist, because women no longer need a compensatory environment, and women's history, African-American history, and all those remedial areas have become people's and world history.

Women achieved parity long ago, so the idea of bean counting is irrelevant. At Harvard, 75 percent of the tenured professors are women, and at nearby Boston College, 30 percent of the tenured faculty is female. History courses cover the relevance of a movement that ended sexual violence against women. Though there is still a throwback incident now and then, men are even more outraged by it than women are. Once a year, there is a party in the quad to commemorate what was once called Take Back the Night.

Women walking through a park at night can feel just as safe as they do during the day, when kids play while white male nannies watch over them, right along with women and men of every group. In fact, it's as common to see a white man taking care of a black or a brown baby as it is to see a woman of color taking care of a white baby.

Sex is separate from procreation. Because there is now a national system of health insurance, birth control and abortions are covered right along with births, and the Hyde Amendment's ban of federal funding for abortions is regarded as a shameful moment in history, much like the time of Jim Crow laws. A judicial decision known as *Doe v. Hyde* effectively affirmed a woman's right to bodily integrity, and went way past the right to privacy guaranteed by *Roe v. Wade*. Abortion isn't morally contested territory because citizens don't interfere with one another's life choices, and women have the right to determine when and whether to have no children, a single child, or five children.

Environmentally sound menstrual products are government-subsidized and cost the same as a month's worth of shaving supplies. After all, women's childbearing capacity is a national asset, and young, sexually active men often opt for freezing their sperm or undergoing a simple vasectomy to control their paternity. Many men choose vasectomies, given that it's the least dangerous and most foolproof form of birth control—as well as the easiest to reverse. Men are screened for chlamydia, human papilloma virus, herpes, and other sexually transmitted diseases during their annual trip to the andrologist. Doctors learn how to detect and treat all of the above, in both men and women. Although the old number of three million or so new cases of STDs each year has dropped to half that amount, STDs are still as common (and about as shameful) as the common cold—and are finally acknowledged as such.

The Equal Rights Amendment has put females in the U.S. Constitution. There are many women of all races in fields or institutions formerly considered to be the province of men, from the Virginia Military Institute and the Citadel to fire departments and airline cockpits. Women are not only free to be as exceptional as men but also as mediocre. Men are as critiqued or praised as women are. Women's salaries have jumped up 26 to 40 percent from pre-equality days to match men's. There are no economic divisions based on race, and the salary categories have been equalized. This categorization is the result of legislation that requires the private sector—even companies that employ fewer than 50 people—to report employees' wages. Many older women are averaging half a million dollars in back pay as a result of the years in which they were unjustly underpaid. Women and men in the NBA make an average of $100,000 per year. Haircuts, dry cleaning, and clothes for women cost the same as they do for men.

The media are accountable to their constituency. Magazines cover stories about congressional hearings on how to help transition men on welfare back into the workforce. Many of these men are single fathers—by choice. Welfare is viewed as a subsidy, just as corporate tax breaks used to be, and receiving government assistance to help rear one's own child is as destigmatized as it is to be paid to rear a foster child. Howard Stern, who gave up his declining radio show to become a stay-at-home granddad, has been replaced on radio by Janeane

Garofalo, who no longer jokes primarily about her "back fat" and other perceived imperfections. (Primary caregiving has humanized Stern so that people no longer have to fear for his influence on his offspring.) Leading ladies and leading men are all around the same age. There is always fanfare around *Time* magazine's Person of the Year and *Sports Illustrated*'s coed swimsuit issue. *Rolling Stone* covers female pop stars and music groups in equal numbers with male stars, and women are often photographed for the cover *with* their shirts on. Classic-rock stations play Janis Joplin as often as they play Led Zeppelin.

Women who choose to have babies give birth in a birthing center with a midwife, a hospital with a doctor, or at home with a medicine woman. Paid child-care leave is for four months, and it is required of both parents (if there is more than one). Child rearing is subsidized by a trust not unlike Social Security, a concept pioneered by the welfare-rights activist Theresa Funiciello and based on Gloria Steinem's earlier mandate that every child have a minimum income. The attributed economic value of housework is figured into the gross national product (which increases the United States' GNP by almost 30 percent), and primary caregivers are paid. Whether you work in or out of the home, you are taxed only on your income; married couples and people in domestic partnerships are taxed as individuals, too. When women retire, they get as much Social Security as men do, and all people receive a base amount on which they can live.

The amount of philanthropic dollars going to programs that address or specifically include women and girls is now pushing 60 percent, to make up for all the time it was about 5 percent.[49] More important, these female-centered programs no longer have to provide basic services, because the government does that.[50] All school meals, vaccinations, public libraries, and museums are government-funded and thus available to everybody. Taxpayers have made their wishes clear because more than 90 percent of the electorate actually votes.

"Postmenopausal zest" is as well documented and as anticipated as puberty. Women in their fifties—free from pregnancy, menstruation, and birth control—are regarded as sexpots and envied for their wild and free libidos. "Wine and women," as the saying goes, "get better with age."

Every man and woman remembers exactly where they were the moment they heard that the Equal Rights Amendment passed. The President addressed the nation on the night of that victory and said, "Americans didn't know what we were missing before today . . . until we could truly say that all people are created equal." The first man stood at her side with a tear running down his face.

The social-justice movement, formerly known as feminism, is now just *life*.

Appendix 1: Manifesta's *Timeline*

A.D. 33

History as it should be: *The First Supper. Eve hangs out with New and Old Testament girlfriends, and gets the picture that she was framed. They rewrite the Bible.*

1405

Christine de Pisan publishes *The Book of the City of Ladies* in France. That's no lady; that's a feminist.

1600

More than five hundred Native American women convene in Seneca Falls, including those for whom the city was named, and try to figure out what to do about these crazy white folks who imported patriarchy.

1648

Margaret Brent goes before the Maryland State Assembly and requests the right to vote, initiating the first recorded step in the women's suffrage movement of the United States.

1792

Mary Wollstonecraft, daughter of a battered woman and sister of a boy who got the better education, publishes *A Vindication of the Rights of Woman* in England.

1835

Ohio's Oberlin College becomes the first college to admit students without regard to race or sex.

1847

Lucy Stone graduates from Oberlin College, the first woman from New England to get a degree. (Later, Barbara Seaman and Jane Pratt graduate from there, too.)

1848

In Seneca Falls, New York, Elizabeth Cady Stanton organizes the first women's rights convention, where she and four sister abolitionists draft the Declaration of Sentiments. One plank is too controversial for almost every progressive in attendance—the right for women to vote.

1855

Lucy Stone marries Henry Blackwell and keeps her own name. Together they issue a protest against the disadvantages of women in marriage.

1860

New York's Married Woman's Property Act gives wives the same right to own property that is enjoyed by their husbands, and gives women the right to joint custody of their children.

1865

One Civil War later, the Thirteenth Amendment abolishes slavery. *The Nation* is founded.

1872

Victoria Woodhull runs for President on the Free Love ticket, with former slave and abolitionist Frederick Douglass listed as vice president.
Susan B. Anthony votes illegally and is arrested.

1893

Matilda Joslyn Gage publishes *Woman, Church and State*, pointing out that many ancient societies were better for women, and Christianity wasn't so great.

1895

Elizabeth Cady Stanton publishes *The Woman's Bible*. Its message creates big-time controversy.

1903

Mother Jones takes children who are forced to work in Philadelphia textile factories to President Theodore Roosevelt's Long Island home to protest child labor.

1906

The term *feminisme* immigrates to the United States from France.

1911

The tragedy of the Triangle Shirtwaist Fire alerts people to the poor working conditions of factory workers, most of whom are immigrant women.

1913

The National Woman's Party is founded by Alice Paul.

1915

A New England nurse named Margaret Sanger publishes her zine, *The Woman Rebel*, and begins disseminating illegal birth-control information, especially to poor women.

1916

In Montana, Jeannette Rankin becomes the first woman to be elected to Congress.
Margaret Sanger opens the first family-planning clinic on the Lower East Side of New York City.

1919

The League of Women Voters is founded.

1920

After seventy-two years of struggle, the Nineteenth Amendment passes. White and black women finally get the right to vote in every state in the Union. On November 2, more than eight million American women vote for the first time.

1923

The Equal Rights Amendment is first introduced to Congress by Alice Paul on the seventy-fifth anniversary of the Seneca Falls Convention.
Helen Gurley Brown is born in Little Rock, Arkansas.

1926

Mae West is arrested for performing her Broadway show *Sex*.

1932

To train labor organizers, the Highlander Research and Education Center (also known as the Highlander Folk School) is co-founded by Myles Horton in Grundy County, Tennessee.

1933

Frances Perkins becomes the secretary of labor, the first woman to head a President's cabinet. She leads the fight for the Social Security Act and initiates unemployment insurance, aid to dependent children, and old-age insurance.

1935

Mary McLeod Bethune and Mabel Keaton Staupers form the National Council of Negro Women to fight racism and sexism.

1942

More than 100,000 Japanese-Americans are sent to internment camps; two-thirds of them are U.S.-born. One is Suki Nishi, a high-school chum of Helen Gurley Brown's.

1945

Girls Incorporated, formerly the Girls Clubs of America, is created.

1946

The United Nations Commission on the Status of Women is formed.

1954

Fourteen-year-old Emmett Till is lynched after allegedly whistling at a white woman.

1955

Rosa Parks, a longtime civil-rights activist who had been trained at the Highlander Folk School, refuses to give up her bus seat to a white man and sparks the Montgomery Bus Boycott.

1957

The Southern Christian Leadership Conference (SCLC) is founded.
The Little Rock Nine integrate all-white Central High School in Little Rock, Arkansas.

1960

Ella Baker, formerly the head of SCLC's Atlanta hub, helps young activists found the Student Nonviolent Coordinating Committee (SNCC).
Following years of unethical testing on women in Puerto Rico, the birth-control pill is approved by the Food and Drug Administration (FDA) for use by U.S. women.
Students for a Democratic Society is founded.

1962

After two decades as a single working woman, newly married Helen Gurley Brown publishes *Sex and the Single Girl*.

1963

Martin Luther King, Jr., gives his "I Have a Dream" speech in Washington, D.C., at the biggest civil-rights march in history.
"Bull" (a.k.a. T. Eugene) Connor, Birmingham's police commissioner, turns fire hoses on civil-rights activists.
The Equal Pay Act passes Congress, acknowledging that men and women in the same job should be paid the same wage.
Betty Friedan publishes *The Feminine Mystique*, urging women to drop their vacuums and head into the paid workforce.
Helen Gurley Brown takes over *Cosmopolitan* and brings unmarried sex into a women's magazine for the first time.

1964

The Civil Rights Act passes.
Barry Goldwater's Presidential campaign and William F. Buckley's *National Review* usher in the conservative right.
The first recorded U.S. shelter for abused women opens in Pasadena, California.
Griswold v. Connecticut, the Supreme Court decision granting married couples legal access to birth control, is handed down.
Chicago activist Heather Booth informally initiates the Jane abortion-referral service after a friend asks her to help his sister, who is pregnant and suicidal.

1966

The National Organization for Women is created in New York City, initially as an invitation-only group for professional women.

1967

Phyllis Schlafly creates the Eagle Forum, the anti-feminist group for conservative women.

Valerie Solanas publishes *The SCUM Manifesto* and sells it on the streets of downtown New York.

In *Loving v. Virginia*, the Supreme Court rules unanimously that laws prohibiting marriage between nonwhites and whites are unconstitutional.

1968

The Equal Employment Opportunity Commission says it's illegal to forcibly retire stewardesses for marrying or reaching the age of thirty-five.

Feminists protest the Miss America Pageant in Atlantic City, New Jersey, tossing symbols of femininity to be burned in a "freedom trash can." The term "bra-burner" is coined by reporter Lindsy Van Gelder, who compares this act to burning one's draft card.

Cell 16 is founded in Boston and Women's Liberation in Washington, D.C., and Gainesville, Florida.

Valerie Solanas shoots Andy Warhol.

1969

Redstockings forms in New York, launches consciousness-raising groups, organizes a speak-out on abortion, and publishes *Notes from the First Year*.

The National Association for the Repeal of all Abortion Laws (NARAL) is founded to decriminalize abortion.

Barbara Seaman's *The Doctors' Case Against the Pill* sparks congressional hearings on the Pill, the feminist health movement, and required patient information for all prescription medicine.

1970

Jennifer and Amy are born.

Ladies' Home Journal editor in chief John Mack Carter finds his office taken over by a group of feminists, who insist that *women* should be editing women's magazines, and articles should reflect women's liberation. They win the right to edit an issue of *Ladies' Home Journal*.

The feminist best-sellers *Sisterhood Is Powerful*, edited by Robin Morgan; *Sexual Politics*, by Kate Millett; and *The Dialectic of Sex: The Case for the Feminist Revolution*, by Shulamith Firestone, are published.

The Women's Action Alliance is formed to promote multicultural, nonsexist early-childhood education and to provide women with organizing information on diverse issues.

Judy Blume's *Are You There, God? It's Me, Margaret* is published.

The first edition of *Our Bodies, Ourselves* is self-published by a group of Boston women, later to become the Boston Women's Health Book Collective.

Women at *Newsweek* file a sex-discrimination complaint with the EEOC.

Susan Brownmiller, Nora Ephron, and Sally Kempton, three New York journalists, propose a new feminist magazine called *Jane*, but funding never materializes.

1971

Lorraine Rothman invents the Del-Em menstrual extraction device out of a mason jar, some tubing, and a syringe.

The National Women's Political Caucus (NWPC) is founded by Bella Abzug, Betty Friedan, Fannie Lou Hamer, Patsy Mink, Gloria Steinem, and others.

1972

Shirley Chisolm runs for President on the Democratic ticket in some states. At the Democratic convention, Sissy Farenthold runs for vice president.

The ERA finally passes the U.S. Senate and the House of Representatives and goes to states for ratification.

Ms. magazine hits the stands; in the preview issue, Jane O'Reilly describes her "click" and soon women around the United States are identifying theirs.

In *Eisenstadt v. Baird*, the Supreme Court extends the right to birth control to single people.

In Chicago, the police bust the Jane Collective. (In its eight years of existence, the organization helped women to find nearly twelve thousand safe and illegal abortions.)

Virginia Slims sponsors the American Woman poll by Louis Harris

Associates, the first national survey of women's opinions on women's issues. Black women turn out to be almost twice as likely to support these issues as are white women.

A "gender gap" emerges in politics during the McGovern-Nixon Presidential race.

Patsy Mink sponsors Title IX of the Education Act Amendments; it passes, guaranteeing a legal basis for equal coeducation.

1973

On January 22, the *Roe v. Wade* decision is handed down by the Supreme Court, guaranteeing women the right to an abortion, after a successful argument by lawyer Sarah Weddington.

Alix Kates Shulman's "A Marriage Agreement" is published in *Ms.*, while her own marriage disintegrates.

Ti-Grace Atkinson's hard-core women's liberation group The Feminists, founded in 1969, falls apart.

1974

The Equal Credit Opportunity Act attacks a wide variety of discriminatory practices against women in getting access to such benefits as loans and mortgages.

Seven women employees bring a sex-discrimination suit against *The New York Times*, risking prestigious careers for the cause.

Free to Be . . . You and Me, a nonsexist, multiracial book of songs and skits, is created by Marlo Thomas and Friends.

The Lesbian Herstory Archives is founded in New York City by Joan Nestle and Deborah Edel.

Girls play in the Little League for the first time.

1975

Dell Williams opens Eve's Garden, a feminist sex store, in New York City.

The Michigan Womyn's Music Festival is created.

1976

In a feat of sister power organized by Patricia Carbine, publisher of *Ms.*, thirty major women's magazines run positive stories on the ERA around the same time.

To distribute women's music, Ladyslipper is founded by Laurie Fuchs in Durham, North Carolina.

1977

The National Women's Conference, the result of legislation introduced by Bella Abzug, convenes meetings of thousands in every state, elects delegates, and hammers out a national political agenda for women at a historic meeting in Houston.

Appalled by the lack of sex toys and the number of female clients who don't have orgasms, sex therapist Joani Blank opens Good Vibrations in San Francisco.

The Hyde Amendment cuts off federal funding for abortions. As a result, Rosie Jimenez, the first woman forced to seek a cheap illegal abortion because of the lack of Medicaid, dies.

1978

The first Take Back the Night march and speak-out is held in San Francisco.

The Pregnancy Discrimination Act makes it illegal to fire or demote a woman because she is pregnant.

1979

Judy Chicago's installation "The Dinner Party" is showcased.

1980

The U.S. Census concedes that "head of household" need not be a male.

1981

The first woman justice, Sandra Day O'Connor, is appointed to the U.S. Supreme Court.

Reagan is shot by a deranged young white guy.

1982

The ERA misses ratification by only three states and goes into hibernation.

Carol Gilligan publishes *In a Different Voice*.

The Valley Girl Handbook, one of the earliest signs of Girlie culture, takes junior high schools by storm.

Elisabeth Subrin attends an Anti-Nuclear Protest in New York.

1983

Sally Ride, the first American woman astronaut, goes into space. (The dozen women who had qualified with John Glenn and the first astronauts had been washed out by NASA's no-women ruling.)

1984

Madonna's second album, *Like a Virgin*, is released.

1985

The Guerrilla Girls, mysterious women in masks, begin picketing, parodying, and exposing sexism in the art world. ("Does a Woman Have to Be Nude to Get into the MET?")

1986

Newsweek says that a single woman in her mid-thirties is more likely to get killed by a terrorist than to find a husband. Later, this turns out to be false information.
The *Challenger* space shuttle blows up, with a civilian, teacher Christa McAuliffe, on board.
Fourteen years after the federal government approved its use, *The New York Times* finally allows the honorific "Ms." to appear in its pages.

1987

Animated by the AIDS epidemic and its effect on the community, more than 500,000 people march on Washington for lesbian and gay rights. This Second National March on Washington (the first was in 1979) would be followed by a third in 1993.

1988

Sassy is launched in the United States by two Australian feminists.
Sarah Lucia Hoagland's *Lesbian Ethics: Toward New Value* coins the word "autokeonony."
At the age of nine, Kory Johnson starts Children for a Safe Environment.
Seventeen-year-old Becky Bell dies—the first recorded incident of a person's dying because parental-consent laws restricted her right to choose an abortion.

1989

A seventeen-year-old mentally disabled woman is gang-raped in New Jersey, in what later became famous as the Glen Ridge Rape Case.

Students looking for freedom of the press protest in Tiananmen Square, Beijing, China. *Ms.* later publishes an exclusive interview with its young woman leader.

The Center for Women's Policy Alternatives convenes Feminist Futures, a national conference by and for women in their twenties.

In *Webster v. Reproductive Health Services*, the Supreme Court upholds a law which supports the presumption of fetal 'viability' at twenty weeks.

Derrick Bell leaves Harvard Law School to protest the lack of tenured black female professors there.

A march on Washington initiated by NOW and the Feminist Majority Foundation to organize on behalf of choice galvanizes six hundred thousand in support of reproductive freedom.

Cornell University student Alexandra Stanton creates Students Organizing Students (SOS).

Ms. Foundation for Women launches the National Girls Initiative.

Mark Lapine guns down fourteen female engineering students at a Montreal university, screaming, "You're all fucking feminists."

1990

Twenty-year-old Ani DiFranco launches Righteous Records, which becomes Righteous Babe Records in 1994.

Two young women in Olympia, Washington, Kathleen Hanna and Tammy Rae Carland, look to each other for truth after reading a *Newsweek* article about feminism being bad for women.

Carol Gilligan, Nona Lyons, and Trudy Hanmer publish their historic study of girls' development, *Making Connections*, at the Emma Willard School.

1991

Young Katie Roiphe's writing first appears on *The New York Times* op-ed page, a harbinger of media acceptance to come.

In February, seven hundred high-school and college-age women attend NOW's Young Feminist Conference in Akron, Ohio.

At the Senate Confirmation Hearings of Clarence Thomas, Anita

Hill throws a temporary wrench in his appointment to the Supreme Court. Three days of hearings become the first national teach-in on sexism.

Several naval officers at Tailhook are charged with sexual harassment.

Amy Cohen's case against Brown University for inequality in sports strengthens Title IX.

The Ms. Foundation publishes its report "Risk, Resiliency, and Resistance: Current Research on Adolescent Girls."

Naomi Wolf publishes *The Beauty Myth* and Susan Faludi publishes *Backlash*.

Susan Sarandon and Geena Davis star in *Thelma & Louise* and a muscled Linda Hamilton stars in *Terminator 2*.

Tali Edut, a student at the University of Michigan and an intern at *Sassy*, starts *HUES*, a magazine that appears on newsstands one year later.

1992

Planned Parenthood of Southeastern Pennsylvania v. Casey affirms *Roe v. Wade*.

Nell Merlino writes a five-page memo to the Ms. Foundation for Women proposing Take Our Daughters to Work Day.

The March on Washington for Reproductive Rights draws 750,000 people.

The Ms. Foundation for Women and the New York Women's Foundation co-sponsor a conference at Hunter College on sexual harassment, at which Anita Hill speaks.

The Rodney King verdict is handed down, and awareness of racism goes up.

Right-wing women create the Independent Women's Forum to support Clarence Thomas.

In Freedom Summer '92, more than 20,000 new voters are registered by 120 young activists. It is the founding project of the Third Wave Foundation.

The Riot Grrrl Convention takes place in Washington, D.C.

The media sees rage from the Anita Hill hearings translating into women running for political office and declares the Year of the Woman.

The Antioch Rape Policy is instituted.

1993

Jody Steinauer founds Medical Students for Choice to ensure that more doctors are trained in performing abortions.

David Gunn, a doctor who performs abortions, is murdered in Pensacola, Florida.

The anti-choice Women's Freedom Network is formed.

The arts collective Fierce Pussy creates actions in response to the Lesbian Chic cover story in *Newsweek*.

Debbie Stoller and Marcelle Karp meet in Tompkins Square Park, and soon *Bust* busts on the scene as their Xerox-and-staple zine.

Nancy Gruver and family launch *New Moon: The Magazine for Girls and Their Dreams*.

Katie Roiphe's *The Morning After: Sex, Fear and Feminism on Campus* is published by editor seeking controversy.

President Clinton allows female pilots to fly in combat.

Jennifer and Amy meet at the offices of *Ms.* magazine.

1994

The Violence Against Women Act passes. Newt Gingrich introduces his Contract with America to roll back progressive legislation.

Twenty-six-year-old Mary Chung founds the National Asian Women's Health Organization.

1995

Barbara Findlen publishes *Listen Up: Voices from the Next Feminist Generation*, an anthology of young feminists, and initiates a spate of Third Wave books.

Fifty thousand activists from all over the world gather at the Beijing Women's Conference.

Tyra Banks goes to MTV to participate in Take Our Daughters to Work Day.

The "new" *Sassy* dies. Lisa Miya-Jervis and Andi Zeisler's zine *Bitch* is born.

1996

Nancy Lublin uses a $5,000 inheritance from her grandfather to start Dress for Success.

Foxfire women's festival takes place in Olympia, Washington.

1997

Lilith Fair does its first tour.

The WNBA has its first season.

Helen Gurley Brown, age seventy-five, retires as editor at *Cosmo* and puts her energy into *International Cosmo*.

The Media and Democracy Forum holds panel: "Girl Power: Progress . . . or the Selling of Feminism Lite?"

1998

British journalist Natasha Walter publishes *The New Feminism*, which incites a vitriolic response, despite being a fairly straight-forward British book.

An international court denounces the rape of women prisoners as a form of torture.

Louisiana heart patient Michelle Lee has to travel to Texas for a lifesaving abortion.

On February 14, Eve Ensler puts on *V-Day*, a star-studded version of her performance piece *The Vagina Monologues*, to benefit anti-violence programs.

In June, *Time* magazine asks, "Is Feminism Dead?"

In July, a celebration is held in Seneca Falls to commemorate the 150th anniversary of the Seneca Falls Convention.

We learn that Monica Lewinsky flashed her thong at President Clinton.

1999

Barbie turns forty.

Samantha Gellar, seventeen, fights anti-lesbian censorship at her Charlotte, North Carolina, high school.

The Independent Women's Forum launches magazines for young women on college campuses. *The Guide: A Little Beige Book for Today's Miss G* debuts at Georgetown.

Ms. magazine relaunches under feminist ownership.

Lilith Fair does its final tour, having given away a million dollars in three years.

On March 8, "A Night of Radical Writings from the Second and Third Waves" is held in New York City.

In May, three hundred girls attend the First Annual Girls' Congress at the Lower Eastside Girls Club.

The U.S. women's soccer team wins the Women's World Cup, with ninety thousand people watching up close and forty million via their TVs.

Bust girls go on the road with their recently published book, *Bust Guide to the New Girl Order.*

Jennifer and Amy have "The Dinner Party."

2000

Manifesta is published.

Nomy Lamm performs *The Transfused 2000*, an anti-corporation rock opera.

Honor the Earth and Third Wave's ROAMS (Reaching Out Across MovementS) Tour raise money and consciousness.

The Michigan Womyn's Music Festival celebrates its twenty-fifth year.

The Beijing Plus Five conference checks up on governments and their promises of equality.

2002

Universal day care is declared a public-health issue. New York pioneers a program offering tax incentives to corporations that provide their employees with on-site day care or day-care benefits.

Women are no longer taxed in their husband's bracket, because the Marriage Penalty is struck down.

The Alan Guttmacher Institute releases a study on how many men have STDs, and the FBI tells how many men are rapists, not just how many women are raped.

Congress ratifies the CEDAW (Commission for the Elimination of Discrimination Against Women), no matter what Jesse Helms says.

The Hyde Amendment is overturned because women turn out to defeat George W. Bush and other politicians who want to nationalize their bodies and take away their reproductive freedom.

Amber still stands at Astor Place, menacing people with her placard.

Appendix 2: A Young Woman's Guide to Revolution—Chapter by Chapter

PROLOGUE: A DAY WITHOUT FEMINISM

To tell the National Honor Scholarship Corporation that it's not fair to butt into teens' sex lives or the National Merit Society that it's not right to have a gender gap in standardized testing, contact:

National Merit Scholarship Corporation
1560 Sherman Avenue
Evanston, Illinois 60201-4897
(847) 866-5100; fax (847) 866-5113
www.kaplan.edu

National Honor Society
c/o National Association of Secondary School Principals
1904 Association Drive
Reston, Virginia 20191-1537
(703) 860-0200; fax (703) 476-5432
www.nassp.org

To discover a women's studies department near you, contact:

National Women's Studies Association
University of Maryland
7100 Baltimore Avenue, Suite 500
College Park, Maryland 20740
(301) 403-0525; fax (301) 403-4137
www.nwsa.org
E-mail: nwsa@umail.umd.edu

Chapter 1: The Dinner Party

If you want to raise community consciousness or create your own consciousness-raising (CR) group, these resources will get you started:

1. Redstockings (see address in Chapter 6 resources)
2. NOW Guidelines (see address in Chapter 6 resources)
3. "One Year Later and a Proposal for the Future"—an Afterword to Gloria Steinem's *Revolution from Within*. (See Primary Sources.)

To learn about ratifying the ERA in your state—especially if you live in Alabama, Arizona, Arkansas, Florida, Georgia, Illinois, Louisiana, Mississippi, Missouri, Nevada, North Carolina, Oklahoma, South Carolina, Utah, or Virginia—contact:

ERA Summit
P.O. Box 113
Chatham, New Jersey 07928
(973) 765-0102; fax (973) 660-0766
www.equalrightsamendment.org
E-mail: era@equalrightsamendment.org

If you need an abortion, contact:

National Abortion Federation (NAF)
1755 Massachusetts Avenue, Suite 600
Washington, D.C. 20036-2188
(800) 772-9100 or (202) 667-5881; fax (202) 667-5890
www.prochoice.org
E-mail: naf@prochoice.org
NAF will refer you to one of its approved clinics across the country.

If you want to share your secret of a sexually transmitted disease (STD) or an abortion, you can write to us (c/o www.manifesta.net). Or to find out if you have an STD or need to have an abortion, contact Planned Parenthood Federation of America, which probably has an affiliate near you. Make sure that the men in your life are getting tested for STDs, too.

Planned Parenthood Federation of America
810 Seventh Avenue
New York, New York 10019
(800) 230-PLAN or (212) 541-7800; fax (212) 245-1845
www.plannedparenthood.org

To learn about setting up a men's and boys' clinic like the one in Washington Heights, New York, contact:

Young Men's Clinic
c/o Bruce Armstrong
Center for Population and Family Health
Joseph L. Mailman School of Public Health
Columbia University
60 Haven Avenue
B-3
New York, New York 10032
(212) 304-5247; fax (212) 304-5209
E-mail: ba5@columbia.edu

If you're Catholic and pro-choice and want to know that you are not alone or if you believe that the problem isn't Catholicism but the Vatican, contact:

Catholics for a Free Choice
1436 U Street, NW, Suite 301
Washington, D.C. 20009-3997
(202) 986-6093; fax (202) 332-7995
www.cath4choice.org
E-mail: cffc@igc.apc.org

To make sure that your medical school includes abortion training and fosters a choice-supportive atmosphere, contact:

Medical Students for Choice
2041 Bancroft Way, Suite 201
Berkeley, California 94704
(510) 540-1195; fax (510) 540-1199
www.ms4c.org

Medical Students for Choice inspired other groups to take similar steps—all under the rubric of the Abortion Access Project:

Nursing Students for Choice and Midwives for Choice
c/o Abortion Access Project
522 Massachusetts Avenue, Suite 215
Cambridge, Massachusetts 02139
(617) 661-1161; fax (617) 492-1915
E-mail: info@repro-activist.org

Other national choice- and feminist-health-care-friendly groups:

Alan Guttmacher Institute
120 Wall Street
New York, New York 10005
(212) 248-1111; fax (212) 248-1952
or
1120 Connecticut Avenue, NW, Suite 460
Washington, D.C. 20036
(202) 296-4012; fax (202) 223-5756
www.agi-usa.org
E-mail: info@agi-usa.org
If you are looking for health statistics, the Alan Guttmacher Insti-tute is the primary authority on statistics related to reproductive health in the United States and worldwide.

**National Abortion and Reproductive Rights
  Action League (NARAL)**
1156 15th Street, NW, Suite 700
Washington, D.C. 20005
(202) 973-3000; fax (202) 973-3096
www.naral.org
E-mail: naral@naral.org

National Black Women's Health Project
600 Pennsylvania Avenue, SE, Suite 310
Washington, D.C. 20003
(202) 543-9311; fax (202) 543-9743
www.nbwhp.org
E-mail: nbwhp@nbwhp.org

National Latina Institute for Reproductive Health
1200 New York Avenue, NW, Suite 206
Washington, D.C. 20005
(202) 326-8970; fax (202) 371-8112
www.nlirh.org
E-mail: nlirh@igc.apc.org

Native American Women's Health Education Resource Center
P.O. Box 572
Lake Andes, South Dakota 57356-0572
(605) 487-7072; fax (605) 487-7964
www.nativeshop.org/nawhere.html

Physicians for Reproductive Choice and Health (PRCH)
1780 Broadway, 10th Floor
New York, New York 10019
(212) 765-2322; fax (212) 246-5134
www.PRCH.org
E-mail: PRCH@aol.com
PRCH publishes an extensive reference, PRCH Reproductive
Health Resource Guide, *which includes a curriculum on abortion
and family planning as well as a listing of videos, organizations,
and facts.*

**Sexuality Information and Education Council
  of the United States (SIECUS)**
130 West Forty-second Street, Suite 350
New York, New York 10036-7802
(212) 819-9770; fax (212) 819-9776
or
1638 R Street, NW, Suite 220
Washington, D.C. 20009-1139
(202) 265-2405; fax (202) 462-2340
www.siecus.org
E-mail: siecus@siecus.org
*SIECUS provides information about sex education and tips on
how to get sex education into a curriculum.*

Voters for Choice (VFC)
1010 Wisconsin Avenue, NW, Suite 410
Washington, D.C. 20007-9301
(202) 944-5080; fax (202) 944-5081
www.voters4choice.org
E-mail: vfc@ibm.net
VFC, *the largest pro-choice political-action committee in the United States, provides information on a candidate's position on choice.*

Beyond the corporate walls of HMV and Tower Records, there is a thriving women's music scene (or womyn's, if you prefer). It exists in defiance of the male-dominated, corporate-controlled industry (though some of our favorite artists are still available via corporate channels). Here are a few that are fighting the good fight on the indie route:

Creative Folk
P.O. Box 8021
Green Bay, Wisconsin 54308
(920) 437-7373; fax (920) 437-7389
www.creativefolk.com
E-mail: Gerri@creativefolk.com
This Web site, created by Gerri Gribi, lists more than a hundred feminist folk songs that are related to domestic violence and sexual assault.

Daemon Records
P.O. Box 1207
Decatur, Georgia 30031
(404) 373-5733; fax (404) 370-1660
www.monsterbit.com/daemon/daemon.html
Owned and started by Indigo Girl Amy Ray in 1989, the artists on this co-op label include Danielle Howle, Three Finger Cowboy, and Rose Polenzani.

Kill Rock Stars
120 NE State Avenue
P.O. Box 418
Olympia, Washington 98501
(360) 357-9732; fax (360) 357-6408

www.killrockstars.com
E-mail: krs@killrockstars.com
This feminist label is most associated with the Riot Grrrl bands of the early nineties. Owned by Slim Moon, artists include Bikini Kill, the Need, Sleater-Kinney, and Mary Lou Lord.

Ladyslipper, Inc.
P.O. Box 3124 R
Durham, North Carolina 27715
For orders: (800) 634-6044; to contact: (919) 383-8773;
    fax (919) 383-3525
www.ladyslipper.org
E-mail: orders@ladyslipper.org
The first—and most comprehensive—distributor of all forms of women's music, from Holly Near and Alix Dobkin to Joan Armatrading to Tribe 8 to Jewel. Founded by Laurie Fuchs, Ladyslipper's primary purpose is to heighten public awareness of women artists.

Mr. Lady Records and Videos
P.O. Box 3189
Durham, North Carolina 27715-3189
(919) 682-1150 phone and fax
www.mrlady.com
E-mail: mrlady@mindspring.com
Mr. Lady, founded and owned by lesbian feminists Tammy Rae Carland and Kaia Wilson, records The Butchies. It was founded to make women's music and videos accessible and affordable.

Olivia Records (a.k.a. Olivia Cruise Line)
c/o Judy Dlugacz
4400 Market Street
Oakland, California 94608
(510) 655-0364
Olivia Records is now the lesbian cruise line and therefore no longer makes new records. But you can order its womyn's music classics, such as Chris Williamson's The Changer and the Changed.

Righteous Babe Records
P.O. Box 95
Ellicott Station
Buffalo, New York 14205
(800) On-Her-Own or (716) 852-8020; fax (716) 852-2741
E-mail: RBRinfo@aol.com
Righteous Babe Records, Ani DiFranco's very own label, has been putting out DiFranco's work since 1990, along with other projects, such as recordings of the spoken-word old-timer Utah Phillips.

Sheeba Records
c/o Jane Siberry
291-238 Davenport Road
Toronto, Ontario, Canada M5R 1J6
(416) 921-1364; fax (416) 921-1024
www.sheeba.ca/lobby
E-mail: siba@sheeba.ca
Jane Siberry left Warner Brothers to strike out on her own and now runs this one-woman show. She even answers the phone.

Thrill Jockey
P.O. Box 476794
Chicago, Illinois 60647
(312) 492-9643
www.brainwashed.com/thrilljockey/
E-mail: info@thrilljockey.com
Bettina Richards owns this co-op label. Thrill Jockey's artists include The Sea and Cake and Freakwater.

Villa Villakula
Tinuviel
200 Broadway
Cambridge, Massachusetts 02139
(617) 776-8196
www.garment_district.com/store/
E-mail: ayal@garment-district.com
Tinuviel, who co-founded Kill Rock Stars, specializes in producing artists' first albums. This "almost all-girl label" features releases by Ruby Falls, Sleater-Kinney, Dame Darcey, and Fresh Fish.

Crystal Echohawk no longer lives in El Paso, Texas, but the National Commission for Democracy in Mexico is still organizing in Chiapas and in the United States:

National Commission for Democracy in Mexico
2001 Montana, Suite B
El Paso, Texas 79903
(915) 779-2003

CHAPTER 2: WHAT IS FEMINISM?

To get the story up till now, you should read the books listed in our Bibliography, and view *Not For Ourselves Alone: Elizabeth Cady Stanton & Susan B. Anthony,* a film by Ken Burns and Paul Barnes. It comes with a curriculum. To order both, contact:

PBS
P.O. Box 75109
Charlotte, North Carolina 28275
(800) 424-7963
www.pbs.org/stantonanthony/resources/

Lilith Fair is taking a hiatus, but its Web site can still provide resources and links to the nonprofit organizations the group funded, as well as contacts with other music tours:

Lilith Fair
www.lilithfair.com
E-mail: lilith@netmedia.com or info@lilithsong.org

Other Tours

The Spitfire Tour
1 Harbor Drive, #200
Sausalito, California 94965
www.colleges.com/spitfire
E-mail: spitfire@onboardent.com
Instigated by Rage Against the Machine front man Zach de la Rocha, this feministy college tour combines grassroots activists (for example, environmentalist Julia "Butterfly" Hill and Zapatista leader Cecilia Rodriquez) and celebrities who are political (such as actor Woody Harrelson, MTV host Kennedy, and rapper Ice-T) to hold town meetings and CR groups on college campuses.

There are dozens of women's music fests every summer, but the mother of them all is the Michigan Womyn's Music Festival. To camp out on the Land—and to hear great womyn artists—you should consider attending:

Michigan Womyn's Music Festival
P.O. Box 22
Walhalla, Michigan 49458
(231) 757-4766, or winter number (510) 652-5441;
    fax (510) 658-3501
www.michfest.com

To ensure that women's soccer becomes as important as the NFL, support your local teams and learn more about how women fare in sports and what you can do to speed up equality in women's sports:

Women's World Cup
www.womensoccer.com
E-mail: womensoc@aol.com

    or

Women's Sports Foundation
Eisenhower Park
East Meadow, New York 11554
(516) 542-4700; fax (516) 542-4716
www.womenssportsfoundation.org
E-mail: wosport@aol.com

To join existing Third Wave and Gen-X groups, contact:

Active Element Foundation
532 LaGuardia Place, #510
New York, New York 10012
(718) 783-6856; fax: (718) 783-1927
www.ActivElement.org
E-mail: HipHopFund@aol.com or activeElement@aol.com
This group makes grants to youth organizers and activists.

Center for Campus Organizing (CCO)
165 Friend Street, M/S #1
Boston, Massachusetts 02114-2025
(617) 725-2886; fax (617) 725-2873
www.cco.org
E-mail: cco@igc.apc.org
CCO also houses the Campus Alternative Journalism Project to counter all the conservative newspapers currently sweeping through college campuses.

Center for Third World Organizing (CTWO)
1218 East Twenty-first Street
Oakland, California 94606
(510) 533-7583; fax (510) 533-0923
www.ctwo.org
E-mail: ctwo@ctwo.org
Contact CTWO to be trained by its Minority Activist Apprenticeship Program (MAAP) and to get in touch with its associated organizations, such as Action for a Better Community and People United for a Better Oakland (PUEBLO).

The Empower Program
1312 Eighth Street, NW
Washington, D.C. 20007
(202) 882-2800; fax (202) 243-1901
www.empowered.org
E-mail: empower@empowered.org
Empower works with young people to end gender violence and build self-esteem.

Home Alive
1400 Eighteenth Street
Seattle, Washington 98112
(206) 720-0606 or (206) 903-9747; fax (206) 720-0396
www.homalive.org
E-mail: Selfdef@homalive.org
A self-defense organization by and for young women, Home Alive was created in response to the death of Mia Zapata, lead singer of the Gits, who was murdered while walking home late one night.

Kilawin Kolektibo
P.O. Box 507
New York, New York 10159-0507
A sociopolitical collective of queer Filipinas, co-founded by Sabrina Margarita Alcantara-Tan from Chapter 1, "The Dinner Party."

New America Foundation
1630 Connecticut Avenue, NW, 7th Floor
Washington, D.C. 20009
(202) 986-2700; fax (202) 986-3696
www.newamerica.net
This public-policy institute seeks to train the next generation of public intellectuals through strategy initiatives and fellowship programs.

Positive Force
3510 North Eighth Street
Arlington, Virginia 22201
(703) 276-9768
www.outersand.com/positive/meetings.html
E-mail: emmausedc@aol.com
A volunteer activist group that uses art to educate and activate young people about political and social issues. It grew out of the D.C. punk-rock scene of the mid-eighties.

Third Wave Foundation
116 East Sixteenth Street, 7th Floor
New York, New York 10003
(212) 388-1898; fax (212) 982-3321
www.thirdwavefoundation.org
E-mail: ThirdWaveF@aol.com
Third Wave is a national organization for young feminist activists, primarily those between the ages of fifteen and thirty. Through grant-making, public-education campaigns, and a national network of members, Third Wave informs and empowers this generation of feminist leaders.

2030 Center
1015 Eighteenth Street, NW, Suite 200
Washington, D.C. 20036
(202) 822-6526; fax (202) 822-1199
www.2030.org
E-mail: 2030@2030.org
An action think tank designed to provide a voice for young people's economic concerns.

The Young Women's Political Caucus
c/o the National Women's Political Caucus
1275 K Street, NW, Suite 750
Washington, D.C. 20005
(202) 785-1100; fax (202) 785-3605
www.nwpc.org
This is the organization's national office, but it also has state chapters. Each chapter seeks to get young women involved in politics.

Young Women's Project
923 F Street, NW
Washington, D.C. 20004
(202) 393-0461; fax (202) 393-0065
www.tidalwave.net/~ywp
E-mail: ywp@tidalwave.net
Provides leadership training for teenage women of color.

Young Women's Work Project
995 Market Street, Suite 1418
San Francisco, California 94103
(415) 974-6296; fax (415) 974-6295
E-mail: YWWP@aol.com
YWWP instigates new economic, educational, spiritual, and leadership opportunities by and for poor and working-class young women with the goal of ending poverty and fostering young women's leadership. It conducts research, organizes a national network of young women fighting for better jobs, and creates affiliate organizations such as Young Women United for a Better Oakland and Young Women's Leadership Foundation in Brooklyn.

Chapter 3: Feminists Want to Know: Is the Media Dead?

Media groups that are combating the seven deadly sins:

About Face
P.O. Box 77665
San Francisco, California 94107
(415) 436-0212
www.about-face.org
A great grassroots campaign dedicated to combating sexist advertising.

Aviva
www.aviva.org
A Britain-based comprehensive site for international women's news. Essential for feminists interested in the world beyond the United States; their stories typically do not make it into The New York Times.

The Center for the Integration and Improvement of Journalism
San Francisco State University
1600 Holloway Avenue
San Francisco, California 94132
(415) 338-2083; fax (415) 338-2084
www.journalism.sfsu.edu/www/ciij/ciijihtm
E-mail: emartine@sfsu.edu
The center's Newswatch Project monitors media coverage of people of color, as well as lesbians and gays. It also wants to become an information clearinghouse on racism and homophobia in the media.

Fairness and Accuracy in Reporting (FAIR)
130 West Twenty-fifth Street
New York, New York 10001
(212) 633-6700; fax (212) 727-7668
www.fair.org
E-mail: fair@fair.org
FAIR offers well-documented criticism of the media. Its Women's Desk, helmed by Third Waver Jennifer Pozner, pays particular attention to how women fare.

Independent Media Institute
77 Federal Street
San Francisco, California 94107
(415) 284-1426; fax (415) 284-1414
E-mail: khayes@alternet.org
An organization that strengthens and promotes alternative media.

The International Women's Media Foundation
1726 M Street, NW, Suite 1002
Washington, D.C. 20036
(202) 496-1992; fax (202) 496-1977
www.iwmf.org
E-mail: IWMF@aol.com
Its study "Voices for the Future" was created in response to the dearth of women of color in the media.

Just Think Foundation
P.O. Box 475638
San Francisco, California 94147
(415) 561-2900; fax (415) 561-2901
www.justthink.org
E-mail: think@justthink.org
The foundation works with students, educators, and the entertainment industry to promote critical thinking about popular media.

Media Education Foundation
26 Center Street
Northampton, Massachusetts 01060
(413) 584-8500 or (800) 897-0089; fax (413) 586-8398
www.mediaed.org
E-mail: mediaed@mediaed.org
The foundation has turned cutting-edge research into accessible videos such as Reviving Ophelia *with Mary Pipher,* Lani Guinier: Democracy in a Different Voice, *and* bell hooks: Cultural Criticism & Transformation.

Progressive Media Project
409 East Main Street
Madison, Wisconsin 53703
(608) 257-4626; fax (608) 257-3373
www.progressive.org/mediaproject.html
E-mail: pmproj@itis.com

The Progressive Media Project provides progressive opinion pieces to daily and weekly newspapers across the United States.

THINKAGAIN
http://members.aol.com/agitart
A group of artists who are fighting greed and retrograde politics.

Third World Newsreel
545 Eighth Avenue, 10th Floor
New York, New York 10018
(212) 947-9277; fax (212) 594-6417
E-mail: twn@twn.org
Committed to creating independent media about social issues, this organization pays particular attention to people of color and to people in developing countries around the world.

We Interrupt This Message
965 Mission Street, Suite 220
San Francisco, California 94103
(415) 537-9437; fax (415) 537-9439
www.interrupt.org
A media training center dedicated to challenging unfair and biased coverage.

Women Make Movies
462 Broadway, #500
New York, New York 10013
(212) 925-0606; fax (212) 925-2052
www.wmm.com
Women Make Movies has a full range of videos by women, including Righteous Babes *and others by Pratibha Parmar, Jocelyn Taylor, and Elisabeth Subrin.*

WOMEN (Women's OnLine, Media and Education Network)
5568 Fremont Street
Oakland, California 94608
(510) 547-1689; fax (510) 668-7051
E-mail: GoLadies@WomenRadio.com
In response to the fact that women and people of color own less than 3 percent of all media, this organization has launched a National Women's Media Campaign to create a media industry and quality programming that reflect cultural diversity.

Women's Wire
www.womenswire.com
This group posts women-related newspaper stories from the wire services.

There are some great alternative magazines, including some that aren't so alternative:

Colorlines
4096 Piedmont Avenue, PMB 319
Oakland, California 94611-5221
(510) 653-3415; fax (510) 653-3427
To order: (888) 458-8588
www.colorlines.com
E-mail: colorlines@arc.org
A quarterly magazine on race, culture, and organizing.

Labyrinth
Westbury Publishing
P.O. Box 58489
Philadelphia, Pennsylvania 19102
(215) 546-6686; fax (215) 546-1156
A local Philadelphia monthly feminist newspaper that covers national and international news.

Lilith
250 West Fifty-seventh Street, #2432
New York, New York 10107
To order: (800) 783-4903
(212) 757-0818; fax (212) 757-5705
www.lilithmag.com
Since it began in 1976, this independent Jewish women's magazine has been providing a link between feminism and Jewish life.

Mother Jones
731 Market Street, Suite 600
San Francisco, California 94103
(800) 438-6656; fax (815) 734-1223
www.motherjones.com
A bimonthly magazine whose mission and name are inspired by Mary Harris "Mother" Jones, a union organizer and "hellraiser."

Moxie
1230 Glen Avenue
Berkeley, California 94708
(510) 540-5510
E-mail: emily@moxiemag.com
This sporadically published magazine has lots of interviews and profiles, and its tag line is For the Woman Who Dares.

Ms.
20 Exchange Place, 22nd Floor
New York, New York 10005
To order: (800) 234-4486
(212) 509-2092; fax (212) 509-2407
www.msmagazine.com
This feminist bimonthly magazine has been in business since 1972, when it was co-founded by Patricia Carbine, Gloria Steinem, and others.

The Nation
33 Irving Place
New York, New York 10003
(212) 209-5400; fax (212) 982-9000
To order: (800) 333-8536
www.TheNation.com
A progressive, political weekly magazine.

off our backs
2337 B Eighteenth Street, NW
Washington, D.C. 20009
(202) 234-8072; fax (202) 234-8092
www.igc.apc.org/oob
E-mail: offourbacks@compuserve.com
A radical feminist news journal, publishing since 1970.

Sojourner
42 Seaverns Avenue
Jamaica Plain, Massachusetts 02130
To order: (888) 475-5996
(617) 524-0415; fax (617) 524-9397
www.sojourner.org
E-mail: info@sojourner.org
A monthly journal featuring feminist news, culture, and commentary.

Utne Reader
1634 Harman Place
Minneapolis, Minnesota 55403
(800) 736-UTNE or (612) 338-5040; fax (612) 338-6043
www.utne.com
An alternative magazine covering social change, politics, and gender.

The Women's Review of Books
Department WWW
Center for Research on Women
Wellesley College
Wellesley, Massachusetts 02481
(781) 283-2087 or (888) 283-8044; fax (781) 283-3645
www.wellesley.edu/WomensReview/
E-mail: lgardiner@wellesley.edu
A monthly review of books by and about women.

The Women's Times
Box 390
Great Barrington, Massachusetts 01230
or
323 Main Street
Great Barrington, Massachusetts 01230
(413) 528-5303; fax (413) 528-8186
E-mail: wtimes@bcn.net
The Women's Times *covers women's issues, specifically in western Massachusetts.*

Z
18 Milifield Street
Wood Hole, Massachusetts 02543
(508) 548-9063; fax (508) 457-0626
www.zmag.org
E-mail: sysop@zmag.org
A bimonthly that presumes its readers are activists.

CHAPTER 4: GIRL, YOU'LL BE A WOMAN SOON

Girlies' Tools. If "Vixens need vibrators," as *Bust* says—and instructions to use them—then call on Betty Dodson, a Second Wave pleasure professor:

Betty Dodson
Box 1933, Murray Hill
New York, New York 10156
www.bettydodson.com
E-mail: site@bettydodson.com
*Betty Dodson has several videos devoted to "erotic sex education
. . . promoting sexual freedom for heterosexuals, bisexuals, ho-
mosexuals, lesbians, transsexuals, intersexuals, and self-sexuals."
All things Dodson, including her book,* Sex for One, *are available
by contacting her.*

Eve's Garden
119 West Fifty-seventh Street, Suite 1201
New York, New York 10019
(212) 757-8651
www.evesgarden.com
*The first feminist, and least intimidating, sex-toy store in New
York City. From Eve's Garden you can purchase vibrators, erotic
books and magazines, and anything that will increase your im-
pulse toward pleasure.*

Good Vibrations
1210 Valencia Street
San Francisco, California 94110
Store: (415) 974-8980; mail order: (415) 974-8990;
    fax (415) 974-8989
or
2504 San Pablo Avenue (@ Dwight)
Berkeley, California 94702
(510) 841-8987
www.goodvibes.com
E-mail: goodvibe@well.com
*Good Vibrations, which was founded by free-love senior citizen
Joani Blank, is the West Coast version of Eve's Garden—erotica
and sexual products galore.*

To paint your nails in the boardroom, buy whatever you need from these great woman-founded companies:

Urban Decay
331 Fairchild Drive
Mountain View, California 94043
(800) 784-URBAN; fax (650) 988-9971
E-mail: www.urbandecay.com
Urban Decay pioneered grunge makeup—and continues to produce great products like roach-colored nail polish. It's run by surfer Wende Zomnir with help from Sandy Lerner, the entrepreneur and animal-rights activist, and co-founder of Cisco Systems. Sadly, it's now owned by Estée Lauder.

Hard Candy
www.hardcandy.com
UCLA sophomore Dineh Mohajer founded this cutesy company in 1995 after she figured out how to make baby-blue nail polish. She's now a millionaire.

To host your Girlie party, you have to start with a Girlie-friendly locale:

Meow Mix
269 East Houston Street
New York, New York 10009
(212) 254-0688
www.meowmixchix.com
Founded and run by Brooke Webster, Meow Mix is a rare breed—a young lesbian-feminist music bar.

Web sites are a part of Third Wave's DNA. Given the rapidly expanding world of the Web, it's impossible to provide a comprehensive list of feminist-friendly sites, but here are a few places for you to get started:

ChickClick
www.chickclick.com
ChickClick is a Web site for teenage girls and young women who are interested in the issues that affect them, from fashion to politics. It merged with EstroNet and houses most of the sites that are germane to Girlie. For instance, www.disgruntledhouse

wife.com and www.bust.com. Chickclick offers free E-mail, home pages, postcards, and even horoscopes.

Cybergrrl
www.cybergrrl.com
Cybergrrl is activist Aliza Sherman's Web consulting center whose mission is transforming women's lives through technology. Sherman is also a resource for other feminist/woman-friendly spaces on the Web.

Disgruntled Housewife
www.disgruntledhousewife.com
Your guide to modern living and intersex relationships.

EchoNYC
www.echonyc.com
One of the first Internet salons—this one started by a woman, Stacy Horn—Echo was dedicated to creating a women-friendly space back when cyberspace was more of a nerdy boys' club.

EstroNet
www.estroclick.chickclick.com
EstroNet offers young women a chance to discuss body, psyche, sex, and how to earn, spend, and inspire.

Feminist.com
www.feminist.com
Feminist.com is an umbrella resource for anything feminist-related. It features links to women-friendly sites and hosts women-owned businesses as well as organizations that can't yet afford or manage their own sites. It is also the home of Ask Amy.

Feminista.com
www.feminista.com
Feminista.com is an on-line journal of women's art, literature, and commentary.

Geekgirl
www.geekgirl.com.au
Geekgirl is from an Australian women's center.

Girls on Film
www.girlsonfilm.com
Girls on Film reviews movies from a woman's perspective.

GreaserGrrls (affiliated with EstroNet)
www.greasergrrls.com
Greasergrrls.com celebrates women motor enthusiasts. The site features stories and cool pictures and is a great way to meet other Greasergrrls around the world. It has a list of women racers, mechanics, and just plain ol' motor lovers—and it offers support from women who are interested in auto mechanics.

gUrl
www.gurl.com
GUrl is a sort of Sassy on-line with free gUrl mail, gUrl pages, and E-cards. Free community with chat and pen-pal lists, poetry, and more!

Maxi Mag
www.maximag.com
Maxi Mag is a Web page for women who are interested in all sorts of issues, from breaking up to punishment for sex offenders, polls, scoops, and more.

Nerve
www.Nerve.com
As this site proclaims, Nerve is an on-line magazine for thoughtful hedonists.

Oxygen
www.Oxygen.com
Oxygen, the first site to offer simultaneous television broadcast, is also the first woman-owned network.

ProActivist.com
www.proactivist.com; opinions@proactivist.com
This site is dedicated to photographically documenting progressive protests and demonstrations, and to assisting activists with their efforts.

Punk Planet
http://punkplanet.com
Punk Planet *is an on-line punk magazine with articles on music and culture.*

Riotgrrl
www.Riotgrrl.com
*Two rs are better than one, but perhaps not as rad as three,
which was the original spelling of Riot Grrrl. This comprehensive
site by Florida chick Nikki seeks to be the hard-core version of*
Seventeen *and* Cosmo.

Wigmag
www.wigmag.com
Wigmag *is a women's on-line magazine that covers arts, sports,
culture, and music.*

Wired Woman
www.wiredwoman.com
*The Wired Woman Society is a nonprofit group where women
can learn and share ideas about technology in a comfortable and
dynamic space.*

Zinerack
www.nrrdgirl.com/zinerack
A link to women's webzines.

Manifesta's manifestos are largely the zines that girls have produced. Some zines are actually just noncorporate or independently
owned magazines. We can't begin to list all of them, but we started
with the ones we mentioned in the book and included a few others
that are hard to find:

Alice: For Women on the Other Side of the Looking Glass
41 Freitas Ct.
Santa Rosa, California 95407
(707) 526-5965; fax (801) 640-8535
E-mail: ecochicks@earthlink.net

Bamboo Girl
c/o Sabrina Margarita Alcantara-Tan
P.O. Box 507
New York, New York 10159-0507
www.bamboogirl.com
E-mail: Bamboogirl@aol.com
Bamboo Girl *is brought to you by Sabrina Margarita Alcantara-
Tan from our dinner party. (See Chapter 1.)*

Bitch: Feminist Response to Pop Culture
3128 Sixteenth Street
Box 143
San Francisco, California 94103
To order: (415) 864-6671
www.bitchmagazine.com

Bust
P.O. Box 1016
Cooper Station
New York, New York 10276
www.bust.com
E-mail: celina@bust.com or BUST@aol.com

Fact Sheet Five
P.O. Box 170099
San Francisco, California 94117
www.factsheet5.com
Fact Sheet Five *is a zine that reviews other zines and is basically the industry rag for the independent media.*

Fabula Magazine
2785 Shasta Road
Berkeley, California 95708
(510) 704-8952
www.fabulamag.com
E-mail: fabula@vdn.com

Girlfriends
P.O. Box 383
Mt. Morris, Illinois 61054-7506
(888) GRL-FRND; fax (415) 648-4705
www.gfriends.com

Hip Mama
P.O. Box 9097
Oakland, California 94613
www.hipmama.com
E-mail: ariel@hipmama.com

Jailhouse Turn Out (JTO)
Available through Mr. Lady
P.O. Box 3189
Durham, North Carolina 27715-3189
www.mrlady.com
JTO *is brought to you by Tammy Rae Carland, the same woman who brought us* I (heart) Amy Carter.

Rockrgrl
7683 SE Twenty-seventh Street, #317
Mercer Island, Washington 98040
(206) 230-4280; fax (206) 230-4288
www.rockrgrl.com
E-mail: info@rockrgrl.com

CHAPTER 5: BARBIE VS. THE MENSTRUAL KIT
Like Web sites, girls' groups have proliferated beyond the scope of this guide. But we can provide you with the groups we refer to in *Manifesta*:

An Income of Her Own
www.anincomeofherown.com
A site for girls and young women under twenty who want to start their own businesses.

Center for Young Women's Health
Children's Hospital
300 Longwood Avenue
Boston, Massachusetts 02115
(617) 355-2994; fax (617) 355-3394
www.youngwomenshealth.org
E-mail: cywh@a1.tch.harvard.edu

The Girls Advisory Board (GAB) of the Empower Program
The Empower Program
1312 Eighth Street, NW
Washington, D.C. 20007
(202) 882-2800; fax (202) 243-1901
www.empowered.org
E-mail: empower@empowered.org

The Girls' Coalition of Greater Boston
c/o PTGSC
95 Berkeley Street
Boston, Massachusetts 02116
(781) 942-3809, phone and fax
www.girlscoalition.com
E-mail: kawheeler@earthlink.net
A coalition of groups whose motto is "Focusing on Girls' Matters . . . Because Girls Matter."

Girls Inc.
120 Wall Street
New York, New York 10005-3902
(212) 509-2000; fax (212) 509-8708
www.girlsinc.org
With hundreds of affiliates, Girls Inc. is dedicated to inspiring girls between the ages of six and eighteen to become strong, smart, and bold.

Girls on the Move/Outward Bound
2582 Riceville Road
Asheville, North Carolina 28805
(800) 437-6071; fax (828) 299-3928
www.obgotm.org
To empower girls to be leaders in their communities.

GirlSource
2121 Bryant Street
San Francisco, California 94110
(415) 824-9050; fax (415) 821-0113
www.girlsource.org
Offers hands-on, paid opportunities for low-income young women.

Girls Speak Out
c/o Andrea Johnston
18200 Sweetwater Springs Road
Guerneville, California 95446
(707) 869-0829; fax (707) 869-0578

Girl Tech
851 Irwin Street, Suite 302
San Rafael, California 94901
(415) 256-1510; fax (415) 256-1515
www.girltech.com
E-mail: girltech@girltech.com

Girls to Women: Empowering Girls to Control Their Destinies
P.O. Box 113
7 Redwood Drive
Ross, California 94957
(415) 459-7112

iEmily
www.iEmily.com
A health-and-wellness Web site for teenage girls.

Lower Eastside Girls' Club
220 East Fourth Street
New York, New York 10009
(212) 982-1633; fax (212) 982-1577
A space where girls ages eight to eighteen can come together to learn and grow.

Young Sisters for Justice
c/o Boston Women's Fund
14 Beacon Street, Suite 805
Boston, MA 02108
(617) 725-0035; fax (617) 725-0277
www.bostonwomen.com
The Young Sisters for Justice program grew out of the Boston Women's Fund's work with girls, and seeks social and economic justice.

Media that are girl-focused and girl-friendly:

BoHoS
Flypaper Press
(888) COMIC-BOOK
www.bohos.flypaperpress.com
A comic-book series created for girls, by a girl—seventeen-year-old Maggie Whorf.

Dream Girl *(The Arts Magazine for Girls)*
P.O. Box 639
Carrboro, North Carolina 27510
E-mail: Fdowell@mindspring.com

Girls Like Us
Point of View (P.O.V.)
220 West Nineteenth Street, 11th Floor
New York, New York 10011
(212) 989-8121; fax (212) 989-8230
www.pbs.org/pov
Girls Like Us *is a documentary film by Tina DiFeliciantonio and June Wagner about five girls growing up in South Philadelphia; it's distributed by Point of View. (P.O.V. has other great videos on a range of topics.)*

New Moon Publishing
P.O. Box 3587
Duluth, Minnesota 55803-3587
(218) 728-5507 or (800) 381-4743; fax (218) 728-0314
www.newmoon.org
E-mail: newmoon@newmoon.org
Besides the magazine itself, New Moon *has a range of other publications available for girls and their parents, including two new books:* New Moon Writing: How to Express Yourself with Passion and Practice, *and* New Moon Money: How to Get It, Spend It, and Save It.

Seventeen
850 Third Avenue
New York, New York 10022
To order: (800) 388-1749
(212) 407-9700; fax (212) 407-9899
A monthly magazine for adolescent girls and young women.

Teen Voices
c/o Women Express, Inc.
P.O. Box 120-127
Boston, Massachusetts 02112-0027
(888) 882-TEEN; fax (617) 262-8937
www.teenvoices.com
E-mail: womenexp@teenvoices.com

CHAPTER 6: THOU SHALT NOT BECOME THY MOTHER
Second Wave groups we love:

Center for Research on Women
106 Central Street
Wellesley, Massachusetts 02431
(781) 283-2500; fax (781) 283-2504
www.wellesley.edu
E-mail: pbauer@wellesley.edu
Conducts research on social issues that affect women in order to affect policy.

Center for Women Policy Studies
1211 Connecticut Avenue, NW, Suite 312
Washington, D.C. 20036
(202) 872-1770; fax (202) 296-8962
www.centerwomenpolicy.org
E-mail: cwps@centerwomenpolicy.org
A feminist policy research and advocacy group that focuses on diversity issues.

Feminist Majority Foundation (FMF)
1600 Wilson Boulevard, Suite 801
Arlington, Virginia 22209
(703) 522-2214; fax (703) 522-2219
www.feminist.org
E-mail: femmaj@feminist.org

Among other things, FMF has been active in attempting to stop the Taliban's maltreatment of women in Afghanistan. Contact the foundation about the status of the proposed Women's Equality Act. FMF also started Rock for Choice.

Guerrilla Girls
Box 1056, Cooper Station
New York, New York 10276
The Guerrilla Girls is an anonymous collective of women in the art world who attempt to shake up this male-dominated institution by creating agitprop art for the feminist revolution.

Ms. Foundation for Women
120 Wall Street, 33rd Floor
New York, New York 10005
(212) 742-2300; fax (212) 742-1653
www.ms.foundation.org
The Ms. Foundation is the first national multi-issue, multiracial public women's fund. The foundation makes grants to projects by and for women in such areas as economic justice, health and safety, AIDS, democracy, and girls, young women, and leadership.

National Council for Research on Women
11 Hanover Square
New York, New York 10005
(212) 785-7335; fax (212) 785-7350
www.ncrw.org
E-mail: ncrw@ncrw.org
An alliance of women's research and policy centers that seeks to enhance the connection between research, policy analysis, and advocacy.

National Organization for Women
733 Fifteenth Street, NW, 2nd Floor
Washington, D.C. 20005
(202) 331-0066; fax (202) 785-8576
www.now.org
E-mail: now@now.org
An organization that advocates political and social equality for women.

National Women's History Project
7738 Bell Road
Windsor, California 95492
(707) 838-6000; fax (707) 838-0478
www.nwhp.org
A clearinghouse for women's history (including Legacy '98) that produces educational materials on women's history.

National Woman's Party
144 Constitution Avenue, NE
Washington, D.C. 20002
(202) 546-1210; fax (202) 546-3997
www.nationalwomanparty.org
Okay, technically NWP is First Wave. This is the group responsible for the ERA, among other First Wave initiatives.

Redstockings
Women's Liberation Archives for Action
Distribution Project
P.O. Box 2625
Gainesville, Florida 32602
Once a revolutionary New York women's liberation group, now a Florida-based archive. Redstockings members are available to do research on behalf of journalists and feminists for a nominal fee.

Refuse & Resist
305 Madison Avenue, Suite 1166
New York, New York 10165
(212) 713-5657
www.calyx.com/~refuse/
E-mail: refuse@calyx.com
A great radical group that organizes, among other things, an annual day of Appreciation for Abortion Providers. Its campaigns support resistance and encourage activism, and they have a strong youth presence.

Washington Feminist Faxnet
Center for Advancement of Public Policy
1735 S Street, NW
Washington, D.C. 20009
(202) 797-0606; fax (202) 265-6245

An essential organizing tool, the WFF is compiled by Martha Burk and her team; they watch Congress, the media, and the President, and then fax a two-page activist tip sheet to subscribers every week.

Women & Philanthropy
1015 Eighteenth Street, NW, Suite 202
Washington, D.C. 20036
(202) 887-9660; fax (202) 861-5483
www.womenphil.org
An association of grant makers dedicated to achieving equity for women and girls.

CHAPTER 7: WHO'S AFRAID OF KATIE ROIPHE?
To organize a Take Back the Night on your campus, see how others do it by going to:

www.members.tripod.com/~tbtn/index.htm or
www.pages.nyu.edu/clubs/womensactivism

To counter the right-wing think tanks, acquaint yourself with the progressive training groups:

The Audre Lorde Project
85 South Oxford Street
Brooklyn, New York 11217
(718) 596-0342; fax (718) 596-1328
E-mail: j.kang@alp.org
The Audre Lorde Project, named for the late poet, is a center for lesbian, gay, bisexual, two-spirit, and transgendered people of color communities.

Center for Gender Equity
c/o Faye Wattleton
25 West Forty-third Street, Suite 1014
New York, New York 10036
(212) 391-7718; fax (212) 391-7720
Started by former Planned Parenthood president Faye Wattleton, this think tank aims to provide bipartisan research that pushes feminism.

Center for the American Woman in Politics
Eagleton Institute of Politics
191 Ryders Lane
New Brunswick, New Jersey 08901-8557
(732) 932-9384; fax (732) 932-6778
www.rci.rutgers.edu/~cawp/newl/ywlihome.htm
The center has a Young Women's Leadership Initiative that educates and empowers young women to participate in politics.

Highlander Research and Education Center
1959 Highlander Way
New Market, Tennessee 37820
(423) 933-3443; fax (423) 933-3424
E-mail: hrec@igc.apc.org
Since its founding in 1932, Highlander has been training community leaders. Highlander trainings were integral to the civil-rights movement.

The Policy Institute
National Gay and Lesbian Task Force
121 West Twenty-Seventh Street, Suite 501
New York, New York 10001
(212) 604-9830; fax (212) 604-9831
www.ngltf.org
E-mail: ngltf@ngltf.org
A think tank dedicated to research, policy analysis, and strategic projects to advance greater understanding of gay, lesbian, bi, and trans people.

The Wellesley Center for Women
Wellesley College
106 Central Street
Wellesley, Massachusetts 02481-8203
(781) 283-2500; fax (781) 283-2504
www.wellesley.edu/wcw
Houses the Center for Research on Women and the Stone Center.

The Woodhull Institute for Ethical Leadership
61 East Eighth Street, Suite 130
New York, New York 10003
(212) 475-5575; fax (212) 475-5627
E-mail: Woodhulli@aol.com

Naomi Wolf, Margot Magowan, and others founded this institute to provide training to women on the following topics: The Basics of Ethical Leadership, Young Women and Voice: How We Lose It, How to Regain It, and Basic Financial Literacy. The retreat center is at Hyperion Farm, in upstate New York.

CHAPTER 8: WHAT IS ACTIVISM?

To replicate the activism being conducted in beauty salons, obtain a copy of the Hairdresser Project Guidelines for $15.00:

Hairdresser Project
16 J Street
New London, Connecticut 06320
(860) 447-0366; fax (860) 440-3327
E-mail: w.cpr@snet.net

To tell the Motion Picture Association of America that you think its board should be more representative of all movie viewers, contact the organization at:

Motion Picture Association of America (MPAA)
1600 Eye Street
Washington, D.C. 20006
(202) 293-1966; fax (202) 296-7410
To influence the gender and racial breakdown of the MPAA board, you have to contact the big companies within the industry directly, including Disney, Fox, MGM, Paramount, Sony, Universal, and Warner Brothers. Each company is responsible for nominating people to the twenty-member board.

To lend your time and energy to the campaign to free Mumia Abu Jamal, contact Refuse & Resist (see Chapter 6 resources) or:

Prison Radio
P.O. Box 411074
San Francisco, California 94141
www.prisonradio.org

To give money to the Literacy Volunteers of America, which the U.S. government isn't:

Literacy Volunteers of America
635 James Street
Syracuse, New York 13203-2214
(315) 472-0001 or (800) LVA-8812; fax (315) 472-0002
E-mail: info@literacyvolunteers.org

To give money to Hale House, as Smashing Pumpkins did:

Hale House
152 West 122nd Street
New York, New York 10027
(212) 663-0700; fax (212) 749-2888

The Jane Collective no longer exists, but the National Network of Abortion Funds does, and it always needs help for poor women seeking abortions:

National Network of Abortion Funds
c/o CLPP
Hampshire College
Amherst, Massachusetts 01002-5001
(413) 559-5645; fax (413) 559-5620
Marlene Fried, the executive director of this program, has successfully brought together intergenerational groups of feminist activists. Each year Hampshire College also hosts an annual reproductive-rights conference.

A few organizations, among many (including those listed in Chapter 2), founded by Third Wave activists:

Melissa Bradley
The Entrepreneurial Development Institute (TEDI)
Washington, D.C.
(202) 822-8334
E-mail: TEDIBDC@Yahoo.com

Mary Chung
National Asian Women's Health Organization
250 Montgomery Street, Suite 410
San Francisco, California 94104
(415) 989-9747; fax (415) 989-9758
www.nawho.org
E-mail: nawho@aol.com

Nancy Lublin
Dress for Success
19 Union Square West, 6th Floor
New York, New York 10003
(212) 989-6373; fax (212) 989-4559
www.dressforsuccess.org

Philip Morris isn't the only company lining the pockets of politicians in the hope of political paybacks. To find out who supports who, contact:

Open Secrets
www.opensecrets.org

To file a complaint or to find out what your legal rights are as an employee or employer, to file a sexual-harassment or discrimination complaint, or to learn if you should be filing a sexual-harassment or -discrimination complaint, contact:

Equal Employment Opportunity Commission
1801 L Street, NW
Washington, D.C. 20507
(800) 669-4000 for the nearest field office.

To help your city pass a version of San Francisco's city ordinance implementing the Convention on the Elimination of All Forms of Discrimination Against Women (CEDAW), contact the group responsible for that city's passage of CEDAW:

Wild
Women's Institute for Leadership Development for Human Rights
340 Pine Street, Suite 302
San Francisco, California 94104
(415) 837-0795; fax (415) 837-1144
E-mail: wild@igc.org

To urge the U.S. government to sign CEDAW or to find out the status of the Beijing Platform for Action, including how to encourage your government and others to begin implementing this document, contact one of the following organizations:

Charlotte Bunch
Center for Women's Global Leadership
Rutgers University
160 Ryders Lane
New Brunswick, New Jersey 08901-8555
(732) 932-8782; fax (732) 932-1180
www.cwgl.rutgers.edu
E-mail: cwgl@igc.apc.org

Equality NOW
250 West Fifty-seventh Street, #826
New York, New York 10107
(212) 586-0906; fax (212) 586-1611
E-mail: info@equalitynow.org

International Women's Tribune Centre
777 United Nations Plaza
New York, New York 10017
(212) 687-8633; fax (212) 661-2704
E-mail: iwtc@igc.org

There are so many international groups doing important work on the most urgent feminist issues—the following are just some of the biggies. Each group knows about hundreds of others who are doing similar work.

International Gay and Lesbian Human Rights Commission
1360 Mission Street, Suite 200
San Francisco, California 94103
(415) 255-8680; fax (415) 255-8662
www.iglhrc.org
E-mail: iglhrc@iglhrc.org

The Global Fund for Women
425 Sherman Avenue, Suite 300
Palo Alto, California 94306
(650) 853-8305; fax (650) 328-0384
www.globalfundforwomen.org
E-mail: gfw@globalfundforwomen.org

The Sisterhood Is Global Institute
1200 Atwater Avenue, Suite 2
Montreal, Quebec, Canada H32 IX4
(514) 846-9366; fax (514) 846-9066
www.sigi.org
E-mail: sigi@qc.aibn.com

Women's Environment and Development Organization
355 Lexington Avenue, 3rd Floor
New York, New York 10017
(212) 973-0325; fax (212) 973-0335
www.wedo.org
E-mail: wedo@igc.apc.org

To replicate the alliance of 80 high schools with gay/lesbian/bisexual/straight alliances:

Student Pride U.S.A.
The National Network of Gay/Straight Alliances
121 West Twenty-seventh Street, Suite 804
New York, New York 10001
(212) 727-0135; fax (212) 727-0254
www.studentprideusa.org
E-mail: studentpride@glsen.org
or
**Boston Alliance for Gay, Lesbian, Bisexual and
 Transgendered Youth (BAGLY)**
www.bagly.org
*BAGLY is one of the oldest community groups for queer and
questioning youth, and it sponsors the oldest gay prom.*

For legal/advocacy help:

National Association for the Advancement of Colored People (NAACP)
39 Broadway, 22nd Floor
New York, New York 10006
(212) 344-7474

National Women's Law Center
11 Dupont Circle, Suite 800
Washington, D.C. 20036
(202) 588-5180; fax (202) 588-5185
www.nwlc.org

Southern Poverty Law Center
400 Washington Avenue
Montgomery, Alabama 36104
(334) 264-0286; fax (334) 264-0629

To end violence against women:

Family Violence Prevention Fund (Domestic)
383 Rhode Island, Suite 304
San Francisco, California 94103
(415) 252-8900 or (888) END-ABUSE; fax (415) 252-8991
The fund helps individual women who are being battered and fa-cilitates community organizing through its Take Action Kits. Its bimonthly newsletter is called Speaking Up, *and is full of information about legislation regarding domestic violence, as well as examples of these injustices:*
Speaking Up
c/o PR Solutions, Inc.
(202) 371-1999; fax (202) 371-9142
E-mail: speakingup@prsolutionsdc.com

Women's Rights Network (International)
106 Central Street
Wellesley, Massachusetts 02481-8203
(781) 283-2500; fax (781) 283-2504
The Women's Rights Network is a network of organizations working around the world, including England's Chiswick Family Rescue.

To radicalize the workplace:

Catalyst
120 Wall Street
New York, New York 10005
(212) 514-7600; fax (212) 514-8470
www.catalystwomen.org
E-mail: info@catalyst.org
Working with businesses to advance women.

National Committee on Pay Equity
1126 Sixteenth Street, NW, Suite 411
Washington, D.C. 20036
(202) 331-7343; fax (202) 331-7406
www.feminist.com/fairpay
E-mail: fairpay@aol.com
A nonprofit organization working to eliminate sex and wage discrimination.

9 to 5: National Association of Working Women
231 West Wisconsin Avenue, Suite 900
Milwaukee, Wisconsin 53203
(414) 274-0925 or for its job survival hotline,
   call (800) 522-0925; fax (414) 272-2870
www.9to5.org
E-mail: NAWW9to5@execpc.com
*9 to 5 is the largest membership organization of working women.
The organization lobbies and advocates for women and workplace
issues. The organization's hotline can help if you encounter
discrimination on the job.*

To start your own business:

National Foundation for Women Business Owners
1411 K Street, NW, Suite 1350
Washington, D.C. 20005
(202) 638-3060; fax (202) 638-3064
www.nfwbo.org
E-mail: nfwbo@worldnet.att.net

Women's Business Center
c/o Small Business Administration
(202) 205-6673 or (800) 827-5722
www.onlinewbc.org
The Small Business Administration has a branch in all fifty states.
Contact the one closest to you for the most up-to-date informa-
tion.

Small Business at Women.com
www.women.com/smallbiz/
Information for a woman who wants to start her own business.

Women's Self-Employment Project
20 N. Clark Street
Chicago, Illinois 60602
(312) 606-8255; fax (312) 606-9215
E-mail: cevans@wsep.com

Women's Venture Fund
240 W. Thirty-fifth Street, #201
New York, New York 10001
(212) 732-7500; fax (212) 868-9116
E-mail: womventure@aol.com

Proving that feminists do support child care, the following organization is among the leaders in the quest for more comprehensive
child-care programs:

Anita Moeller
Acre Family Day Care Corporation
14 Kirk Street
Lowell, Massachusetts 01852
(978) 937-5899; fax (978) 937-5148

To get funding for your good projects/ideas:

Women's Funding Network
332 Minnesota Street, Suite E840
St. Paul, Minnesota 55101-1320
(651) 227-1911; fax (651) 227-2213
www.wfnet.org
E-mail: wfn@wfnet.org

This membership organization includes funding sources such as Ms. Foundation for Women, the Sister Fund, and the Third Wave Foundation.

The Foundation Center
79 Fifth Avenue, 2nd Floor
New York, New York 10003
(212) 620-4230; fax (212) 691-1828
www.fdncenter.org
This center is a resource bank for funding for all issues, organizations, or individuals.

EPILOGUE: A DAY WITH FEMINISM
Here's how we can all help to get to "A Day with Feminism":

A to-do list for everyday activists:

- Speak up. When you hear a racist or homophobic joke, dare to say, "That's not funny." If someone says, "All feminists hate men," respond with "Name one." Think of snappy answers to sexist questions and street harassment. *Why don't we have Take Our Sons to Work Day?* For the same reason we don't have White History Month. *How are you today, baby?* Armed. *Feminism teaches women to leave their husbands, kill their children, destroy capitalism, practice witchcraft, and become lesbians!* And . . . what's your point?

- Write a letter to an advertiser telling the company how offensive you think its ad is. Advertisers are notoriously conservative, so if you like an ad, let them know that, too. Like an insecure teenager, they need reinforcement for their every act. Every letter an advertiser receives represents thousands of potential consumers. (See Chapter 3 resources for groups that can help you do this.)

- Write letters or call your local representatives and ask them to oppose or support legislation that represents your values. Politicians do pay attention to their constituents, and every phone call is recorded in a book or file by a legislative intern. (Call them at the U.S. House of Representatives and the U.S.

Senate at (202) 225-3121.) Take the time to thank them for voting the right way—they also make note of approbation and could use the love. This shouldn't apply only to federal elections but also to your city council or the school board. To find out about state initiatives, contact your state capitol. For local politics, try Town Hall or City Hall.

- Don't put your money toward companies that don't support you. Use your purchasing power toward the revolution, and especially give to women-owned or independently owned stores and restaurants. For greater purchasing power:

   The Feminist Dollar: The Wise Woman's Buying Guide, by Phyllis A. Katz and Margaret Katz (New York: Plenum Trade, 1997), lists companies that are good to women. To rule out the companies that are bad to women, as well as to the environment and to human rights, see *Boycott Quarterly*, a journal with a list of boycotted products. Published by the Center for Economic Democracy, P.O. Box 30727, Seattle, Washington 98103-0727.

   If you want to undermine the male-owned chain bookstores such as Barnes & Noble and Amazon.com, order all your books from feminist bookstores or other independent bookstores. For a list, go to: www.fembooknet.com. (*The Ruminator Review* also has a complete listing). In addition, support women-owned/women-friendly presses, such as:

   The Feminist Press
   365 Fifth Avenue, 5th Floor
   New York, New York 10016
   (212) 817-7915; fax (212) 817-1593
   www.feministpress.org
   Devoted to reprinting women's literature from the United States and around the world and to developing new such pieces of work as well as other education resources.

Girl Press
c/o Pam Nelson
8273 Clinton
Los Angeles, California 90048
(323) 651-0880
www.girlpress.com
E-mail: Girlpress@Earthlink.net

Seal Press
3131 Western Avenue, Suite 410
Seattle, Washington 98121
(206) 283-7844; fax (206) 285-9410
www.sealpress.com
E-mail: seapress@sealpress.com

- Give your time to something you care about. Volunteer at a local clinic or an after-school program; it will make a difference both in your life and in the lives of others. (But don't stop agitating for important work to be economically valued as well.)

- Inform your community. Organize a speak-out, a panel, a media campaign, or leaflet your neighborhood about an issue you care about. (See Appendix 3, "How to Put the Participatory Back into Participatory Democracy," for tips about how to do this.)

- Vote or do voter-registration, education, or get-out-the-vote drives. (More on this in Appendix 3.)

- Dare to say, "I am a feminist."

Appendix 3: How to Put the Participatory Back into Participatory Democracy

We have spent much of this book waxing poetic about the joys, power, righteousness, and general necessity of activism. What we haven't dealt with so much is how, practically speaking, you can put feminism to work. So that you can skip some of the trial and error that we put ourselves through, we thought we would leave you with a sample action: organizing a voter-registration drive.

The vote, which was the goal of the first seventy-two years of feminist struggle, is actually controversial among some activists we know. Some feminists argue that the system is so damaged and corrupt that it should be revolutionized, not sustained by encouraging the participation of its citizens. The fact is, most aspects of our lives are influenced by the government: our schools, the condition of our roads, the state of the economy, how much our milk and cigarettes cost, and so on. But the vast majority of people who don't vote are not doing it as a political protest. Many people aren't voting because they don't have access to registration, don't know that they can vote, or are unable to get to the polls. That's why it's imperative for us, as feminists and organizers, to register voters, to understand the system and the issues, and to help people to exercise their right to vote. Once we have this basic foundation accounted for, we can lobby for better information on candidates and for more representative candidates. In addition, most of the steps outlined below are universal and can be applied to other campaigns if voting isn't really your thing:

IDENTIFY A PROBLEM (A.K.A. WHAT'S WRONG WITH THIS PICTURE?):

You notice that young people aren't voting. In 1994, only 37 percent of people aged eighteen to twenty-four were registered voters, and only 22 percent of women aged eighteen to twenty-four voted. Only 36 percent of the eligible voting population actually cast a ballot for President in 1996, and just 6 percent of everyone who voted in 1994 was under the age of thirty.

DETERMINE YOUR GOALS:
If even 60 percent of the women who could vote did, and voted in their own best interests, the face of the electorate would be changed. This should be both part of your message and your goal.

IDENTIFY YOUR CONSTITUENCY (WHO DOES THIS ISSUE AFFECT?):
How many people do you want to register? Be realistic. If you are doing it solo, registering one person a day is great. Is there a particular, under-registered community that you want to target? Do you want to target a neighborhood? A segment of the population? Perhaps your goal isn't registering but encouraging people to vote—voter awareness or voter education. If you want to get one hundred people out to vote on Election Day, you need a plan to find those one hundred people.

- If you live in or near a college town, an obvious place to both register people and encourage them to vote is on campus. Set up a table at the dining hall, lobby to make voter registration a part of new-student registration, or petition to keep forms at the library and anywhere else that students gather.

- Off campus, target grocery stores, welfare offices, malls, the line outside the women's bathroom at movies, and anywhere else that people congregate and loiter.

- If you choose to go door-to-door outside your community, you may want to collaborate with a local group (i.e., a church or Project South, which works in rural Georgia and urban Atlanta) in order to have a recognizable and trusted name behind you.

- After you pick a place and a date, consult the management or administration to make sure that you don't need a permit.

- Besides the constituency you are trying to reach, who is going to help you? Get a group of committed volunteers—from the League of Women Voters, your friends, student groups, your slacker cousin, or your retired lawyer mother—and delegate some of the implementation steps.

RESEARCH:
Each state has different laws governing voter registration, so call your local Board of Elections. (The number is in your phone book.) The League of Women Voters (LWV) also has this information. Ask the local Board of Elections or the LWV:

Who can/can't register to vote?
Myths about who can vote get in the way of the act of registering. For instance, when Amy did Freedom Summer in 1992, an eighty-year-old woman told her that she was too old to vote. Amy met two women who were told by someone in authority that although they were U.S. citizens they couldn't vote because they weren't born in this country. Homeless people often don't know that they can vote, and others think that because they were once imprisoned they can't vote, either. Actually, all of these people probably can vote. Another myth trumpeted by many to make our generation seem lame is the fact that 1972 had the highest turnout among young voters—without mentioning that this was the first election after Nixon lowered the voting age from twenty-one to eighteen. You want the numbers up? The government should try lowering the age to seventeen.

For now, in all states you must be eighteen or older to vote. In some states you can register to vote before you turn eighteen, as long as you will be eighteen by the time of the election. Most states have restrictions on people who have been convicted of a crime and on those who are currently serving time. States differ on the voting rights of convicted felons, but most allow them to vote once they're out of prison and off parole.

How do you register to vote?

- In most states there is a simple form available through the local Board of Elections that you will use in your drive. Filling out this form enables a citizen to vote in all elections—local, state, and federal.

- In 1993, Clinton signed the National Voter Registration Act, which introduced a National Voter Registration form that you pick up when you go to get your driver's license or when you sign up for welfare. (Colloquially, the act is known as "Motor Voter.") Many states allow you to fill out this form to register for all elections. However, states that haven't fully implemented this law allow you to use this form only for federal elections (President, U.S. Senate, and U.S. House of Representatives).

- Forms are available in different languages. Choices vary, but you can usually get them in Spanish and Chinese, which you should have on hand for your drive. If you are planning to do a large-scale voter-registration drive, you should call ahead to the Board of Elections to make sure that it will have enough registration forms available.

- Sometimes you must be over eighteen and a U.S. citizen in order to register others to vote. If you learn that your state allows only a "state-certified registrar" to register voters, refocus your attentions to a voter-education drive (the specifics of which are coming up).

When to register?

Most states require that registration be done at least thirty days prior to the election. Minnesota, however, has same-day registration, which is one of the reasons that Jesse Ventura was able to win the gubernatorial race in 1998. Citizens who had stayed away from the polls for years were able to participate in this election spontaneously. (Once you have registered, you will be able to vote for any and all elections. You have to re-register if you have changed addresses or your name, or if you registered but didn't vote in the previous two elections.)

VOTER REGISTRATION:

When registering voters, keep in mind that the easier you make it for people to register, the more effective your drive will be. Some people may not be able to read but would rather not admit it. Others may not speak English (which is why you should have forms in as many languages as possible). Still others may claim to be just too busy and be annoyed that you're adding one more thing to their day.

- Offer to fill the form out for them, or help them fill it out.

- Some people don't want to register because they believe they will then be eligible for jury duty. Assuage their fears by telling them that, in reality, there are many other ways of becoming eligible for jury duty—one's driver's license, taxes, and being on public assistance, for example.

- Don't forget to tell potential voters that the Board of Elections will be sending them a voter-registration card in the mail in the coming weeks and that they should save it.

- Once you have finished, make sure you mail the forms to the appropriate place, most likely the Board of Elections. You should keep copies (or, at least, contact information) of every form you filled out so that you can follow up ("get out the vote") with the same people you registered.

VOTER EDUCATION:

Most people won't register to vote or go to polls unless they have a reason to do so. Local issues are the ones that are most likely to inspire people to vote. Other issues that drive people to vote may have personal reasons behind them—violence, education, and reproductive rights, for example. Research local issues, candidates' positions on those issues, and which referendums will be on the upcoming ballot.

- Get information from the candidates and see which issues are central to their campaigns.

- Campaign materials are often presented in dense, confusing language—you should translate it into clear points. Your role is simply to give voters information about a candidate's position. They, in turn, need to determine how well the candidate will represent them. The following resources can help you research local and other issues on-line:
  Women's Voting Guide (www.womenvote.org) is sponsored by the Women Leaders OnLine Fund and tracks how well candidates will represent women's issues.
  Voters for Choice (www.voters4choice.org) can provide

you with information on how candidates rate on reproductive rights.
Project Vote Smart (www.vote-smart.org or http://www.
selectsmart.com/PRESIDENT/) is a nonpartisan, nonprofit voter-education site with great information about
every candidate. You can also call (800) 622-7627 and
talk to a knowledgeable student volunteer.

• You may want to prepare your own local voting guide. Contact the Third Wave Foundation for sample Voter Education
Guides (see Chapter 2 resources for contact information).

GET OUT THE VOTE!
In recent elections, the biggest problem was actually getting people
to the polls. The week before the election (general elections, not including special elections, are always held on the first Tuesday in
November), you should call those people you registered and everyone else you know and remind them that it is Election Day. Encourage them to vote with their conscience and their consciousness
raised.

• Be prepared to tell them where they must go to vote. (The information is on their voter-registration card, or you can direct
them to the Board of Elections.) And give people enough reason to vote.

• Most people are nervous that they might pull the wrong lever
or that they don't know what they're doing. Let them know
that you are, too.

• The superactivists among you can actually get people to the
polls by being an escort for the elderly or for those with disabilities, helping to organize baby-sitting for parents of young
children, or arranging transportation for people who don't
have cars.

• Last, but not least, vote.

Notes

PROLOGUE: A DAY WITHOUT FEMINISM

1. Phyllis Rosser pioneered the research that named the gender gap in SAT and PSAT scores. She wrote to us as we were finishing the book that in the past couple of years "the gender gap on the PSAT has narrowed from 45 to 20 points (in SAT terms). This means that women will receive about $1,500,000 more in scholarship money in 2000 than in previous years." See Rosser's book, *The SAT Gender Gap: Identifying the Causes*, published by the Center for Women's Policy Studies (1989) for more information.

2. In 1999, the Women's Rights Project of the American Civil Liberties Union (ACLU) won a landmark Title IX case. Two high-school girls from Covington, Kentucky, brought suit against the National Honor Society for ignoring their qualifying GPAs in light of their pregnancy and parental status. The school district argued that the girls weren't denied admission because of their parental status (and implicitly acknowledged that such a practice would be unlawful) but because "they engaged in premarital sex." The school relied solely on pregnancy as proof of sexual activity, though, a determining factor that can apply only to women. (No males had ever been excluded from the school's chapter of the National Honor Society on grounds of having had sex—Title IX prevailed!)

3. Beauty contests are still the largest source of college scholarships for women. For example, the Miss America winner receives upward of $50,000, and the Miss America Organization has given more than $100 million in grants since 1945, when it began awarding scholarships. It remains the largest "scholarship organization" in the world.

4. Anonymous was a woman, as were the translators of most "great" works. For instance, the first English translation of *The Communist Manifesto* was done by a woman, Helen McFarlane. We intend to have any translations of *Manifesta* done by a man.

391

5. Before 1969, there were no women's studies departments, and very few individual courses. As of 2000, the National Women's Studies Association counted 728 women's studies courses in their database in the United States alone.

6. The McGovern-Nixon election of 1972 marked the emergence of a "gender gap," the first election in which there was a clear difference between men's and women's voting patterns. During the 1980 Carter-Reagan election, the gap had become wide enough for politicians to worry about getting the women's vote. (Only 46 percent of women voted for Reagan, according to the Gallup poll, but 54 percent of men did.)

7. Statistics and facts from "A Day without Feminism" come from a few sources: *The American Woman 1994–95: Where We Stand, Women and Health,* edited by Cynthia Costello and Anne J. Stone for the Women's Research and Education Institute (New York: W. W. Norton, 1994); *The Book of Women's Firsts,* by Phyllis J. Read and Bernard L. Witlieb (New York: Random House, 1992); *Mothers on Trial: The Battle for Children and Custody,* by Phyllis Chesler; *The Reader's Companion to U.S. Women's History*; and the U.S. Bureau of Labor Statistics. (For full citations of all other books mentioned, see the Bibliography.)

1. THE DINNER PARTY

8. Nearly two thousand years later, women did notice that the Bible was a little sinister. In 1895, Elizabeth Cady Stanton published *The Woman's Bible,* a best-seller that also rendered Stanton a heretic and a less acceptable suffragist. The women's movement was divided into those who wanted to take on organized religion along with everything else and those who thought taking on the political patriarchy was tough enough. The latter camp won out. Matilda Joslyn Gage, Stanton's friend, had already published an even more radically feminist book about women and religion called *Women, Church, and State.* Instead of *The Woman's Bible,* with its Creation story in which Adam and Eve were born at the same instant in the image of an androgynous God, Gage observed that God made creatures from the most base to the most wonderful; therefore woman must have been created after man.

9. Redstockings member Kathie Sarachild, née Amatniek, created most of the early pamphlets on consciousness-raising and is generally considered to be its principal architect. Anne Koedt's "The Myth of the Vaginal Orgasm" is reprinted in *Radical Feminism.*

10. The full roster of women and goddesses seated at Judy Chicago's Dinner Party is as follows: Primordial Goddess, Fertile Goddess, Ishtar, Kali, Snake Goddess, Sophia, Amazon, Hatshepsut, Judith, Sappho, Aspasia, Boadicea, Hypatia, Marcella, Saint Bridget, Theodora, Hrosvitha, Trotula, Eleanor of Aquitaine, Hildegarde of Bingen, Petronilla de Meath, Christine de Pisan, Isabella d'Este, Elizabeth R., Artemisia Gentileschi, Anna van Schurman, Anne Hutchinson, Sacagawea, Caroline Herschel, Mary Wollstonecraft, Sojourner Truth, Susan B. Anthony, Elizabeth

Blackwell, Emily Dickinson, Ethel Smythe, Margaret Sanger, Natalie Barney, Virginia Woolf, and Georgia O'Keeffe. For more about this work, read *The Dinner Party: A Symbol of Our Heritage* by Judy Chicago.

11. STD statistics are according to the 1999 Alan Guttmacher Institute/Kaiser Family Foundation report on the U.S. epidemic of STDs. To obtain the full report, contact the Alan Guttmacher Institute. (See Appendix 2: A Young Woman's Guide to Revolution for contact information.)

12. The statistics on who has abortions come from the 1996 Fact Sheet "Women Who Have Abortions," prepared by the National Abortion Federation, a D.C.–based organization that promotes access to and education about abortion. (See Appendix 2 for contact information.)

13. We actually do have the ERA. Even though its deadline is past, women's-rights groups have devised a strategy whereby three more states are needed to ratify it. (Congress accepted a 203-year ratification process for an amendment on congressional pay raises, so we have some leverage.) Ratification bills have been introduced in Illinois, Mississippi, Missouri, Oklahoma, and Virginia; lobby your state legislators, if you live in any of those states, to ratify. Once the trio of states sign on, we must all lobby Congress to acknowledge the amendment.

14. Alix Kates Shulman's "Marriage Agreement" appeared in the preview issue of *Ms.* (Spring 1972, page 72). Shulman writes about her creation—titling it "The Marriage Disagreement," since the Agreement's rhetoric surpassed the reality—in *The Feminist Memoir Project*.

15. Read "The Housewife's Moment of Truth," by Jane O'Reilly, in the preview issue of *Ms.* (Spring 1972, page 54).

16. "The Politics of Housework," by Pat Mainardi, was another groundbreaking article from the Second Wave. It is available today in Robin Morgan's anthology, *Sisterhood Is Powerful*.

17. Since Phyllis Chesler published *Mothers on Trial: The Battle for Children and Custody* in 1986, the situation for women in relationship to custody and divorce has improved only minimally. For instance, then and now, in 60 to 82 percent of the instances when a father asks for custody of his child, the courts grant him custody, regardless of his track record as a parent. This injustice is more glaring when you consider that fathers don't ask that often, and that custody is often based on nothing more than men's greater earning power or likelihood to remarry.

2. WHAT IS FEMINISM?

18. Henricus Cornelius Agrippa is quoted in Ian Mclean's *The Renaissance Notion of Woman* (New York: Cambridge University Press, 1980). Page 80.

19. More on the history of *feminism* can be found in *Women Imagine Change: A Global Anthology of Women's Resistance from 600 B.C.E. to the Present*, edited by Eugenia DeLamotte, Natania Meeker, and Jean O'Barr, page 10.

20. Andrea Dworkin and her compatriot, University of Michigan Law School professor Catharine MacKinnon, are often the subjects of feminist "urban myths." For example, after they wrote an anti-pornography ordinance for Minneapolis and MacKinnon was asked to consult on Canada's law, news stories insisted that the law was causing works of erotica, including those by lesbian feminists, to be censored and confiscated. According to Canadian journalist Michelle Landburg, it wasn't the Dworkin-MacKinnon statute that banned such materials but preexisting customs regulations. For more on this case, look to *In Harm's Way: The Pornography Civil Rights Hearing*, edited by MacKinnon and Dworkin.

21. Shulamith Firestone is best known for her aforementioned 1970 work of feminist political theory, *The Dialectic of Sex*, published when she was twenty-five. Like Alice Paul, Firestone is one of those brilliant minds who changed the terms of the debate but was never properly recognized, in part because the media picked up on Kate Millett's *Sexual Politics*, published the same year. Firestone went to art school in Chicago in the late sixties, couldn't get a job in the sexist art establishment when she graduated, and hooked up with the emerging radical-feminist movement in Chicago. In 1968, she moved to New York City and helped found a number of influential groups such as Redstockings, New York Radical Women, and New York Radical Feminists. (She edited the Redstockings' publication, *Notes*.) At the height of her activism, she retired from public life and now lives quietly in New York, where she writes.

22. In 1997, the Census Bureau reported that men with less than a ninth-grade education make, on average, $22,748, while women who have a high-school diploma make $90 less than that. A man who has graduated from high school makes more than a woman with some college education or even an associate's degree.

23. "This is not consciousness-raising or yuppie networking from hell," said Naomi Wolf of her short-lived women's media group, Culture Babes. Instead, it was a group experimenting with Wolf's ideas of "power feminism." Her latest venture—the Woodhull Institute for Ethical Leadership—seeks to increase the number of women leaders for the Third Wave through a three-day training program. Wolf initiated this organization with the help of others, including Margot Magowan, a young woman who is a radio producer living in San Francisco, and Erica Jong, the Second Wave author.

3. FEMINISTS WANT TO KNOW: IS THE MEDIA DEAD?

24. *Ms.* has had five owners. In 1987, its original all-female ownership sold it to the Australian company Fairfax, whose feminist editor-publisher team also started *Sassy*. In 1989, Dale Lang bought *Sassy* and agreed to publish *Ms.* in an ad-free format. In 1996, after hatcheting the much-loved *Sassy*, this mini-media magnate sold *Working Woman, Working Mother* and *Ms.* to Jay MacDonald. Finally in 1999, after nine years of uninterested and abusive male ownership, *Ms.* was purchased by a cartel of feminists, a publishing venture aptly named Liberty Media for Women.

25. As we write this chapter, there is a proliferation of magazines—big and small. Hearst alone has launched Tina Brown's *Talk, Cosmo Girl,* and Oprah Winfrey's *O.* Cable stations devoted to women (to compete with the stale programming on Lifetime), such as Oxygen, are also in the works. While it's exciting to create more choices and opportunities, the danger is that rather than change the status quo (which requires work, diligence, and political consciousness within the existing media), people are opting to start their own magazines (or foundations or whatever) in their own image. It leads us to more choices, but all are competing for the same advertising money, saddled with the same advertising constraints.

26. There are so many examples of women's independent media—with varying degrees of success in terms of content and financial stability—that we hesitate to even begin compiling names. A short list includes the Philadelphia magazine *Labyrinth, The Women's Times, The Women's Review of Books,* and numerous Third Wave fanzines that grew up in the petri dish of feminism. There are also countless now defunct but once great magazines, such as *HUES, Women of Power, Plexus,* and *On the Issues.* These alternative publications are freer in the sense that they don't have to kowtow to advertisers. But they are so on the margins that readers can hardly find them, and so underfunded that writers can hardly rely on them for their careers. Writing and publishing them is more like volunteer work, something women have no trouble finding.

27. We didn't count associate and assistant editors, where there tends to be more gender parity (and where there also tends to be less money and decision-making power).

28. *The San Francisco Chronicle,* among others, declared, "Preventative Mastectomies Found to Work." As one respondent to this piece astutely pointed out, "If dealing with breast cancer is so simple, why do 44,000 women die of the disease each year?"

29. The original report, issued by the National Association for Perinatal Addiction Research and Education, found, in a survey of births in thirty-six hospitals, that 11 percent of the babies were affected by their mother's use of illegal drugs.

30. Two days before the *Ladies' Home Journal* sit-in, forty-six women at *Newsweek* filed a sex-discrimination complaint with the Equal Employment Opportunity Commission. Women at *The New York Times* and *Time* magazine followed suit, so to speak, that same year.

31. Advertiser control of women's magazines was exposed in Gloria Steinem's essay "Sex, Lies, and Advertising," published in the first ad-free issue of *Ms.* (July/August 1990). An updated version appears in Steinem's *Moving Beyond Words.* Things haven't changed much since Steinem wrote her exposé. In a random issue of *Glamour* (November of 1997), we counted 244 pages of ads in a 334-page magazine. In a random issue of *GQ* (May of 1997), we counted 278 pages, 136 of which were ads. The editorial pages, especially in the women's magazine, had obvious ties to

the ad pages. When we asked Steinem about this, she underscored *strongly* that advertiser control, not focus groups or misogynist editors, is the reason feminist media hasn't thrived.

32. *Ms.*'s "success" in running various opinions within feminism is debatable. See former editor Ellen Willis's essay "Why I Quit *Ms.*" in *Feminist Revolution,* a Redstockings collective book, which is out of print but available at the library. It's always been next to impossible for *Ms.* to run pieces that took a complex view of pornography, sex work, and S/M, even though many feminists (i.e., Susie Bright, COYOTE, Pat Califia, Danzin) do positive work in those arenas.

33. Editorial didn't make cosmetic suggestions, but when it came to covers, the publisher, or business side, of *Ms.* often did—even after the magazine went ad-free. The 1995 July/August issue featured a black woman's hand holding six candles to represent the anniversary of six ad-free years. The publisher, bowing to industry lore that black covers don't sell, was angry because it wasn't a white woman's hand.

34. *Time* editor Priscilla Painton reiterated the day-care concern at a meeting with activists from NOW and the Third Wave Foundation following publication of the story. Painton's insistent cries about day care might have been more symbolic than actual, since she, like most of the top editors at *Time*, has a private nanny to care for her tykes in tony Bronxville.

35. Penny Penrose's Good Faith Fund, one terrific example among many, has disbursed more than 250 loans to seed businesses of entrepreneurs deemed "pre-bankable." It has also offered training in basic business skills—from how to do market research to bookkeeping—to more than 700 individuals. The largest inner-city, worker-owned cooperative home-care provider in the country, Cooperative Home Care Associates, is located in the Bronx. Nearly 400 formerly low-income or welfare recipients are now full-time home-health workers; 250 of these workers also own a piece of the business.

36. In 1995, the United Nations hosted the Fourth World Conference on Women in Beijing, China. Running simultaneous to this meeting was the Non-Governmental Forum on Women. (The former was solely for governments, and the latter for more grassroots constituencies.) A Platform for Action resulted from the forum, a document listing twelve areas of concern for women around the world. Each country committed to independently implementing these "platforms."

4. GIRL, YOU'LL BE A WOMAN SOON

37. Katie's premise that men are too wimpy now, and women want to revel in their stilettos, is seemingly a bit of a "Fuck you" to Mom. In other ways, however, Katie's anti-feminism feminism is right in line with her mother's modus operandi. For example, the elder Roiphe wrote a homophobic exposé of Sarah Lawrence College in the late eighties that "accused" the predominantly female school of essentially turning female students into lesbians.

38. Don't underestimate the power of sending aesthetic signals. Mary Clarke, recalling the day she applied for a job in the *Sassy* art department, says, "I was so tired of pulling together my Condé Nast suit so I just thought, I am going to wear whatever the hell I want. I looked nice but very 'me.' I said something to Jane [Pratt] like, 'I really get what you're doing.' And she said, 'Oh, yes. I can tell by what you're wearing.' "

39. Gloria Steinem recalls that *Ms.* wouldn't have gotten any investors either, except that she and the other editors did a sample issue for free. *New York* magazine used it as a special issue, and all 300,000 copies sold out almost immediately. This evidence of a women's community, hungry for smart, political content, didn't prompt people with money to try to fund competitors, though. Apparently, only one overtly feminist magazine was allowed back then. Oh, and also now.

5. BARBIE VS. THE MENSTRUAL KIT

40. A lucky intersection with Gloria Steinem and *Parade* magazine launched the Take Our Daughters to Work Day program into 37 million homes. "The first day I ever met Gloria," says Merlino, "I gave her a one-pager on Take Our Daughters to Work Day to sort of explain to her what it was about. She took it and as she was throwing her cape over her shoulder, she said, 'You know, I'm going to lunch with Walter Anderson [the publisher of *Parade* magazine], and if he asks me what's new, I'll give him this.' "

41. The stars must have been in alignment when Nancy Gruver and Joe Kelly slammed up against the typical feminist quandary: whose name to give to the kids. Both are devoted to equality, so they decided to flip a coin. Nancy won, which meant the first child would get her last name, the second his, and who cares if people won't assume the kids are from the same family. But they had identical twins, so Mavis, the firstborn, is a Gruver, Nia is a Kelly, and no one looking at the two would ever think they weren't sisters.

6. THOU SHALT NOT BECOME THY MOTHER

42. Recent movement histories include: *The Feminist Memoir Project: Voices from the Women's Liberation Movement,* edited by Rachel Blau DuPlessis and Ann Snitow, Susan Brownmiller's *In Our Time,* Judith Hennesee's biography of Betty Friedan called *Her Life,* Robin Morgan's *Saturday's Child: A Memoir of Work, Love, and Politics,* Bonnie Watkins and Nina Rothchild's *In the Company of Women: Voices from the Women's Movements,* and Mary Thom's history of *Ms.* magazine, *Inside* Ms., among others. (See the Bibliography for more books to add to your reading pile.)

43. After we wrote this chapter, Gloria Steinem took a complementary approach in advising her generation on how to forge alliances with younger feminists. In the February/March 2000 issue of *Ms.* magazine, Steinem's regular column was devoted to "Advice to Old Fems." She

wrote: "Just as you and I didn't become feminists out of guilt or gratitude, young women won't either."

7. WHO'S AFRAID OF KATIE ROIPHE?

44. A more comprehensive and useful definition of rape can be found in the 1999 United States Criminal Code, USC 2241-2244. It states that drugging and intoxicating a woman so that she passes out or is unable to control her conduct with the intent to have sexual intercourse (which includes oral and anal sex) without her consent is rape.

45. "Recall of Childhood Trauma: A Prospective Study of Women's Memories of Child Sexual Abuse," by Linda Meyer Williams, was presented at the Annual Meeting of the American Society of Criminology in Phoenix, Arizona, on October 27, 1993, and is available through the Family Research Laboratory, University of New Hamsphire, 126 Horton Social Science Center, Durham, New Hampshire 03824.

8. WHAT IS ACTIVISM?

46. The wording of the ERA that was passed by Congress in 1972, and went to the states for ratification, was "equality of rights under the law shall not be abridged or denied . . . on account of sex."

47. Some inequalities do still exist in Scandinavia and the presumption of equality sometimes silences those who want to break down remaining barriers. In the words of a twenty-one-year-old Finnish student in an article called "Finland's Flawed Utopia," by Mia Spangenberg (*Women's International Net Magazine*, no. 12, available at http://www.winmagazine. org), "Finland is ruled by the collective illusion that men and women are equal so that even women dare not see the discrepancies around them. If a woman admits that there is inequality, she also has to admit to herself that she isn't as successful and equal as she would like to believe."

48. "Making Differences Matter: A New Paradigm for Managing Diversity," by David A. Thomas and Robin J. Ely. *Harvard Business Review,* September/October, 1996.

EPILOGUE: A DAY WITH FEMINISM

49. In 1997, according to research undertaken by Women & Philanthropy, only 5.7 percent of philanthropic dollars went to programs specifically benefiting women and girls.

50. At present, some of life's basic necessities are either not available to those who need them or must be paid for with private funding. For example, between 21 and 23 percent of U.S. adults are functionally illiterate, according to the Literacy Volunteers of America. Yet this organization, the largest literacy-training initiative in America, doesn't get a dime from the government and is funded almost exclusively by individual donors and corporations.

Manifesta's *Lexicon*

After we wrote *Manifesta*, we asked some of our colleagues and friends to read it. From their comments, we realized that our use of language sometimes revealed a generation gap—or at least a vocabulary gap. Some friends didn't know what we meant by Third Wave, a term that we use almost interchangeably with *young feminist*. Others challenged our use of language that the Second Wave had dissected and found sexist: words like *girl*, when used to address an adult woman, and *cunt* and *suffragette*. Some young women today can and do confidently use words that were previously forbidden or that have been used against women in the past. This is a good thing. However, we don't want our vernacular to be confusing to the reader. Therefore this glossary is intended to tip you off to word usage throughout the book.

bitch (noun): *Webster's* says a bitch is a female dog. Many note that when a woman is tough she's called a bitch and men of the same quality are just, you know, tough. Well, self-determination is on the feminist menu, and *bitch* is not an aspersion in this book (nor is it in Elizabeth Wurtzel's 1998 book, *Bitch*). Given female socialization, a not-nice woman can be a beautiful thing.

crip rights (noun): Self-named term for the goal of some in the disabled-rights movement. Specifically, the amputee and activist Hilary Russian uses the term in her amazing zine *Ring of Fire*.

cunt (noun): These four letters are known as the *c* word, a word so hateful that it can scarcely be uttered. In the past few years *Bust*, a Girlie magazine, has published a tart, incisive reclaiming of the

399

word as a term of grudging respect ("You bought those red leather pants—you *cunt*"), and it still can indicate a bad-assed bitch ("Madonna? She's a cunt, but I like her"). It's used when ordinary words don't have enough *ooomph*. Inga Muscio, a Third Wave lady, also grabbed the word back for us with her sunny, square 1999 book, *Cunt: A Declaration of Independence.*

First Wave (noun): The suffragists/suffragettes are considered to be the First Wave of the feminist movement, although they didn't know that the organized push for women's rights would ever fly and need to be identified by its subsequent surges of political and cultural action. This wave originated in the mid-1800s and ended in 1920 with the Nineteenth Amendment, which guaranteed women the right to vote.

girl (noun): A girl can be a female under the age of eighteen. Yes, in the sixties (and before), calling a grown woman "girl" was belittling, as in "I'll get the new girl to get us some coffee." The only problem with banishing the term was that women didn't have any familiar, relaxed way of referring to other members of their sex— anything akin to "guy" for men. In the past few years, *girl* or *gal* has become that jocular word. From Riot Grrrls to Girlies to girl-friends, *girl* no longer conveys anything retrograde or, when coming from a peer or a friend, any disrespect.

Girlie (adjective and noun): A Girlie-girl can be a stereotypically feminine one—into manicures and hairstyles and cooking and indoorsy activities. Girlie is also a feminist philosophy put forth most assertively by the folks at *Bust*. Girlies are adult women, usually in their mid-twenties to late thirties, whose feminist principles are based on a reclaiming of girl culture (or feminine accoutrements that were tossed out with sexism during the Second Wave), be it Barbie, housekeeping, or girl talk.

lady or ladies (noun): Casual, alternative term for a *woman* or *women*, not only those who adhere to prissy, white-glove, upper-crusty stereotypes. For example, "Do you know Nomy Lamm? That punk-rock lady is so damn smart."

out (adjective and verb): This useful term usually refers to whether a gay, lesbian, or bisexual person is public, as opposed to secretive, about her or his sexual identity (i.e., "out of the closet"). We use the word colloquially to mean conscious and public expression of any political or disparaged aspect of one's identity. For example, Jennifer is out about having an STD, Amy is out about having had an abortion, and Sarah McLachlan is out about being a feminist.

queer (adjective and noun): There's *lesbian* and *gay* and *bi* and *transsexual* . . . and then there's *queer*—the word that attempts to capture them all and reclaim a slur in one fell swoop.

Second Wave (noun): The Second Wave of the women's movement originated in the 1960s and was a full-on force throughout the seventies. These activists, both radical and reformist, shepherded in abortion reform, equal pay, and credit legislation, and consciousness of sexism as a tool of cultural and political oppression. Second Wavers, now in their forties through seventies, are still active and, indeed, run most of the institutions of the women's movement, from NOW to NARAL to women's studies to *Ms.*

slut (noun): A slut is a woman whose sexuality belongs to no man. (Rounding out our triumvirate of Third Wave books that reclaim slurs and dash stereotypes is *Slut! Growing Up Female with a Bad Reputation*, by Leora Tanenbaum.)

suffragette (noun, derivation of *suffrage*, or "right to vote"): Suffragist is the preferred term of historians and academics for the nineteenth- and twentieth-century ladies who fought for voting and other citizenship rights for all women. In America, the term *suffragette* was typically used by contemptuous patriarchs who wished to belittle these women. In England, however, during the same time period, the women's-rights revolutionaries (who were radical and also got the vote before their American sisters did) were called suffragettes, and they liked it fine. In *Manifesta*, we prefer *suffragette* because it sounds more hard-core (and lends itself to rock and roll), which Elizabeth Cady Stanton and Matilda Joslyn Gage, among many others, indisputably were. Besides, it is a sign of confidence that we can reclaim a former slight.

Third Wave (noun): No, it's not the techno-crazy theory put forth by Alvin and Heidi Toffler, the couple who were unfortunately picked to be Newt Gingrich's gurus. Third Wave means the core mass of the current women's movement in their late teens through their thirties, roughly speaking—the ones who grew up with Judy

Blume books, *Free to Be . . . You and Me*, and *Sesame Street*. Another way of looking at Third Wave is as the "daughters," both real and metaphorical, of the Second Wave, the women who read *Ms.* magazine, *Our Bodies, Ourselves*, and lobbied for *Roe v. Wade* and the ERA.

zines (noun): These homemade, xeroxed, independent publications are the communications arm of the DIY (do-it-yourself) punk scene, the DIY women's scene, and other revolutionary groups. In the early nineties, Riot Grrrls learned about one another from loose zine networks where a dollar and a couple of stamps meant a young feminist writer or artist would send you the news of her community and her own life. Decades earlier, similar mail-order publications, such as *The Furies* and *First Things First*, connected women to the burgeoning radical women's movement.

Bibliography

PRIMARY SOURCES
Books we relied on to write this book

Bell Scott, Patricia, Gloria Hull, and Barbara Smith. *All the Women Are White, All the Blacks Are Men, But Some of Us Are Brave: Black Women's Studies*. New York: Feminist Press at the City University of New York, 1982.

Brown, Helen Gurley. *Sex and the Single Girl*. New York: Avon Books, 1983.

Brownmiller, Susan, *Against Our Will: Men, Women and Rape*. New York: Fawcett Books, 1993. Originally published in 1975.

——. *In Our Time: Memoir of a Revolution*. New York: Dial Press, 1999.

Chesler, Ellen. *Woman of Valor: Margaret Sanger and the Birth Control Movement in America*. New York: Simon & Schuster, 1992.

Chesler, Phyllis. *Mothers on Trial: The Battle for Children and Custody*. New York: Harcourt Brace, 1991.

——. *Letter to a Young Feminist*. New York: Four Walls Eight Windows, 1998.

Davis, Angela Y. *Women, Race, and Class*. New York: Random House, 1983.

Delamotte, Eugenia, Natania Meeker, and Jean O'Barr, eds. *Women Imagine Change: A Global Anthology of Women's Resistance from 600 B.C.E. to the Present*. New York: Routledge, 1997.

Douglas, Susan. *Where the Girls Are: Growing Up Female with the Mass Media*. New York: Random House, 1994.

DuPlessis, Rachel Blau, and Ann Snitow, eds. *The Feminist Memoir Project: Voices from Women's Liberation*. New York: Three Rivers Press, 1998.

Dworkin, Andrea. *Intercourse*. New York: Free Press, 1987.

Faludi, Susan. *Backlash*. New York: Crown, 1991.

——. *Stiffed*. New York: William Morrow, 1999.

Fielding, Helen. *Bridget Jones's Diary*. New York: Viking Press, 1998.
Firestone, Shulamith. *The Dialectic of Sex: The Case for Feminist Revolution*. New York: William Morrow, 1970.
Friedan, Betty. *The Feminine Mystique*. Reprint, New York: W. W. Norton, 1997.
Funiciello, Theresa. *Tyranny of Kindness: Dismantling the Welfare System to End Poverty in America*. New York: Atlantic Monthly Press, 1994.
Gage, Matilda Joslyn, and Sally Roesch Wagner, eds. *Woman, Church and State*. Aberdeen, SD: Sky Carrier Press, 1998. Originally published in 1893. (To order, contact: Sky Carrier Press, P.O. Box 2135, Aberdeen, SD 57402. $20 plus $4.95 for shipping.)
Gilligan, Carol. *In a Different Voice: Psychological Theory and Women's Development*. Cambridge: Harvard University Press, 1993. Originally published in 1982.
Greer, Germaine. *The Female Eunuch*. New York: McGraw-Hill, 1971.
Hardisty, Jean. *Mobilizing Resentment: Conservative Resurgence from the John Birch Society to the Promise Keepers*. Boston: Beacon Press, 1999.
Hennessee, Judith Adler. *Betty Friedan: Her Life*. New York: Random House, 1999.
Hine, Darlene Clark. *Black Women in America: An Historical Encyclopedia*. Brooklyn: Carlson Publishing, 1993.
Hoagland, Sarah Lucia. *Lesbian Ethics: Toward New Value*. Chicago: Institute of Lesbian Studies, 1988. (To order, contact Hoagland directly: P.O. Box 25568, Chicago, IL 60625.)
Hole, Judith, and Ellen Levine. *Rebirth of Feminism*. New York: Quadrangle Books, 1971.
hooks, bell. *Ain't I a Woman: Black Women and Feminism*. Boston: South End Press, 1981.
Koedt, Anne, Ellen Levine, and Anita Rapone, eds. *Radical Feminism*. New York: Quadrangle Books, 1973. (This anthology includes essays such as Anne Koedt's "The Myth of the Vaginal Orgasm.")
Lerner, Gerda. *The Creation of Patriarchy*. Reprint, New York: Oxford University Press, 1987.
Lorde, Audre. *Sister Outsider: Essays and Speeches*. Freedom, Calif.: Crossing Press, 1984.
MacKinnon, Catharine. *Feminism Unmodified: Discourses on Life and Law*. Reprint, Cambridge: Harvard University Press, 1988.
———, and Andrea Dworkin, eds. *In Harm's Way: The Pornography Civil Rights Hearings*. Cambridge: Harvard University Press, 1998.
Mankiller, Wilma, Gwendolyn Mink, Maryssa Navarro, Barbara Smith, and Gloria Steinem. *The Reader's Companion to U.S. Women's History*. Boston: Houghton Mifflin, 1998.
Millett, Kate. *Sexual Politics*. New York: Simon & Schuster, 1990. Originally published in 1970.
Morgan, Robin, ed. *Sisterhood Is Powerful: An Anthology of Writings from the Women's Liberation Movement*. New York: Random House, 1970.
Redstockings. *Feminist Revolution*. New York: Random House, 1975.

Roberts, Dorothy. *Killing the Black Body: Race, Reproduction, and the Meaning of Liberty*. New York: Pantheon Books, 1997.

Seaman, Barbara. *The Doctors' Case Against the Pill*. Alameda, Calif.: Hunter House, 1995. Originally published in 1969.

Shulman, Alix Kates. *Memoirs of an Ex–Prom Queen*. New York: Penguin Books, 1997. Originally published in 1972.

Steinem, Gloria. *Outrageous Acts and Everyday Rebellions*. New York: Henry Holt, 1995. Originally published in 1983.

———. *Revolution from Within*. New York: Little, Brown, 1992.

———. *Moving Beyond Words*. New York: Simon & Schuster, 1994.

Thom, Mary. *Inside Ms.: 25 Years of the Magazine and the Feminist Movement*. New York: Henry Holt, 1997.

Thomas, Marlo, and Friends. *Free to Be . . . You and Me*. Philadelphia: Running Press, 1974.

Walker, Alice. *In Search of Our Mothers' Gardens: Womanist Prose*. Orlando: Harcourt Brace Jovanovich, 1983.

SECONDARY SOURCES
Books that are a foundation of the movement or related to this book

Acker, Kathy. *Pussy, King of the Pirates*. New York: Grove Press, 1997.

Anzaldúa, Gloria, and Cherríe Moraga, eds. *This Bridge Called My Back*. Brooklyn: Kitchen Table: Women of Color Press, 1983.

Bank, Melissa. *The Girls' Guide to Hunting and Fishing*. New York: Viking Press, 1999.

Brown, Rita Mae. *Rubyfruit Jungle*. New York: Bantam Books, 1983.

———. *Rita Will: Memoir of a Literary Rabble-Rouser*. New York: Bantam Doubleday, 1999.

Callenbach, Ernest. *Ecotopia*. New York: Bantam Books, 1990.

Chesler, Phyllis. *Women and Madness*. New York: Four Walls Eight Windows, 1997. Originally published in 1972.

Chicago, Judy. *The Dinner Party: A Symbol of Our Heritage*. Garden City: Anchor Press, 1979.

Daly, Mary. *Gynecology: The Metaethics of Radical Feminism*. Boston: Beacon Press, 1990.

———. *Beyond God the Father: Toward a Philosophy of Women's Liberation*. Boston: Beacon Press, 1985.

de Beauvoir, Simone. *The Second Sex*. New York: Vintage Books, 1989.

de Pizan, Christine. *The Book of the City of Ladies*. New York: Persea Books, 1998.

Ehrenreich, Barbara. *Fear of Falling: The Inner Life of the Middle Class*. New York: HarperCollins, 1990.

———, Gloria Jacobs, and Elizabeth Hess. *Re-Making Love: The Feminization of Sex*. New York: Anchor, 1987.

Ensler, Eve. *The Vagina Monologues*. New York: Villard Books, 1998.

Estes, Ralph W. *The Tyranny of the Bottom Line: Why Corporations Make Good People Do Bad Things*. San Francisco: Berrett-Koehler, 1996.

French, Marilyn. *The Women's Room.* New York: Summit Books, 1977.

Greer, Germaine. *The Whole Woman.* New York: Alfred Knopf, 1999.

The Guerrilla Girls. *The Guerrilla Girls' Bedside Companion to the History of Western Art.* New York: Penguin, 1998.

Hall, Radclyffe. *The Well of Loneliness.* Reprint, New York: Anchor Books/Doubleday, 1990.

Hancock, Emily. *The Girl Within.* New York: Fawcett Columbine, 1989.

Jordan, June. *Affirmative Acts: Political Essays.* New York: Anchor Books/Doubleday, 1998.

Millett, Kate. *Flying.* New York: Simon & Schuster, 1990. Originally published in 1979.

Morgan, Robin, ed. *Sisterhood Is Global: The International Women's Movement Anthology.* New York: Feminist Press at the City University of New York, 1996. Originally published in 1984 by Anchor/Doubleday.

Pollitt, Katha. *Reasonable Creatures: Essays on Women and Feminism.* New York: Alfred A. Knopf, 1994.

Rilke, Rainer Maria. *Letters to a Young Poet.* New York: Vintage Books, 1987.

Rosen, Ruth. *The World Split Open: How the Modern Women's Movement Changed America.* New York: Viking, 2000.

Sanchez, Sonia. *Does Your House Have Lions?* Boston: Beacon Press, 1998.

Schneir, Miriam, ed. *Feminism in Our Time: The Essential Writings, World War II to the Present.* New York: Vintage Books, 1994.

————, ed. *Feminism: The Essential Historical Writings.* New York: Vintage Books, 1994. Originally published in 1972.

Smith, Barbara, ed. *Home Girls: A Black Feminist Anthology.* New Brunswick: Rutgers University Press, 2000. Originally published in 1983.

Stanton, Elizabeth Cady. *The Woman's Bible.* Boston: Northeastern University Press, 1993. Originally published in 1895–1898.

Wallace, Michele. *Black Macho and the Myth of the Superwoman.* New York: Verso Books, 1999.

Watkins, Bonnie, and Nina Rothchild. *In the Company of Women: Voices from the Women's Movement.* St. Paul: Minnesota Historical Society Press, 1996.

Wollstonecraft, Mary. *Vindication of the Rights of Woman.* New York: Konemann, 1999. Originally published in 1792.

Woolf, Virginia. *A Room of One's Own.* New York: Harcourt Brace, 1990.

TERTIARY SOURCES
Books that are antagonistic to feminism but important to read, especially if you are going to launch a counterattack

Crittenden, Danielle. *What Our Mothers Didn't Tell Us: Why Happiness Eludes the Modern Woman.* New York: Touchstone Books, 2000.

Denfeld, Rene. *The New Victorians: A Young Woman's Challenge to the Old Feminist Order*. New York: Warner Books, 1996.

Paglia, Camille. *Sexual Personae: Art and Decadence from Nefertiti to Emily Dickinson*. New Haven: Yale University Press, 1990.

Roiphe, Katie. *The Morning After: Sex, Fear and Feminism on Campus*. New York: Little, Brown, 1993.

Shalit, Wendy. *A Return to Modesty: Discovering the Lost Virtue*. New York: Free Press, 1999.

Sommers, Christina Hoff. *Who Stole Feminism? How Women Have Betrayed Women*. New York: Simon & Schuster, 1994.

THIRD WAVE'S READING ROOM
Books we used that are from or about our generation

Arnoldi, Katherine. *The Amazing "True" Story of a Teenage Single Mom*. New York: Hyperion, 1998.

Bagby, Meredith. *We've Got Issues: Election 2000: A Guide for 20- and 30-Somethings*. New York: Public Affairs, 2000.

Bail, Kathy, ed. *DIY Feminism*. St. Leonards, Australia: Allen & Unwin, 1996.

Bartlett, John W. *The Future Is Ours*. New York: Owl Books, 1996.

Belle, Jennifer. *Going Down*. New York: Riverhead, 1996.

Block, Francesca Lia, and Hillary Carlip. *Zine Scene: The Do It Yourself Guide to Zines*. Los Angeles: Girl Press, 1998.

Bright, Susie. *Susie Sexpert's Lesbian Sex World*. San Francisco: Cleis Press, 1990.

Chambers, Veronica. *Mama's Girl*. New York: Riverhead Books, 1997.

Chideya, Farai. *The Color of Our Future*. New York: William Morrow, 1999.

———. *Don't Believe the Hype: Fighting Cultural Misinformation About African Americans*. New York: Plume, 1995.

Coupland, Douglas. *Generation X: Tales for an Accelerated Culture*. New York: St. Martin's Press, 1991.

Daly, Meg, ed. *Surface Tension: Love, Sex, and Politics Between Lesbians and Straight Women*. New York: Touchstone, 1996.

Daly, Meg, and Anna Bodoc, eds. *Letters of Intent: Women Cross the Generations to Talk about Family, Work, Sex, Love and the Future of Feminism*. New York: Free Press, 1999.

Daly, Steven, and Nathaniel Wice. *alt.culture: an a-to-z guide to the '90s—underground, online, and over-the-counter*. New York: HarperPerennial, 1995.

Danticat, Edwidge. *Breath, Eyes, Memory*. New York: Soho Press, 1994.

———. *KrikKrack!* New York: Vintage Books, 1991.

Drill, Esther, Heather McDonald, and Rebecca Odes. *Deal with It: A Whole New Approach to Your Body, Brain, and Life as a Teenage Gurl*. New York: Pocket Books, 1999.

Ducombe, Stephen. *Notes from Underground: Zines and the Politics of Alternative Culture*. London: Verso, 1997.

Edut, Ophira, ed. *Adiós, Barbie: Young Women Write about Body Image and Identity*. Seattle: Seal Press, 1998.

Findlen, Barbara, ed. *Listen Up: Voices from the Next Feminist Generation*. Seattle: Seal Press, 1995.

Fine, Michelle, and Lois Weis. *The Unknown City: The Lives of Poor and Working-Class Young Adults*. Boston: Beacon Press, 1998.

Gore, Ariel. *The Hip Mama Survival Guide*. New York: Hyperion Books, 1998.

Green, Karen, and Tristan Taormino, eds. *A Girl's Guide to Taking Over the World. Writings from the Girl Zine Revolution*. New York: St. Martin's Press, 1997.

Heywood, Leslie, and Jennifer Drake, eds. *Third Wave Agenda: Being Feminist, Doing Feminism*. Minneapolis: University of Minnesota Press, 1997.

Horn, Stacy. *Cyberville: Clicks, Culture and the Creation of an Online Town*. New York: Warner Books, 1998.

Inness, Sherrie A. *Delinquents & Debutantes: Twentieth-Century American Girls' Cultures*. New York: New York University Press, 1998.

Kalma, Veronika. *Start Your Own Zine, Everything You Need to Know to Put into Print*. New York: Hyperion Books, 1997.

Kamen, Paula. *Feminist Fatale: Voices from the "Twentysomething" Generation Explore the Future of the "Women's Movement."* New York: Donald I. Fine, 1991.

Klein, Naomi. *No Logo: Taking Aim at the Brand Bullies*. Toronto: Knopf Canada, 2000.

Leblanc, Lauvaine. *Pretty In Pink: Girls' Gender Resistance in a Boys' Subculture*. New Brunswick: Rutgers University Press, 1999.

Looser, Devoney, and E. Ann Kaplan. *Generations: Academic Feminists in Dialogue*. Minneapolis: University of Minnesota Press, 1997.

Lublin, Nancy. *Pandora's Box: Feminism Confronts Reproductive Technology*. New York: Rowman & Littlefield, 1998.

Mitchell, Michelle. *A New Kind of Party Animal: How the Young Are Tearing Up the American Political Landscape*. New York: Simon & Schuster, 1998.

Morgan, Joan. *When Chickenheads Come Home to Roost: A Hip-Hop Feminist Breaks It Down*. New York: Touchstone, 2000.

Muscio, Inga. *Cunt*. Seattle, Washington: Seal Press, 1999.

Nelson, Rob, and Jon Cowan. *Revolution X*. New York: Penguin Books, 1994.

Palac, Lisa. *The Edge of the Bed: How Dirty Pictures Saved My Life*. New York: Little, Brown, 1998.

Raphael, Amy. *GRRRLS: Women Rewrite Rock*. New York: St. Martin's Griffin, 1995.

Roberts, Tara, ed. *Am I the Last Virgin? Ten African American Reflections on Sex and Love*. New York: Simon & Schuster, 1997.

Sapphire. *Push*. New York: Knopf, 1996.

Scholinski, Daphne, with Jane Meredith Adams. *Last Time I Wore a Dress*. New York: Riverhead Books, 1997.

Senna, Danzy. *Caucasia*. New York: Riverhead Books, 1999.
Shah, Sonia, ed. *Dragon Ladies: Asian American Feminists Breathe Fire*. Boston: South End Press, 1997.
Sherman, Aliza. *A Woman's Guide to the World Wide Web*. New York: Ballantine Books, 1998.
Stoller, Debbie, and Marcelle Karp, eds. *The* Bust *Guide to the New Girl Order*. New York: Penguin Books, 1999.
Tanenbaum, Leora. *Slut! Growing Up Female with a Bad Reputation*. New York: Seven Stories Press, 1999.
Walker, Rebecca, ed. *To Be Real: Telling the Truth and Changing the Face of Feminism*. New York: Anchor Books, 1995.
Walter, Natasha. *The New Feminism*. London: Little, Brown, 1998.
Wiseman, Rosalind. *Defending Ourselves*. New York: Farrar, Straus and Giroux, 1995.
Wolf, Naomi. *The Beauty Myth: How Images of Beauty Are Used Against Women*. New York: William Morrow, 1991.
———. *Fire with Fire: The New Female Power and How to Use It*. New York: Fawcett Books, 1994.
———. *Promiscuities: The Secret Struggle for Womanhood*. New York: Fawcett Books, 1998.
Wurtzel, Elizabeth. *Prozac Nation: Young and Depressed in America*. New York: Riverhead Books, 1997.
———. *Bitch: In Praise of Difficult Women*. New York: Doubleday, 1998.

MOTHERS AND DAUGHTERS
We surely weren't the first to explore the complex mother-daughter relationship

Beard, Patricia. *Good Daughters: Loving Our Mothers as They Age*. New York: Warner Books, 1998.
Edelman, Hope. *Motherless Daughters*. New York: Delta, 1995.
Friday, Nancy. *My Mother, Myself*. Reprint, New York: Delta, 1997.
Kline, Christina Baker, and Christina Looper Baker. *The Conversation Begins: Mothers and Daughters Talk about Living Feminism*. New York: Bantam, 1996.
Koppelman, Susan, ed. *Between Mothers and Daughters: Stories Across a Generation*. New York: Feminist Press at the City University of New York, 1985.
Lerner, Harriet Goldhor. *The Mother Dance: How Children Change Your Life*. New York: HarperCollins, 1998.
McCrindle, Jean, and Sheila Rowbotham. *Dutiful Daughters: Women Talk about Their Lives*. Austin: University of Texas Press, 1977.
Shulman, Alix Kates. *A Good Enough Daughter*. New York: Schocken Books, 1999.
Wilson, Marie C., Idelisse Malavé, and Elizabeth Debold, *Mother Daughter Revolution: From Good Girls to Great Women*. New York: Bantam Doubleday Dell, 1994.

THE GIRLS' ROOM
The cottage industry of girls' low self-esteem produced lots of books and workbooks. All are good-hearted, and some are really interesting

Blume, Judy. *Are You There, God? It's Me, Margaret.* New York: Laurel Leaf Library, 1974.

Brooks, Susan M. *Any Girl Can Rule the World.* Minneapolis: Fairview Press, 1998.

Brown, Lyn Mikel. *Raising Their Voices: The Politics of Girls' Anger.* Cambridge: Harvard University Press, 1998.

Brumberg, Joan. *Fasting Girls: The Emergence of Anorexia Nervosa as a Modern Disease.* Cambridge: Harvard University Press, 1988.

————. *The Body Project: An Intimate History of American Girls.* New York: Random House, 1999.

Carlip, Hillary. *Girl Power: Young Women Speak Out.* New York: Warner Books, 1995.

Dee, Catherine. *The Girls' Guide to Life: How to Take Charge of the Issues that Affect YOU.* New York: Little, Brown, 1997.

Gadesberg, Jeanette. *Brave New Girls: Creative Ideas to Help Girls Be Confident, Healthy, and Happy.* Minneapolis: Fairview Press, 1997.

Gilligan, Carol, Nona P. Lyons, and Trudy J. Hanmer, eds. *Making Connections: The Relational Worlds of Adolescent Girls at the Emma Willard School.* Cambridge: Harvard University Press, 1990.

Gray, Heather M., and Samantha Phillips. *Real Girl/Real World: Tools for Finding Your True Self.* Seattle: Seal Press, 1998.

Hughes, K. Wind, and Linda Wolf. *Daughters of the Moon, Sisters of the Sun: Young Women and Mentors on the Transition to Womanhood.* Gabriola Island, BC, Canada: New Society Publishers, 1997.

Johnston, Andrea. *Girls Speak Out: Finding Your True Self.* New York: Scholastic Press, 1997.

Karnes, Frances A., and Suzanne M. Bean. *Girls and Young Women Leading the Way. Twenty Stories about Leadership.* Minneapolis: Free Spirit, 1993.

Kravetz, Stacy. *Girl Boss: Running the Show Like the Big Chicks.* Los Angeles: Girl Press, 1999.

Mann, Judy. *The Difference: Growing Up Female in America.* New York: Warner Books, 1994.

McCune, Bunny, and Deb Traunstein. *Girls to Women, Women to Girls.* Berkeley: Celestial Arts, 1998.

Misiroglu, Gina, ed. *Girls Like Us: 40 Extraordinary Women Celebrate Girlhood in Story, Poetry, and Song.* New York: New World Library, 1999.

Pipher, Mary. *Reviving Ophelia: Saving the Selves of Adolescent Girls.* New York: Putnam, 1994.

Sadker, Myra and David. *Failing at Fairness: How America's Schools Cheat Girls.* New York: Charles Scribner's Sons, 1994.

Shandler, Sara, ed. *Ophelia Speaks: Adolescent Girls Write about Their Search for Self.* New York: HarperPerennial, 1999.

Index